SILVER BURDETT & GINN
MATHEMATICS

AUTHORS

Grades K-2 Team
Herbert P. Ginsburg
Deborah B. Gustafson
Larry P. Leutzinger

Grades 3-8 Team
Ruth I. Champagne
Carole E. Greenes
William D. McKillip
Lucy J. Orfan
Fernand J. Prevost
Bruce R. Vogeli
Marianne V. Weber

Problem Solving Team
Lucille Croom
Gerald A. Goldin
Stephen Krulik
Henry O. Pollak
Jesse A. Rudnick
Dale G. Seymour

SILVER BURDETT GINN
MORRISTOWN, NJ • NEEDHAM, MA
Atlanta, GA • Deerfield, IL • Irving, TX • San Jose, CA

ISBN 0-382-28235-3
ISBN 0-382-23953-9

1 2 3 4 5 6 7 8 9-RRD-99 98 97 96 95 94 93

Table of Contents

Introducing . . .
MATHEMATICS Exploring Your World

c.2

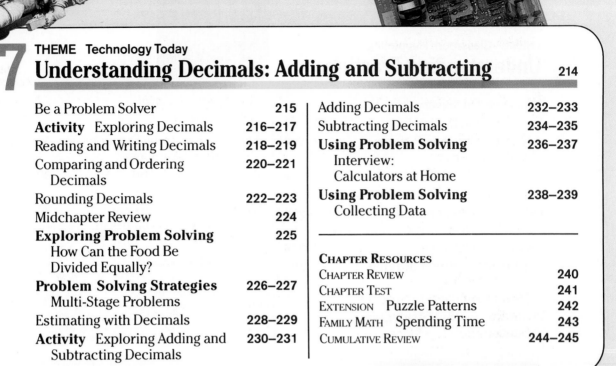

7 THEME Technology Today
Understanding Decimals: Adding and Subtracting   214

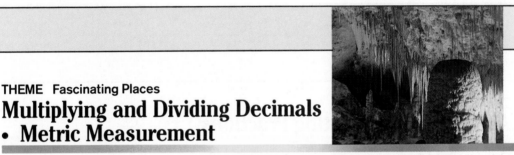

8 THEME Fascinating Places
Multiplying and Dividing Decimals • Metric Measurement   246

13
THEME Learning from Experiments
Ratio • Percent • Probability

414

ix:b. Alexander Calder. 1947. Wood, string, metal, polychrome paint. 36½ x 60 x 21 inches. Collection of Whitney Museum of American Art. Purchase, with funds from the Howard and Jean Lipman Foundation, Inc.

Mathematics *is* HAPPENING...

Japan

USA

all
around
the world!

Sudan

By 31 B.C., the Maya of **Central America** were using a place-value number system that allowed calculations involving millions.

Zimbabwe

Ireland

In **China**, around A.D. 375, circular coins, marked with weight and value, were used for trade.

Thailand

USA

By 1400 B.C., water clocks were being used in **Egypt**.

Morocco

In 1975, spacecraft from the **Soviet Union** and the **United States** linked up for the first international space mission.

USA

In 1626, Santorio Santorio, a doctor in **Italy**, was measuring human temperature with a thermometer.

By 950 B.C., the Chaldeans of **Babylonia** were using water filled cubes to measure weight, length, and time.

Journal Writing

Write a short story describing what our world would be like if mathematics had never been developed.

Cuba

1 Building Number Sense • Place Value •

Adding and Subtracting

THEME   The USA Yesterday and Today

Sharing What You Know

You've come a long way, U.S.A.! Our country is very different today from the way it was when it became a nation in 1776. In what ways do you think the United States has grown and changed? How has the way we use mathematics changed?

Using Language

In 1780 there were about two million, seven hundred eighty thousand people living in the United States. In **standard form** that's 2,780,000. By 1988, the U.S. population had grown to about two hundred forty-seven million, one hundred thousand (247,100,000). A million is one thousand thousands. A billion is one thousand millions. Where else do people use such large numbers in everyday life?

Words to Know: million, billion, periods, standard form, expanded form

Be a Problem Solver

UNITED STATES POPULATION	
Year	Number of People
1950	151,000,000
1960	179,000,000
1970	203,000,000
1980	226,000,000
1990 (estimated)	250,000,000
2000	

Predict the United States population in the year 2000, based on the data.

Write what you think your life will be like in the year 2000.

1

Use the digits 0, 2, 5, and 7. Write as many four-digit numbers as you can. Each digit can be used only once in each number.

Place Value to Millions

Alexander Graham Bell's first telephone conversation was with Mr. Watson in 1876. Today there are about 679,000,000 telephone conversations each day in the United States.

A place-value chart can help you read the number.

Millions			Thousands			Ones		
hundreds	tens	ones	hundreds	tens	ones	hundreds	tens	ones
6	7	9,	0	0	0,	0	0	0

Standard form **679,000,000**
     Read 679 million
    Write six hundred seventy-nine million

Numbers are separated by commas into groups of three digits, called **periods**.

The value of a digit depends on its place in the number.

Use the place-value chart to find the value of each digit.

The digit 6 is in the hundred millions place.
The value of the digit 6 is 600,000,000.

The digit 7 is in the ten millions place.
The value of the digit 7 is 70,000,000.

What is the value of the digit 9?

You can show the value of each digit by writing a number in expanded form. Here is the expanded form for 679,000,000.

Expanded form **600,000,000 + 70,000,000 + 9,000,000**

Read each number. Then write each in words.

1. 50,708   **2.** 16,160,106   **3.** 3,450,500   **4.** 22,811,095

Share Your Ideas How many thousands are there in the greatest six-digit number?

Read each number. Then write each in words.

5. 84,238   **6.** 244,308   **7.** 47,713   **8.** 807,486

9. 3,395,061   **10.** 59,841,348   **11.** 862,559,271   **12.** 200,020,002

Give the value of the digit 4 in each number.
Then write each number in expanded form.

13. 6,742   **14.** 14,650   **15.** 40,085   **16.** 345,600

17. 24,876,500   **18.** 104,387,210   **19.** 240,000,000   **20.** 460,709,009

Write each number in standard form, using commas.

21. 708374798   **22.** 4666853   **23.** 96508321   **24.** 10000000

25. three million, two hundred thousand

26. thirteen million, one thousand four

27. six hundred thousand, five hundred

28. one hundred million, twelve thousand

29. 20,000,000 + 4,000,000 + 80,000 + 3,000 + 500

30. 900,000,000 + 7,000,000 + 100,000 + 50 + 6

31. 20,000 more than 1,230,500

32. 100,000 less than 8,750,000

Problem Solving

33. Look back at **25–30**. Decide which numbers can be shown on a calculator with an 8-digit display.

34. How many thousands are there in one million?

Logical Thinking

35. Use the clues below. Who am I?
- My thousands digit is one-half my ones digit.
- My hundreds digit is 2 times my ones digit.
- My tens digit is 5 more than my hundreds digit.
- My ones digit is 2.

In the number 539,684,701 which digit is in the hundred millions place? ten thousands place?

SUMMING UP

Exploring Billions

In 1925 the federal budget was about 3 billion dollars a year. Today the United States spends more than this each day! How big is a billion?

Working together

Use mental math, paper and pencil, or a calculator.

A. Estimate the number of dollar signs that would cover this entire page.

B. About how many dollar signs would fit on all the pages of this book?

C. About how many books like this one would it take to show a million dollar signs if all the pages were covered with dollar signs?

D. The next period after millions is billions. If one book contains approximately 1,000,000 dollar signs, about how many books do you think it would take to show a billion dollar signs?

$$$
$$$
$$$
$$$
$$$

Sharing Your Results

1. Describe to your classmates how your group estimated the answer to each question.

2. Which method of estimating do you prefer? Why?

Practice

Work with a partner. Use a calculator if you like.

3. How many groups of 100 do you need to make 1,000?

4. How many groups of 1,000 do you need to make 1,000,000?

5. If you had 1 million pennies, would you be able to carry them? Use real pennies to help you estimate.

6. How tall would a stack of 1,000,000,000 sheets of paper be? Would it be as tall as you? as tall as a building? as tall as a mountain? Describe a way to estimate how tall the stack of 1,000,000,000 sheets of paper would be.

Summing Up

7. Discuss how big a billion is. How many millions is it?

8. DATA Do you think a billion people live in the United States? in the world? Use an almanac to find out.

9. If you used a calculator, explain how it helped you.

10. Create your own activity to show a billion. Describe your activity.

Look at the numbers 659,832,147 and 6,598,321,470. How did the zero change the value of the digits?

Place Value to Billions

Every year about 1,197,000,000 books are checked out of public libraries in the United States.

Billions			Millions			Thousands			Ones		
h	t	o	h	t	o	h	t	o	h	t	o
		1,	1	9	7,	0	0	0,	0	0	0

Standard form 1,197,000,000

Read 1 billion, 197 million

Write one billion, one hundred ninety-seven million

Expanded form 1,000,000,000 + 100,000,000 + 90,000,000 + 7,000,000

Another Example

standard form 20,130,004,805

write twenty billion, one hundred thirty million, four thousand, eight hundred five

expanded form 20,000,000,000 + 100,000,000 + 30,000,000 + 4,000 + 800 + 5

What digit is in the billions place?

What digit is in the ten-millions place?

What digit is in the thousands place?

Check Your Understanding

Read each number. Then write each in words.

1. 28,419
2. 2,857,902
3. 31,000,400,041
4. 670,504,000

Give the values of the digits 3 and 8.

5. 10,182,315,000
6. 3,541,077,802
7. 84,003,655,047

Share Your Ideas Look back at 7. Compare the values of the digit 4. Compare the values of the digit 5.

Read each number. Then write each in words.

8. 30,405   **9.** 9,809   **10.** 20,457,000   **11.** 8,200,070

12. 357,609,840   **13.** 650,000,400,000   **14.** 898,809,600   **15.** 72,050,000,000

Write each number in standard form and expanded form.

16. 5040261873   **17.** 601208007   **18.** 1093621785   **19.** 7035093281

20. twenty million, four hundred five thousand

21. one hundred three billion

22. seventy-five thousand, eight hundred twelve

Choose the correct standard form.

23. five billion, four hundred twenty-six thousand

     a. 5,000,426   **b.** 5,000,426,000   **c.** 5,426,000   **d.** not given

24. 20,000,000 + 7,000,000 + 5

     a. 27,500   **b.** 27,000,500   **c.** 27,000,005   **d.** not given

25. one hundred thousand less than one million

     a. 900,000   **b.** 1,100,000   **c.** 90,000   **d.** not given

Problem Solving

Play this game with a partner.

26. Write a ten-digit number using each of the digits 0–9 exactly once. Do not show your partner the number.

Give your partner clues such as "There is a 7 in the millions place." Give clues in any order. Cross out each digit as you give its clue.

See if your partner can match your number!

Use words to write the least possible ten-digit number that can be made using the digits 0–9 only once.

SUMMING UP

Which number in each pair is greater?
256   259
6,248   6,428

Comparing and Ordering Numbers

In 1846, an American, Richard Hoe, invented the rotary printing press. Today, most newspapers are printed on rotary presses.

Look at the table on the right. If you wanted to place an ad in the *County News* or *The Messenger*, which newspaper would give your ad the greater circulation?

Newspaper	Daily Circulation
County News	5,879
The Reporter	5,089
The Messenger	5,350

> means is greater than
< means is less than

You can use place value to compare the numbers. Compare 5,879 and 5,350.

Start at the left and compare digits in the same place.

The *County News* has a greater circulation than *The Messenger*.

5,879
5,350
↓ ↓
same ↓
8 > 3
so **5,879 > 5,350.**

List these numbers in order from least to greatest.
23,851   21,385   123,640

To order numbers, compare them two at a time.

21,385 < 23,851
23,851 < 123,640   The whole number with more digits is greater.

So 21,385 < 23,851 < 123,640.
The numbers from least to greatest are 21,385; 23,851; 123,640.

Check Your Understanding

Compare. Use >, <, or = for ⬤.

1. 6,750 ⬤ 675

2. 304,812 ⬤ 340,812

3. 38,902,040 ⬤ 38,902,400

Share Your Ideas   In your own words, explain how to compare 67,453 and 67,543.

Practice

Compare. Use >, <, or = for ⬤.

4. 430 ⬤ 403

5. 720 ⬤ 7,020

6. 845 ⬤ 841

7. 9,020 ⬤ 9,200

8. 6,359 ⬤ 6,395

9. 2,117 ⬤ 2,119

10. 23,405 ⬤ 23,400

11. 39,000 ⬤ 3,999

12. 18,600 ⬤ 19,200

13. 643,643 ⬤ 643,364

14. 100,005 ⬤ 100,500

15. 36,007,000 ⬤ 36,700,000

16. 80,509,000 ⬤ 80,509,000

List in order from least to greatest.

17. 3,824   3,248   3,482

18. 2,056   2,506   2,605

19. 32,005   320,005   32,050

20. 782,100   728,100   872,100

21. Which number is greater, 1,000 thousands or 10 million? Explain how you decided.

22. Explain what you would do to order more than three numbers.

Problem Solving

DATA The table shows some of the American inventions developed between 1800 and 1900. A **time line** shows dates on a number line.

Invention	Year
camera	1888
microphone	1875
sewing machine	1846
typewriter	1867
washing machine	1858
steamboat	1807

1800   1810   1820   1830   1840   1850   1860   1870   1880   1890   1900

23. Copy the time line above. Make a mark on your time line to show approximately the date for each invention. Write the name of the invention.

24. List the inventions in the order they occurred, from earliest to latest.

25. **Look back** at **24.** Are the inventions listed from oldest to newest or from newest to oldest?

These numbers are in order from greatest to least. Could all three hidden digits be the same? Could two be the same? Explain. 2■,450 > 2■,900 > 2■,695

9

Name some numbers that are closer to 400 than to 300. Name some numbers that are closer to 400 than to 500. How can you tell?

Rounding Whole Numbers

The population of Denver is between 400,000 and 500,000. It is closer to 500,000. The population of Denver rounded to the nearest hundred-thousand is 500,000.

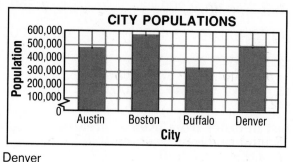

CITY POPULATIONS

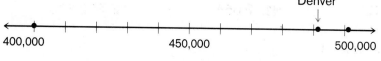

A rounded number tells about how many.

Round 492,694 to the nearest thousand.

What is the population of Austin rounded to the nearest hundred-thousand? of Boston? of Buffalo?

Step 1	Find the rounding place.	492,694
Step 2	Look at the digit to the right. If it is less than 5, leave the digit in the rounding place unchanged.	↓ 492,694
	If it is 5 or more, increase the digit in the rounding place by 1.	6 > 5
Step 3	Change each digit to the right of the rounding place to 0.	493,000

Another Example

Round money the same way you round whole numbers.
Round $1,852 to the nearest ten dollars.
$1,852 _rounds to_ $1,850

Check Your Understanding

Round 78,156 to the place named.

1. nearest hundred

2. nearest thousand

3. nearest ten thousand

Share Your Ideas Which of these numbers would round to 600 if rounded to the nearest hundred? Explain.

568   635   678   550   529

Round to the nearest ten.

4. 72   **5.** 85   **6.** 349   **7.** 523

Round to the nearest hundred.

8. 910   **9.** 462   **10.** 171   **11.** 10,250

Round to the nearest thousand.

12. 6,406   **13.** 7,399   **14.** 8,500   **15.** 9,705

Round to the nearest ten thousand.

16. 89,450   **17.** 62,512   **18.** 7,654   **19.** 350,698

Round to the nearest hundred dollars.

20. $245   **21.** $171.20   **22.** $4,981   **23.** $53.75

24. A number is between 230 and 240. It rounds to 240. What could the number be?

25. A number is between 23,750 and 23,760. What could the number be if it rounds to 23,750?

Problem Solving

26. Which city has the greatest population?

27. Which city has the least population?

28. Which cities have populations over 400,000?

29. Round the population of each city to the nearest ten thousand.

30. Newspapers sometimes use rounded numbers. Why might a newspaper report that '10,000' people instead of 12,876 people attended a concert?

POPULATIONS OF 10 U.S. CITIES	
City	Population
Atlanta, GA	421,910
Austin, TX	466,550
Buffalo, NY	324,820
Cleveland, OH	535,830
Kansas City, MO	441,170
Minneapolis, MN	356,840
Omaha, NE	349,270
Pittsburgh, PA	387,490
Seattle, WA	486,200

31. Joan said, "I live at about 300 Elm Street." What problems does Joan create by giving a rounded number? Discuss examples of other numbers you would never round.

Describe at least two reasons for using rounded numbers.

Midchapter Review

Write each number in words. pages 2–3, 6–7

1. 15,723,143
2. 899,462,986
3. 6,869,000,000

Write each number in standard form and expanded form. pages 2–3, 6–7

4. 6045689034
5. 29984320648
6. 2060345885

Give the place value of the digit 9 in each number. pages 2–3, 6–7

7. 90,046,482
8. 6,928,564
9. 29,600,543,000

Write <, >, or = for each ●. pages 8–9

10. 586 ● 5,850
11. 56,902 ● 56,802
12. 698,423 ● 699,423

List in order from least to greatest. pages 8–9

13. 56,030   56,301   56,299
14. 984,500   982,500   983,986

Round to the place named. pages 10–11

thousands	15. 634	16. 8,456	17. 10,831
ten thousands	18. 48,142	19. 8,948	20. 840,986
hundred dollars	21. $832	22. $1,590	23. $82.20

Use the words in the box to complete the sentence.

24. In _____ , numbers are separated by commas into groups of three digits, called _____ .

Words to Know
periods
standard form
expanded form

Solve.

25. In 1946 the national income was one hundred eighty-one billion dollars. Four years later it was $242,000,000,000. In what year was the national income greater?

26. In the 1948 presidential election, Thomas Dewey received 24,200,000,000 popular votes, and Harry Truman received 24,100,000,000. Who received more popular votes?

Exploring Problem Solving

How Many Different Stamp Arrangements?

The students in the Conservation Club are collecting special stamps. The students each bought 4 stamps. The stamps are attached to each other at the edges as shown at the right.

Thinking Critically

How many different arrangements of the four stamps can you make?

Work in a small group. You may want to make drawings or use manipulatives to help you solve this problem.

Analyzing and Making Decisions

1. How many stamps are in each arrangement? How are they connected?

2. When you make a new arrangement, how can you make sure it is not like one you have already made?

3. How might listing all the arrangements with two rows help? What kinds of groupings would help you make sure you list every arrangement?

4. Show all the arrangements you can. How many did you find?

Look Back Try to put your arrangements into groups. Describe your groups. How many are in each group?

Problem Solving Strategies

SNEAKER SALE

Runner's Best	$40.00
High-Fliers	$39.00
High Tops	$50.00
Tenny Pro	$38.00

Socks on Sale

All wool	$5.00/pair
Heavy Duty	$3.50/pair
Tube Socks	$5.00/4pairs

Facts from Pictures and Text

"It's time to buy shoes," said Mother.
"I'll need socks, too," said Dennis, "lots of them."
"Right," said Mother. "Now I don't want to spend more than 45 dollars all together, Dennis."
"These High-Flyers look great," said Dennis.
"Fine," said Mother.
How many socks could Dennis buy after he bought the shoes?

Sometimes you can solve a problem by looking at pictures and reading text.

CHOICES

Solving the Problem
Use a calculator where appropriate.

Think   What is the question?

Explore   What information do you need to answer the question? How much money do they have to spend? What is the price of the High-Flyers? the socks?

Solve   How much is left from the $45 after Dennis buys the High-Flyers? Does Dennis have a choice of socks? Are there several possible answers? Explain.

Look Back   Which socks do you think Dennis might buy? Explain.

Share Your Ideas

1. Which other shoes might Dennis have bought and still have had enough money to buy socks?

Practice

THINK
EXPLORE
SOLVE
LOOK BACK

Solve. Use a calculator where appropriate.

Use the information below to solve 2–3.

Livestock Population in the United States			
	1950	1970	1988
Cattle, Beef	77,963,000	112,369,000	98,984,000
Sheep	29,826,000	20,423,000	10,774,000
Dairy Cows	23,853,000	13,303,000	10,307,000

2. Which farm animal population was greater in 1988 than in 1950?

3. Which farm animal population decreased the most between 1950 and 1988?

The State Forest Commission records its monthly attendance by rounding to the nearest thousand.

4. In July, 12,473 people went to the parks. What number did the State Forest Commission record?

5. In August, the Commission recorded that there were 11,000 visitors. The actual number of visitors was between what two numbers?

Mixed Strategy Review

Use the table at the right to solve 6–7.

6. In which presidential election was the popular vote closer? Explain.

7. What if you were a candidate in the 1884 election and received more votes than William S. Hancock but less than James A. Garfield? Give a vote total you could have received.

Presidential Elections Number of Votes	
1884	
James A. Garfield	4,449,053
William S. Hancock	4,442,035
1892	
Grover Cleveland	5,556,918
Benjamin Harrison	5,176,108

Create Your Own
Write a problem about an election. Make up your own vote totals if you wish.

15

Find each sum mentally. Explain your thinking.
2 + 8   12 + 18   22 + 28   32 + 38

Mental Math: Using Properties

The 13 original colonies became the first states in the United States. Since then, 37 new states have been added.

Compatible numbers are numbers that are easy to compute mentally. 13 and 37 are compatible numbers for addition.

13 + 37 = 50   Why is it easy to
addends   sum   add 13 and 37?

The properties of addition can help you compute mentally.

Commutative Property

The order in which numbers are added does not change the sum. **6 + 15 + 4 = 25**
6 + 4 + 15 = 25
In which order is it easier to add mentally? Why?

Associative Property

The way in which numbers are grouped does not change the sum.

Compatible numbers

(17 + 25) + 5 = ▮   17 + (25 + 5) = ▮
42 + 5 = 47   17 + 30 = 47

Identity Property

The sum of any number and zero is that number.
18 + 0 = 18   31 + 0 = 31

Check Your Understanding

Find each sum mentally.

1. 3 + 19 + 7   **2.** 27 + 0   **3.** 36 + 20 + 80   **4.** 70 + 99 + 30

Share Your Ideas Make up an addition problem that has three numbers and can be solved mentally, using the associative property. Explain how you would solve it.

Find each sum mentally.

5. 4 + 38 + 6

6. 12 + 8 + 29

7. 42 + 0

8. 5 + 19 + 5

9. 17 + 11 + 9

10. 13 + 0 + 4

11. 40 + 38 + 60

12. 7 + 13 + 18

13. 0 + 78

14. 80 + 36 + 20

15. 42 + 8 + 29

16. 25 + 14 + 75

17. 24 + 39 + 6

18. 77 + 25 + 23

Find each missing addend. Name the property you used.

19. 13 + ▮ = 9 + 13

20. ▮ + 0 = 24

21. 15 + (▮ + 26) = (15 + 5) + 26

22. (9 + 6) + 27 = ▮ + 27

23. 26 + 27 + 14 = 26 + ▮ + 27

24. 93 + ▮ = 93

25. 7 + (23 + 8) = ▮ + 8

26. 7 + (33 + 46) = ▮ + 46

27. 62 + (25 − 25) = 62 + ▮

28. 176 + 358 + 0 = ▮ + 358

Problem Solving

29. There are two branches of the U.S. Congress. In 1800 there were 32 members in the Senate and 106 members in the House of Representatives. How many senators and representatives were there in all?

30. In 1988 there were 100 senators and 435 representatives in Congress. How many members were there in 1988?

Analyze 14 + 0 + 56 + 4. Describe different ways to compute the answer mentally, using properties.

Mixed Review

Give the value of the digit 3 in each number.

1. 203,902,702

2. 341,476

3. 56,311

4. 8,325,401

5. 843

6. 35,670,109

7. 3,962

8. 45,087,238,075

Write in expanded form.

9. 102,801,601

10. 431,365

11. 45,100

12. 7,324,301

13. 703

14. 84,560,109

15. 32,072,126,005

Write in words.

16. 2,258

17. 62,007

18. 620,070

19. 4,006,005

20. 4,010,305,000

21. 7,000,000,460

22. 2,395,467,159

SUMMING UP

2 + 7 = 9, 7 + 2 = 9, 9 − 7 = 2, and 9 − 2 = 7 are a family of facts. Write a family of facts for 12, 13, and 25.

Relating Addition and Subtraction

Each machine at the function factory follows a rule. This machine adds 5 to the input numbers and sends out a new number. This table shows what the machine has done.

Rule: Add 5.

Input	Output
21	26
22	27
23	28

What would the output be if you input 6?

Part of the label for the second machine is missing. How can you find the rule?

40 + *n* = 67   *n* stands for the missing number.

You can solve the addition problem by writing a related subtraction problem.

67 − 40 = 27, so 40 + 27 = 67.

The rule is: Add 27.

▶ You can subtract to find a missing addend because addition and subtraction are **inverse operations.**

Check Your Understanding

Find *n*.

1. 8 + *n* = 25   **2.** *n* + 10 = 33   **3.** 30 + *n* = 76   **4.** 901 + 10 = *n*

Share Your Ideas Write a related subtraction sentence for △ + □ = ○.

Practice

Find *n*.

5. $n + 6 = 43$ **6.** $25 + n = 34$ **7.** $n + 18 = 21$ **8.** $10 + n = 803$

9. $n + 20 = 20$ **10.** $30 + n = 90$ **11.** $n + 17 = 38$ **12.** $59 + 7 = n$

13. $18 + 44 = n$ **14.** $112 - n = 4$ **15.** $n - 16 = 33$ **16.** $n - 23 = 60$

Complete. Use mental math, paper and pencil, or a calculator. Explain your choices.

Rule: Add 20.

	Input	Output
17.	20	
18.	30	
19.	50	
20.	80	

Rule: Subtract 9.

	Input	Output
21.	28	
22.	27	
23.	143	
24.	90	

25. Find the rule.

Input	Output
13	21
16	24
18	26
22	30

Rule: Add 17.

	Input	Output
26.	9	
27.	26	
28.	39	
29.	51	

Rule: Subtract 15.

	Input	Output
30.	25	
31.	40	
32.	55	
33.	90	

34. Find the rule.

Input	Output
26	7
39	20
57	38
93	74

Problem Solving

Play this game with a partner. Use a calculator to find the mystery number.

35. One player writes an addition example. The sum cannot be greater than a two-digit number. Do not show your partner the example.

Give your partner the sum and one addend. Your partner has to find the missing addend. Change roles for the next game.

Make your own Input-Output chart. Write the rule above it.

If ——— represents a distance of about 200 miles, give a visual estimate of the length of the Chisholm Trail from San Antonio to Abilene.

Estimating Sums

Long ago, cowboys drove cattle up the Chisholm Trail. Today you can drive close to the old trail in a car. Use the map to estimate the distance from San Antonio, Texas, to Abilene, Kansas.

270 + 207 + 246

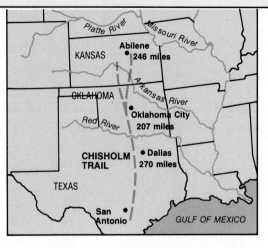

▶ You can estimate by adding the value of the front digits.

```
  270
  207
+ 246
  600  ← Remember, you are
          adding hundreds.
```

▶ To get a closer estimate, the first estimate can be adjusted by using the digits to the right of the front digits.

```
  270 ↖
  207   about 100
+ 246 ↙
  600 + 100 = 700  ← adjusted estimate
```

Both 600 and 700 are good estimates for the total number of miles.

Do you think the actual answer will be more than or less than 700? Why?

Describe how you could use rounding to estimate the sum.

Check Your Understanding

Estimate. Describe your method.

1.	2.	3.	4.	5.
36	320	$208	1,450	480 *500*
+26	+475	+ 89	+7,450	285 *300*
				+627 *600*

Share Your Ideas Look back at **4–5**. Explain why your estimate will be more than or less than the actual sum.

Estimate each sum.

6. 43 +38	**7.** $58 + 29	**8.** 52 +77	**9.** 89 +69	**10.** 97 +96
11. 765 + 55	**12.** 345 + 52	**13.** 449 + 99	**14.** 428 +125	**15.** $812 + 995
16. 306 +449	**17.** 680 +225	**18.** $350 + 450	**19.** 419 +585	**20.** 4,010 + 655
21. 1,312 + 190	**22.** $4,500 + 598	**23.** 2,400 +5,550	**24.** 6,240 +3,780	**25.** 7,186 +8,192

**Read the following. State whether you need an exact
number or an estimate in each situation. Explain.**

26. You are a cashier at a store and need to give change.

27. You want to know the population of Texas.

28. You want to know the distance around a garden in order to buy fencing.

29. You are ordering tickets to the planetarium for a class trip.

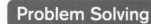

Problem Solving

30. Use the map on page 20. About how far was a trip from San Antonio to Oklahoma City and back?

31. Pioneers traveled west along the Oregon Trail. It was 1,156 miles from Independence, Missouri, to Fort Hall. It was another 1,041 miles from Fort Hall to Oregon City. About how long is the Oregon Trail?

32. Use the BASIC program below to find the sum of the numbers 1 to 10, then 1 to 100. Look for a pattern. Predict the sum of the numbers 1 to 1000. Then use the computer program to find the sum.

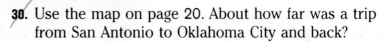
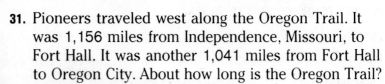

```
10 INPUT "SUM OF 1 TO WHAT NUMBER? ";N
20 SUM = N * (N + 1) / 2
30 PRINT SUM
```

How do you use place value when you estimate
with front digits? with rounding?

SUMMING UP

Write the number that shows 13 hundreds.

Adding

The Wabash Cannon Ball traveled 299 miles from Detroit, Michigan, to Danville, Illinois, and then another 189 miles to St. Louis, Missouri. How long was the route?

called the   Wa – bash   Can – on   Ball.

Step 1 Add ones. Regroup.	**Step 2** Add tens. Regroup.	**Step 3** Add hundreds.	Estimate to be sure your answer makes sense.
1 **299** **+189** 18 ones = **8** 1 ten 8 ones	1 1 **299** How do you **+189** write 18 tens? **88**	1 1 **299** **+189** **488**	300 +200 500

The Wabash Cannon Ball route was 488 miles long.

Another Example

Add 408 + 97 + 532.

1 1
408   ↖ Look for compatible
 97   ↙ numbers.
+532
1,037

You can check by adding up.

1 1
408 ↑
 97 |
+532 |
1,037

Check Your Understanding

Add. Estimate to be sure your answer makes sense.

1. 375 + 268

2. 49 + 185

3. 271 + 396 + 84

Share Your Ideas Look back at **3**. Explain in your own words how you found the sum.

Add. Estimate to be sure your answer makes sense.

4.	36 +56	**5.**	820 +906	**6.**	75 +67	**7.**	136 + 55
8.	795 +345	**9.**	847 + 29	**10.**	446 + 38	**11.**	529 +273
12.	676 94 +203	**13.**	42 259 +118	**14.**	499 86 + 57	**15.**	350 127 +536

Add. Use mental math, paper and pencil, or a calculator. Explain your choices.

CHOICES

16. 525 + 70 + 30   **17.** 852 + 978

18. 28 + 159 + 76 + 241   **19.** 220 + 320 + 60

20. 605 + 398   **21.** 29 + 86 + 427 + 986

22. Copy and complete the figure. Use the digits 1–9. Make the sum along each line equal 15.

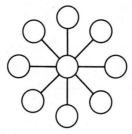

23. An engineer worked 29 hours one week and 37 hours the next week. How many hours did he work those two weeks?

24. A Wabash Domeliner train traveled 278 miles from St. Louis to Kansas City. Then it continued for another 639 miles to Denver. How far was the train ride from St. Louis to Denver?

25. It will take 87 hours to repair some railroad track. If 4 people each work 8 hours and another 7 people work 9 hours can they finish the job?

Create an addition problem where an exact answer is needed. Solve. Which method of computation did you use?

Mixed Review

Round to the nearest hundred.

1. 845

2. 1,675

3. 78

4. 972

5. 249

6. 904

7. 3,954

Round to the nearest thousand.

8. 6,495

9. 12,621

10. 7,985

11. 2,567

12. 841

13. 19,963

14. 5,098

Compare. Use >, <, or = for each ●.

15. 106 ● 160

16. 5,500 ● 5,250

17. 100,005 ● 105,000

18. 67,980 ● 67,980

19. 2,384 ● 976

20. 15,048 ● 104,211

SUMMING UP

23

When regrouping, how many hundreds do you need to make 1,000?

Adding Greater Numbers

In 1820, 7,197 males and 3,114 females immigrated to the United States. What was the total number of immigrants in 1820?

One way to find the sum is shown below.

Step 1 Add ones. Regroup.	Step 2 Add tens. Regroup.	Step 3 Add hundreds.	Step 4 Add thousands.
1 7,197 +3,114 1	11 7,197 +3,114 11	1 1 7,197 +3,114 311	1 1 7,197 +3,114 10,311

The total number of immigrants was 10,311.

More Examples

Another way to add greater numbers is to use a calculator.
Find $237.53 + $649.37

Estimate.

$237.53 → rounds to → $200.00
+ 649.37   600.00
                     $800.00

Calculate.

$237.53 + $649.37 = | 886.9 |

How would you write the answer displayed on the calculator using a dollar sign and decimal point?

Check Your Understanding

Estimate. Then use a calculator to find each sum.

1. 9,075 + 2,186

2. 45,698 + 7,950

3. $650.45 + $399.70

Share Your Ideas   How would you find the answer to 1,986 + 3,266 on your calculator if the 6 key was broken? Use a calculator to test your ideas.

Estimate. Then use a calculator to find each sum.

4.	4,329 +2,671	5.	45,329 + 6,750	6.	$32.45 + 89.76	7.	135,098 +688,145	8.	$156.25 + 495.50

9.	75,050 + 7,850	10.	$245.12 + 308.29	11.	82,130 +44,965	12.	271,500 + 58,500	13.	$499.25 + 75.95

14. 37,298 + 156,295

15. 40,270 + 429 + 5,321

16. $1,273.50 + $864.95

17. $149.80 + $82.99 + $325.50

18. 279,584 + 1,498,215

19. 26,390 + 4,567,987 + 683,574

Find each missing digit. Use mental math, paper and pencil, or a calculator. Explain your method.

20.	1,8■4 +4,■67 ■,40■	21.	34,618 +2■,7■■ 63,327	22.	2■,145 + 9■■ ■3,■43

23. In which year did the greatest number of immigrants come to the U.S.?

24. How many people in all immigrated to the U.S. in 1840 and 1860?

25. Estimate the total number of immigrants for the years 1820, 1840, 1860, and 1880. Use a calculator to find the actual sum.

26. The Statue of Liberty has welcomed millions of immigrants arriving in New York Harbor. The figure is 151 feet tall, the pedestal is 89 feet tall, and the base is 65 feet tall. How tall is the Statue of Liberty from the base to the top of the figure?

U. S. IMMIGRANTS	
Year	**Number**
1820	10,311
1840	92,207
1860	179,691
1880	457,257

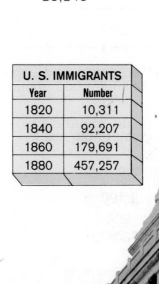

Use the digits 3, 6, 7, 4, 8 to write the greatest possible number using each digit once. Then write the least possible number. Find their sum.

SUMMING UP

Why are maximum weights posted in elevators?
When would you need that information?

Estimating Differences

In 1854, an American, Elisha G. Otis invented the first elevator with a safety device. Today, we still use elevators to move people and freight.

If the piano weighs 1,155 pounds, about how much more weight can the elevator carry?

► Estimate a difference by rounding each number before subtracting.

Estimate 2,400 − 1,155.

Round to the nearest thousand.

$$\begin{array}{r} 2,400 \\ -1,155 \\ \end{array} \xrightarrow{\text{rounds to}} \begin{array}{r} 2,000 \\ -1,000 \\ \hline 1,000 \end{array}$$

The elevator can hold about 1,000 pounds more.

► To get a closer estimate, round each number one more place to the right.

Round to the nearest hundred.

$$\begin{array}{r} 2,400 \\ -1,150 \\ \end{array} \xrightarrow{\text{rounds to}} \begin{array}{r} 2,400 \\ -1,200 \\ \hline 1,200 \end{array}$$

Check Your Understanding

Estimate each difference.

1.	2.	3.	4.	5.
83	600	$200	2,150	9,500
− 29	− 438	− 76	− 680	− 4,325

Share Your Ideas Can you find a closer estimate for **4** and **5**? Explain why you might need a close estimate in everyday life.

Estimate each difference.

6. 62
    -18

7. 91
    -75

8. 87
    -48

9. 34
    -9

10. $925
    -675

11. 789
    -267

12. 655
    -278

13. 705
    -215

14. $350
    -87

15. 100
    -34

16. 2,386
    $-1,799$

17. 9,291
    $-7,850$

18. $7,450
    $-6,500$

19. $5,000
    -624

20. 3,450
    -775

Estimate to compare. Use >, <, or = for ●.

21. 685 − 260 ● 500

22. 358 − 46 ● 200

23. 2,361 − 1,472 ● 800

24. 1,874 − 526 ● 1,400

25. Use eight different digits. Create two numbers whose difference is about 3,000.

26. Use ten different digits. Create two numbers whose difference is about 15,000.

Problem Solving

27. Anna has 5,526 balloons. 3,491 are red and the rest are blue. She must have at least 2,100 blue balloons for a rock concert. Should she estimate by rounding to thousands? Explain.

28. Dan shipped 2,518 balloons from a supply of 3,449. He rounded to the nearest thousand to find how many balloons he had left. What answer did he get? What should he do? Explain the problem and your solution.

Test Taker

29. Sometimes you can save time by estimating answers for a multiple-choice test. Use estimation and ending digits to help you choose the correct answer.

    437 + 454

    a. 791
    b. 889
    c. 891
    d. 982

    874 − 825

    a. 149
    b. 1,699
    c. 51
    d. 49

Give 3 different estimates for 6,840 − 2,173. Explain your method for each.

SUMMING UP

How many tens are in 120?

Subtracting

In 1919 an army scouting plane set an American speed record of 164 miles per hour. A modern Boeing 747B jumbo jet can travel at a speed of 625 miles per hour. How much faster than the scouting plane can a Boeing 747B fly?

Subtract to find the difference.

Step 1 Subtract ones.	**Step 2** Regroup 1 hundred. Subtract tens.	**Step 3** Subtract hundreds.	Check by adding.
$\begin{array}{r} 625 \\ -164 \\ \hline 1 \end{array}$	$\begin{array}{r} \overset{5\ 12}{6\cancel{2}5} \\ -164 \\ \hline 61 \end{array}$ 6 hundreds 2 tens = 5 hundreds 12 tens	$\begin{array}{r} \overset{5\ 12}{6\cancel{2}5} \\ -164 \\ \hline 461 \end{array}$ ← difference	$\begin{array}{r} \overset{1}{164} \\ +461 \\ \hline 625 \end{array}$

A Boeing 747B can fly 461 miles per hour faster than the scouting plane.

Another Example

Find $5.00 − $3.65.

$\begin{array}{r} \overset{\quad\ 9}{\overset{4\ \ 10\,10}{\$\cancel{5}.\cancel{0}\,\cancel{0}}} \\ -\ \ 3.65 \\ \hline \$1.35 \end{array}$ Write the dollar sign and decimal point in the answer.

If you are making change, sometimes it is easier to count up.

$$\underset{\$3.65}{} \overset{+10\text{¢}}{\curvearrowright} \underset{\$3.75}{} \overset{+25\text{¢}}{\curvearrowright} \underset{\$4.00}{} \overset{+\$1\ =\ \$1.35}{\curvearrowright} \underset{\$5.00}{}$$

Check Your Understanding

Subtract. Add to check.

1. $\begin{array}{r} 83 \\ -29 \\ \hline \end{array}$

2. $\begin{array}{r} 602 \\ -438 \\ \hline \end{array}$

3. $\begin{array}{r} 299 \\ -\ 76 \\ \hline \end{array}$

4. $\begin{array}{r} \$9.34 \\ -\ 5.13 \\ \hline \end{array}$

5. $\begin{array}{r} 521 \\ -486 \\ \hline \end{array}$

Share Your Ideas Subtract 700 − 283. In your own words, explain how you found the answer.

Subtract. Add to check.

6. 62 −18	**7.** 91 −75	**8.** 87 −48	**9.** 34 − 9	**10.** $92 − 67
11. 100 − 32	**12.** 455 −138	**13.** 705 −215	**14.** $4.90 − 1.75	**15.** 361 −284
16. 789 −267	**17.** 622 −378	**18.** $605 − 399	**19.** $3.50 − .87	**20.** 211 −117
21. 500 −176	**22.** 489 − 39	**23.** $499 − 236	**24.** 846 − 9	**25.** 989 −594

Subtract. Use mental math, paper and pencil, or a calculator. Explain your choices.

26. $4.00 − $3.25

27. $3.00 − $2.78

28. $5.00 − $.95

29. 200 − 99

30. 76 − 9

31. 352 − 99

32. 705 − 117

33. 471 − 80

34. 578 − 235

Problem Solving

35. Would $40 be enough to buy both model airplanes? Estimate to find out. Explain.

36. What change would you receive from $40 if you bought the more expensive model? the less expensive model? Use counting up to help you.

37. How much more money would you need if you wanted to buy both models?

Visual Thinking

38. Complete the bottom row for each pattern.

A.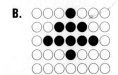

B.

C.

Explain why place value is important when you subtract.

Find each missing digit.
$$\begin{array}{r} 1,\blacksquare 3 \\ -\ 27\blacksquare \\ \hline 1,207 \end{array}$$

Subtracting Greater Numbers

Native Americans have lived on the land we call Arizona for 12,000 years.

The Bureau of Indian Affairs recently recorded 8,421 Apaches and 9,040 Hopis living in Arizona. What is the difference in these populations?

One way to find the difference is to subtract, as shown below.

Step 1	Step 2	Step 3
Regroup. Subtract ones.	Subtract tens.	Regroup. Subtract hundreds.
$\begin{array}{r} {\scriptstyle 3\ 10} \\ 9{,}04\!\!\!/0 \\ -8{,}421 \\ \hline 9 \end{array}$	$\begin{array}{r} {\scriptstyle 3\ 10} \\ 9{,}04\!\!\!/0 \\ -8{,}421 \\ \hline 19 \end{array}$	$\begin{array}{r} {\scriptstyle 8\ 10\ 3\ 10} \\ 9{,}04\!\!\!/0 \\ -8{,}421 \\ \hline 619 \end{array}$

There are 619 more Hopis than Apaches.

More Examples

Another way to subtract greater numbers is to use a calculator.

Estimate.

$$\begin{array}{r} 504{,}678 \\ -\ 72{,}769 \end{array} \xrightarrow{\text{rounds to}} \begin{array}{r} 500{,}000 \\ -100{,}000 \\ \hline 400{,}000 \end{array}$$

Calculate.

$504{,}678 - 72{,}769 =$ | 431909 |

Check Your Understanding

Estimate. Then use a calculator to find each difference.

1. $43{,}172 - 38{,}098$ 2. $28{,}672 - 9{,}451$ 3. $55{,}000 - 39{,}949$

4. $\$1{,}458.05 - \$645.95$ 5. $350{,}065 - 24{,}196$ 6. $\$13{,}956 - \$8{,}725$

Share Your Ideas   Look back at **3**. Explain how you could do this mentally.

Estimate. Then use a calculator to find each difference.

7. 2,982 − 1,760	**8.** 25,980 − 12,640	**9.** $862.12 − 59.95	**10.** $799.99 − 480.98
11. 345,609 − 263,712	**12.** 316,400 − 299,300	**13.** 50,000 − 48,132	**14.** $800.00 − 79.99
15. 86,040 − 6,982	**16.** 485,907 − 2,659	**17.** 45,001 − 29	**18.** 681,000 − 9,000

Estimate. Then find *n*.

19. $54{,}906 - 3{,}678 = n$ **20.** $\$925.50 - \$12.50 = n$

21. $212{,}090 - 16{,}252 = n$ **22.** $19{,}467 - 92 = n$

23. $960{,}900 - 4{,}199 = n$ **24.** $86{,}147 - 47{,}888 = n$

Problem Solving

Choose the numbers below that would make sense in this story.

25. Carla's odometer reading was _____ at the beginning
26. of the trip. She traveled _____ miles in the morning
27. and _____ miles in the afternoon. Her odometer
28. reading was _____ when she stopped in Phoenix.

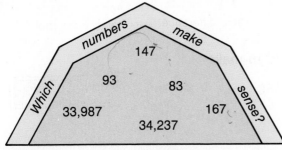

Which numbers make sense?

147
93   83
33,987   167
34,237

29. Calculators are often used to subtract greater numbers. Give examples of some situations in which it is faster to use paper and pencil or mental math rather than a calculator to subtract greater numbers.

Common Error

These problems look like subtraction problems. How would you answer each question?

30. Your teacher assigns exercises 5–15 for homework. How many exercises do you have to do?

31. Sally had $12,000 in her budget at work. She has spent $3,000. How much money did Sally use from her budget?

Write a six-digit number that has a 0 in the ten thousands and hundreds places. Use the digits 5–9 to write a five-digit number. Subtract.

Which is easier to subtract, 25 − 18 or 27 − 20? Explain.

Mental Math: Subtracting

Look at each problem.
Are the answers the same for both?
Which problem is easier to do mentally?

$$\begin{array}{r} 72 \\ -39 \end{array} \qquad \begin{array}{r} 73 \\ -40 \end{array}$$

Sometimes subtraction can be made easier by adding to both numbers.

$$72 \xrightarrow{+1} 73 \leftarrow \text{Add 1 to 72 to}$$

Add one to 39 to get 40 → $\underline{-39} \xrightarrow{+1} \underline{-40}$ balance the problem.

40 is easier to subtract $\;33\qquad\quad 33$

same difference

More Examples

$$92 \xrightarrow{+3} 95$$
$$\underline{-47} \xrightarrow{+3} \underline{-50}$$
$$45 \qquad\; 45$$

same difference

Think Add 3 to 47.
50 is easier to subtract.

Add 3 to 92 to balance the problem.

$$131 \xrightarrow{+2} 133$$
$$\underline{-\;88} \xrightarrow{+2} \underline{-\;90}$$
$$43 \qquad\quad 43$$

same difference

Think Add 2 to 88.
90 is easier to subtract.

Add 2 to 131 to balance the problem.

How can you determine what number to add to make the subtraction easier?

Check Your Understanding

Solve mentally.

1.	28	29	2.	34	36	3.	153	155	4.	232	235
	− 9	−10		−18	−20		− 48	− 50		− 17	− 20

5. 56 − 39   6. 192 − 85   7. 347 − 199   8. 517 − 19

Share Your Ideas Look back at **1–4**. Tell what number was added in each problem to make it easier to subtract.

Practice

Find each difference.
Tell what number you would add to solve mentally.

9.	40	44	**10.**	52	54	**11.**	73	79
	− 16	− 20		− 18	− 20		− 24	− 30

12.	81	85
	− 36	− 40

13. 94 − 39   **14.** 100 − 43   **15.** 200 − 46   **16.** 160 − 35

17. 142 − 57   **18.** 164 − 29   **19.** 223 − 98   **20.** 350 − 245

Subtract mentally. Choose the correct answer.

21. 31 − 14 = ☐
   a. 27
   b. 17
   c. 23
   d. 28

22. 62 − 49 = ☐
   a. 111
   b. 11
   c. 13
   d. 23

23. 200 − 54 = ☐
   a. 136
   b. 254
   c. 156
   d. 146

24. 172 − 135 = ☐
   a. 137
   b. 37
   c. 307
   d. 47

Subtract. Use mental math, paper and pencil, or a calculator. Explain your choices.

25. 87 − 29 = ☐   **26.** 99 − 46 = ☐   **27.** 28 − 19 = ☐

28. $53 − $38 = ☐   **29.** 159 − 57 = ☐   **30.** $345 − $296 = ☐

31. 578 − 69 = ☐   **32.** 999 − 543 = ☐   **33.** 2,016 − 0 = ☐

34. 5,984 − 84 = ☐   **35.** 6,000 − 2,153 = ☐   **36.** 8,065 − 59 = ☐

Problem Solving

Solve. Use mental math where appropriate.

37. Jan wants to buy the items below. Estimate to find about how much they will cost.

Laundry Detergent	$3.49
Shampoo	2.89
Film	1.59
Bread	1.49
Milk	1.69

38. Jan has a $10 bill. Find the exact total of the items. How much more money does Jan need?

39. Suppose Jan decided not to buy the film. How much change would she receive from her $10 bill?

Write a subtraction problem that can be solved mentally by adding to both numbers.

SUMMING UP

33

Using Problem Solving

Collecting Data

This time line describes the typical day of a child in the 1890s.

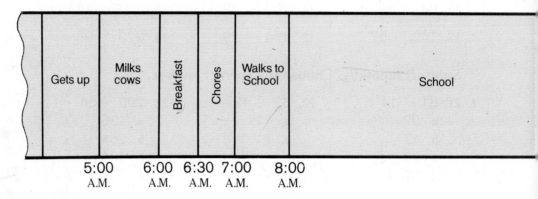

	Milks cows	Breakfast	Chores	Walks to School	School
Gets up					

5:00 A.M.   6:00 A.M.   6:30 A.M.   7:00 A.M.   8:00 A.M.

How would you describe the typical day of a child in the 1990s?

Working together

A. One way to find out about the daily activities of a child in the 1990s is to survey your classmates. Find out the activities of each person and the times that they are done.

B. Look at the lists of activities. Which are done by everybody? Are they always done at the same time? If not, what is a reasonable time for each?

C. Which activities that are not done by everybody would you include in your description of a typical day? Why? Give a reasonable time for each.

D. List the activities that you would include in a typical day for a child in the 1990s. Show the time when each activity is done.

Sharing Your Ideas

1. Compare your group's description of a typical day with those of other groups in the class. Make any necessary changes in your description.

2. How do the activities of the 1890s differ from the activities of the 1990s?

Practice

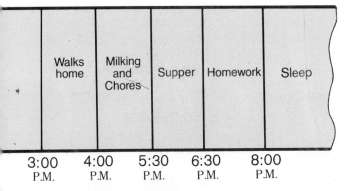

| Walks home | Milking and Chores | Supper | Homework | Sleep |

| 3:00 P.M. | 4:00 P.M. | 5:30 P.M. | 6:30 P.M. | 8:00 P.M. |

Follow these steps to make a time line to show a typical day for a child in the 1990s. Use your description from page 34. You will need a ruler.

3. What is the earliest time shown on the time line for a child in the 1890s? What is the earliest time that you need to show?

4. What is the latest time shown on the time line for the 1890s? What is the latest time that you need to show on your time line?

5. How many activities are shown on the 1890s time line? How many activities do you need to show?

6. Draw a line across a sheet of paper. Mark the earliest time on the left end and the latest on the right end.

7. How many hours are there between the earliest and latest times? Mark equal intervals on the line for the hours.

8. Complete the time line by writing each activity at the appropriate place on the line.

Summing Up

9. Write a description comparing the activities of a child in the 1890s with that of a child in the 1990s.

Chapter Review

Choose the correct number in standard form for each. pages 2–3, 6–7

1. sixty-three million, nine hundred twenty-eight thousand
   a. 63,928,000   **b.** 63,900,280   **c.** 63,090,028

2. forty-eight billion, seven hundred twenty-six million, eight hundred forty-nine thousand, three hundred fifty-six
   a. 48,702,684,356   **b.** 48,726,849,356   **c.** 48,706,849,356

3. 500,000 + 20,000 + 9,000 + 800 + 40 + 3
   a. 500,298,403   **b.** 529,843   **c.** 50,298,403

Compare. Use >, < or = for each ●. pages 8–9

4. 25,691 ● 24,914   5. 326,891 ● 326,957   6. 50,108,000 ● 50,108,000

Round 486,375 to the place named. pages 10–11

7. hundreds   8. thousands   9. tens   10. hundred thousands

Find each missing addend. Name the property you used. pages 16–17

11. $7 + 22 + 4 = 7 + \square + 22$ 12. $48 + \square = 48$ 13. $25 + (4 + 1) = (25 + \square) + 1$

Find n. pages 18–19

14. $15 - n = 5$ 15. $n + 20 = 36$ 16. $n - 5 = 20$ 17. $28 + 17 = n$

Estimate each sum or difference. pages 20–21, 26–27

18.	19.	20.	21.	22.
473 +526	7,357 +4,986	$643.89 + 289.63	858,742 −262,844	99,465 − 1,498

Add or subtract. pages 22–25, 28–31

23.	24.	25.	26.	27.
$9.58 − 2.62	9,465 − 1,498	83,546 +31,678	389,563 − 9,672	89,402 + 6,985

Solve. pages 13–15

28. How much money was raised altogether?

29. How many more dollars were raised by Memorial than by Washington?

MONEY RAISED FOR THE ENVIRONMENT	
School	**Dollars**
Eisenhower	$ 1,258
Washington	$10,620
Johnson	$ 8,498
Memorial	$16,904

Chapter Test

Choose the correct number in standard form for each.

1. three million, twenty-nine thousand
   a. 32,900   **b.** 3,029,000   **c.** 329,000,000,000

2. one billion, two hundred million, fifty thousand
   a. 1,250,000   **b.** 1,200,050,000   **c.** 1,002,050,000

3. 2,000,000,000 + 50,000 + 4,000 + 2
   a. 2,050,004,002   **b.** 2,000,504,002   **c.** 2,000,054,002

Compare. Use >, < or = for each ⬤.

4. 52,176 ⬤ 51,987   5. 26,403 ⬤ 26,410   6. 123,160 ⬤ 99,878

Round 246,843 to the place named.

7. tens   8. hundreds   9. thousands   10. hundred thousands

Find each missing addend. Name the property you used.

11. 8 + 19 + 6 = 8 + □ + 19   12. 35 + □ = 35   13. 29 + (2 + 5) = (29 + □) + 5

Find n.

14. $28 - n = 16$ 15. $n + 10 = 23$ 16. $n - 6 = 24$ 17. $35 + 17 = n$

Estimate each sum or difference.

18. $492 - 203$ 19. $46.48 + 28.53$ 20. $3,475 - 2,556$ 21. $675 + 47 + 114$

Add or subtract.

22. 425
    -175

23. 413
    -337

24. $2,572$
    $-1,821$

25. 86.24
    -24.86

26. $6,975$
    $-3,925$

27. 901
    $+309$

28. $3,223$
    $+3,727$

29. 267.75
    $+384.25$

30. 260
     148
    $+652$

31. 352
     237
    $+411$

Solve.

32. The World Trade Center is 1,350 feet tall. The Chrysler Building is 304 feet shorter. What is the height of the Chrysler Building?

33. Mr. and Mrs. Bevans took two children to the South Street Seaport. How much did it cost?

Museum Tickets	
Adults	$5.00
Children	$2.00

THINK Find the missing digits. $2\square\square + 231 = \square72 - 415$

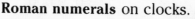

Roman Numerals

The Romans used a numeration system that is different from ours. Sometimes you see these **Roman numerals** on clocks.

Use the clock. Write the Roman numeral for each number.

1. 5   **2.** 4   **3.** 6   **4.** 7   **5.** 8

6. 10   **7.** 9   **8.** 11   **9.** 12   **10.** 3

11. In the Roman numeral system, combinations of only 3 different numerals are used to express the numbers on the clock. What are they?

12. Look at the Roman numerals for the numbers 4, 5, and 6. How does placing the I before the V change its value? How does placing the I after the V change its value?

13. Look at the Roman numerals for 9, 10, and 11. Does the same rule apply? What is the greatest number of times any numeral is used?

The **Roman Numeral System** uses addition and subtraction instead of place value to write its numbers.

Addition is used when the values of the symbols are the same or decrease from left to right.

VIII $= 5 + 1 + 1 + 1 = 8$
MDCCX $= 1,000 + 500 + 100 + 100 + 10 = 1,710$

Subtraction is used when the value of the symbol on the left is less than the value of the symbol on the right.

XL $= 50 - 10 = 40$ **CD** $= 500 - 100 = 400$

The same Roman numeral is never used more than three times in a row.

BASIC ROMAN NUMERALS	
I	1
V	5
X	10
L	50
C	100
D	500
M	1,000

A BAR CALLED A VINCULUM MEANS TO MULTIPLY BY 1,000	
$\overline{IV}$	4,000
$\overline{V}III$	6,007
$\overline{C}$	100,000
$\overline{C}M$	101,000

Write each number in standard form.

14. CMXII   **15.** DCXCIX   **16.** XIX   **17.** MLIV   **18.** $\overline{DC}$

19. CDXCIV   **20.** MCMLI   **21.** CDXC   **22.** MMMDIII   **23.** $\overline{C}XV$

24. Use Roman numerals to write the year in which you were born.

Maintaining Skills

Choose the correct answer. Write A, B, C, or D.

1. What is the value of 6 in 56,342?

   A 60,000   **C** 6,000

   B 600   **D** not given

2. What is the standard number for 8 million, 742 thousand, 18?

   A 87,420,018   **C** 874,218

   B 8,742,018   **D** not given

3. What property is used?

   $3 + (4 + 7) = (3 + n) + 7$

   A Identity   **C** Commutative

   B Associative   **D** not given

4. Compare. 43,004,563 ⬤ 6,892,611

   A $<$ **C** $=$

   B $>$ **D** not given

5. Round 56,354 to the nearest thousand.

   A 56,000   **C** 6,000

   B 57,000   **D** not given

6. Find n. $7 + n = 15$

   A 6   **C** 8

   B 9   **D** not given

7. Estimate. 6,744 + 2,206

   A 10,000   **C** 12,000

   B 4,000   **D** 9,000

8.   615
    + 263

   A 452   **C** 862

   B 878   **D** not given

9. 86,103 + 25,538

   A 111,641   **C** 101,661

   B 101,631   **D** not given

10. Estimate. 8,000 − 362

   A 4,000   **C** 7,600

   B 5,000   **D** 600

11. $8.00 − $2.45

   A $6.45   **C** $5.55

   B $6.65   **D** not given

Solve. Use the picture for **12.**

12. What statement helps to find the total number of boats on the lake?

   A $6 \times 5 = n$ **C** $6 - 5 = n$

   B $6 + 5 = n$ **D** not given

2 Multiplying Whole Numbers

THEME   People at Work

Sharing What You Know

Who's been working on the railroad? Students 10 to 14 years old, that's who! The Pioneer Railway in Hungary takes travelers to a ski resort, to a campsite, and to a park where there are open-air stages. Students have run the Pioneer Railway for more than 30 years and there has never been an accident. What kinds of jobs do you think the Pioneers do to run their railroad? How do you think they could use multiplication in their work?

Using Language

Most travelers don't realize all the details that go into running a railway. Talk about some of the details. The final product of the students' work is to operate a dependable train system. **Product** means the result of work. In mathematics, the **product** is the answer when you multiply. For example, the product of 3 and 6 is 18. How are these meanings alike? How are they different?

Words to Know: product, factor, multiple, common multiple, least common multiple, identity property, associative property, commutative property, zero property

Á.E.V.
BÖRZSÖNYI ÚTTÖRŐVASÚT

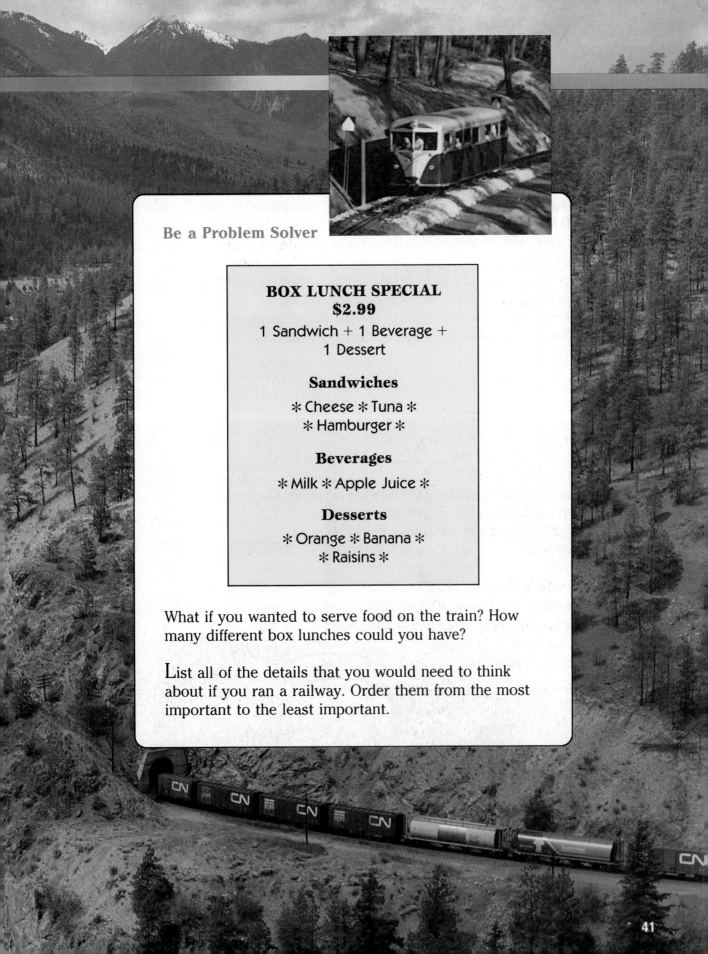

BOX LUNCH SPECIAL
$2.99
1 Sandwich + 1 Beverage +
1 Dessert

Sandwiches
* Cheese * Tuna *
* Hamburger *

Beverages
* Milk * Apple Juice *

Desserts
* Orange * Banana *
* Raisins *

What if you wanted to serve food on the train? How
many different box lunches could you have?

List all of the details that you would need to think
about if you ran a railway. Order them from the most
important to the least important.

Which is easier to multiply mentally:
(9 × 2) × 5 or 9 × (2 × 5)? Explain your
thinking.

Mental Math: Using Properties

Last night the fifth-grade class had 25
multiplication problems for homework.
Clyde worked on them until dinner. Suzie
used mental math and finished earlier.

The multiplication properties helped
her solve this problem mentally.

$$2 \times 7 \times 5 = \underbrace{2 \times 5}_{} \times 7$$
$$= \quad 10 \quad \times 7$$
$$= 70$$

factors → **2 × 7 × 5 = 70** ← product

Explain what Suzie did.
Name the properties
she used.

COMMUTATIVE PROPERTY

The order in which numbers
are multiplied does not change
the product.

$$2 \times 14 = 14 \times 2$$
$$28 = 28$$

ASSOCIATIVE PROPERTY

the way in which numbers
are grouped does not
change the product.

$$\underbrace{7 \times 2}_{14} \times 3 = 7 \times \underbrace{2 \times 3}_{6}$$
$$14 \quad \times 3 = 7 \times \quad 6$$
$$42 = 42$$

IDENTITY PROPERTY

The product of 1 and any
number is that number.

$$1 \times 6 = 6$$

ZERO PROPERTY

The product of zero and
any number is zero.

$$13 \times 7 \times 0 = 0$$

What if the problem was (13 − 12) × 2 × 7?

Describe how you would find the product
mentally.   Remember to do the work inside
the parentheses first.

Check Your Understanding

Find each product mentally.

1. 8 × 4 × 0   **2.** 1 × 856   **3.** 7 × 2 × 4   **4.** 9 × 2 × 5 × 1   **5.** 8 × 2 × 3

Share Your Ideas   Look back at **4**. Tell how you found
the product.

Practice

Find each product mentally.

6. 927×0 **7.** 236×1 **8.** $5 \times 5 \times 2$

9. $3 \times 2 \times 5 \times 1$ **10.** $2 \times 3 \times 9$ **11.** $4 \times 9 \times 2$

12. $50 \times 3 \times 0$ **13.** 365×1 **14.** $3 \times 0 \times 7 \times 9$

15. $6 \times 2 \times 3$ **16.** $2 \times 9 \times 5$ **17.** $8 \times 1 \times 9$

18. $3 \times 4 \times 3$ **19.** $8 \times 3 \times 3$ **20.** $7 \times 2 \times 4$

21. $4 \times 4 \times 2$ **22.** $2 \times (7 - 7)$ **23.** $10 \times 7 \times 0$

Find *n*. Name the property that you used.

24. $3 \times n = 7 \times 3$ **25.** $91 \times 0 = n$

26. $45 \times n = 45$ **27.** $32 \times n = 3 \times 32$

28. $68 \times n = 0$ **29.** $(3 \times 4) \times 2 = 3 \times (n \times 2)$

Problem Solving

Describe more than one way to find each product.

30. $2 \times 3 \times 4$ **31.** $3 \times 5 \times 2$

32. $4 \times 1 \times 7 \times 2$ **33.** $1 \times 6 \times 7$

34. Fill in the circles. Use each of the numbers 1, 2, 3, 4, 5, 6, and 12 once. The product of the three numbers on each line is 60.

Name the properties that help you find each product mentally.
a. $9 \times 6 \times 0 \times 8$ **b.** $3 \times 2 \times 7 \times 5$

Mixed Review

1.   58
  $+32$

2.   126
  $+\ 25$

3.   89
  -54

4.   408
  -205

5.   3,880
  $+9,940$

6.   6,000
  $-2,715$

7.   4,792
  $-\ \ 304$

8.   5,965
  $+2,819$

Answer each question.

9. How many zeros appear in a calculator display when you enter 1 million?

10. How much money do you have if you have seven quarters?

11. Today, 7,854 people came to the ball game. Round this number to the nearest hundred.

SUMMING UP

43

Mental Math: Multiplication Patterns

Mathematicians look for patterns in numbers. Look at the table. What patterns can you find in the numbers? Use the patterns to predict the missing numbers.

x	3	30	300	
6	18	180	1,800	
60	180	1,800		
600	1,800			
6,000				

Basic facts and patterns can help you find some products quickly.

a. $2 \times 4 = 8$
$2 \times 40 = 2 \times 4 \times 10 = 80$
$2 \times 400 = 2 \times 4 \times 100 = 800$
$2 \times 4,000 = 2 \times 4 \times 1,000 = 8,000$

b. $20 \times 4 = 80$
$20 \times 40 = 800$
$20 \times 400 = 8,000$
$20 \times 4,000 = 80,000$

c. $40 \times 5 = 200$
$40 \times 50 = 2,000$
$40 \times 500 = 20,000$
$40 \times 5,000 = 200,000$

What rule can you state for multiplying by tens, hundreds, and thousands?

Check Your Understanding

Find each product mentally. Use a multiplication fact and patterns.

1. 5×7
   5×70
   5×700
   $5 \times 7,000$

2. 9×8
   9×80
   9×800
   $9 \times 8,000$

3. 30×2
   30×20
   30×200
   $30 \times 2,000$

4. 70×6
   70×60
   70×600
   $70 \times 6,000$

Share Your Ideas Explain how multiplication patterns help you compute 60×300 mentally.

Find each product mentally. Use patterns.

5. $\begin{array}{r} 8 \\ \times 7 \\ \hline \end{array}$
6. $\begin{array}{r} 80 \\ \times 7 \\ \hline \end{array}$
7. $\begin{array}{r} 80 \\ \times 70 \\ \hline \end{array}$
8. $\begin{array}{r} 800 \\ \times 70 \\ \hline \end{array}$
9. $\begin{array}{r} 8,000 \\ \times 70 \\ \hline \end{array}$

10. $\begin{array}{r} 60 \\ \times 3 \\ \hline \end{array}$
11. $\begin{array}{r} 70 \\ \times 40 \\ \hline \end{array}$
12. $\begin{array}{r} 900 \\ \times 70 \\ \hline \end{array}$
13. $\begin{array}{r} 1,000 \\ \times 20 \\ \hline \end{array}$
14. $\begin{array}{r} 4,000 \\ \times 50 \\ \hline \end{array}$

Find each product. Use mental math, paper and pencil, or calculator. Explain your choices.

CHOICES

15. $8 \times 9,000$
16. 50×50
17. 40×80
18. 300×900

19. $400 \times 6,000$
20. $200 \times 100,000$
21. $7,000 \times 5,000$
22. $600,000 \times 600,000$

23. $5 \times 30 \times 2$
24. $70 \times 4 \times 50$
25. $6 \times 80 \times 900$
26. $2 \times 600 \times 60$

27. $5 \times 70 \times 40$
28. $8 \times 6 \times 500$
29. $50 \times 900 \times 20$
30. $25 \times 4 \times 40$

Find n.

31. $n \times 30 = 300$
32. $60 \times n = 6,000$
33. $n \times 900 = 9,000$

34. $n \times 40 = 4,000$
35. $900 \times n = 18,000$
36. $8,000 = n \times 2$

37. $3,000 = 1 \times n$
38. $500 \times n = 10,000$
39. $n \times 800 = 400,000$

Problem Solving

Write a rule for each.

40.

Input	Output
50	15,000
7	2,100
300	90,000
20	6,000
8	2,400

41.

Input	Output
20	18,000
7	6,300
9,000	8,100,000
80	72,000
6	5,400

42. Create your own rule. Use it to make an input/ output table like **40–41**. Challenge a classmate to discover your rule by looking at the input and output.

Describe how you would use mental arithmetic to solve $5 \times 70 \times 2$.

SUMMING UP

Describe a situation where an estimate would be more useful than an exact answer.

Estimating Products: Rounding

The educational director at the science museum is ordering materials for a workshop on making paper. He needs 4 pounds of wood pulp for each of the 487 students registered for the workshop. About how many pounds of pulp should he buy?

Does the director need an exact answer in this case? Give some reasons why an estimate makes sense.

One way to estimate a product is to use rounding. Then, multiply.

$$\begin{array}{c} 487 \\ \times\ \ 4 \end{array} \xrightarrow{\text{rounds to}} \begin{array}{c} 500 \\ \times\ \ 4 \\ \hline 2,000 \end{array}$$

The director should order about 2,000 pounds of pulp.

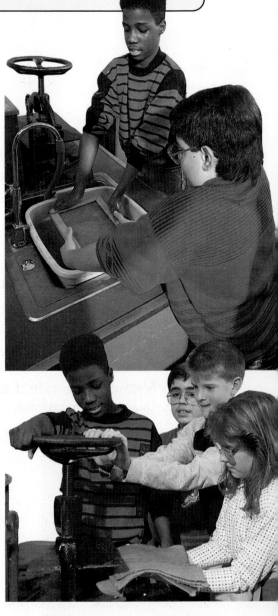

More Examples

a. Estimate 43 × 682.

$$\begin{array}{c} 682 \\ \times\ 43 \end{array} \xrightarrow[\hspace{1cm}]{\text{rounds to}} \begin{array}{c} 700 \\ \times\ 40 \\ \hline 28,000 \end{array}$$

b. Estimate 9 × 2,389.

$$\begin{array}{c} 2,389 \\ \times\ \ \ \ \ 9 \end{array} \rightarrow \begin{array}{c} 2,000 \\ \times\ \ \ \ \ 9 \\ \hline 18,000 \end{array}$$

Check Your Understanding

Estimate each product.

1. $\begin{array}{r} 53 \\ \times\ 7 \\ \hline \end{array}$

2. $\begin{array}{r} 694 \\ \times\ 8 \\ \hline \end{array}$

3. $\begin{array}{r} 26 \\ \times\ 8 \\ \hline \end{array}$

4. $\begin{array}{r} 391 \\ \times\ 72 \\ \hline \end{array}$

5. $\begin{array}{r} 1,458 \\ \times\ 46 \\ \hline \end{array}$

Share Your Ideas 3,500 is an estimate for 7 × 459. Is this estimate greater than or less than the actual product? Explain.

Estimate each product.

6. 48
   × 3

7. 24
   × 5

8. 82
   × 2

9. 63
   × 6

10. 18
    × 4

11. 535
    × 36

12. 753
    × 18

13. 842
    × 3

14. 105
    × 5

15. 1,254
    ×   4

16. 2 × 66

17. 5 × 412

18. 26 × 4

19. 108 × 643

Estimate to choose the correct answer.

20. 3 × 57   a. 141   b. 171   c. 180

21. 6 × 74   a. 404   b. 524   c. 444

22. 8 × 325   a. 2,600   b. 2,400   c. 3,200

23. 6 × 148   a. 888   b. 588   c. 618

24. 5 × 727   a. 3,435   b. 4,250   c. 3,635

25. 7 × 291   a. 2,137   b. 2,037   c. 1,427

For each situation, decide if an estimate or an exact answer is more appropriate. Explain your answers.

26. Give change for a purchase.

27. Decide if you can afford 3 or 4 new shirts.

28. Determine the number of cars that use a bridge each day.

29. Predict the number of people coming to the baseball game.

Problem Solving

30. The 5th-grade class is planning a trip to the Franklin Institute. The cost of the trip is $4 per student. There are 27 students in the class, and $100 has been collected. Estimate to find out whether all the money has been collected.

31. There are 4,326 visitors to the museum on a typical weekday. About twice as many come on each weekend day. Estimate the total number of visitors during a 7-day week.

Write a problem for which you would estimate the product.

SUMMING UP

What if you had to add 309 four times? Could you use mental math? Explain?

Multiplying by a One-Digit Factor

Luis is ordering supplies for his kite store. He plans to make 2 dragon kites. To support each kite he will need 38 inches of thin wood strips. How many inches of wood strips does he need in all?

Luis multiplies 2 × 38.

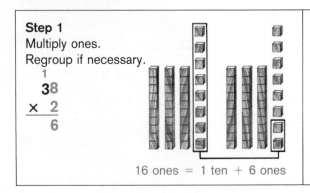

Step 1
Multiply ones.
Regroup if necessary.

```
  1
  38
×  2
───
   6
```

16 ones = 1 ten + 6 ones

Step 2
Multiply tens.
Add any extra tens.

```
  1
  38
×  2
───
  76
```

6 tens + 1 ten = 7 tens

Luis estimates to make sure his answer makes sense.

```
  38   rounds to    40
×  2   ──────→    ×  2
```

80 is close to 76.
The answer makes sense.

Luis needs 76 inches of wood strips for the kites.

More Examples

a. 6 × 157

```
 3 4
 157
×  6
────
 942
```
Why is the 9 in the hundreds place?

b. 7 × 2,009

```
    6
 2,009
×    7
──────
14,063
```

Check Your Understanding

Multiply. Estimate to be sure each answer makes sense.

1. 6 × 32   **2.** 5 × $42   **3.** 6 × 150   **4.** 8 × 781   **5.** 9 × 5,072

Share Your Ideas Describe, step by step, how to multiply 7 × 58.

Practice

Estimate first. Then multiply.

6. 46
× 3

7. 82
× 7

8. $21
× 4

9. $45
× 8

10. 30
× 7

11. 875
× 3

12. 612
× 8

13. 908
× 4

14. $510
× 5

15. 671
× 6

16. 3,150
× 9

17. 6,009
× 4

18. $2,017
× 4

19. 6,995
× 3

20. 1,951
× 8

Find *n*.

21. $3 \times \$96 = n$

22. $9 \times 48 = n$

23. $83 \times 6 = n$

24. $59 \times 3 = n$

25. $9 \times 110 = n$

26. $8 \times \$673 = n$

27. $4 \times 609 = n$

28. $5 \times 231 = n$

29. $2 \times 4,007 = n$

30. $3 \times 6,150 = n$

31. $5 \times n = 5,500$

32. $4 \times n = 8,080$

Problem Solving

33. Estimate. Would 8 feet of wood strips be enough to make the vertical supports in this kite?

34. How many inches of wood strips are needed to make all the supports for this kite?

35. **What if** basswood strips cost $3.00 for a 4-foot length? What would it cost to buy the wood supports for this kite?

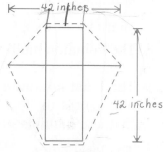

Remember:
12 inches = 1 foot

42 inches

42 inches

14 inches

36. Use your calculator to find three factors for each product. Do not use 1 as a factor.

   a. 70   **b.** 24

Write a multiplication exercise that requires regrouping. Then write one that does not. How did you decide which numbers to use?

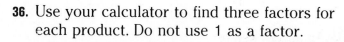

SUMMING UP

49

If batteries are sold 4 in a package, can you buy exactly 6 batteries?

Multiples

Imagine that you are programming a laser light show. You plan to use a yellow light every 4 seconds. If you use a red light every 6 seconds, when will both colors be on at the same time?

Knowing about multiples can help you find the answer.

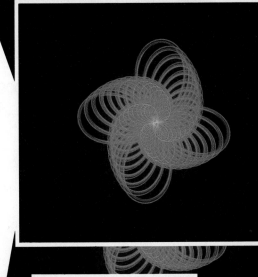

▶ When you multiply a number by 0, 1, 2, 3, ...,
the product is a **multiple** of that number.

	0×4	1×4	2×4	3×4
multiples of 4:	0	4	8	12

▶ **Common multiples** of two or more numbers are multiples that are the same.

Multiples of 4: 0, 4, 8, 12, 16, 20, 24, ...

Multiples of 6: 0, 6, 12, 18, 24, 30, 36, ...

The common multiples of 4 and 6 are 0, 12, 24, ...

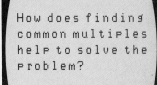

How does finding common multiples help to solve the problem?

▶ The **least common multiple** (LCM) of two or more numbers is the least nonzero number that is a multiple of each number.

The least common multiple of 4 and 6 is 12. Both colors will be on at the same time every 12 seconds.

List the first five multiples of each.

1. 3   **2.** 5   **3.** 12   **4.** 8

Find the least common multiple (LCM).

5. 10, 25   **6.** 2, 11   **7.** 3, 6   **8.** 4, 7

Share Your Ideas Explain how to find the least common multiple of 3 and 10.

List the first six multiples of each.

9. 9   **10.** 1   **11.** 2   **12.** 10   **13.** 7

14. 20   **15.** 100   **16.** 30   **17.** 25   **18.** 1,000

Name two common multiples other than zero for each.

19. 2, 4   **20.** 6, 2   **21.** 4, 3   **22.** 5, 2   **23.** 8, 10

Find the LCM.

24. 4, 5   **25.** 9, 4   **26.** 2, 8   **27.** 10, 6   **28.** 3, 7

29. 5, 8   **30.** 9, 12   **31.** 10, 35   **32.** 10, 14   **33.** 15, 25

34. 3, 4, 6   **35.** 4, 2, 8   **36.** 3, 5, 2   **37.** 10, 12, 8   **38.** 5, 6, 20

Write *true* or *false* for each statement.
Explain your thinking.

39. 24 is a multiple of 1, 3, 8, and 12.

40. Any multiple of 9 is also a multiple of 3.

41. 45 is not a multiple of 3 or 9.

42. The LCM of 8 and 12 is 36.

Problem Solving

43. Rob must buy the same number of blue and orange light bulbs. Blue bulbs are sold 6 in a package. Orange bulbs are sold 8 in a package. What is the least number of bulbs of each color that he must buy?

44. The least common multiple of 3 and 4 is 12. Without listing the multiples, how can you determine what the next common multiple after the LCM will be?

Visual Thinking

45. Count the dots. Use the pattern to draw the next three triangles.

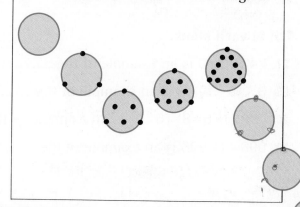

Is this statement always, sometimes, or never true? The LCM of two numbers is the product of the two numbers.

SUMMING UP

Midchapter Review

Find *n*. Name the property that you used. pages 42–43

1. $6 \times 17 = n \times 6$

2. $2 \times 8 \times 3 = 8 \times n \times 3$

3. $1 \times n = 23$

4. $15 \times n = 0$

Compute mentally. Write each product. pages 44–45

5. 6×50

6×500

$6 \times 5,000$

6. 4×700

4×70

$4 \times 7,000$

7. 900×3

90×3

$9,000 \times 3$

Find *n*. pages 44–45

8. $6 \times n = 60$

9. $n \times 8 = 4,000$

10. $n \times 4 = 120$

11. $n \times 700 = 700$

12. $1,900 \times n = 0$

13. $300 \times 2 \times 60 = 2 \times n \times 300$

Estimate each product. Tell whether each actual product will be more than or less than the estimate. pages 46–47

14. 7×82

15. 56×3

16. $4,926 \times 2$

17. $\$530 \times 8$

Estimate each product. Then multiply. pages 48–49

18. $\begin{array}{r} 96 \\ \times\ 3 \\ \hline \end{array}$

19. $\begin{array}{r} \$704 \\ \times\ \ \ 6 \\ \hline \end{array}$

20. $\begin{array}{r} 9,352 \\ \times\ \ \ \ 8 \\ \hline \end{array}$

21. $\begin{array}{r} 3,009 \\ \times\ \ \ \ 7 \\ \hline \end{array}$

Find the first three common multiples. Underline the LCM. pages 50–51

22. 2, 5

23. 3, 4

24. 3, 9

25. 6, 9

26. 4, 6

Fill in each blank.

27. $743 \times 0 = 0$ is an example of the _____.

28. $3 \times 19 = 19 \times 3$ is an example of the _____.

29. $(8 \times 5) \times 6 = 8 \times (5 \times 6)$ is an example of the _____.

30. $996 \times 1 = 996$ is an example of the _____.

Words to Know
identity property
associative property
commutative property
zero property

Solve.

31. The benefit concert was attended by 6,000 people who each paid $20. How much money was taken in?

32. Firefighters sold 185 tickets to the pancake breakfast. If each serving includes 4 pancakes, how many pancakes should be cooked?

Exploring Problem Solving

What Do You Order?

It is time to reorder some popular exercise equipment for your store.

Thinking Critically

Write your order but do not spend more than $1,500. Work in a small group. Keep a written record of your work so you can share your thinking.

Analyzing and Making Decisions

Use a calculator where appropriate.

1. Look at each low inventory item.
   a. How many were ordered last month?
   b. How many were sold last month?

2. What other information would you like to have? What information do you have that is not needed?

3. You are out of stock on Exercise Bike A and Rower B. Of which item should you order more?

4. Which items should you consider first when planning your order? Which items require the most from your $1,500 budget?

5. Write the order for your store. Find the total cost.

Look Back What were your most difficult decisions? How did you make them?

LAST MONTH'S ORDER			
Item	Number	Cost	Total
Exercise Bike A	5	$110	$ 550
Exercise Bike B	1	$200	$ 200
Rower B	2	$150	$ 300
Rower C	5	$ 95	$ 475
Weight Set 110#	8	$ 30	$ 240
Heating Pad	15	$ 8	$ 120
Total			$1885

ITEMS WITH LOW INVENTORY	
Item	Number
Exercise Bike A	0
Rower B	0
Weight Set 110#	2
Heating Pad	2

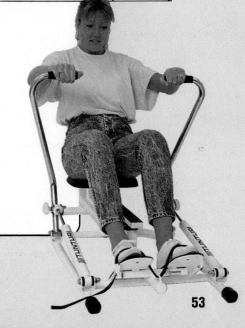

53

Problem Solving Strategies

Too Much or Too Little Information

Mr. Cole, the baseball coach, bought new equipment. He bought 8 baseball caps, 9 baseballs, 6 baseball bats, 3 soccer balls, and 4 footballs.

a. How much money was spent on baseball equipment?

b. How much money does he have left in his baseball budget?

Sometimes too little or too much information is given. Knowing what the question is can help you decide what information you need.

Solving the Problem

Use a calculator where appropriate.

CHOICES

Think What must you find out? How many questions are there?

Sneakers	$40.00
Baseball Cap	$ 2.00
Baseball	$ 7.00
Baseball Bat	$ 8.00
Soccer Ball	$10.00
Football	$12.00
Award Pin	$ 2.50

Explore Is there information you don't need? Do you need the information about soccer and football equipment? Is there information you are missing? Explain. Do you know what Mr. Cole's baseball budget is?

Solve How much will the baseball equipment cost? How much does Mr. Cole have left in his baseball budget?

Look Back Estimate to make sure your total for the baseball equipment makes sense. How could you find out how much Mr. Cole has left in his baseball budget?

Share Your Ideas

1. Write this problem so that it will not have too much information.

2. Often a problem doesn't have all the information you need. What can you do in real life if a problem does not have all the information you need?

Practice

Solve. Use a calculator where appropriate. If too little information is given, tell what is needed to solve.

CHOICES

3. Each Saturday, Andy Miles plays 6 albums in the morning and 4 albums in the afternoon on station WXTR. Each album has 9 songs. How many albums are played on 16 Saturdays?

4. A compact disc costs the station double the price of an album. Last month the station bought 65 new compact discs. What was the total cost?

5. About how many songs does Andy play in 19 hours?

6. Station WXTR is on the air 24 hours each day. How many songs are played in five days?

Mixed Strategy Review

7. Last week it cost $537.75 to repair the turntable. The cassette player cost $149.88 for repairs. How much more did it cost to repair the turntable?

8. Andy Miles personally owns 152 jazz records, 289 classical records, 329 blue-grass records, 571 rock records, and 164 inspirational records. Estimate how many records he owns.

9. Andy works 48 hours a week. He has one day off. For 3 days he works 8 hours a day. During the next 2 days he works 9 hours a day. How many hours does he work the last day of the week?

10. Look at problem **9**. Rewrite the problem, but give Mr. Miles two days off.

Create
Your Own

What if you were a disc jockey with a two-hour morning show on WXTR? Write a problem about your show.

The meteorologist reports a storm traveling at 37 miles per hour. Do you think that this is an exact speed or an estimate?

Estimating Products: Find a Range

A meteorologist is tracking a storm that is traveling at 37 miles per hour. She needs to alert cities in the path of the storm. About how far will the storm travel in the next 6 hours?

Since the speed of the storm is not constant, the meteorologist needs to allow for both a decrease and an increase in speed. She determines a **range** by rounding.

Round down
$$\begin{array}{r} 37 \\ \times\ 6 \end{array} \rightarrow \begin{array}{r} 30 \\ \times\ 6 \end{array}$$
$6 \times 30 = 180$

Round up
$$\begin{array}{r} 37 \\ \times\ 6 \end{array} \rightarrow \begin{array}{r} 40 \\ \times\ 6 \end{array}$$
$6 \times 40 = 240$

The storm will most likely travel within a **range** of 180 to 240 miles in 6 hours.

Another Example

$$\begin{array}{r} 457 \\ \times\ 20 \end{array} \xrightarrow{\text{round down}} \begin{array}{r} 400 \\ \times\ 20 \\ \hline 8{,}000 \end{array} \qquad \begin{array}{r} 457 \\ \times\ 20 \end{array} \xrightarrow{\text{round up}} \begin{array}{r} 500 \\ \times\ 20 \\ \hline 10{,}000 \end{array}$$

The range is from 8,000 to 10,000.

Check Your Understanding

Give a range for each product.

1. $\begin{array}{r} 55 \\ \times\ 3 \end{array}$

2. $\begin{array}{r} 627 \\ \times\ 4 \end{array}$

3. $\begin{array}{r} 79 \\ \times 10 \end{array}$

4. $\begin{array}{r} \$643 \\ \times\ 70 \end{array}$

5. $\begin{array}{r} 5{,}639 \\ \times\ 8 \end{array}$

Share Your Ideas Look back at the range for the storm. If the storm continues to travel at 37 miles per hour for the next 6 hours, why is it sure to travel 180 miles? Why is it impossible for the storm to go 240 miles?

Practice

Give a range for each product.

6.	7.	8.	9.	10.
46 × 2	98 × 3	345 × 5	$550 × 60	82 ×40

11.	12.	13.	14.	15.
93 ×10	15 ×20	146 × 30	126 × 50	17 ×80

Look at the range. Choose the numbers whose product falls within that range.

16. 480–560   **a.** 8 × 63   **b.** 5 × 49   **c.** 7 × 58   **d.** not given

17. 350–420   **a.** 6 × 46   **b.** 9 × 32   **c.** 7 × 54   **d.** not given

18. 400–450   **a.** 4 × 87   **b.** 5 × 86   **c.** 9 × 37   **d.** not given

19. 180–270   **a.** 3 × 91   **b.** 5 × 62   **c.** 4 × 75   **d.** not given

Estimate to find the greater product. Use > or < for ⬤.

20. 8 × 69 ⬤ 7 × 87   21. 8 × 54 ⬤ 9 × 38

22. 3 × 240 ⬤ 2 × 420   23. 3 × $5.25 ⬤ 4 × $4.98

Problem Solving

Look at the map. This storm is traveling at about 68 miles an hour in a northeasterly direction. Make the following predictions for the next 4 hours.

24. Which cities is the storm likely to reach?

25. Which cities is the storm not likely to reach?

26. Which cities are you not sure about?

Look back at **24–26**. Describe how finding a range helped you to make predictions.

SUMMING UP

57

What is 2 × 13? What is 10 × 13? Tell how you could use these products to find the product of 12 × 13.

Multiplying by a Two-Digit Factor

An animator creates 24 pictures for each second of an animated cartoon. How many pictures are drawn to make a cartoon that is 45 seconds long?

One way to find out is to multiply.

Step 1	Step 2	Step 3
Multiply by ones.	Multiply by tens.	Add.
$\quad$ 2 $\quad$ 24 $\times$ 45 120	$\quad\overset{1}{\overset{2}{\,}}$ $\quad$ 24 $\times$ 45 120 960 ← Why is this product 960 rather than 96?	$\quad\overset{1}{\overset{2}{\,}}$ $\quad$ 24 $\times$ 45 120 960 1,080

The animator creates 1,080 pictures to make a 45-second cartoon.

When you multiplied 45 × 24 in the example above, you really multiplied by two numbers. What were they?

More Examples

a.
$$
\begin{array}{r}
\overset{2}{\overset{4\ 1}{472}} \\
\times\ 36 \\
\hline
2832 \\
14160 \\
\hline
16{,}992
\end{array}
$$
2832 ← 6 × 472
14160 ← 30 × 472

b.
$$
\begin{array}{r}
\overset{4\ 2}{\overset{5\ 2}{3{,}084}} \\
\times\ \ 57 \\
\hline
21588 \\
154200 \\
\hline
175{,}788
\end{array}
$$
21588 ← 7 × 3,084
154200 ← 50 × 3,084

Check Your Understanding

Multiply. Estimate to be sure each answer makes sense.

1. $\begin{array}{r} 25 \\ \times\ 38 \\ \hline \end{array}$
2. $\begin{array}{r} \$93 \\ \times\ 26 \\ \hline \end{array}$
3. $\begin{array}{r} 861 \\ \times\ 45 \\ \hline \end{array}$
4. $\begin{array}{r} 2{,}047 \\ \times\ 19 \\ \hline \end{array}$
5. $\begin{array}{r} 6{,}540 \\ \times\ 63 \\ \hline \end{array}$

Share Your Ideas Write a multiplication example with two factors that has the same answer as (7 × 251) + (30 × 251).

Multiply. Estimate to be sure each answer makes sense.

| 6. | 78
 ×62 | 7. | 43
 ×34 | 8. | 50
 ×90 | 9. | 87
 ×83 | 10. | $460
 × 13 |

| 11. | 250
 × 44 | 12. | 139
 × 87 | 13. | $99
 × 75 | 14. | $55
 × 16 | 15. | 600
 × 80 |

| 16. | 912
 × 23 | 17. | 406
 × 58 | 18. | 8,094
 × 54 | 19. | 7,008
 × 67 | 20. | 524
 × 39 |

21. 36 × 88

22. 14 × 70

23. 28 × 568

24. 67 × 148

25. 60 × 300

26. 19 × 8,390

27. 17 × 5,000

28. 400 × 500

29. Look back at **11–15.** Tell which exercises you could do using mental math. Explain how you would do it.

Compare. Use mental math, paper and pencil, calculator, or estimation. Use >, <, or = for each ⬤. Explain your choices.

30. 25 × 44 ⬤ 1,200

31. 20,000 ⬤ 54 × 376

32. 18 × 25 ⬤ 2 × 250

33. 50 × 40 ⬤ 4 × 2 × 250

34. 4 × 386 ⬤ 23 × 82

35. 8 × 100 × 50 ⬤ 80 × 25 × 200

Problem Solving

36. A cartoon commercial uses 24 drawings a second. The animator multiplies 35 × 24 to find how many drawings are needed in all. How long is the commercial?

37. The first motion picture was recorded in 1882, in France. The camera took 12 pictures a second. Use these facts to write a problem that can be solved using multiplication.

Common Error

38. What if Maria multiplied 72 × 35 this way? How would you use estimation to show her that 315 is *not* a reasonable answer? Help Maria do the problem correctly.

```
  3
  1
 35
×72
 70
245
315  ← incorrect
```

Describe step by step how to multiply 25 × 46.

If you have 15 dimes, how much money do you have?

Multiplying Money

Ray and Ben wash windows after school. They charge $2.75 a window. Mr. Sparkle asked them to wash the 26 windows in his house. They multiplied to find out how much they will earn.

$$\begin{array}{r} \$2.75 \\ \times\ \ \ 26 \\ \hline 1650 \\ 5500 \\ \hline 7150 \end{array}$$

Ben wants to know how much money this is. $7,150? $71.50? $7.50?

Ray uses estimation to show Ben about how much money they could expect to earn.

$2.75 is between $2.00 and $3.00.
26 × $2 = $52   26 × $3 = $78
$71.50 is between $52.00 and $78.00.

When you multiply money, remember to write the dollar sign and place the decimal point to show cents.

$$\begin{array}{r} \$2.75 \\ \times\ \ \ 26 \\ \hline 1650 \\ 5500 \\ \hline \$71.50 \end{array}$$

Ben and Ray will earn $71.50.

Check Your Understanding

Estimate each product. Then multiply.

	1.	2.	3.	4.	5.
	$1.49	$10.48	$.59	$1.98	$17.50
	× 8	× 6	× 2	× 40	× 39

Share Your Ideas   In your own words, state a rule for multiplying money.

Practice

Estimate each product. Then multiply.

6. $.24 $\times$ 3	**7.** $5.17 $\times$ 7	**8.** $8.90 $\times$ 6	**9.** $1.36 $\times$ 6

6. $.24
  × 3

7. $5.17
  × 7

8. $8.90
  × 6

9. $1.36
  × 6

10. $.46
  × 20

11. $7.32
  × 90

12. $1.20
  × 58

13. $50.39
  × 26

14. $1.05
  × 9

15. $10.99
  × 8

16. $.75
  × 24

17. $6.87
  × 35

18. $3.48
  × 60

19. $12.23
  × 41

20. $36.80
  × 27

21. $19.99
  × 53

Multiply mentally. Follow the rule.

Rule: Multiply by 4.

	Input	Output
22.	$ 25.	
23.	$300.	
24.	$ 80.	
25.	$125.	

Rule: Multiply by 2.

	Input	Output
26.	$3.50	
27.	$1.10	
28.	$ .75	
29.	$6.25	

30. **Look back** at **25** and **28**. Describe the method you used to find each product.

Problem Solving

Use a calculator where appropriate.

CHOICES

31. Clearview Company charges $7.50 a window to wash office windows. The medical building has 126 windows. How much will it cost to have them washed?

32. A famous architect, Mies Van Der Rohe, designed a Baltimore office with 2,100 windows. At $7.50 each, how much will it cost to have the windows washed? If the windows are washed 4 times a year, what is the annual cost for cleaning the windows?

When multiplying money, how does estimation help you place the decimal point?

SUMMING UP

Mixed Review

1. $8 + 7 = n$

2. $11 - 6 = n$

3. $6 + n = 32$

4. $7 \times 7 = n$

5. $n - 8 = 19$

6. $37.42
  − 16.20

7.   451
  216
  + 1,420

8.   3,054
  + 7,045

9.   387
  + 29

10.   256
  − 83

11. $45.87
  + 2.56

12.   8,090
  + 347

13.   3,000
  − 1,451

Estimate.

14. $295.50
  − 87.35

15.   65,195
  + 61,767

Describe the steps you would use to multiply 768 by 23.

Multiplying Greater Numbers

A helicopter air-taxi service carries about 185 passengers a day from one airport to another. At this rate how many passengers does it carry in a year?

$365 \times 185 = n$

One way to find the product is to multiply as shown below.

Step 1 Multiply by ones.	Step 2 Multiply by tens.	Step 3 Multiply by hundreds.	Step 4 Add.
185 $\times$ 365 925 $\leftarrow$ 5 $\times$ 185	185 $\times$ 365 925 11100 $\leftarrow$ 60 $\times$ 185	185 $\times$ 365 925 11100 55500 $\leftarrow$ 300 $\times$ 185	185 $\times$ 365 925 11100 55500 67,525

The air-taxi service carries about 67,525 passengers in a year.

Another Example

Another way to multiply greater numbers is to estimate, then use a calculator. Find 389×504.

Estimate.

504	rounds to	500
$\times$ 389	$\longrightarrow$	$\times$ 400
		200,000

Calculate.

$389 \times 504 =$ | 196056 |

Check Your Understanding

Estimate first. Then use a calculator to multiply.

1. 751
   $\times$ 602

2. 638
   $\times$ 304

3. 204
   $\times$ 510

4. 324
   $\times$ 679

5. 3,459
   $\times$ 108

Share Your Ideas What three separate multiplications do you use to find 728×439?

Practice

Estimate first. Then use a calculator to multiply.

6. $\begin{array}{r} 179 \\ \times\,305 \end{array}$ 7. $\begin{array}{r} 785 \\ \times\,107 \end{array}$ 8. $\begin{array}{r} 247 \\ \times\,480 \end{array}$ 9. $\begin{array}{r} \$3.68 \\ \times\,\,\,\,502 \end{array}$ 10. $\begin{array}{r} 169 \\ \times\,700 \end{array}$

11. $\begin{array}{r} 519 \\ \times\,294 \end{array}$ 12. $\begin{array}{r} 245 \\ \times\,653 \end{array}$ 13. $\begin{array}{r} 6,008 \\ \times\,\,\,\,689 \end{array}$ 14. $\begin{array}{r} \$19.07 \\ \times\,\,\,\,906 \end{array}$ 15. $\begin{array}{r} 2,413 \\ \times\,\,\,\,701 \end{array}$

16. 195×372 17. 471×587 18. 239×695 19. 860×614

20. $755 \times 2,863$ 21. $226 \times 1,267$ 22. $444 \times 9,824$ 23. $853 \times 2,518$

Find _n_.

24. $300 \times 367 = n$ 25. $(803 \times 145) \times 1 = n$ 26. $408 \times 2,378 = n$

27. $(520 \times 289) \times 10 = n$ 28. $6 \times (74 \times 568) = n$ 29. $2 \times (210 \times 7,463) = n$

Compare. Use mental math, calculator, or estimation. Use >, <, or = for ⬤.

CHOICES

30. 320×307 ⬤ 320×308 31. $50 \times 7,000$ ⬤ $60 \times 6,000$

32. 682×254 ⬤ 978×200 33. $7,896 \times 432$ ⬤ $3,948 \times 864$

Problem Solving

Use a calculator where appropriate.

CHOICES

34. Air food Service prepares 1,800 inflight meals every day. How many meals do they prepare yearly?

35. Twelve tank trucks each deliver jet fuel 15 times a day. They carry 675 gallons each. How many gallons of fuel are delivered daily?

36. Explain how you can solve each by using mental math.
    a. $25 \times 400 = n$
    b. $1,005 \times 30 = n$

Mathematics and History

37. The first arithmetic book was published in Treviso, Italy, in 1478. The × symbol for multiplication was introduced 140 years later. Analyze this old example. Use a calculator to help you find the factors and the product. Rewrite the multiplication as we do it today.

$$\begin{array}{r} 852 \\ \hline 5964 \quad 7 \\ 852 \quad 1 \\ 1704 \quad 2 \\ \hline 184,884 \end{array}$$

Describe an easy way to find the product of 777×249 using multiplication patterns.

SUMMING UP

63

Using Problem Solving

Interview: Calculators at the Zoo

Working with numbers is part of a zookeeper's job. Jim Murtaugh is the curator of animals at the Central Park Zoo, in New York City.

"We use calculators to help us order the correct amount of food for each animal. Budgeting food costs is also easier with a calculator."

How many pounds of fish are needed to feed all the penguins at the zoo for a year? Use a calculator to multiply.

2 × 40 = 80

80 × 365 = 29,200
⎿ days in a year

Animal	Food	Daily amount for one animal	Number of animals
Penguin	fish	2 pounds	40
Polar bear	bear chow	20 pounds	2
	fish	2 pounds	
	chicken	2 pounds	
Sea lion	fish	10–18 pounds	5
Seal	fish	3–10 pounds	3

The penguins eat 29,200 pounds of fish a year.

Explain how estimation can help you decide if this answer is reasonable.

Sharing Your Ideas

Use the information in the chart above to answer each question.

1. How much bear chow do the two polar bears eat in 2 days?

2. What is the least amount of fish needed for the sea lions each year?

3. If fish costs $.65 per pound, how much does the zoo spend on fish for the bears each year?

4. Male sea lions eat about 18 pounds of fish a day. How much food does a zoo buy for 3 males in 1 year?

Practice

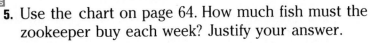

Solve. Use mental math, paper and pencil,
or a calculator. Explain your choices.

CHOICES

5. Use the chart on page 64. How much fish must the zookeeper buy each week? Justify your answer.

6. At $.65 per pound, what does a week's supply of fish cost?

7. The zookeeper plans to add four harbor seals to the seal exhibit. How much more fish will he need to order each week?

8. The zookeeper wants to know how much the new seals will cost the zoo for the first year. What will the food cost be for one year? What other costs do you think he might take into consideration?

Chlorine is put into swimming pools at the zoo every day. Use the information in the chart to answer **9** and **10**.

	Gallons of water	Gallons of chlorine used each week in winter	Gallons of chlorine used each week in summer
Seal Pool	60,000	5	15
Polar Bear Pool	90,000	7	21
Sea Lion Pool	100,000	10	30

9. What is the total amount of chlorine used in 12 weeks in the summer? in the winter?

10. **What if** chlorine costs $.79 per gallon? How much does the chlorine for the bear pool cost in 12 weeks of summer? in 12 weeks of winter?

Summing Up

11. Is using a calculator always the fastest way to find an answer? Explain your thinking.

12. Plan ahead! Create a 90-day budget for feeding the penguins and polar bears at the Central Park Zoo. Bear chow costs $.25 per pound. Chicken costs $.45 per pound. Fish costs $.65 per pound. Record your budget in a chart. Use estimation to check your results.

Using Problem Solving

Consumer Skills

"We have only $2.95 and we need 3 packages of hot dogs. How can we decide if we have enough money?," asked Fred.

"There is a way to do this in your head," said Steve.

Think
$$\$1.00 \times 3 = \$3.00$$
$$\$1.00 - \$.97 = \$.03$$
$$\$.03 \times 3 = \$.09$$
$$\$3.00 - \$.09 = \$2.91$$

"We have enough money," said Fred.

Hot Dogs $.97

A. Use the grocery ad shown on page 67 or a food circular. Make a small shopping list that shows multiple purchases of items.

Example: 5 packages of hot dogs
4 lb watermelon
4 jars of mustard
$3\frac{1}{2}$ gal of lemonade

B. Use mental math to find the total cost for each item purchased. Then use a calculator to find the total cost for each item. Which way made more sense? Why?

C. Make a new shopping list. Find the total cost of each item by using mental math and a calculator.

Sharing Your Ideas

1. What are reasons why it might be helpful to use mental math?

2. Do you think you could find some prices faster mentally than with a calculator or pencil and paper? Explain.

Practice

Use mental math, paper and pencil, or calculator.

CHOICES

3. Plan a picnic for your class. You have $2.00 to spend per person. Make your shopping list and determine your total. Use mental math whenever it will help.

Paper Cups ..... pkg. of 30 $1.89	Hamburger or Hot Dog Buns.......
Hamburger ....1 lb $1.59	pkg. of 8 $ .93
Muffins.............. pkg. of 6 $ .89	Hot Dogs........... pkg. of 8 $ .97
Potato Salad..............1 lb $ .57	Cole Slaw..................1 lb $ .68
Apple Juice.............. $\frac{1}{2}$ gal $1.39	Orange Juice .... $\frac{1}{2}$ gal $1.99
Apples .... bag of 10 $ .95	Lemonade................ $\frac{1}{2}$ gal $ .99
Mustard ....$ .23	Oranges .... 5 for $ .79
Peanuts ....2-lb bag $1.95	Watermelon ....1 lb $ .19
Napkins ....pkg. $ .85	Paper Plates ... pkg. of 10 $1.93

Summing Up

4. How did you determine how much of each item to buy?

5. Which prices were easiest to determine mentally? with paper and pencil? with a calculator?

6. How did you determine your total cost? Explain.

Chapter Review

Find *n*. Name the property that you used.
pages 42–43

1. $58 \times 76 = 76 \times n$

2. $19 \times (4 \times 23) = (19 \times n) \times 23$

3. $n \times 148 = 0$

4. $800 = n \times 800$

5. $92 \times 85 = 85 \times n$

6. $(21 \times 13) \times 5 = 21 \times (n \times 5)$

Find *n*. pages 44–45

7. $7 \times n = 70$

8. $n \times 9 = 4,500$

9. $n \times 3 = 150$

10. $10 \times n = 200$

11. $n \times 100 = 5,000$

12. $1,000 \times n = 6,000$

Estimate each product. Then multiply.
pages 46–49, 58–59, 62–63

13. 8×26

14. 6×507

15. $95 \times 1,467$

16. $3 \times 8,092$

17. 93×85

18. 400×367

19. 56×736

20. 20×605

Write the LCM for each pair. pages 50–51

21. 3, 10

22. 5, 10

23. 4, 6

24. 6, 8

25. 5, 9

Multiply. pages 60–61, 66–67

26.
$$\begin{array}{r} \$19.25 \\ \times \quad 4 \\ \hline \end{array}$$

27.
$$\begin{array}{r} \$8.50 \\ \times \quad 25 \\ \hline \end{array}$$

28.
$$\begin{array}{r} \$20.75 \\ \times \quad 16 \\ \hline \end{array}$$

29.
$$\begin{array}{r} \$3.99 \\ \times \quad 5 \\ \hline \end{array}$$

30.
$$\begin{array}{r} \$42.00 \\ \times \quad 65 \\ \hline \end{array}$$

Fill in the blank. pages 56–57

31. A low estimate for 7×35 is 210. A high estimate is 280. Numbers between 210 and 280 are in the _____ .

Solve. pages 53–55

32. The bowling club met on Friday. Only 81 members paid their dues of $10.50. What were the total dues paid? Can you calculate the dues that still need to be paid? Explain.

33. Twenty carpenters each worked 30 hours one week. Fifteen apprentices also worked 30 hours each that week. How many hours was that altogether?

Chapter Test

Find _n_. Name the property that you used.

1. $672 \times n = 672$

2. $(385 \times 27) \times 6 = (n \times 385) \times 6$

3. $n \times 55 = 0$

4. $21 \times (6 \times 81) = (21 \times n) \times 81$

Find each missing number.

5. $54 \times n = 5,400$

6. $n \times 4 = 240$

7. $16 \times 100 = n$

Multiply.

8. 9×77

9. 6×351

10. $87 \times 1,007$

11. $6 \times \$5.99$

12. $4 \times \$3.25$

13. 29×300

14. $\begin{array}{r} 3,050 \\ \times \quad 63 \\ \hline \end{array}$

15. $\begin{array}{r} 325 \\ \times 631 \\ \hline \end{array}$

16. $\begin{array}{r} \$6.37 \\ \times \quad 52 \\ \hline \end{array}$

17. $\begin{array}{r} \$367.00 \\ \times \qquad 8 \\ \hline \end{array}$

Write the LCM for each pair.

18. 3, 9

19. 5, 7

20. 4, 10

Estimate.

21. 6×34

22. 5×444

23. $9 \times 5,500$

Solve.

24. Franklin School has 26 classrooms. If each class donates 149 cans of food to charity, how many cans will be donated?

25. Stamps are printed 100 to a sheet. If the postmaster sold 72 sheets in 10 days, how many stamps did he sell? What information is not needed to solve this problem?

THINK The Associative Property works for addition and multiplication. Does it work for subtraction? Give two examples to support your answer.

Exponents

A shortcut for writing
$2 \times 2 \times 2 = 8$ is $2^3 = 8$.

base $\rightarrow$ 2^3 $\leftarrow$ **exponent:** This number is written above and to the right of another number.

Read 2^3 two to the third power

▶ The **exponent** tells you how many factors to write.

▶ The **base** tells you which number to use for each of the factors.

$2^3 =$ _____ × _____ × _____	$2^3 = 2 \times 2 \times 2$
$3^4 =$ _____ × _____ × _____ × _____	$3^4 = 3 \times 3 \times 3 \times 3$

Explain why 3^4 is 81.

Use a base and an exponent to write each in a shorter way.

1. 6×6

2. 9×9

3. $5 \times 5 \times 5$

4. $7 \times 7 \times 7$

5. $2 \times 2 \times 2 \times 2$

6. $3 \times 3 \times 3 \times 3 \times 3$

Find n. Use mental math, paper and pencil, or a calculator.

CHOICES

7. $5^2 = n$

8. $7^2 = n$

9. $9^3 = n$

10. $6^4 = n$

11. $8^n = 64$

12. $2^n = 64$

13. $2^n = 512$

14. $4^n = 1,024$

15. $3^n = 2,187$

16. Does $3^4 = 4^3$? Why or why not?

Maintaining Skills

Choose the correct answers. Write A, B, C, or D.

1. What is the value of 9 in 89,854,370?

   A 900,000   C 9,000,000

   B 90,000,000   D not given

2. Write the standard number for 82 billion, 18 million, 362 thousand, 492.

   A 82,180,362,492   C 8,218,362,492

   B 82,018,362,492   D not given

3. Compare. 13,806 ⬤ 13,860

   A <   C =

   B >   D not given

4. Round 13,892 to the nearest hundred.

   A 13,900   C 13,800

   B 14,000   D not given

5. Find *n*.   6 + *n* = 14

   A 7   C 9

   B 20   D not given

6. 208,765 + 218,036

   A 416,791   C 426,801

   B 426,701   D not given

7. What property is used?
   (2 × 4) × 5 = *n* × (4 × 5)

   A Associative   C Identity

   B Commutative   D not given

8. Estimate. 685 × 6

   A 360   C 4,200

   B 500   D 42,000

9. 8,214
   ×   3

   A 24,642   C 24,632

   B 24,542   D not given

10. Find the LCM of 10 and 5.

    A 15   C 50

    B 10   D not given

11. 479 × 36

    A 16,144   C 17,244

    B 17,246   D not given

Solve. Use the picture for 12.

12. Paula and Harry went to the pet store to buy a pet. How much more expensive was Harry's choice?

    A $60.75   C $36.15

    B $33.95   D not given

3 Understanding Division

Glow by Josef Albers USA 15c

Learning never ends

Viking missions to Mars

Expanding human knowledge USA 15c

Martin Luther King Jr.

Black Heritage USA 15c

Sharing What You Know

Do you know that collectors have special names? Philatelists (Fill-AY-tuh-lists) collect stamps. Numismatists (New-MIZ-muh-tists) collect coins. Do you collect anything? Talk about how you would use mathematics in organizing your collection. How could using division help collectors?

Using Language

Numismatists divide coins by date and value. They also use divided cases to hold the coins. **Divide** means to separate. In mathematics, to **divide** is to separate into equal parts. 16 divided by 8 is 2. How are the two meanings of **divide** alike? How are they different?

Words to Know: dividend, divisor, quotient, remainder, average, divisible, inverse operations

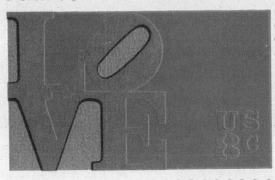

Be a Problem Solver

Anna and Henry want to arrange 36 stamps on an album page. How could they do this so that the stamps on the page look attractive?

Write about how you would organize a brand-new collection of stamps, coins, shells, or anything else.

3 × 4 = 12 and 12 ÷ 3 = 4 are part of the fact family for 3, 4, and 12. Write two other related facts for the family.

Relating Multiplication and Division

Caitlin is repairing a multiplication machine at the function factory.
If she inputs 4, the output should be 20. Find the rule.

Let *n* represent the number by which the machine is multiplying. **n × 4 = 20**

Use the relationship between multiplication and division to find *n*.

related facts   **20 ÷ 4 = 5   5 × 4 = 20**
                 20 ÷ 5 = 4   4 × 5 = 20

The rule is to multiply by 5.

▶ You can divide to find a missing factor because multiplication and division are **inverse operations**.

Help Caitlin decide if the division machines are broken. When she input 0 the output was 0.

0 ÷ 4 = 0   Think **0 × 4 = 0**
0 ÷ 7 = 0   Think **0 × 7 = 0**

The machines are not broken.

▶ Zero divided by any number, except zero, is zero.

Explain why a number can never be divided by zero. Write some related multiplication facts with zero.

Check Your Understanding

Find *n*.

1. 3 × n = 21   **2.** n × 6 = 48   **3.** 54 ÷ 6 = n   **4.** 35 ÷ n = 5

Share Your Ideas   What related fact did you use to solve example **4**? Explain your answer.

Find *n*.

5. $n \times 6 = 12$ 6. $8 \times n = 8$ 7. $18 \div 3 = n$ 8. $28 \div n = 7$

9. $5 \times n = 40$ 10. $n \times 9 = 63$ 11. $0 \div 8 = n$ 12. $n \div 2 = 9$

13. Write a multiplication fact and two related division facts that are illustrated by this picture.

Write two related division examples for each.

14. 4×5 15. 8×4 16. 5×9 17. 9×8 18. 3×8

Complete. Follow each rule, if given.

Rule: Multiply by 6.

	Input	Output
19.	3	
20.	7	
21.		24
22.		36

Rule: Divide by 3.

	Input	Output
23.	9	
24.	21	
25.		6
26.		10

27. Find the rule.

Input	Output
2	14
7	49
4	28
5	35

28. **Look back** at **27**. Explain how you found the rule.

29. Use a calculator to divide a number by zero. What answer do you get? Explain.

30. Chen placed a total of 24 stickers on 3 pages of his album. If each page had an equal number of stickers, how many were on a page?

31. Carlos has 18 stickers to place in an album. If each page holds 9 stickers, how many pages will he need?

32. Samantha gave 5 stickers to each of her 4 friends. How many stickers did she give away?

33. When Samantha gave each of her 4 friends 5 stickers, she had 2 left over. How many stickers did she have originally?

Think of a number between 1 and 9. Multiply it by 5. Divide the product by 5. What number do you get? Explain.

SUMMING UP

Multiply 5 × 3, 5 × 30, and 5 × 300. Describe the pattern you see.

Mental Math: Division Patterns

Carol collects one set of 5 United States coins for each year. She has 100 coins. How many sets of coins does she have?

100 ÷ 5 = *n*

Use a basic division fact to find the quotient.

Think $5\overline{)10}$ with quotient 2

$$5\overline{)100}$$

20 ← quotient
divisor → 5)100 ← dividend

Look at the pattern.

10 ÷ 5 = 2

| 100 ÷ 5 = 20 | She has 20 sets of coins.

1,000 ÷ 5 = 200

Basic facts and patterns can help you divide mentally. Describe the patterns you see.

54 ÷ 9 = 6	40 ÷ 8 = 5	10 ÷ 1 = 10
540 ÷ 9 = 60	400 ÷ 8 = 50	20 ÷ 1 = 20
5,400 ÷ 9 = 600	4,000 ÷ 8 = 500	30 ÷ 1 = 30
54,000 ÷ 9 = 6,000	40,000 ÷ 8 = 5,000	40 ÷ 1 = 40

Check Your Understanding

Find each quotient mentally.

1.	36 ÷ 4	2.	12 ÷ 6	3.	32 ÷ 8	4.	25 ÷ 5
	360 ÷ 4		120 ÷ 6		320 ÷ 8		250 ÷ 5
	3,600 ÷ 4		1,200 ÷ 6		3,200 ÷ 8		2,500 ÷ 5

5. $7\overline{)28}$ 6. $7\overline{)280}$ 7. $7\overline{)2,800}$ 8. $7\overline{)28,000}$

Share Your Ideas Use 42 ÷ 6 = 7 to write 3 division examples that can be solved using division patterns.

Practice

Find each quotient mentally.

9. $9 \div 3$
$90 \div 3$
$900 \div 3$

10. $45 \div 9$
$450 \div 9$
$4{,}500 \div 9$

11. $24 \div 4$
$240 \div 4$
$2{,}400 \div 4$

12. $21 \div 7$
$210 \div 7$
$2{,}100 \div 7$

13. $9\overline{)270}$

14. $2\overline{)400}$

15. $5\overline{)40{,}000}$

16. $8\overline{)72{,}000}$

17. $3\overline{)600}$

18. $5\overline{)300}$

19. $60\overline{)600}$

20. $20\overline{)1{,}400}$

Choose the division that you can solve mentally by using a division fact. Give the quotient.

21. a. $160 \div 3$
b. $160 \div 4$
c. $160 \div 5$
d. $160 \div 6$

22. a. $4\overline{)350}$
b. $6\overline{)350}$
c. $7\overline{)350}$
d. $8\overline{)350}$

23. a. $6\overline{)2{,}000}$
b. $8\overline{)2{,}000}$
c. $5\overline{)2{,}000}$
d. $7\overline{)2{,}000}$

24. a. $9\overline{)27{,}000}$
b. $9\overline{)26{,}000}$
c. $9\overline{)25{,}000}$
d. $9\overline{)28{,}000}$

25. Divide. Find the pattern. Explain.

$2 \div 2$ $4 \div 4$ $5 \div 5$ $7 \div 7$ $9 \div 9$ $25 \div 25$

Problem Solving

26. Rosa paid $56 for eight 1939 World's Fair coins. How much did each coin cost, if she paid the same amount for each?

27. The Coin Mart received 1,600 Indian head pennies to be sold in sets of 8. How many sets will they have for sale?

V isual Thinking

28. Which piece completes the circle?

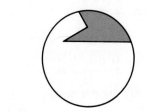

a.   **b.**

c.   **d.**

Find $63{,}000 \div 7$. Show the basic fact and pattern that give the quotient.

Describe a situation where only an estimate is necessary. Explain your thinking.

Estimating Quotients

Andrew has collected 500 baseball cards. He wants to keep them in a binder. He plans to put 8 cards on a page. About how many pages will Andrew need to buy?

Here is one way to estimate 500 ÷ 8.

Use **compatible numbers** that are close to the original numbers. Compatible numbers can be divided mentally.

$$8\overline{)500}$$ Think What division fact is close to 50 ÷ 8? $$8\overline{)480}^{\,60}$$

Explain why each conclusion is true.

• The quotient is in the 60's.

• Andrew will need more than 60, but less than 70 pages.

More Examples

a. Estimate 91 ÷ 4.

$$4\overline{)91}$$ Think $$4\overline{)80}^{\,20}$$

A good estimate is 20.

b. Estimate 286 ÷ 5.

$$5\overline{)286}$$ Think $$5\overline{)300}^{\,60}$$

A good estimate is 60.

Check Your Understanding

Estimate each quotient.

1. $3\overline{)84}$ **2.** $6\overline{)91}$ **3.** $8\overline{)326}$ **4.** $4\overline{)295}$ **5.** $5\overline{)160}$

Share Your Ideas   Which example would you use to estimate $3\overline{)200}$? Explain your choice.

a. $3\overline{)180}$ **b.** $3\overline{)210}$ **c.** $3\overline{)300}$

Practice

Estimate each quotient.

6. $4\overline{)90}$ 7. $2\overline{)56}$ 8. $5\overline{)59}$

9. $3\overline{)80}$ 10. $6\overline{)500}$ 11. $7\overline{)155}$

12. $6\overline{)450}$ 13. $4\overline{)195}$ 14. $8\overline{)766}$

15. $9\overline{)300}$ 16. $2\overline{)130}$ 17. $2\overline{)154}$

18. $7\overline{)612}$ 19. $4\overline{)150}$ 20. $5\overline{)283}$

21. $299 \div 6$ 22. $486 \div 5$ 23. $135 \div 3$

24. $400 \div 9$ 25. $588 \div 11$ 26. $746 \div 10$

Explain why each quotient is greater than $70 or less than $70.

27. $5\overline{)\$360}$ 28. $7\overline{)\$480}$ 29. $6\overline{)\$395}$

Estimate to choose the correct quotient.

30. $92 \div 4$
   a. 13
   b. 23
   c. 33

31. $416 \div 8$
   a. 42
   b. 52
   c. 502

32. $141 \div 3$
   a. 27
   b. 37
   c. 47

Problem Solving

33. Jennifer has 250 baseball cards. She plans to buy 30 plastic sheets that hold 8 cards each. Will she be able to put all her baseball cards in the sheets? Why or why not?

34. Lenny gives each of his 4 friends 20 baseball cards. He keeps 10 for himself. How many baseball cards did Lenny have originally?

Explain why you can estimate a quotient without completing the division.

Mixed Review

Find *n*.

1. $1,090 + n = 5,000$

2. $4 \times 185 = n$

3. $263 - 117 = n$

4. $n \times 7 = 56$

5. $48 \div n = 8$

6. $n + 532 = 1,603$

7. $n \div 6 = 0$

8. $752 + n = 827$

Give a range for each product.

9. 7×39

10. 4×82

11. 10×43

12. 6×251

13. 20×18

14. $30 \times \$440$

Write in words.

15. 4,200

16. 685

17. 10,060

18. 110,100

19. 3,020,000

20. 608,304

SUMMING UP

Exploring Division

How can you divide $396 equally among 3 people?

Working together

Materials: Play money (ten $100-bills, twenty $10-bills, twenty $1-bills) for each group.

A. Use your play money to show $396.

- Divide the money among 3 people so that each gets the same amount. Which bills will you share first? Why?

- How many $100-, $10-, and $1-bills did each person get?

B. Now use your play money to show $168.

- Can you divide $168 among 3 people so that each gets the same amount? How many $100-bills will each person get? What must you do before the money can be divided?

- How much money did each person get?

Sharing Your Results

1. Describe how your group shared $396 among 3 people. Did you have to exchange any bills before completing the division? Explain.

2. Describe how your group shared $168 among 3 people. Did you have to exchange any bills before completing the division? Explain.

Practice

Work with a partner. Use your play money to show $35.

The picture shows how the $35 was divided into 2 equal groups.

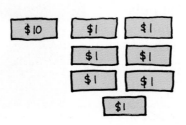

3. How many $10-bills are in each group? What do you do with the extra $10-bill?

4. How many $1-bills are in each group? Do you have any extra bills?

The division for this example can be written

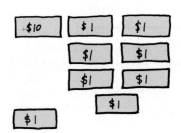

$17 R1
2)$35 — remainder of $1
— make 2 equal groups

5. Could you also share the remainder? Explain how.

Use or draw play money to model each division example. Then solve.

6. 6)$138   7. 2)$402   8. 4)$86   9. 5)$118

Summing Up

10. Divide 46 into 3 equal groups. Remember 46 is 4 tens and 6 ones. Describe how to do the division. Record your work.

11. Divide 275 into 8 equal groups. 275 is 2 hundreds, 7 tens, and 5 ones. Describe how to do the division. Record your work.

12. This picture shows one way to divide 12 stickers into equal groups. How many groups are there? How many stickers are in each group? Show some other ways to make equal groups.

13. Explain how to share an extra $100-, $10-, or $1-bill among 5 people.

What remainders are possible when a number is divided by 4? How do you know?

Dividing Two-Digit Numbers

Mr. Anderson is one of the 20 million philatelists in the United States. He collects stamps. Mr. Anderson wants to place 67 stamps on 3 pages. If he puts the same amount on each page, how many stamps will there be on each page? How many stamps will be left?

Divide 67 by 3 to find the answer.

Step 1	Step 2	Step 3
Estimate to place the first digit in the quotient.	Divide tens. Then multiply.	Subtract and compare.
$\square$ 20 3)67 Think 3)60	2 3)**67** Think 3)6 6 ← 2 × 3	2 3)67 −6 0 0 < 3 The difference must be less than the divisor.

Step 4
Bring down the ones.
Repeat the steps.

  22 **R1**
3)67
 6↓   Think
 07   3)7
− 6 ← 2 × 3
  1   1 < 3 Write the remainder in the quotient.

Check by multiplying.

   22
× 3
  66
+ 1
  67

22 is the quotient of the above division example. What part of the division example are the numbers 3, 1, and 67?

There will be 22 stamps on each page and 1 stamp left.

Check Your Understanding

Divide. Check by multiplying.

1. 4)52   **2.** 3)87   **3.** 5)19   **4.** 8)99   **5.** 7)20   **6.** 2)45

Share Your Ideas   Describe the steps you would use to find 7)91.

Divide. Check by multiplying.

7. 4)56 8. 3)96 9. 6)95 10. 2)29 11. 5)46 12. 1)47

13. 7)62 14. 8)51 15. 4)92 16. 5)66 17. 6)59 18. 4)76

19. 9)71 20. 1)32 21. 7)78 22. 2)90 23. 4)61 24. 8)97

25. 3)76 26. 2)47 27. 7)98 28. 5)77 29. 6)88 30. 4)42

31. 7)84 32. 5)86 33. 1)62 34. 8)60 35. 3)59 36. 5)53

Find *n*.

37. $2 \times n = 38$

38. $n \times 5 = 75$

39. $6 \times n = 78$

40. $(n \times 2) + 1 = 27$

41. $(n \times 6) + 5 = 89$

42. $(n \times 9) + 8 = 98$

Choose the correct answer by looking only at the remainder. Explain your choice.

43. $89 \div 5$
   a. 17 R6 b. 17 R5 c. 17 R8 d. 17 R4

44. $50 \div 4$
   a. 12 R7 b. 12 R2 c. 12 R4 d. 12 R5

Problem Solving

The division key on Jordan's calculator was broken. The work in the box shows how Jordan found $27 \div 6$.

45. What calculator key did Jordan use?

46. How did Jordan know the quotient was 4?

47. How did Jordan know the remainder was 3?

48. Use a calculator to find $49 \div 9$ using Jordan's method.

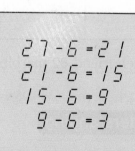

$$27 - 6 = 21$$
$$21 - 6 = 15$$
$$15 - 6 = 9$$
$$9 - 6 = 3$$

$$27 \div 6 = 4 \, R3$$

List three numbers that have a remainder of 2 when you divide by 6.

SUMMING UP

Use the digits 3, 4, and 5 once to find the missing digits.   8 R3
□)□□

Dividing Three-Digit Numbers

In *The Contest Kid Strikes Again*, Harvey wins a collection of 575 marbles. How can he give this collection equally to 7 friends?

575 ÷ 7 = n

Step 1 Estimate to place the first digit in the quotient. $$\begin{array}{r}\sqcup \qquad 80 \\ 7\overline{)575}\end{array}$$ Think $7\overline{)560}$	**Step 2** Divide tens. Then multiply. $$\begin{array}{r}8 \\ 7\overline{)575} \\ 56 \quad\leftarrow 8\times 7\end{array}$$ How many tens is 5 hundreds 7 tens? **Think** $7\overline{)57}$	**Step 3** Subtract and compare. $$\begin{array}{r}8 \\ 7\overline{)575} \\ -56 \\ \hline 1 \quad 1<7\end{array}$$
Step 4 Bring down ones. Divide. Then multiply. $$\begin{array}{r}82 \\ 7\overline{)575} \\ 56\downarrow \\ \hline 15 \\ 14 \leftarrow 2\times 7\end{array}$$ Think 1 ten 5 ones = 15 ones $7\overline{)15}$	**Step 5** Subtract and compare. $$\begin{array}{r}82\ R1 \\ 7\overline{)575} \\ 56 \\ \hline 15 \\ -14 \\ \hline 1 \quad 1<7\end{array}$$	Check $$\begin{array}{r}82 \\ \times\ 7 \\ \hline 574 \\ +\ 1 \\ \hline 575\end{array}$$

Harvey can give each friend 82 marbles. One marble would be left.

Check Your Understanding

Find each quotient.

1. $5\overline{)635}$ **2.** $4\overline{)512}$ **3.** $3\overline{)379}$ **4.** $8\overline{)571}$

Share Your Ideas   Look back at **1** and **4**. Explain how you  determined where to place the first digit in the quotient.

Divide. Check by multiplying.

5. 7)855	**6.** 6)734	**7.** 3)162	**8.** 4)908	**9.** 5)393
10. 8)927	**11.** 4)136	**12.** 3)68	**13.** 5)867	**14.** 6)350
15. 2)586	**16.** 7)614	**17.** 4)868	**18.** 2)125	**19.** 3)467
20. 6)220	**21.** 2)79	**22.** 1)513	**23.** 8)681	**24.** 3)566

25. 748 ÷ 6   **26.** 146 ÷ 3   **27.** 210 ÷ 9   **28.** 599 ÷ 4

29. 580 ÷ 7   **30.** 324 ÷ 5   **31.** 708 ÷ 5   **32.** 238 ÷ 8

Write and solve a division problem that matches each multiplication check.

33.	**34.**	**35.**	**36.**
317 × 2 634	24 × 7 168 + 3 171	87 × 3 261 + 2 263	425 × 2 850 + 1 851

Problem Solving

37. Lyle keeps his collection of 187 marbles in 4 boxes. He puts the same number of marbles in each box and any extras go in the fourth box. How many marbles are in each box?

38. In *The Contest Kid Strikes Again*, Harvey won second place by guessing there were 550 marbles in the jar. His friend Woody guessed 800 marbles. There were really 575 marbles in the jar. How far off was each boy's guess?

Logical Thinking

39. How many marbles are in the jar?

When the number is divided by 2 or 3, the remainder is 1. There is no remainder when it is divided by 5. There are more than 40 but less than 60 marbles in the jar.

You are dividing a three-digit number by a one-digit number. Explain how you can tell whether the quotient will have two digits or three digits.

SUMMING UP

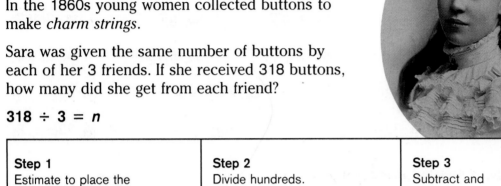

30 ÷ 3 = 10. Write three other division examples that have a one-digit divisor and a quotient of 10.

Zeros in the Quotient

In the 1860s young women collected buttons to make *charm strings*.

Sara was given the same number of buttons by each of her 3 friends. If she received 318 buttons, how many did she get from each friend?

318 ÷ 3 = *n*

Step 1
Estimate to place the
first digit in the quotient.
 	
    □   100
3)318 Think 3)300
	Step 2
	Divide hundreds.
	Then multiply.
	
	   1
	3)318 Think 3)3
	  3 ← 1 × 3
		Step 3
		Subtract and
		compare.
		
		  1
		3)318
		 −3
		  0 0 < 3

Step 4
Bring down tens.
Divide.
 	
  10
3)318
 −3↓
  01 Think 3)1. There are
             not enough tens to
             divide. Write 0 in the
             quotient.
	Step 5
	Bring down ones.
	Divide. Then multiply.
	
	  106
	3)318 Think
	 −3 ↓ 1 ten 8 ones = 18 ones
	 018 3)18
	  18←6 × 3
		Step 6
		Subtract and
		compare.
		
		  106
		3)318
		 −3
		 018
		 −18
		   0 0 < 3

Sara received 106 buttons from each friend.

Check Your Understanding

Divide. Check by multiplying.

1. 3)92   **2.** 4)83   **3.** 4)428   **4.** 2)817   **5.** 5)402

Share Your Ideas Look back at **4**. What if you forgot to write the 0 in the quotient? How would you know that the answer is not reasonable?

Divide. Check by multiplying.

6. $6\overline{)64}$ 7. $2\overline{)61}$ 8. $6\overline{)725}$ 9. $5\overline{)525}$ 10. $4\overline{)830}$

11. $7\overline{)843}$ 12. $3\overline{)782}$ 13. $9\overline{)951}$ 14. $4\overline{)139}$ 15. $2\overline{)181}$

16. $7\overline{)495}$ 17. $4\overline{)723}$ 18. $5\overline{)600}$ 19. $8\overline{)911}$ 20. $7\overline{)356}$

21. $3\overline{)911}$ 22. $6\overline{)284}$ 23. $4\overline{)785}$ 24. $2\overline{)720}$ 25. $9\overline{)914}$

26. $652 \div 6$ 27. $122 \div 3$ 28. $273 \div 4$ 29. $703 \div 5$

30. $941 \div 2$ 31. $376 \div 8$ 32. $982 \div 9$ 33. $562 \div 4$

Find *n*. Use mental math, paper and pencil, or calculator. Explain your choices.

CHOICES

34. $408 \div 4 = n$ 35. $156 \div 3 = n$ 36. $791 \div 7 = n$

37. $510 \div 3 = n$ 38. $n \div 4 = 203$ 39. $410 \div n = 205$

Problem Solving

40. Lisa had 125 buttons to divide equally among 6 friends. How many buttons did Lisa give to each friend? How many buttons did Lisa keep for her collection?

41. The Tingue button was named after John H. Tingue. He had challenged 3 friends to make a string of 2,500 buttons in 30 days. They made one of 2,700 buttons. If each friend put on the same number of buttons, how many buttons did each put on?

Common Error

42. When Brian divided 812 by 3, he got an incorrect answer of 27 R2. Why is his answer not reasonable? Explain. What is the correct answer? What did Brian do wrong?

Explain why estimating before you divide 528 by 5 helps you decide where to place the first digit in the quotient.

SUMMING UP

Midchapter Review

Find *n*. pages 74–75

1. $n \times 7 = 63$ **2.** $64 \div n = 8$ **3.** $42 \div 6 = n$ **4.** $0 \div 7 = n$

Write two related divisions for each. pages 74–75

5. 6×3 **6.** 4×8 **7.** 7×3 **8.** 9×6 **9.** 4×5 **10.** 2×1

Complete. Follow each rule, if given. pages 74–75

Rule: Divide by 5.

	Input	Output
11.	5	
12.	10	
13.		5
14.		8

Rule: Multiply by 6.

	Input	Output
15.	7	
16.		48
17.	3	
18.		18

19. Find the rule.

Input	Output
3	12
9	36
6	24
8	32

Divide. pages 76–77

20. $49{,}000 \div 7$ **21.** $4\overline{)3{,}600}$ **22.** $6\overline{)1{,}800}$ **23.** $63{,}000 \div 9$

Estimate. Then divide. Check by multiplying. pages 78–79, 82–87

24. $98 \div 7$ _____   **25.** $85 \div 6$ _____   **26.** $38 \div 3$ _____   **27.** $83 \div 4$ _____

28. $6\overline{)618}$ **29.** $7\overline{)569}$ **30.** $9\overline{)675}$ **31.** $3\overline{)426}$

32. $188 \div 3$ **33.** $4\overline{)932}$ **34.** $6\overline{)613}$ **35.** $9\overline{)926}$

Choose the correct word to complete the sentence.

36. In a division problem the answer is called the _____ .

37. Multiplication and division are _____ .

38. In the exercise $936 \div n$, *n* is the _____ .

Words to Know
inverse operations
divisor
quotient
dividend

Solve.

39. Becky wants to divide her 257 tropical fish equally into 3 tanks. How many will be in each tank? How many are left?

40. Brad has 238 stamps. If he buys 9 pages that each hold 25 stamps will he be able to place all his stamps on pages?

Exploring Problem Solving

What Should the Page Look Like?

The Transportation Series of stamps, which the United States began to issue in 1981, had 36 different stamps by 1989. A page in a stamp album contains 52 squares across and 72 squares down. A stamp is 6 squares wide by 8 squares high.

Thinking Critically

Decide how to place all 36 stamps on a page. Show at least two different ways to display the stamps on the page. You may wish to use Workmat 1 to help you.

Analyzing and Making Decisions

Use a calculator where appropriate.

1. Will 9 stamps fit across a page? Explain. Will 8 stamps fit across a page? Explain. If they will fit, how many squares are blank?

2. How can a table like this help you plan the layout of the page? Is it useful to know the number of squares left over? Explain.

Stamps in each row	Squares used for stamps	Squares left over
4	24	28

3. The table above shows the number of stamps in a row. How can you make a table that shows the number of rows on a page? How many rows of squares are there?

4. Make at least two plans for placing the stamps on a page 52 squares across and 72 squares down.

Look Back How did you solve the problem? How would a drawing help?

Problem Solving Strategies

Making and Using Tables

Mary Lou is collecting pennies, nickels, and dimes. She wants to collect one coin of each kind for the years 1970 through 1991. She has already collected coins for these years:

Pennies: 1970–71, 1974–76, 1978–82, 1985–90.
Nickels: 1972–76, 1979–81, 1983–85, 1988–90.
Dimes:　1970–76, 1978, 1981–83, 1987–89.

If she collects three coins every month, how long will it take her to finish her collection?

Sometimes there are many facts in a problem. Using a table is one way to organize these facts.

Solving the Problem

Think　What is the question? What else do you need to find out?

Explore　How would putting the information you know in a table like this help you?

COINS COLLECTED			
	1970	1971	1972
Pennies	X	X	
Nickels			X
Dimes	X	X	X

Copy and complete the table for the years 1970 through 1991. How many coins does Mary Lou need to finish her collection? How can you tell how long it will take her to collect these coins at the rate of three coins a month?

Solve　How many months will it take Mary Lou to finish her collection?

Look Back　If you divided to find out, what does the remainder tell you?

Share Your Ideas

1. Write another problem that uses the information given in the table.

Practice

Solve. Use a calculator where appropriate.

CHOICES
The traffic on Maple and Elm Streets was counted to see if a traffic light is needed at that intersection. The table below shows the information recorded.

NUMBER OF CARS AND TRUCKS					
	Mon.	Tues.	Wed.	Thurs.	Fri.
Maple Street	165	182	173	164	173
Elm Street	145	151	136	142	157

2. On which day is the traffic heaviest on Maple and Elm Streets?

3. To get a traffic light, there must be over 1,500 cars and trucks traveling on the streets from Monday through Friday. Should the intersection of Maple and Elm streets receive a light? Explain.

This table shows how much money the band and the Math Club raised each week at a car wash.

4. How much in all was raised by both groups?

	Week 1	Week 2	Week 3
Band	$126	$138	$145
Math Club	$123	$135	$140

5. The groups divided the money equally among the Activity Fund, the Charity Drive Fund, and the Class Trip Fund. How much did each fund receive?

Mixed Strategy Review

6. The Pep Club sold 53 pennants and 24 buttons at a rally. How much money did the Pep Club make on the sales?

7. Bobby earned $108 in 5 days, working part-time as a package handler. He earns $6 per hour. How many hours did he work that week?

Create **Your Own**

Create your own problem that uses the information about the band and the Math Club.

91

Do these calculations mentally. Multiply 6 by 7. Then subtract the product from 47. What answer do you get?

Short Division

The Museum of the American Indian has a collection of 700 kachina dolls. The museum curator wants to display the dolls in 5 showcases. If she puts the same number of dolls in each showcase, how many dolls will there be in each?

You can use the short form of division to find $700 \div 5$. Multiply and divide mentally for each step. Write the remainders in the dividend. Write the last remainder in the quotient.

Step 1 Estimate.	Step 2 Divide hundreds.	Step 3 Divide tens.	Step 4 Divide ones.
$\square$ $5)\overline{700}$ Think $\dfrac{100}{5)\overline{500}}$	1 $5)\overline{7^2 00}$ Think $1 \times 5 = 5$ $7 - 5 = 2$	$1\ 4$ $5)\overline{7^2 0^0 0}$ Think $4 \times 5 = 20$ $20 - 20 = 0$	$1\ 4\ 0$ $5)\overline{7^2 0^0 0}$ Think $0 \div 5 = 0$ Write 0 in the quotient.

There will be 140 dolls in each showcase.

Another Example

Find $6,175 \div 3$.

Step 1	Step 2	Step 3	Step 4
2 $3)\overline{6,^0 175}$ Think $2 \times 3 = 6$ $6 - 6 = 0$	$2,\ 0$ $3)\overline{6,^0 1^1 75}$ Think $0 \times 3 = 0$ $1 - 0 = 1$	$2,\ 0\ 5$ $3)\overline{6,^0 1^1 7^2 5}$ Think $5 \times 3 = 15$ $17 - 15 = 2$	$2,\ 0\ 5\ 8\ R1$ $3)\overline{6,^0 1^1 7^2 5}$ Think $8 \times 3 = 24$ $25 - 24 = 1$

Check Your Understanding

Divide, using the short form.

1. $4)\overline{56}$ **2.** $2)\overline{297}$ **3.** $3)\overline{192}$ **4.** $5)\overline{7,140}$ **5.** $7)\overline{3,195}$

Share Your Ideas Look back at **Another Example**.
Write the long division for $6,175 \div 3$.

Practice

Divide, using the short form.

6. 3)89

7. 9)197

8. 2)1,946

9. 4)508

10. 5)507

11. 7)7,611

12. 5)2,135

13. 4)726

14. 6)18,300

15. 3)8,120

16. 8)21,795

17. 5)7,500

18. 1,298 ÷ 5

19. 681 ÷ 6

20. 4,850 ÷ 2

21. 32,480 ÷ 8

22. 20,360 ÷ 7

23. 84,780 ÷ 9

Estimate each quotient, then divide. Use mental math, long division, or short division. Explain your choices.

CHOICES

24. 186 ÷ 3

25. 522 ÷ 3

26. 1,827 ÷ 9

27. 8,505 ÷ 7

28. 14,296 ÷ 4

29. 40,000 ÷ 6

Problem Solving

30. The Museum of the American Indian has a collection of 22,000 Apache objects. If the collection is displayed in 5 rooms, about how many objects must be in each room?

31. The Museum also has a collection of 1,500 prehistoric pots found at a site in Mexico. Half the collection is in storage. An equal number of pots is stored in each of 5 crates. How many pots are in each crate?

Discuss the advantages and disadvantages of using the short form of division.

1. 4,000
    − 2,589

2. 3,076
    + 984

3.   587
    ×   6

4. $42
    ×   29

5.   603
    ×   57

6. 8)1,036

Find the LCM.

7. 3 and 5

8. 4 and 6

9. 2 and 10

10. 6 and 8

Compare. Use >, <, or = for ●.

11. 1,032 ● 1,302

12. 45,987 ● 45,789

13. 8 + 19 ● 30 − 2

14. 3 × 15 ● 4 × 12

15. 4 × 25 ● 82 + 19

SUMMING UP

Jane has $1.24 in pennies. How many pennies does Jane have? She divides the pennies into two groups. How many pennies are there in each group?

Dividing Money

Lauren collects compact discs. She bought 3 discs for $26.91. What was the price of 1 disc?

Estimate to see about how many dollars.

$$\begin{array}{r} \$\ 8.00 \\ 3)\overline{\$26.91} \end{array} \quad \text{Think} \quad 3)\overline{\$24.00}$$

Divide money the same way you divide whole numbers.

$$\begin{array}{r} \$\ 8.97 \\ 3)\overline{\$26.91} \\ -24\downarrow \\ \hline 29 \\ -27\downarrow \\ \hline 21 \\ -21 \\ \hline 0 \end{array}$$

Remember to write the dollar sign and the decimal point in the quotient.

Check
$$\begin{array}{r} \$8.97 \\ \times\quad 3 \\ \hline \$26.91 \end{array}$$

One disc costs $8.97.

More Examples

a.
$$\begin{array}{r} \$\ .64 \\ 6)\overline{\$3.84} \\ -36\downarrow \\ \hline 24 \\ -24 \\ \hline 0 \end{array}$$

b.
$$\begin{array}{r} \$2.09 \\ 3)\overline{\$6.27} \\ -6\downarrow\downarrow \\ \hline 0\ 27 \\ -27 \\ \hline 0 \end{array}$$

c.
$$\begin{array}{r} \$1\ 3.\ 4\ 5 \\ 7)\overline{\$9^24.^31^35} \end{array}$$

Divide.

1. 8)$.56

2. 2)$17.50

3. 9)$72.45

4. 4)$92.68

Share Your Ideas Explain how dividing $4.75 by 5 is like dividing 475 by 5. How is it different?

Practice

Divide.

5. $7\overline{)\$9.03}$

6. $5\overline{)\$.75}$

7. $3\overline{)\$5.40}$

8. $6\overline{)\$19.20}$

9. $9\overline{)\$34.65}$

10. $3\overline{)\$1.35}$

11. $8\overline{)\$93.76}$

12. $4\overline{)\$15.56}$

13. $7\overline{)\$14.63}$

14. $5\overline{)\$14.00}$

15. $6\overline{)\$.54}$

16. $4\overline{)\$59.12}$

17. $\$.72 \div 3$

18. $\$.84 \div 6$

19. $\$2.60 \div 4$

20. $\$43.25 \div 5$

21. $\$94.15 \div 7$

22. $\$90.72 \div 9$

23. $\$38.80 \div 8$

24. $\$16.90 \div 2$

**Estimate, then explore with a calculator.
Find each divisor.**

25. $\$3.00 \div n = \$1.50$

26. $\$19.00 \div n = \$4.75$

27. $\$78.90 \div n = \$26.30$

28. $\$43.25 \div n = \$8.65$

29. $\$239.40 \div n = \$34.20$

30. $\$157.68 \div n = \$17.52$

Problem Solving

Shoppers use unit price to compare the costs of different-sized packages. **Unit price** is the price per single item, per ounce, per pound, and so on.

31. What is the unit price for the package of brand X tapes? (Hint: Find the price of 1 tape.)

32. What is the unit price for the package of brand Y tapes?

33. To find the better buy, shoppers compare unit prices. If both brands of tape are the same quality, which is the better buy? Why?

34. Explain when a lower price may not be the better buy.

DATA 35. Look in the newspaper to find ads for packages of 2, 3, 4, or more items. Find their unit prices.

Brand X
2 for $7.00

Brand Y
3 for $8.97

Discuss the meaning of this statement, using your own examples: Whether you are dividing money or other amounts, you always use place value to divide.

SUMMING UP

Using Problem Solving

Interpreting Remainders

Problems may have the same numbers but have different answers.

How do you tell what the answer should look like?

Solving these problems may help you.

A. A group of 34 people need taxis to take them to the airport. Each taxi can take no more than four people. How many taxis are needed? Will each taxi carry 4 riders? Explain.

B. Roy is putting books on a library shelf. He has a space that is 34 cm wide. Each book in a series is 4 cm thick. How many of the books can Roy fit on the shelf? How did you decide on your answer?

C. Angela has 34 muffins. She is packing 4 muffins in each box. She is packing as many full boxes as she can and keeping the extra muffins. How many boxes does she pack? How many muffins does she keep? How did you find out?

Sharing Your Ideas

1. How could dividing 34 by 4 help you answer each question?

2. Look back at **A.** Would $8\frac{1}{2}$ taxis be a good answer for this problem? Explain.

3. Which problem was answered by increasing the quotient? Which problem was answered by decreasing the quotient? In which problem was the remainder part of the answer?

4. Why did each problem have a different answer?

98

Practice

5. The shop sent enough supplies to make 34 sandwiches for 4 people on their week-long camping trip. How many sandwiches is that per person? What can be done with some of the sandwiches to be sure that there are no leftovers?

6. Four runners are in a 34 km long-distance relay. The runners will divide up the distance equally. How far will each runner travel? Have the four runners together covered the 34 km? Explain.

7. Belinda has collected 115 stamps. She can put 8 stamps on a page in her album. How many pages will she need to display the stamps?

8. Kai made 6 birdhouses in about 21 hours. If he used about the same amount of time to build each birdhouse, how long did it take to build one?

Summing Up

9. Look back at problems **A**, **B**, and **C** on page 98 and at problems **5** and **6** above. Each of these problems could be solved by dividing 34 by 4, yet each problem has a different answer. Why does this happen?

10. What hints would you give to someone to help them answer the problems on these pages?

Move some dots from one group to another so that each group has the same number.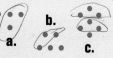

Estimating and Finding Averages

The scouts collected aluminum cans for recycling. What is the average number of cans collected by the troops?

ALUMINUM CANS COLLECTED	
Troop	Number of cans
A	129
B	190
C	203

The **average** tells you the number of cans that each troop would have collected if each troop collected the same number.

Estimate the average. Would it be less than 100 cans? more than 200 cans? Explain.

▶ To find an average, add to find the sum.

```
   129
   190
 + 203
   522
```

▶ Then divide the sum by the number of addends.

```
     174  ← average
  3)522
   -3
    22
   -21
    12
   - 12
     0
```

The troops collected an average of 174 cans.

Another Example

Find the average of $3.45, $2.25, $4.15, and $3.39.

Estimate. $3 + $2 + $4 + $3 = $12
$12 ÷ 4 = $3

$3.45 + $2.25 + $4.15 + $3.39 = $13.24

```
     $ 3.31
  4)$13.24
```

The average is $3.31.

Find each average.

1. 98, 98, 112, 100

2. 80, 56, 38

3. $17.50, $18.00

Share Your Ideas Marybeth received scores of 75, 80, and 85 on three quizzes. She estimates her average to be 70. Is she correct? Why or why not?

Find each average.

4. 74, 60, 64

5. 40, 65, 54

6. 315, 325

7. 10, 17, 9, 12

8. 26¢, 28¢, 27¢

9. 655, 652, 652

10. 8, 9, 11, 12

11. 89, 93, 97

12. $12.50, $17.98

13. 600, 711, 858

14. 74, 72, 84, 78

15. 79, 96, 89, 60

16. $5.25, $5.32, $5.15

17. 32, 31, 35, 30, 37

18. $9.75, $10.18, $9.34, $10.97

19. 116, 136, 129, 143, 131

20. Look back at **8.** How can you find the average mentally?

21. Look back at **10.** How can you find the average mentally?

Problem Solving

22. Use the chart on page 100. If Troop D collected the same number of cans as Troop B, what is the average number of cans collected by the 4 troops?

23. If each scout troop collected 200 cans, what would be the average number of cans collected by the troops? Explain.

24. Ted received these scores on his spelling quizzes. What is his average for these quizzes? Explain what the average means.

25. Ted had an average of 88 after taking his fourth quiz. What score did Ted get on the fourth quiz?

Jeremy and Carla said they collected an average of 46 aluminum cans. How many cans could each of them have collected? Give several possible answers.

SUMMING UP

Exploring Divisibility

A number is **divisible** by another number when the remainder is 0. There are rules to tell if a number is divisible by certain other numbers. See if you can discover some **rules of divisibility**.

Working together

Materials: calculator

18	90	344
32	114	456
54	128	480
60	136	506
86	272	518

A. The list shows numbers that are divisible by 2. Examine the numbers.

- What do the final digits of all the numbers have in common?

- Can you find a rule for divisibility by 2? Use the calculator and test your rule.

- Use your rule to write some numbers that should be divisible by 2. Check by dividing.

B. Can you discover the rule for divisibility by 5?

- Pick 3 numbers and multiply each by 5. Will the products be divisible by 5? Explain.

- Examine the numbers. How can you tell if a number is divisible by 5? Test your rule.

Sharing Your Results

1. Write your divisibility rules for 2 and 5. Share them with the class. Have students test your rules.

2. Write a rule for divisibility by 10. Use the rule for divisibility by 5 as a model. Show that the rule works.

Practice

Work on your own.

3. A number is divisible by 3 if the sum of its digits is divisible by 3. Is that rule correct? Test this rule with these numbers. Check the results with a calculator.

    a. 72   **b.** 48   **c.** 125   **d.** 345   **e.** 8,025

4. A number is divisible by 4 if the last two digits are divisible by 4. Test this rule with these numbers.

    a. 324   **b.** 634   **c.** 172   **d.** 600   **e.** 522

5. Try to write rules for divisibility by 6 and 9. Use the divisibility rules for 2 and 3 as models. Show that the rules work.

Summing Up

Divisibility Challenge Match

Two players take turns covering a number on the grid. Each time a player covers a number, the opponent can earn points. The opponent must correctly list the numbers by which the covered number is divisible.

50	51	52
53	54	55
56	57	58
59	60	61
62	63	64

Example: Player A covers 50, player B earns 8 points because 50 is divisible by 1, 2, and 5.

1 point for divisibility by 1
2 points for divisibility by 2
3 points for divisibility by 3
4 points for divisibility by 4
5 points for divisibility by 5

Try to be the player with the most points after the grid is covered.

Build a winning strategy. Consider these questions.

6. What numbers give the most points? the least points?

7. What numbers limit your opponent to 1 point?

8. Is it best to be the first or the second player in the game?

Chapter Review

Find *n*. pages 74–75

1. $8 \times n = 40$ **2.** $49 \div 7 = n$ **3.** $9 \times n = 81$ **4.** $0 \div 6 = n$

Divide. pages 76–77

5. $4\overline{)800}$ **6.** $9\overline{)900}$ **7.** $4\overline{)360}$ **8.** $7\overline{)21,000}$ **9.** $6\overline{)48,000}$

Estimate each quotient. pages 78–79

10. $32 \div 3$ **11.** $330 \div 5$ **12.** $386 \div 6$ **13.** $116 \div 2$ **14.** $196 \div 4$

15. $6\overline{)81}$ **16.** $7\overline{)501}$ **17.** $4\overline{)231}$ **18.** $4\overline{)315}$ **19.** $3\overline{)225}$

Divide. Check by multiplying. pages 80–87, 92–93, 96–97

20. $85 \div 5$ **21.** $695 \div 8$ **22.** $98 \div 7$ **23.** $893 \div 4$ **24.** $764 \div 5$

25. $8\overline{)82}$ **26.** $4\overline{)\$9.12}$ **27.** $5\overline{)451}$ **28.** $9\overline{)919}$ **29.** $3\overline{)336}$

30. $6,992 \div 4$ **31.** $56,882 \div 7$ **32.** $\$98.19 \div 3$ **33.** $18,642 \div 8$

Use short division to find each quotient. pages 94–95

34. $5\overline{)365}$ **35.** $7\overline{)7,490}$ **36.** $3\overline{)6,844}$ **37.** $9\overline{)81,909}$ **38.** $7\overline{)526}$

Find each average. pages 100–101

39. $89.16, $35.22, $65.19

40. 66, 36, 55, 79

41. 108, 263, 391, 608, 345

42. 28, 82, 63, 42, 55

Solve. pages 89–91, 98–101

43. Alice arranged 3 vases on the first shelf, 5 on the second, 8 on the third, and 12 on the fourth. Make a table to show how many vases will be on the seventh shelf if the pattern continues.

44. Alice decided to sell four antique bottles from her collection. She received $9.20, $8.65, $7.52, and $5.32. What was the average price she received?

Chapter Test

Find _n_.

1. $8 \times n = 40$ 2. $42 \div 7 = n$ 3. $0 \div 5 = n$ 4. $35 \div 7 = n$

Estimate each quotient.

5. $3\overline{)48}$ 6. $5\overline{)89}$ 7. $2\overline{)58}$ 8. $8\overline{)817}$ 9. $2\overline{)\$2.12}$

Divide. Check by multiplying.

10. $81 \div 9$ 11. $236 \div 6$ 12. $109 \div 9$

13. $7\overline{)6,241}$ 14. $6\overline{)3,368}$ 15. $3\overline{)9,876}$

16. $18,227 \div 5$ 17. $54,000 \div 9$ 18. $79,844 \div 4$

Use short division to find each quotient.

19. $545 \div 5$ 20. $2,489 \div 3$ 21. $83,203 \div 8$

Find each average.

22. 75, 86, 92, 79   23. $1.72, $2.63, $3.13, $4.47, $6.35

Solve.

24. The Museum of Early Trades and Crafts has 129 tools dating from 1780–1864. If the museum divides them equally among 5 local libraries, how many would each library have to exhibit? How many items would not be exhibited?

25. Fred has these pennies; 1983, 1988, 1981, 1987, and 1983. He wants to collect one penny for each of the years 1980 through 1990. How many more pennies does he need? Make a table. Which pennies does he need?

THINK The Museum of Broadcasting in New York City has 30,000 tapes. The museum plans to lend half of them to three other libraries. How many tapes will each receive if the tapes are divided equally among the libraries?

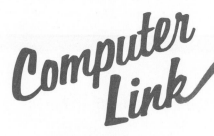

Computer Link

Dividing in Logo

What Logo commands could you use to turn the turtle around exactly one full turn, ending at the same heading at which it started?

AT THE COMPUTER

Materials: Logo

A. Enter this command to turn the turtle around exactly one full turn. How many degrees does the turtle turn in all?

`REPEAT 4 [RIGHT 90]`

B. Find as many REPEAT commands as you can that turn the turtle around exactly one full turn, or 360°. Record each pair of numbers you find in a list like the one below.

`REPEAT ____ [RIGHT ____]`
`REPEAT ____ [RIGHT ____]`
`REPEAT ____ [RIGHT ____]`

C. Compare your results with other teams. How many different REPEAT commands did you find?

Sharing Your Results

1. What strategies did you use to find number pairs?

2. How can you organize your work to find the greatest number of different REPEAT commands?

3. List the pairs of numbers that you found in **B**. The pairs are called factor pairs. How many factor pairs did you find?

Extending the Activity

You can use Logo to find factor pairs by dividing. The symbol for division is /. Logo can find the remainder as well as the quotient. PR means print.

PR 65 / 5   Logo divides 65 by 5 and prints 13.
PR 70 / 6   Prints the quotient 11.
PR REMAINDER 70 / 6   Prints 4, the remainder of 70 ÷ 6.

4. Use the PRINT and REMAINDER commands to find all the possible factor pairs for each.

   a. 24   **b.** 60   **c.** 180

5. Compare these commands. Will the computer print the same result for each? Why or why not?

   a. PR 95 + 85 + 90 / 3   **b.** PR (95 + 85 + 90) / 3

6. What if you enter PR 10 + 15 / 5. What do you expect the computer to print? Why?

7. The computer does multiplication and division left to right before it does addition and subtraction. Parentheses are used to change that order. Would you need parentheses to get each result shown? Try each in a PRINT statement to find out.

   a. 2 + 3 * 5 = 17   **b.** 2 + 3 * 5 = 25
   c. 5 + 25 / 5 = 10   **d.** 85 − 10 / 15 = 5

Summing Up

8. Look back at **3** on page 106. Did you find all possible pairs? How do you know?

9. Explain how the computer finds the value of each.

   a. 15 − 2 * 3   **b.** (15 + 3) / 3
   c. 17 − 5 * 6 / 2   **d.** 18 − 6 / 3 + 1

Order of Operations

Solve. $9 + 6 \times 9 \div 3 - 2 = n$

What answer did you get? What answers did your classmates get? Explain how you each arrived at your answer.

Why do you suppose there seem to be several possible answers?

When a number sentence includes more than one operation, the operations must be performed in the correct order.

Order of Operations

1.( ) Do the operations that are inside the parentheses ( ) first.

$3 \times (10 + 5) + (48 \div 6) \div 4 - 7 = n$

2.×÷ Then do all multiplication and division from left to right.

$3 \times 15 + 8 \div 4 - 7 = n$

3.+ - Then do all addition and subtraction from left to right.

$45 + 2 - 7 = n$
$47 - 7 = n$
$40 = n$

Puzzle Practice

Each sentence has the same answer. Use the order of operations to find this answer.

$(14) - (2) \times (5) + (3)$

$(16) \div (8) \times (10) - (13) = ?$

$(5) \times (5) - (36) \div (2)$

> **My Dear Aunt Sally**
>
> A mnemonic (ni mon′ ik) is a device that helps the memory. This mnemonic will help you to remember the order of operations.
>
> *My Dear* → *M*ultiply and *D*ivide
> *Aunt Sally* → *A*dd and *S*ubtract

Solve.

1. $3 + 4 \times 6 - 8 = n$ **2.** $6 \times (7 + 3) + 15 = n$ **3.** $25 - 5 \times 6 \div 2 = n$

Use +, −, ×, or ÷ for each ●.

4. $8 \times 6 ● 4 ● 2 = 10$

5. $8 ● 6 + 4 ● 2 = 20$

6. $8 ● 6 ● 4 \div 2 = 20$

7. $8 + 6 ● 4 ● 2 = 30$

Family Math

We have finished the first three chapters in our mathematics book. In these chapters, we studied adding, subtracting, multiplying, and dividing whole numbers.

Let's Go Shopping!

Does one person in your family do all the grocery shopping? Try planning the next shopping trip as a group.

Work together to look in the newspaper for food advertisements. Clip the grocery items that you would like to purchase.

Make a grocery list like the one shown. Round the actual price to find the estimated total price for each item.

GROCERY LIST

Item	Price	Quantity	Estimated total price
bread	$1.79	2	$4.00
bacon	.99	1	1.00
soup	.49	5	2.50
cereal	2.89	2	6.00

Estimate the total cost of your groceries.

How would you round each price if you wanted to be sure to have enough money when you went shopping?

Cumulative Review

Choose the correct answer. Write A, B, C, or D.

1. What is the value of 4 in 40,185,365?

   A 4,000,000   C 400,000,000

   B 40,000,000   D not given

2. Write 8,000,000 + 50,000 + 4,000 + 800 + 3.

   A 8,540,830   C 85,483

   B 8,054,803   D not given

3. Compare. 208,000 ● 280,000

   A <   C =

   B >   D not given

4. What property of addition is used?
17 + 0 = 17

   A Associative   C Identity

   B Commutative   D not given

5. 305 + 46 + 172

   A 513   C 423

   B 413   D not given

6. Estimate. 916 − 128

   A 800   C 700

   B 1,000   D 300

7. 30,621 − 18,546

   A 12,165   C 28,125

   B 12,075   D not given

8. Name the property used.
425 × 0 = n

   A associative   C identity

   B commutative   D not given

9. 60 × 500

   A 30,000   C 300,000

   B 3,000   D not given

10.
$$\begin{array}{r} 63 \\ \times\ 5 \\ \hline \end{array}$$

   A 305   C 308

   B 315   D not given

11. Find the LCM of 8 and 5.

   A 24   C 40

   B 13   D not given

12. Estimate. 5 × 387

   A 150   C 2,000

   B 20,000   D 200

13.
$$\begin{array}{r} 806 \\ \times\ 17 \\ \hline \end{array}$$

   A 13,604   C 6,448

   B 13,702   D not given

14. 40 × $23.20

   A $928.00   C $9.28

   B $828.00   D not given

Choose the correct answer. Write A, B, C, or D.

15. Find *n*. $6 \times n = 36$

    A 8   **C** 5

    B 7   **D** not given

16. Estimate. $621 \div 9$

    A 9   **C** 20

    B 70   **D** not given

17. $276 \div 4$

    A 68   **C** 59

    B 69   **D** not given

18. $4\overline{)923}$

    A 230 R3   **C** 23 R12

    B 23 R3   **D** not given

19. $10{,}726 \div 6$

    A 174 R2   **C** 1,704 R2

    B 176   **D** not given

20. $\$19.44 \div 6$

    A \$3.26   **C** \$.32

    B \$3.24   **D** not given

21. Find the average. 16, 25, 76

    A 39   **C** 38

    B 37   **D** not given

Solve.

22. What statement helps to find the number of black horses?

    A $6 + 5 = n$ **C** $11 - 5 = n$

    B $11 - 6 = n$ **D** not given

23. The total number of lunches purchased for the week was 2,396. If 704 students bought their lunch on Monday, 611 on Tuesday, and 425 on both Wednesday and Thursday, how many lunches were bought on Friday?

    A 242   **C** 153

    B 231   **D** not given

What fact is needed to solve 24?

24. Tony bought record albums at the store for a total of \$24.80. How many did he buy?

    A cost of the albums   **C** cost of each album

    B amount of time in the store   **D** not given

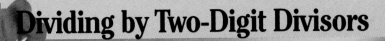

Dividing by Two-Digit Divisors

THEME   Spotlight on Sports

Sharing What You Know

The game is on. "What's the score?" The race is over. "What was the winning time?" The trophies are being handed out. "How will they divide the prize money?" It is hard to talk about sports without using mathematics. Discuss how division is used in your favorite sports.

Using Language

Have you ever heard about sports stars who are "in their prime?" **Prime** means the best part or first-rate. Can you think of another phrase that uses the word **prime**? In mathematics, a **prime** number is a number greater than 1 that has only itself and 1 as factors. These are some prime numbers: 2, 3, 5, 7, 11. How is a prime number like something that is one-of-a-kind and unique?

Words to Know: divisor, quotient, dividend, greatest common factor, common factor, factors, prime, composite.

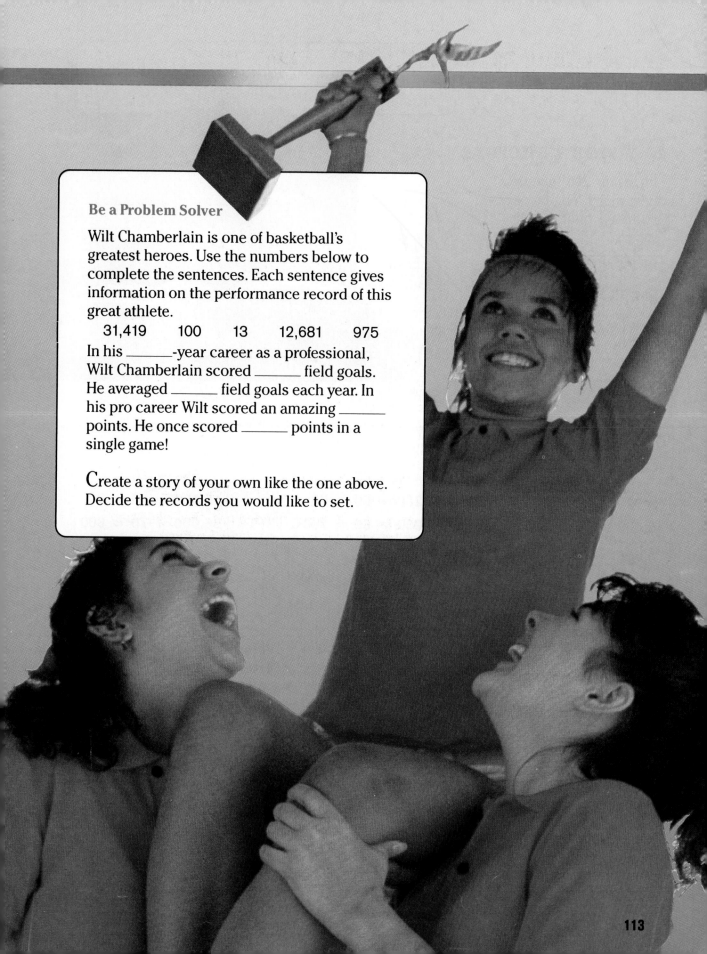

Be a Problem Solver

Wilt Chamberlain is one of basketball's greatest heroes. Use the numbers below to complete the sentences. Each sentence gives information on the performance record of this great athlete.

   31,419   100   13   12,681   975

In his _____-year career as a professional, Wilt Chamberlain scored _____ field goals. He averaged _____ field goals each year. In his pro career Wilt scored an amazing _____ points. He once scored _____ points in a single game!

Create a story of your own like the one above. Decide the records you would like to set.

Multiply 20 × 40, 20 × 400, and 20 × 4,000.
Describe the pattern you see.

Division Patterns

Jill swam 200 meters.
How many lengths of a
50-meter pool did she
swim?

Divide 200 by 50.

Use a basic fact to find
the quotient.

20 ÷ 5 = 4
200 ÷ 50 = 4

Jill swam 4 lengths of the
pool.

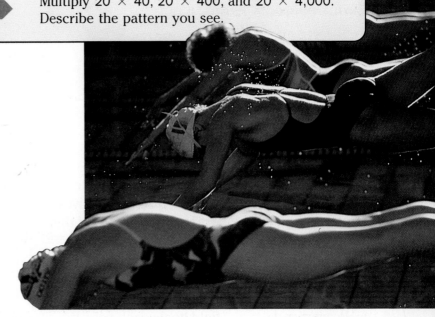

Look at the patterns. Explain how you can use basic
facts and patterns to divide mentally.

90 ÷ 30 = 3	420 ÷ 60 = 7	560 ÷ 70 = 8
900 ÷ 30 = 30	4,200 ÷ 60 = 70	5,600 ÷ 70 = 80
9,000 ÷ 30 = 300	42,000 ÷ 60 = 700	56,000 ÷ 70 = 800

More Examples

Examine the patterns. Use multiplication patterns to
check the quotients.

a. $\overset{2}{40\overline{)80}}$ $\overset{20}{40\overline{)800}}$ $\overset{200}{40\overline{)8,000}}$

b. $\overset{3}{90\overline{)270}}$ $\overset{30}{90\overline{)2,700}}$ $\overset{300}{90\overline{)27,000}}$

Divide. Check by multiplying.

1. 60 ÷ 20
   600 ÷ 20

2. 210 ÷ 30
   2,100 ÷ 30

3. 640 ÷ 80
   6,400 ÷ 80

4. 350 ÷ 70
   3,500 ÷ 70

5. $40\overline{)40}$ $40\overline{)400}$ $40\overline{)4,000}$

6. $50\overline{)450}$ $50\overline{)4,500}$ $50\overline{)45,000}$

Share Your Ideas Look back at **5.** What basic division
fact did you use to find the quotients? Explain how
you knew how many digits there were in the quotients.

Practice

Divide. Check by multiplying.

7. 80 ÷ 20	**8.** 150 ÷ 30	**9.** 400 ÷ 80	**10.** 540 ÷ 60
800 ÷ 20	1,500 ÷ 30	4,000 ÷ 80	5,400 ÷ 60

11. 90)‾6‾3‾0‾   **12.** 90)‾6‾,‾3‾0‾0‾   **13.** 40)‾2‾8‾0‾   **14.** 40)‾2‾,‾8‾0‾0‾

15. 20)‾1‾,‾6‾0‾0‾   **16.** 30)‾2‾7‾0‾   **17.** 40)‾1‾6‾0‾   **18.** 50)‾4‾,‾0‾0‾0‾

19. 80)‾7‾,‾2‾0‾0‾   **20.** 90)‾5‾,‾4‾0‾0‾   **21.** 70)‾7‾,‾0‾0‾0‾   **22.** 30)‾6‾,‾0‾0‾0‾

Complete. Follow each rule, if given.

Rule: Divide by 50.

	Input	Output
23.	150	
24.	250	
25.	3,000	
26.	4,500	

Rule: Divide by 80.

	Input	Output
27.	240	
28.	320	
29.		10
30.		20

Find the rule.

	Input	Output
31.	120	4
	240	8
	1,500	50
	2,700	90

Problem Solving

32. Carl swam 350 meters. How many lengths of a 50-meter pool did Carl swim?

33. Mrs. Ramirez wants to cash a $180 check. She asks the bank teller for $20 bills. How many $20 bills will Mrs. Ramirez receive?

34. At the 1988 Summer Olympics, Janet Evans of the United States won 3 gold medals in swimming. She placed first in the 400-meter freestyle, 800-meter freestyle, and 400-meter individual medley. How many lengths of the 50-meter pool did Janet swim in winning the 3 medals?

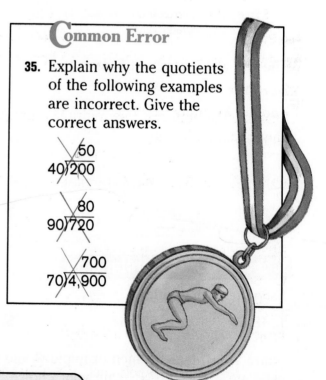

Common Error

35. Explain why the quotients of the following examples are incorrect. Give the correct answers.

$$\frac{\cancel{50}}{40)200}$$

$$\frac{\cancel{80}}{90)720}$$

$$\frac{\cancel{700}}{70)4,900}$$

Look back at your answers for **7–10.** Examine the number of zeros in the divisor, quotient, and dividend. Explain any patterns you see.

SUMMING UP

How can you estimate these quotients mentally:
44 ÷ 7   242 ÷ 4   292 ÷ 5? Explain.

Estimating Quotients

It is 189 kilometers from Falcon Lake on the Rio Grande, down river to Mission, Texas. If you canoe 35 kilometers a day, about how many days will it take to reach Mission?

189 ÷ 35 = n

▶ One way to estimate a quotient is to round the divisor. Use a compatible number for the dividend. Then use mental math to find the quotient.

$35\overline{)189}$ $\xrightarrow{\text{rounds to}}$ $40\overline{)189}$

 5 estimated quotient
Think $40\overline{)200}$
40 and 200 are compatible numbers. Why?

The trip will take about 5 days.

Another Example

Estimate 4,754 ÷ 82.

 60 estimated quotient
$82\overline{)4,754}$ $\xrightarrow{\text{rounds to}}$ $80\overline{)4,754}$ **Think** $80\overline{)4,800}$

Check Your Understanding

Estimate each quotient.

1. $18\overline{)85}$ 2. $62\overline{)245}$ 3. $41\overline{)\$256}$ 4. $23\overline{)3,926}$ 5. $39\overline{)1,568}$

Share Your Ideas Which example would you use to estimate 379 ÷ 86? Explain your choice.

a. $80\overline{)400}$ b. $90\overline{)380}$ c. $90\overline{)360}$

Estimate each quotient.

6. $21\overline{)130}$ 7. $19\overline{)83}$ 8. $25\overline{)87}$ 9. $12\overline{)90}$ 10. $28\overline{)195}$

11. $37\overline{)72}$ 12. $55\overline{)\,\$549}$ 13. $22\overline{)155}$ 14. $57\overline{)495}$ 15. $14\overline{)61}$

16. $32\overline{)1,300}$ 17. $54\overline{)344}$ 18. $43\overline{)3,200}$ 19. $40\overline{)350}$ 20. $35\overline{)1,720}$

21. $85\overline{)\,\$910}$ 22. $79\overline{)4,380}$ 23. $33\overline{)\,\$269}$ 24. $68\overline{)1,500}$ 25. $29\overline{)\,\$200}$

26. $67\overline{)3,650}$ 27. $75\overline{)3,562}$ 28. $60\overline{)4,348}$ 29. $94\overline{)1,950}$ 30. $65\overline{)4,400}$

31. $98 \div 18$ 32. $212 \div 52$ 33. $5,000 \div 82$ 34. $1,625 \div 46$

35. $5,792 \div 67$ 36. $20,413 \div 51$ 37. $11,289 \div 45$ 38. $28,000 \div 88$

39. The Outing Club has 19 members. Estimate each member's share of each trip expense below.

   a. transportation $195   b. food $385

   c. canoe rentals $675   d. other $310

40. Juan and Rosita can paddle 18 km a day. About how many days will it take them to canoe the length of Amistad Reservoir, 138 km?

41. Kathy's outboard motor goes 12 km on a liter of gasoline. About how many liters will she need to go 142 km?

Test Taker

Sometimes you waste time by calculating exact answers instead of estimating answers for a multiple choice test. Estimate each quotient to help you choose the answer.

42. $456 \div 47$

   a. 10 R15   b. 9 R33

   c. 8 R30   d. 9 R50

43. $432 \div 72$

   a. 7   b. $6\frac{1}{2}$

   c. 6   d. $5\frac{3}{4}$

Why are compatible numbers used to estimate a quotient?

SUMMING UP

What are the possible remainders when you divide by 10? by 20? Explain how you know.

Dividing by Tens

Ramón is making a pictograph. Each symbol represents 20 students. Hockey was the favorite sport of 51 students. How many symbols should Ramón put next to hockey on the graph?

Divide 51 by 20 to find the answer.

Favorite Sports at Clarke School

Football	🧍🧍🧍
Tennis	🧍🧍
Hockey	
Baseball	

Each 🧍 represents 20 students.

Step 1	Step 2	Step 3	Check
Estimate to place the first digit in the quotient.	Divide. Then multiply.	Subtract and compare.	20 × 2 40 + 11 51
$20\overline{)51}$ Think $20\overline{)40}$ (with 2 estimated)	$\begin{array}{r} 2 \\ 20\overline{)51} \\ 40 \end{array}$ ← 2 × 20	$\begin{array}{r} 2\ R11 \\ 20\overline{)51} \\ -40 \\ \hline 11 \end{array}$ 11 < 20	

Ramón should draw 2 symbols and about one half of another symbol next to hockey on the pictograph.

Another Example

Find 475 ÷ 70.

Step 1

$70\overline{)475}$ Think $70\overline{)420}$ (with 6 estimated)

Step 2

$\begin{array}{r} 6 \\ 70\overline{)475} \\ 420 \end{array}$ ← 6 × 70

Step 3

$\begin{array}{r} 6\ R55 \\ 70\overline{)475} \\ -420 \\ \hline 55 \end{array}$ 55 < 70

Check Your Understanding

Divide. Check by multiplying.

1. $30\overline{)74}$
2. $20\overline{)159}$
3. $40\overline{)181}$
4. $80\overline{)249}$
5. $90\overline{)600}$

Share Your Ideas Describe the steps you would use to find $60\overline{)285}$.

Divide. Check by multiplying.

6. 40)96 **7.** 10)75 **8.** 20)117 **9.** 60)285 **10.** 90)270

11. 80)130 **12.** 70)564 **13.** 30)100 **14.** 50)100 **15.** 40)173

16. 30)67 **17.** 80)402 **18.** 50)72 **19.** 30)286 **20.** 70)432

21. 20)124 **22.** 80)200 **23.** 70)429 **24.** 40)220 **25.** 30)48

26. 90)810 **27.** 60)316 **28.** 20)84 **29.** 80)593 **30.** 60)540

31. 50)315 **32.** 30)240 **33.** 90)555 **34.** 10)27 **35.** 60)270

36. 812 ÷ 90 **37.** 150 ÷ 20 **38.** 720 ÷ 80 **39.** 657 ÷ 80

40. 390 ÷ 70 **41.** 303 ÷ 50 **42.** 421 ÷ 60 **43.** 340 ÷ 40

44. Use the numbers below to write three division examples.

Divisors	Dividends	Quotients	Remainders
60	739	9	65
70	415	5	19
80	458	7	38

45. Look back at **44.** Explain your method for finding the division examples.

DATA **Use the pictograph on page 118.**

46. Ramón found that 76 students liked baseball. How many figures would you draw for baseball on the pictograph?

47. About how many students chose tennis as their favorite sport?

48. What if each figure represented 30 students? How many figures would there be for football?

When you divide by tens, how can you tell whether or not there will be a remainder?

SUMMING UP

119

What does the word *average* mean? How do you find the average of a set of numbers?

One-Digit Quotients

Larry plays on the high-school basketball team. He scored a total of 152 points in 19 games. What was the average number of points that Larry scored per game?

$$152 \div 19 = n$$

Step 1	Step 2
Estimate to place the first digit in the quotient.	Divide. Then multiply. Subtract and compare.
$19\overline{)152}$ Think $20\overline{)160}^{\,8}$	$\begin{array}{r} 8 \\ 19\overline{)152} \\ -152 \leftarrow 8 \times 19 \\ \hline 0 \quad 0 < 19 \end{array}$

Larry scored an average of 8 points per game.

More Examples

a. $68 \div 21 = n$

$$\begin{array}{r} 3 \text{ R5} \\ 21\overline{)68} \\ -63 \\ \hline 5 \end{array} \quad \text{Think } 20\overline{)60}^{\,3}$$

b. $413 \div 75 = n$

$$\begin{array}{r} 5 \text{ R38} \\ 75\overline{)413} \\ -375 \\ \hline 38 \end{array} \quad \text{Think } 80\overline{)400}^{\,5}$$

Check Your Understanding

Divide. Check by multiplying.

1. $17\overline{)42}$ **2.** $31\overline{)95}$ **3.** $53\overline{)106}$ **4.** $78\overline{)734}$ **5.** $63\overline{)391}$

Share Your Ideas Look back at **1–5**. Tell what numbers you used to estimate each quotient.

Practice

Divide. Check by multiplying.

6. $42\overline{)252}$ **7.** $23\overline{)119}$ **8.** $41\overline{)375}$

9. $17\overline{)43}$ **10.** $44\overline{)264}$ **11.** $58\overline{)186}$

12. $62\overline{)186}$ **13.** $45\overline{)301}$ **14.** $52\overline{)218}$

15. $22\overline{)179}$ **16.** $32\overline{)227}$ **17.** $73\overline{)369}$

18. $56\overline{)193}$ **19.** $64\overline{)320}$ **20.** $72\overline{)580}$

21. $459 \div 51$ **22.** $138 \div 33$ **23.** $544 \div 68$

24. $453 \div 69$ **25.** $162 \div 27$ **26.** $220 \div 39$

Divide. Use mental math or paper and pencil. Explain your choices.

CHOICES

27. $40\overline{)360}$ **28.** $12\overline{)108}$ **29.** $92\overline{)736}$

30. $44\overline{)226}$ **31.** $81\overline{)405}$ **32.** $29\overline{)91}$

33. $21\overline{)84}$ **34.** $23\overline{)71}$ **35.** $26\overline{)128}$

36. $376 \div 53$ **37.** $195 \div 59$ **38.** $84 \div 28$

Find each missing number.

39. $n \div 31 = 4$ R2 **40.** $n \div 67 = 6$ R13

Problem Solving

41. There were 215 people who needed a ride to the game. Each bus held 48 passengers. How many buses were needed?

42. Plennie Wingo, age 81, walked backwards from Santa Monica to San Francisco. He walked 452 miles in 85 days. Did he average more than or less than 5 miles a day? Explain.

Explain how you can tell where to place the first digit in a quotient.

SUMMING UP

Mixed Review

1. $346 - 47$

2. $320 \div 8$

3. $469 - 249$

4. $3{,}511 + 89$

5. $4 \times \$.35$

6. 2×24

7. 3×230

8. $4{,}175 + 25$

9. $6{,}100 - 50$

10. $800 \div 4$

Give two related multiplication facts for each.

11. $9\overline{)63}$ **12.** $7\overline{)28}$

13. $6\overline{)54}$ **14.** $9\overline{)72}$

15. $8\overline{)56}$ **16.** $5\overline{)35}$

17. $6\overline{)42}$ **18.** $8\overline{)48}$

Find the average for each set of numbers.

19. 5, 8, 8, 7

20. 17, 21, 19

121

Many things are packaged by the dozen. How many items are in 1 dozen? 2 dozen? 4 dozen?

Changing Quotient Estimates

The Little League needs 96 baseballs to start the season. If the balls are packed 16 to a box, how many boxes should be ordered?

$96 \div 16 = n$

Sometimes your first estimate is not enough.

Step 1	**Step 2**	**Step 3**
Estimate to place the first digit in the quotient.	Try to divide. Change the estimate.	Divide. Then multiply. Subtract and compare.
$16\overline{)96}$ Think $\begin{array}{r} 5 \\ \hline 20\overline{)100} \end{array}$	$\begin{array}{r} 5 \\ 16\overline{)96} \\ -80 \\ \hline 16 \end{array}$ The remainder must be less than the divisor. 5 is not enough. Try 6.	$\begin{array}{r} 6 \\ 16\overline{)96} \\ -96 \\ \hline 0 \end{array}$ ← 6 × 16 $0 < 16$

Six boxes should be ordered.

Another Example

Find $379 \div 54$.

Sometimes your estimate is too much.

Step 1	**Step 2**	**Step 3**
Estimate to place the first digit in the quotient.	Try to divide. Change the estimate.	Divide. Then multiply. Subtract and compare.
$54\overline{)379}$ Think, $50\overline{)400}$ with 8	$\begin{array}{r} 8 \\ 54\overline{)379} \\ -432 \end{array}$ $432 > 379$ 8 is too much. Try 7.	$\begin{array}{r} 7R1 \\ 54\overline{)379} \\ -378 \\ \hline 1 \end{array}$ ← 7 × 54 $1 < 54$

Check Your Understanding

Divide.

1. $19\overline{)98}$
2. $43\overline{)85}$
3. $35\overline{)105}$
4. $93\overline{)640}$
5. $64\overline{)575}$

Share Your Ideas How do you know if your first quotient estimate is too much or not enough?

Divide.

6. $18\overline{)72}$ **7.** $15\overline{)85}$ **8.** $32\overline{)91}$ **9.** $29\overline{)87}$ **10.** $31\overline{)242}$

11. $47\overline{)249}$ **12.** $93\overline{)730}$ **13.** $75\overline{)225}$ **14.** $58\overline{)349}$ **15.** $54\overline{)161}$

16. $21\overline{)188}$ **17.** $34\overline{)299}$ **18.** $17\overline{)140}$ **19.** $32\overline{)91}$ **20.** $24\overline{)100}$

21. $37\overline{)78}$ **22.** $22\overline{)163}$ **23.** $36\overline{)278}$ **24.** $54\overline{)483}$ **25.** $85\overline{)694}$

26. $861 \div 96$ **27.** $600 \div 65$ **28.** $342 \div 68$ **29.** $132 \div 12$

30. $699 \div 15$ **31.** $345 \div 23$ **32.** $8,690 \div 79$ **33.** $5,440 \div 17$

Estimate each quotient. The correct answers spell a baseball word.

34. $22\overline{)85}$ **m.** 3   **b.** 4   **o.** 2

35. $58\overline{)302}$ **a.** 5   **u.** 4   **i.** 6

36. $41\overline{)291}$ **x.** 6   **r.** 8   **t.** 7

Estimate to compare. Use >, <, or = for ●.

37. $260 \div 94$ ● $262 \div 92$

38. $800 \div 80$ ● $800 \div 82$

39. $48 \div 16$ ● $108 \div 36$

40. Will you need more boxes to pack 180 baseballs 15 to a box or 12 to a box? Explain.

41. A bag of 9-dozen baseballs includes 3 damaged balls. How many good baseballs are there?

Visual Thinking

42. Which piece completes the puzzle?

1   2

3   4

Are there more groups of 12 in 720 or in 760?
How can you tell without dividing?

Midchapter Review

Divide. Check by multiplying. pages 114–115

1. $90 \div 30$
   $900 \div 30$

2. $160 \div 40$
   $1,600 \div 40$

3. $630 \div 90$
   $6,300 \div 90$

4. $720 \div 80$
   $7,200 \div 80$

Estimate each quotient. pages 116–117

5. $30)\overline{265}$

6. $72)\overline{4,824}$

7. $26)\overline{3,394}$

8. $46)\overline{4,862}$

Divide. Check by multiplying. pages 118–121

9. $70)\overline{665}$

10. $60)\overline{378}$

11. $90)\overline{562}$

12. $20)\overline{63}$

13. $50)\overline{264}$

14. $40)\overline{168}$

15. $30)\overline{132}$

16. $80)\overline{744}$

17. $19)\overline{42}$

18. $19)\overline{121}$

19. $56)\overline{187}$

20. $74)\overline{374}$

21. $51)\overline{207}$

22. $66)\overline{497}$

23. $43)\overline{261}$

24. $91)\overline{834}$

Divide. pages 122–123

25. $21)\overline{99}$

26. $56)\overline{449}$

27. $26)\overline{77}$

28. $84)\overline{754}$

29. $41)\overline{244}$

30. $65)\overline{585}$

31. $91)\overline{538}$

32. $87)\overline{698}$

Estimate to compare. Use >, <, or = for ⬤. pages 122–123

33. $364 \div 92$ ⬤ $148 \div 72$

34. $400 \div 40$ ⬤ $400 \div 38$

35. $280 \div 70$ ⬤ $2,800 \div 70$

Choose the word that best completes each sentence.

36. The answer in division is the _____.

37. The number to be divided is the _____.

38. The number by which another number is to be divided is the _____.

Words to Know
divisor
quotient
dividend

Solve.

39. Santiago Sport Store has an order for 289 basketballs. If basketballs come in crates of 25 each, how many crates must they order?

40. The recreation department has 294 baseballs. How many can they give to each team if there are 36 teams in the town? How many baseballs will they have left over?

124

Exploring Problem Solving

Who's the Better Base Stealer?

Use a calculator where appropriate.

CHOICES
Both Ty Cobb and Maury Wills were excellent baseball players. They led their leagues in the number of stolen bases in the years listed below.

Thinking Critically

Who do you think was the better base stealer? Work in a small group. Use the table and questions to help you solve the problem.

	Year	Hits	Walks	Steals
Cobb	1907	212	24	49
	1909	216	48	76
	1911	248	44	83
	1915	208	118	96
	1916	201	78	68
	1917	225	61	55
Wills	1960	152	35	50
	1961	173	59	35
	1962	208	51	104
	1963	159	49	40
	1964	173	41	53
	1965	186	40	94

Analyzing and Making Decisions

1. How many years did each player lead his league? What was the total number of steals each player had during these leading years? Who stole the greater number of bases in one season?

2. To have a chance to steal, a player must be on base. Both hits and walks put a player on base. For each year, how many chances did Cobb and Wills have a chance to steal a base?

3. About how many times was each person on base for every stolen base he made?

4. Who do you think is the better base stealer? Explain why you think so.

Look Back   Of the years listed above, which was the best for stolen bases?

Problem Solving Strategies

Experiment

Mitch put 20 pennies in a row on his desk. He replaced every fifth penny with a dime. Next he replaced every third coin with a nickel. Then he replaced every fourth coin with a quarter. How much are the 20 coins on his desk worth now?

Sometimes the best way to solve a problem is to experiment. You do the action to find the answer.

Solving the Problem

Think   What is the problem? Can you actually do this problem to solve it? Explain.

Explore   What materials will you need to do the problem? How many of these materials will you need? If you do not have these materials, how can you still do the problem?

Solve   Do the experiment. What is the total value of the money on the desk?

Look Back   How can you solve this problem without doing an experiment?

Share Your Ideas

1. **What if** you had a row of 40 pennies and then did this problem? How much would your coins be worth?

2. Can all problems be solved by doing an experiment? Explain.

Practice

Solve. Use a calculator where appropriate.
Use pennies, dimes, and a ruler for **3-4**.

3. Would you rather have your height in pennies stacked, or in dimes standing on end?

4. Look back at **3**. About how much money would you receive?

Use this information for 5-6.
Debbie, Steve, Mark, and Connie are running in a relay.

5. Show the different ways they can run if Debbie is always first.

6. Show the different ways they can run if Debbie is first and Mark is third or fourth.

THINK
EXPLORE
SOLVE
LOOK BACK

Mixed Strategy Review

7. Mr. David bought a pair of basketball shoes for $32.95, a pair of running shoes for $47.90, and a baseball bat for $12.50. How much did he spend?

8. Look at **7**. Rewrite the question so that the problem has too much information.

The class kept this record of the daily high and low temperatures for a week.

Temperature in Degrees Fahrenheit	Mon.	Tues.	Wed.	Thurs.	Fri.	Sat.	Sun.
High temperature	80	82	77	75	84	88	88
Low temperature	62	66	60	56	70	71	68

9. On which day of the week was there the greatest difference in temperature?

10. On which day of the week was there the least difference in temperature?

Create Your Own

Write a problem that uses information given in the temperature chart above.

Using Problem Solving

What Does Your Answer Mean?

Bill runs a store. He has 84 boxes of baseball cards in stock. He usually sells 6 boxes of baseball cards a day. The store is open 6 days a week. Does Bill have enough boxes for two weeks, or should he order more cards?

A. Try to solve this problem by dividing 84 boxes by 12 days. How would you label the answer? How would you use that answer to solve the problem?

B. Now try to solve this problem by dividing 84 boxes by 6 boxes. How would you label the answer? How would you use that answer to solve the problem?

C. Try to find other ways to solve this problem. Record your methods.

Sharing Your Ideas

1. What different ways were you able to solve the problem?

2. Which method did you prefer for solving the problem? Explain.

Practice

3. Bill has 240 boxes of cards in stock. If he sells about 6 boxes a day, how long will the supply last?

4. A summer camp requested that 3 boxes of cards be delivered on each of the 6 days the store is open for 5 weeks. Will the 240 boxes last 5 weeks?

5. At the end of the season Bill has 72 boxes of baseball cards. He decides to have a sale. He is sure that he will sell at least 6 boxes a day, but not more than 12 boxes. He is planning to have his sale last a week. Is that a reasonable amount of time for the sale? Explain.

6. Bill has 105 loose baseball cards. He made 15 sets of 7 cards each. But he soon found that sets with this few cards did not sell well. How can he make sets with more cards?

7. Bill can buy a case of cards (8 boxes) from one supplier for $120. He can buy the cards for $16 per box from a different supplier. Which supplier has the less expensive cards? From whom should Bill buy the cards? Why?

8. Create your own problem about the store. Give it to a partner to solve.

Summing Up

9. How were you able to solve these problems? Why was it possible to use different methods to solve some of the problems?

10. When dividing, why is it important to know what your answer means? Give an example.

List all the divisors of 48 that give you a remainder of zero.

Factors

The high school band will march with 16 twirlers in front of the 48 musicians. An equal number of students will be in each row. Here is one possible arrangement.

Draw another arrangement that the band director can use. Use what you know about the divisors of 16 and 48 to help you.

▶ **Factors** are numbers that are multiplied to give a product.

Factors of a number divide the number without a remainder.

Factors of 16: 1, 2, 4, 8, 16
Factors of 48: 1, 2, **3**, 4, **6**, 8, **12**, 16, **24**, **48**

▶ **Common factors** of two or more numbers are factors that are the same for each.

Why are 1, 2, 4, 8, and 16 called common factors of 16 and 48?

▶ The **greatest common factor (GCF)** of two or more numbers is the greatest number that is a factor of each. Explain why the GCF of 16 and 48 is 16.

Check Your Understanding

List the factors of each number.

1. 12   **2.** 18   **3.** 24   **4.** 36   **5.** 10

Find the common factors and the GCF.

6. 12 and 18   **7.** 12 and 24   **8.** 18 and 24

Share Your Ideas What is the fewest number of rows the band director can make? Explain how you can use what you learned in this lesson to find out.

List the factors of each number.

9. 6   **10.** 30   **11.** 27   **12.** 8   **13.** 15

14. 32   **15.** 54   **16.** 60   **17.** 14   **18.** 13

Find the common factors and the GCF.

19. 6 and 21   **20.** 15 and 24   **21.** 10 and 15   **22.** 18 and 27

23. 6 and 27   **24.** 6 and 16   **25.** 12 and 48   **26.** 72 and 24

27. 6 and 60   **28.** 16 and 60   **29.** 27 and 48   **30.** 25 and 50

31. 27 and 54   **32.** 48 and 60   **33.** 16 and 54   **34.** 45 and 63

35. 48 and 54   **36.** 16, 48, and 60   **37.** 6, 16, and 27   **38.** 36, 48, and 72

Answer *true* **or** *false*. **Use a calculator, if you wish. Explain your answer.**

CHOICES

39. A factor of 432 is 144.   **40.** The GCF for 72 and 576 is 36.   **41.** Two factors of 68 are 16 and 8.

42. A common factor of 900 and 480 is 18.   **43.** All the multiples of 37 have 37 as a factor.   **44.** The GCF for 25 and 100 is 25.

Problem Solving

45. What if you were the band director? How could using common factors help you find all the possible marching arrangements?

46. What if the band director has 28 twirlers and 42 musicians next year? Describe all the possible marching arrangements that can be made.

47. Draw a number line to show that 15 is a factor of 30.

48. Draw a number line to show that 14 is not a factor of 32.

What is the least factor that any number can have? What is the greatest factor that any number can have?

SUMMING UP

Exploring Prime and Composite Numbers

Which numbers have several factors? Try this activity to find out.

Working together

Materials: 20 square tiles or grid paper

A. For each number, 1 to 20, create as many rectangles as possible. For each number, use that many tiles.

Rectangles can be made horizontally or vertically. Sides must touch. Hint: Squares are rectangles, too.

Rectangles for the number 6 are shown. There are 4 different rectangles: 1 × 6, 6 × 1, 2 × 3, and 3 × 2.

B. Record each number and its rectangles. Find the number of rectangles.

C. Look for patterns in the chart.

6 × 1

1 × 6

2 × 3

3 × 2

Number	Rectangles	Number of Rectangles
1		
2		
3		
4		
5		
6	1 × 6, 6 × 1, 2 × 3, 3 × 2	4
7		

Sharing Your Results

1. Compare your chart with others. Discuss answers that do not agree. Discuss patterns in your chart.

2. Use the chart to help you classify the numbers 1 to 20. Explain your categories.

3. Which numbers have an odd number of rectangles? How are those numbers different from the others?

4. Count the factors for each number. Write your answer next to the number of rectangles for that number. What do you notice?

Practice

Use your chart to help you solve each.

5. Which numbers have only 2 rectangles? These numbers are **prime** numbers.

6. Which numbers have more than 2 rectangles? These numbers are **composite** numbers.

7. Which number has only 1 rectangle? This number is neither prime nor composite.

8. Which number has the most rectangles? Which number has the most factors?

Write *prime* or *composite*. Use grid paper or tiles, if needed.

9. 39   **10.** 41   **11.** 49   **12.** 65   **13.** 111

A **prime** number is a whole number greater than 1 with only two factors—itself and 1.

A **composite** number is a whole number greater than 1 that has more than two factors.

▶ A **factor tree** shows the prime factors of a number.

$$51$$
$$3 \times 17$$
$$51 = 3 \times 17$$

$$63$$
$$7 \times 9$$
$$7 \times 3 \times 3$$
$$63 = 7 \times 3 \times 3$$

$$70$$
$$7 \times 10$$
$$7 \times 2 \times 5$$
$$70 = 7 \times 2 \times 5$$

Make a factor tree for each.

14. 27   **15.** 35   **16.** 42   **17.** 44   **18.** 54

Summing Up

19. Explain how each helps you decide if 111 is prime or composite.
   a. factor tree for 111
   b. divisibility rules
   c. 111 tiles

20. Name the only even prime number. Explain why all other even numbers must be composite.

21. Do you think there are more composite numbers than prime numbers? Support your answer.

Chapter Review

Divide. Check by multiplying. pages 114–115, 118–119

1. $60\overline{)315}$ 2. $30\overline{)94}$ 3. $90\overline{)810}$ 4. $80\overline{)6,400}$

Estimate each quotient. pages 116–117

5. $19\overline{)67}$ 6. $74\overline{)449}$ 7. $49\overline{)348}$ 8. $68\overline{)512}$

Divide. Check by multiplying. pages 120–123, 128–133

9. $32\overline{)98}$ 10. $63\overline{)563}$ 11. $64\overline{)2,128}$ 12. $53\overline{)11,503}$

13. $84\overline{)907}$ 14. $78\overline{)7,959}$ 15. $19\overline{)9,937}$ 16. $48\overline{)24,192}$

List the common factors for each. Circle the GCF. pages 136–137

17. 15 and 20   18. 6 and 18   19. 8, 16, and 36

List all the factors of each number. Then tell if the number is prime or composite. pages 138–139

20. 16   21. 17   22. 30   23. 22

Choose the word or phrase that best completes each sentence.

24. _____ are numbers that you multiply to find a product.

25. _____ are factors that are the same for two or more numbers.

26. The _____ is the greatest number that is a factor of each of two or more numbers.

Words to Know
greatest common factor
common factors
factors

Solve. pages 125–127

27. Juan wants to arrange his deck of 52 cards in stacks with the same number in each stack. Show 3 ways he can do this.

28. Eva took 110 pictures at the Bear's game. Each roll of film had 36 exposures. How many rolls did she use? How many exposures were left?

Chapter Test

Divide. Check by multiplying.

1. 50)165

2. 40)320

3. 70)431

4. 90)458

Estimate each quotient.

5. 22)96

6. 56)465

7. 48)552

8. 75)5,734

Divide. Check by multiplying.

9. 28)221

10. 54)605

11. 37)542

12. 35)4,550

13. 21)5,886

14. 16)8,786

15. 12)8,424

16. 23)9,271

List the common factors for each. Circle the GCF.

17. 27 and 45

18. 16 and 24

19. 18, 36, and 54

Fill in the blank with a word or phrase that best completes the sentence.

20. 1, 3, and 9 are _____ of 27 and 36, with 9 being their _____ .

List all the factors for each number. Then tell if the number is prime or composite.

21. 19

22. 51

23. 38

Solve.

24. The 41 swimmers and 15 divers from Davis School will march in the opening ceremony for the swim meet. They must be arranged in rows with the same number of athletes in each row. Show 3 ways this can be done.

25. Sara covered about 50 miles a day on a cross-country biking trip. How many days had she traveled when she completed 1,000 miles?

THINK   A famous mathematician, Christian Goldbach, stated that every even number (except 2) is equal to the sum of two prime numbers. This has never been proven. Test the even numbers between 60 and 70.

Solving Equations

Guess-n-Games

The same number appears on the back of each card.
Can you find that number?

   **+11=17**

You can write this equation to help you find *n*.

$$3n + 11 = 17$$

↑

means *n* + *n* + *n*, or 3 × *n*

What number added to 11 equals 17?

3 × *n* must equal 6. So *n* = 2.

Find *n* for the following Guess-n-Games.

1. 32 +   = 50

2.   = 72

3. − 20 = 10

4.   − 15 = 85

5. **Look back** at **1–4**. Write an equation for each.

Find *n* for each equation.

6. $n + 7 = 10$

7. $2n + 3 = 11$

8. $n - 2 = 18$

9. $3n = 54$

10. $3n - 1 = 14$

11. $2n + 6 = 20$

Create Your Own Guess-n-Game for a friend to solve.

Maintaining Skills

Choose the correct answers. Write A, B, C, or D.

1. $70 \times 80 \times 3$

   A 5,600   **C** 16,800

   B 168   **D** not given

2. 3,946
   $\times\ \ 5$

   A 17,730   **C** 15,500

   B 19,730   **D** not given

3. Find the LCM of 6 and 8.

   A 24   **C** 12

   B 14   **D** not given

4. 126×455

   A 1,764   **C** 56,330

   B 57,330   **D** not given

5. Find n. $n \div 5 = 7$

   A 30   **C** 35

   B 25   **D** not given

6. $3,200 \div 4$

   A 8   **C** 800

   B 80   **D** not given

7. $304 \div 6$

   A 50 R4   **C** 5 R4

   B 54   **D** not given

8. $5\overline{)1,382}$

   A 366 R2   **C** 374 R2

   B 376 R2   **D** not given

9. Estimate. $46\overline{)529}$

   A 40   **C** 90

   B 10   **D** not given

10. $1,673 \div 62$

   A 27 R1   **C** 26 R61

   B 26 R19   **D** not given

11. $26\overline{)2704}$

   A 104   **C** 140

   B 14   **D** not given

Use the table for 12.

Number of Subway Passengers			
	Week 1	Week 2	Week 3
South St.	850	1,000	925
4th Ave.	500	875	900

12. How many more subway passengers used South St. than 4th Ave. during the three-week period?

   A 500   **C** 775

   B 525   **D** not given

Sharing What You Know

How would you complete this bumper sticker? Think of your favorite activity.

How much time do you spend doing your favorite activity? Explain how time influences your activity. Name some activities that must be done at certain times. Why? Discuss the importance of keeping track of time.

Using Language

A.M. is the time from midnight to noon. It is an abbreviation for the Latin phrase *ante meridiem,* which means "before noon." Describe the meaning of **P.M.** Can you guess its Latin root? Many words in mathematics have Latin roots. How does knowing the Latin root help you understand the meaning?

Words to Know: A.M., P.M., data, mean, median, mode, range

Be a Problem Solver

Gary spends twice as much time listening to music as Melissa. Melissa spends twice as much time as Wendy. Altogether they spend 14 hours a week. How much time does each person spend listening to music each week?

Survey your class to find out how much time each person spends listening to music. Decide how to organize and display the data.

Do you prefer to use a standard clock or a digital clock? What are the advantages and disadvantages of each?

Units of Time

Many airports display clocks showing the time in different parts of the world.

The clock for Rome, Italy shows the time as one forty or twenty minutes to two.

What is the time in New York? How would a digital clock display these times?

New York   **Rome**   **Tokyo**

These units are used to measure time.

60 seconds (s) = 1 minute (min)
60 minutes = 1 hour (h)
24 hours = 1 day (d)
7 days = 1 week (wk)

12 months (mo) = 1 year (yr)
52 weeks = 1 year
365 days = 1 year
366 days = 1 leap year

▶ To change to a smaller unit, multiply.

4 h = _____ min
4 × 60 = 240   Why multiply by 60?
4 h = 240 min

▶ To change to a larger unit, divide.

40 mo = _____ yr
40 ÷ 12 = 3 R4   Why divide by 12?
40 mo = 3 yr 4 mo

Check Your Understanding

Complete.

1. 7 wk = _____ d   **2.** 156 wk = _____ yr   **3.** 60 h = _____ d _____ h

Share Your Ideas   Compare 8:50 A.M. and 8:50 P.M. How are they alike? How are they different?

Write the time shown in 2 ways.

4.  5.   6.  7.

Write *multiply* or *divide*.

8. change hours to years   9. change days to minutes   10. change hours to seconds

Complete. Use paper and pencil, mental math, or a calculator.

CHOICES

11. 72 h = __ d   12. 9 yr = __ d   13. 5 yr = __ mo

14. 4 d = __ h   15. 7 min = __ s   16. $2\frac{1}{2}$ yr = __ wk

17. 2 min 4 s = __ s   18. 50 mo = __ yr __ mo   19. 620 s = __ min __ s

20. 500 d = __ yr __ d   21. 525 wk = __ yr __ d   22. 4,205 s = __ h __ min __ s

Use a calculator to find each number.

23. seconds in an hour   24. minutes in a week   25. minutes in a year

26. hours in a year   27. days you have lived   28. hours you have lived

Problem Solving

29. Two possible times that can appear on a digital clock are 4:52 and 10:35. How many possible times can be shown in hours and minutes on a digital clock? Be sure to include all A.M. and P.M. times. Explain your answer.

30. The years of 1980, 1984, 1988, and 1992 are all leap years. Find the pattern. Will the year 2000 be a leap year?

Logical Thinking

31. How many times does the hour hand go around the clock each day? Explain.

32. How many times does the minute hand go around the clock each day? Explain.

33. How many times does the second hand go around the clock each day? Explain.

Write an explanation of how to change one unit of time to another unit of time.

SUMMING UP

> About how long is it from the start of school until lunch? Explain your estimate.

Working With Time

The Clark Family enjoys watching movies. Joey recorded times for the movies he would like to see.

How long is *Marvelous Adventures*?

One way to find elapsed time is to think of a clock and count forward from the starting time.

Movie	Start	End
Marvelous Adventures	5:40	7:00
Journey into Space	6:45	
Camp Out	6:15	

Count hours. Count minutes.

5:40 P.M.   6:40 P.M.   7:00 P.M.

　　　1 h　　　　　20 min

Marvelous Adventures is 1 h 20 min long.

▶ Times can be added.
What if *Journey into Space* is 1 h 32 min long? What time will it end?

```
   6 h    45 min
 + 1 h    32 min
 ─────────────────
   7 h    77 min      Think 77 min =
or 8 h    17 min      1 h 17 min
```

Journey into Space will end at 8:17 P.M..

▶ Times can be subtracted.
What if Joey cannot see *Camp Out* at 3:40 P.M.? How long must he wait before the next show at 6:15 P.M.?

```
   5 h  75 min        Think 1 hr = 60 min
   6 h  15 min          60 + 15 = 75
 − 3 h  40 min
 ─────────────────
   2 h  35 min
```

Joey must wait 2 h 35 min.

Check Your Understanding

Find the elapsed time.

1. from 6:25 A.M. to 8:10 P.M.

2. from 9:03 A.M. to 1:27 P.M.

Add or subtract.

3.　1 h 20 min
　　+ 3 h 35 min

4.　4 min 28 s
　　+ 　　55 s

5.　5 h 15 min
　　− 3 h 47 min

Share Your Ideas   Explain how you found elapsed time in **1** and **2**. How did you account for A.M. and P.M.?

148

Find the elapsed time.

6. from 3:25 P.M. to 5:00 P.M.

7. from 6:15 A.M. to noon.

8. from 10:10 A.M. to 1:00 P.M.

9. from noon to 3:27 P.M.

10. from 2:25 P.M. to 7:15 P.M.

11. from 5:40 A.M. to 2:20 P.M.

12. from 11:12 A.M. to 1:45 P.M.

13. from 8:05 A.M. to 9:50 A.M.

Add or subtract.

14.	2 h 10 min	15.	3 h 40 min	16.	1 h 27 min	17.	6 h
	+ 1 h 35 min		− 1 h 16 min		− 55 min		− 2 h 20 min

Complete.

	Rule: 50 min later	
	Input	Output
18.	12:30 P.M.	1:20
19.	1:15 A.M.	2:05
20.	7:40 P.M.	8:30
21.	3:17 A.M.	4:13

	Rule: 1 h 10 min earlier	
	Input	Output
22.	7:15 A.M.	6:05
23.	3:40 P.M.	2:30
24.	6:00 A.M.	4:50
25.	4:25 P.M.	3:15

Problem Solving

26. The ticket taker at the theater works from 3:45 P.M. to 11:45 P.M. If he is paid $5.75 per hour, how much money does he make in one day?

27. *Future Worlds*, a new movie, starts at 7:20 P.M. and ends at 9:08 P.M. Is this movie longer or shorter than *Marvelous Adventures*? Justify your answer.

DATA
28. Plan your own Field Day. Make a schedule of events starting at 9:20 A.M. and ending at 2:40 P.M. List starting and ending times for each event. Record the length of time it takes for each activity.

29. Last month Joey Clark watched 3 movies. The length of the movies varied from 1 h 32 min to 2 h 40 min. Did Joey spend more than 7 h watching movies? Explain.

How is adding and subtracting time the same as adding and subtracting numbers? How is it different?

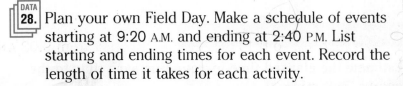

SUMMING UP

Estimating Time

The LaSordas want to hike from about 9:00 A.M. to 1:30 P.M.

If they want to hike two trails in this time period, which trails can they choose? Estimate to find out.

One way to estimate time is to round to the nearest half hour.

Trail	Miles	Average Hiking Time
▲ Red	3.5	55 min
▲ Blue	6.4	2 h 10 min
▲ Green	7.1	2 h 25 min
△ Yellow	11.0	3 h 40 min
▲ Orange	11.1	3 h 50 min

Rounds to

▲ 55 min ⟶ 1 hour

▲ 2 h 10 min ⟶ 2 hours

▲ 2 h 25 min ⟶ $2\frac{1}{2}$ hours.

△ 3 h 40 min ⟶ $3\frac{1}{2}$ hours.

▲ 3 h 50 min ⟶ 4 hours.

Think
9:00 A.M. to 1:30 P.M. is $4\frac{1}{2}$ hours

▲ 1 hour + △ $3\frac{1}{2}$ hours = $4\frac{1}{2}$ hours.

▲ 2 hours + ▲ $2\frac{1}{2}$ hours = $4\frac{1}{2}$ hours.

The LaSordas should choose the red and yellow trails, or the blue and green trails.

Another Example

Estimate the hiking time if the hike began at 8:48 and ended at 3:23.

8:48 is about 9:00.   3:23 is about 3:30.

From 9:00 to 3:30 is $6\frac{1}{2}$ hours.

Check Your Understanding

Estimate the elapsed time by rounding each time to the nearest half hour.

1. from 8:25 A.M. to 11:05 A.M.

2. from 2:40 P.M. to 5:10 P.M.

3. from 11:35 A.M. to 4:20 P.M.

Share Your Ideas   If you were to estimate the sum of 2 h 15 min and 2 h 45 min, why might you round one addend up and the other one down?

Practice

Round each time to the nearest half hour.

4. 3:27 A.M.   **5.** 5:42 P.M.   **6.** 1:11 P.M.   **7.** 12:18 A.M.   **8.** 10:48 A.M.

Estimate the time to the nearest half hour.

9. from 6:25 A.M. to 9:10 A.M.

10. from 4:07 P.M. to 10:17 P.M.

11. from 12:13 A.M. to 8:50 A.M.

12. from 7:17 A.M. to 9:25 A.M.

13. 2 h 12 min after 6:25 P.M.

14. 1 h 55 min after 5:19 P.M.

15. 3 h 45 min after 8:20 A.M.

16. 3 h 45 min before 11:55 A.M.

17. 4 h 25 min before 8:10 P.M.

Choose the best time estimate for each activity.

18. walk a mile
  a. 20 s
  b. 20 min
  c. 1 h

19. wait at a stop light
  a. 45 s
  b. 5 min
  c. 45 min

20. buy stamps at the post office
  a. 5 h
  b. 10 min
  c. 1 d

Which hours of the day are busiest for each? Explain.

21. telephone operators   **22.** gas station attendants   **23.** bank clerks

Problem Solving

24. At 4:20 P.M., Nina and Bill started a campfire for dinner. It was put out at 9:50 P.M. How long did the fire burn?

25. Two hikers want to be at the last campsite by 4:00 P.M. The hike will take 3 h 10 min. About what time should they begin?

26. The hikers left camp the next day at 8:15 A.M. They hiked 2 miles each hour. If the next campsite is 9 miles away, did they reach it by noon? Explain your answer.

In your own words, explain how to estimate time.

SUMMING UP

Why would you use a graph in place of a chart? Where are graphs used?

Bar Graphs and Pictographs

Would you like to travel into space? If so, for how long?

Fifth-graders in Swampscott, Massachusetts, asked their classmates that question. The results are graphed 2 ways.

Bar Graph

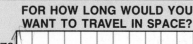

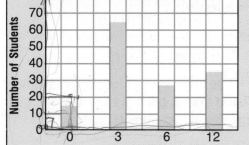

How many students wanted to spend 12 months in space?

- Find the bar marked 12 months.
- Follow the bar to the end.
- Look across to the vertical axis to read the number.

36 students preferred 12 months in space. How many months in space were preferred by 27 students?

How many students wanted to spend 3 months in space?

- There are 11 🛸 for 3 months.
- Multiply 11 by 6.

66 students preferred 3 months in space.

Pictograph

FOR HOW LONG WOULD YOU WANT TO TRAVEL IN SPACE?	
0 months	🛸🛸🛸
3 months	🛸🛸🛸🛸🛸🛸🛸🛸🛸🛸🛸
6 months	🛸🛸🛸🛸
12 months	🛸🛸🛸🛸🛸

Each 🛸 stands for 6 students.

Check Your Understanding

Use the graphs above to answer each question.

1. Which length of time was most popular? Least popular?

2. Find the total number of students surveyed. Which graph did you use? Why?

3. Which graph do you feel presents the data better? Why?

Share Your Ideas How are bar graphs and pictographs the same? How are they different?

Practice

Use the graphs on page 152 to complete each statement.

4. ▮ students wanted to spend 6 mo in space.

5. Exactly ▮ more students wanted to spend 3 mo rather than 6 mo in space.

6. 36 students wanted to spend ▮ mo in space.

7. Just under half of the students surveyed preferred ▮ mo in space.

Use the graphs on page 152. Explain each answer.

8. How does knowing the multiples on a scale make it easier to read the bars on a bar graph?

9. **What if** the topics on the vertical and horizontal axes of the bar graph were exchanged? What items would be changed?

10. How could you tell which time period was most popular? Which graph is easier to use?

11. Can you tell whether students would want to travel in space more than once?

12. How could you tell if students preferred more than 12 mo in space?

13. **What if** you became part of the survey? How would each graph change?

Problem Solving

Use the graph below.

14. Which was the longest flight? shortest flight?

15. How many flights were less than 200 days in length? more than 200 days?

16. Use estimation to find the number of days Soyuz-32 was in space.

17. Actual flight lengths are not easy to read. How can this be corrected?

18. About how many days did Skylab-3 and Skylab-4 travel in space?

19. Write 2 questions that can be answered from the graph, and 2 that cannot be answered.

20. **What if** a new spacecraft spends 6,168 *hours* in space? How would this data be put into the graph?

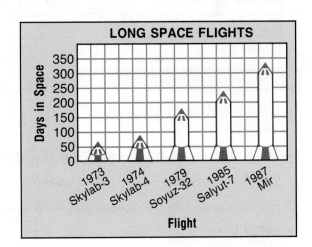

Name one disadvantage each for bar graphs and pictographs.

Yellowstone was our first national park. It was established in 1872. How old is the national park system now?

Line Graphs and Circle Graphs

Americans have a choice of many national parks to visit. These two graphs display different kinds of data about national parks and national seashores.

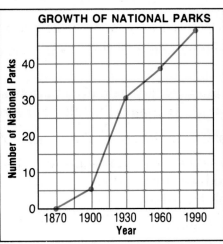

GROWTH OF NATIONAL PARKS

- A **line graph** shows changes over a period of time.

- The **vertical axis** shows the number of national parks.

- The **horizontal axis** shows the years from 1870 to 1990. What does each space represent on the vertical axis? on the horizontal axis? How many parks were there in 1930?

- A **circle graph** shows how a whole is divided. How many national seashores are there in all?

- Circle graphs are good for comparing parts of a whole. How many coasts have national seashores? Which coast has the most?

NUMBER OF NATIONAL SEASHORES

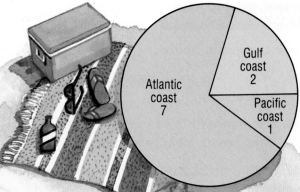

Atlantic coast 7
Gulf coast 2
Pacific coast 1

Check Your Understanding

1. About how many parks were created in the first 30 years?

2. What was the period of greatest growth in national parks?

3. Which coast has the fewest national seashores?

4. What kinds of questions cannot be answered from these graphs?

Share Your Ideas List some reasons for using a line graph to display data. When might you prefer to use a circle graph?

Practice

Use the graphs on page 154. Explain each answer.

5. Can you tell where the national parks are located?

6. Can you tell whether more parks were acquired before or after 1931?

7. Can you tell how many more national parks than national seashores there are?

Which graph would be more appropriate? Write line graph or circle graph. Explain your answer.

8. to show the increase of the price of a cassette tape

9. to show how a town voted at the presidential election

10. to show how you spend the hours of your weekend

Problem Solving

Three thousand fifth graders were asked which foreign continent they would most like to visit. The results are shown in the circle graph.

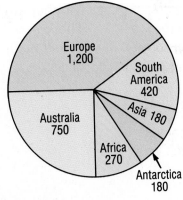

11. Which continent was most popular?

12. How many students were most interested in Africa?

13. Write 4 more questions that can be answered by using the graph.

14. Write 2 questions about interest in foreign continents that cannot be answered by using the graph.

15. Write a title for the graph.

What other kind of graph could be used to display the data about foreign continents? Explain your choice.

Mixed Review

1. 7,965
   − 1,321

2. 27,883
   ×   4

3. 1,954 ÷ 6

4.   75
   × 43

5. 62 × 414

6. 62)750

7.   752
      634
   + 804

Find the least common multiple (LCM).

8. 6, 24   9. 8, 12
10. 5, 8   11. 10, 15
12. 10, 25   13. 25, 30

Tell how much money each person gets if 3 people share equally.

14. $336

15. $453

16. $2,409

17. $30.69

18. $.81

19. $45

20. $81.48

SUMMING UP

155

Exploring Collecting and Organizing Data

Each Sunday, the *Boston Globe* publishes the results of polls taken by elementary school students.
What if you conducted a survey of your class?
How would you do it?

Working together

Materials: index cards or slips of paper

A. Each group should decide on one interesting topic that would help newspaper readers learn more about the class.

B. Create one survey question for your topic. The question can be a short-answer or multiple choice.

C. Each group should write their question on the chalkboard.

D. Number each question to identify it. There should be the same number of questions as there are groups in the class.

Sharing Your Results

Discuss each question below as a class.

1. Is each survey question clear and easy to understand? Rewrite those questions that are not.

2. Will the survey present an interesting view of your class? Explain your answer.

3. Discuss various ways to conduct this survey.

Practice

4. Each student should complete a separate survey card for each question on the chalkboard. Each card should include the student's name, the question number, and the student's response.

5. Collect the survey cards for your question. Organize them in stacks according to the response.

6. Record the data by making a frequency table like the one below. Use one tally mark for each response.

A **frequency table** is used to record and summarize data. The **frequency** is the number of times something occurs. **Tally marks** record the frequency of the data.

#5 If you could meet a famous person, which would you choose?		
answer	tally	frequency
politician	⁣卌 ‖	7
scientist	卌 卌 ‖	12
musician	卌 ‖‖	8

7. Check your frequency table. Is the total frequency the same as the number of students in the class? If not, obtain the missing votes and adjust your results.

8. Draw 2 conclusions from your frequency table.

9. Not all surveys consist of answers to questions. For some surveys, one person records the actions of others. What are the advantages of this type of survey? the disadvantages?

Summing Up

What if your group is to plan a class trip?

10. How would a survey help make the trip a success?

11. Outline the steps for conducting a survey.

Exploring Making Graphs

You can present data in an interesting way by using a graph. Will a bar graph, line graph, or pictograph work best for the date collected in the previous lesson?

Working together

Continue to work with the group from page 156. Choose the best kind of graph for your data. Then use the hints below to make a rough sketch of the graph.

Materials: large paper or poster board, ruler, markers

A. Make these decisions for a pictograph.

- What symbol will you use?
- What amount will the symbol represent?
- Will you need half of a symbol?
- What labels will be used?
- What is the title of your graph?

B. Make these decisions for a bar graph.

- Will the bars be horizontal or vertical?
- How many bars are needed?
- What number scale will you use? (Start at 0.)
- What labels will be used?
- What is the title of your graph?

C. Make these decisions for a line graph.

- What will each axis show?
- What number scale will you use?
- How many points will be connected?
- What labels will you use?
- What is the title of your graph?

Sharing Your Results

1. Display the sketch of your graph. Explain why your group chose the particular kind of graph.

2. Look at each group's sketch. Is each sketch complete? Offer suggestions for improvement.

Practice

Work with your group.

3. Use the suggestions the class made to improve your sketch.

4. Make a clear, complete graph from your sketch.

5. Write a description of your survey and its findings. State a few conclusions.

6. Are your conclusions the same as those drawn from the frequency table? Justify your answer.

Tell how each graph in 7–10 can be improved.

7.

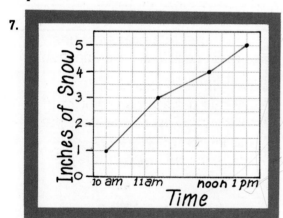

8.

Milk purchased at 2 Schools

Allen School MiLK MiLK

Center School MiLK

Each MiLK stands for 200 cartons

9.

10.

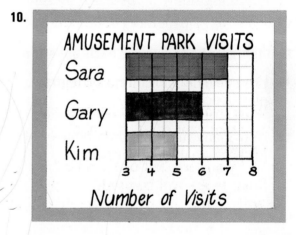

Summing Up

Display all the class graphs.

11. How are the graphs alike? How are they different?

12. Which graphs are easiest to read? Which are most interesting? Explain each answer.

13. Write a description of the students in your class. Use the data gathered in the class surveys.

Midchapter Review

Use words to write each time in two different ways. pages 146–147

1. 12:14   **2.** 9:21   **3.** 7:42   **4.** 1:53   **5.** 5:36   **6.** 8:25

Complete. pages 146–147

7. 60 mo = _____ yr   **8.** 120 min = _____ h   **9.** 1 yr = _____ wk

Estimate the time to the nearest half hour. pages 148–151

10. 8:15 A.M.
to 4:40 P.M.

11. 7:35 A.M.
to 10:15 A.M.

12. 6:20 P.M.
to 9:55 P.M.

13. 1:50 P.M.
to 5:35 P.M.

Add or subtract. pages 148–149

14. 8 h 45 min
    +6 h 55 min

15. 4 h 25 min
    −3 h 35 min

16. 9 h
    −4 h 25 min

17. 2 h 10 min
    +1 h 50 min

Use the graphs to answer each question. pages 152–155

18. How many children registered to play soccer?

19. How many more children registered for basketball than softball?

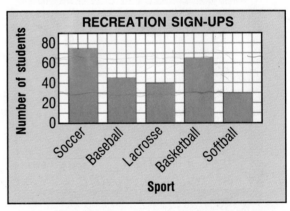

20. How many animal books were sold?

21. How many more sports books were sold than mystery books?

22. How many books were sold in all?

Solve.

23. The Lacrosse game started at 1:30 P.M. The game took 2 h and 15 min to play plus a half hour intermission. At what time did the game end?

24. It took Jan $3\frac{1}{2}$ hours to cut the grass. If she started at 2:35 P.M., at what time did she finish mowing the lawn?

Exploring Problem Solving

What Will People Buy?

"It is difficult to predict what people will buy," said Mr. Warburton. "These buttons sell for $2.00 and these caps sell for $3.00. Can you guess how many of each I have sold?"

"How much money did you get?" asked Beth.

"Forty-six dollars," he said.

Thinking Critically

How many buttons and caps could Mr. Warburton have sold?

Analyzing and Making Decisions

1. How much does a button cost? How much does a cap cost?

2. How much money did Mr. Warburton receive?

3. Could Mr. Warburton have sold only one cap and all the rest buttons? Explain.

4. How many buttons and caps could have been sold? List all the possibilities.

Look Back   What if 19 items were sold altogether? How many would have been buttons? How many caps?

161

Problem Solving Strategies

Guess and Test

At Snow Hill there were 47 people waiting to ride the bobsleds. Some of the bobsleds held 5 people and some held 4 people. Only full sleds went down the hill. All 47 people went down in 10 sleds. How many sleds of each kind were used?

Some problems can be solved by guessing. After you make a guess based on what you know, you must test it. If that guess is not correct, make a guess that will bring you closer to the answer.

Solving the Problem

Think   What is the question? How many people did each sled hold? Were all the sleds full?

Explore   What if you guessed that there were 5 sleds of each kind? These sleds would hold 45 people. That's too few people. In order to hold more people, should there be more five-person sleds or more four-person sleds? Explain.

• Make a new guess. Test it.

• Guess until you solve the problem.

How do you know when your guess solves the problem?

Solve   How many sleds of each kind were used?

Look Back   Would 10 five-person sleds be a good first guess? Explain.

Share Your Ideas

1. For this problem, if you need to make the rider total greater, what should you do? If you need to make the rider total less, what should you do?

2. Why should you test your guess after you have made it?

Practice

Solve. Use a calculator where appropriate.

CHOICES

3. Susan and Teresa together have two dozen golf balls. Susan has 4 more than Teresa. How many golf balls does each girl have?

4. The golf pro distributed 14 golf tees among three people. He gave some to Bernie and twice as many to Matt. To Jesse, he gave twice the number that he gave to Matt. How many golf tees did he give to Matt?

5. **Look back** at **4**. What if Bernie, Matt, and Jesse have 28 golf tees all together? How many would each have?

6. Roland bought 2 ping-pong paddles and 1 package of ping-pong balls for $9.00. Sara bought 1 paddle and 2 packages of ping-pong balls for $6.00. What is the cost of 1 paddle and 1 package of ping-pong balls?

Mixed Strategy Review

7. Wyatt wants to save $25 for summer camp. He saves $1 the first week and 3 times as much the next week. After that, he saves $2 a week. How many weeks must he save to be sure he has saved $25?

8. A camp counselor has Andrew, Bob, Carmelinda and Denise in her group. The counselor makes two-person teams for canoe races. Andrew and Bob race against Carmelinda and Denise. List the other possible races.

9. Bill's mother buys 12 gallons of gas at $1.10 per gallon. How much does she spend?

10. Bill's father wants to buy 15 gallons of gas at $1.10 per gallon. Is $15 enough to pay for the gas? Explain.

Create **Your Own**

11. Three people caught some fish. Write a guess and test problem about this situation.

The numbers in a chart are 71, 56, 62, 77, and 38. What scale would you use to graph the data? Explain your choice.

Displaying Data in Different Ways

By changing the scale on a graph, a different impression can be given. Look closely at each pair of graphs.

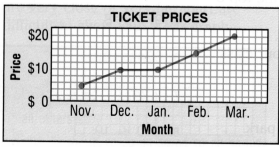

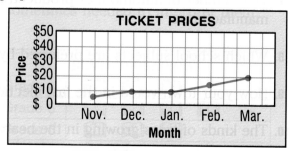

- Are the ticket prices on both graphs the same?
- How are the scales on the graphs different?
- Write a possible headline for each graph.

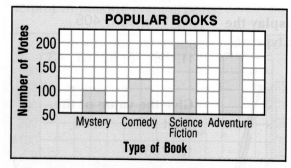

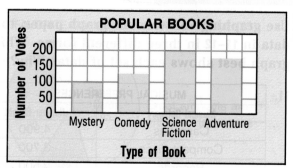

- Do both graphs display the same number of votes?
- Why should the length of the bar for science fiction books be twice as long as the bar for mystery books?
- How are the scales on the graph different?

Discuss.

1. How important is it for a scale to start at 0? Give an example to support your position.

2. Explain how a graph may be misleading if it is not read carefully.

Share Your Ideas   Is each graph accurate? Which presents a clearer representation of the data? Explain.

Write a comparison of each pair of graphs.

3.
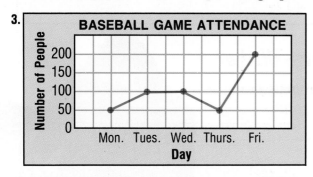
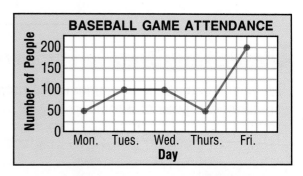

4.
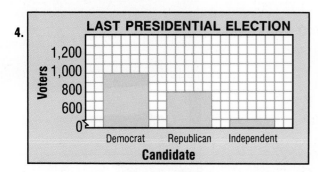
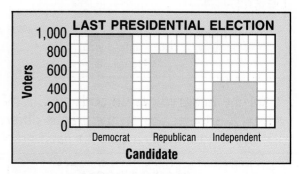

5. Use the data in the table to make a bar graph. Explain the steps you used.

LEADING MANUFACTURED PRODUCTS IN THE UNITED STATES	
Product	Value (in millions)
Transportation equipment	$114
Nonelectrical machinery	$112
Electrical machinery	$110
Food products	$98
Chemicals	$95

Problem Solving

6. Can pictographs and circle graphs be as misleading as bar and line graphs? Explain.

7. A popular news magazine contains 12 bar graphs and line graphs. There are 6 more line graphs than bar graphs. How many line graphs are there?

Write a paragraph to explain how a graph can show data in a misleading way.

SUMMING UP

For what kinds of things would you want to know an average? Explain how you could find it.

Describing Data

Mrs. Scott recorded and summarized the results of the spelling test given to her class.

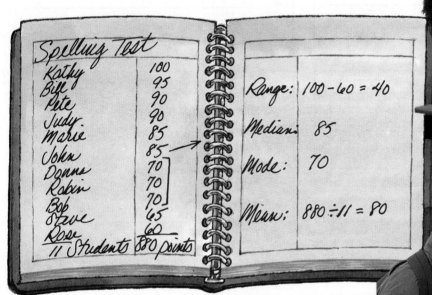

Spelling Test

Kathy	100
Bill	95
Pete	90
Judy	90
Marie	85
John	85
Donna	70
Robin	70
Bob	70
Steve	65
Rose	60
11 Students	880 points

Range: 100 - 60 = 40

Median: 85

Mode: 70

Mean: 880 ÷ 11 = 80

▶ The **range** is the difference between the greatest and least numbers.

▶ The **median** is the middle number or average of the two middle numbers when the data are arranged in order.

▶ The **mode** is the number that occurs most often.

▶ The **mean** is the average of the numbers.

Check Your Understanding

Find the range, median, mode, and mean for the following.

1. 8, 5, 11, 5, 6   **2.** 28, 33, 19, 28   **3.** 16, 8, 11, 8, 17

Share Your Ideas   Which of the four ways to summarize data do you think would be used most often? Why?

Find the range, mode, median, and mean for each table below.

4.

RAINFALL	
Month	Inches
January	2
February	0
March	2
April	5
May	3
June	0

5.

KENNEDY SCHOOL	
Grade	Students
1	41
2	46
3	51
4	46
5	56

6.

RUNS SCORED	
Inning	Runs
1	0
2	4
3	6
4	3
5	6
6	8
7	1

Find the missing number.

7. The median of 3 numbers is 40. Two numbers are 10 and 75. What is the third number?

8. The mean of 4 numbers is 23. Three numbers are 36, 21, and 17. What is the fourth number?

9. The mode of 5 numbers is 3. Four of the numbers are 3, 7, 9, and 5. What is the fifth number?

10. The range of 4 numbers is 10. Three of the numbers are 6, 12, and 2. What could the fourth number be?

Problem Solving

Range, *mode*, and *mean* can also be found by looking at a bar graph.

11. Find the **range** by subtracting the value of the lowest bar from the value of the highest bar.

12. Find the **mean** by leveling out the bars. Rearrange the boxes on the bars so all six heights are the same. You may wish to use counters.

13. How can you find the **mode** by looking at the graph?

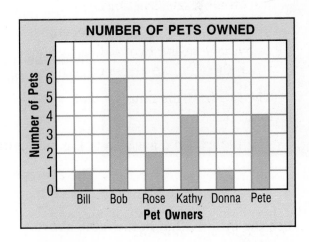

What if your math scores were 60, 80, 80, 90, and 100? Would you prefer the range, median, mode, or mean to be your final grade? Explain.

SUMMING UP

Using Problem Solving

Interview: Calculators in the Cafeteria

Santa Yawger is Food Service Manager for the cafeteria in a large building.

"We use calculators every day to find our total number of customers and sales dollars. Then we average the weekly totals and get the data needed for ordering more food supplies."

CAFETERIA REPORT			WEEK OF DECEMBER 14
Day	Customers	Daily Sales	Monthly Sales to Date
Monday	153	$ 476 08	$4,751 93
Tuesday	156	499 20	5,251 13
Wednesday	168	495 63	
Thursday	152	456 17	
Friday	171	501 92	
Weekly totals	800		Signed _____
Daily average	160		Date _____

The facts in the table can be used to calculate the average daily number of customers for the week of December 14.

Divide the total number of customers by the number of days in the week.

$$153 + 156 + 168 + 152 + 171 = \boxed{800}$$

$$800 \div 5 = \boxed{160}$$

The average daily number of customers is 160.

Sharing Your Ideas

Use the information in the table above.

1. What is the weekly sales total?

2. What is the daily sales average?

3. How would you find the monthly sales to date for Wednesday?

4. Complete the table to find the monthly sales to date as of Friday.

Practice

Use the information in the graph to solve. Use mental math, paper and pencil, or a calculator.

CHOICES

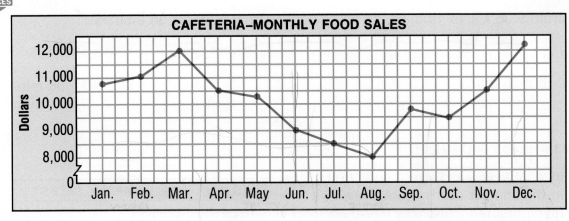

CAFETERIA–MONTHLY FOOD SALES

5. In what season of the year were sales generally high?

6. What three months had the lowest sales?

7. About what is the difference between the highest and the lowest sales months?

8. About how much is the total sales for the year?

9. About what is the average number of sales dollars per month?

10. How might the drop in sales during the summer be explained?

Summing Up

DATA Use the information in the chart to solve.

11. What is the daily average number of customers?

12. What is the daily sales total for Friday?

CAFETERIA REPORT			
Day	Customers	Daily Sales	Monthly Sales to Date
Monday	217	$503.44	$5,650.95
Tuesday	246	570.75	6,221.70
Wednesday	205	475.60	6,697.30
Thursday	241	558.50	7,255.80
Friday	196		
Weekly totals		2,575.65	Signed
Daily average			_____

MILK

171

Chapter Review

Complete. pages 146–147

1. 6 h = _____ min

2. 48 mo = _____ years

3. 7 d = _____ h

Estimate. Then find the elapsed time. pages 148–149, 150–151

4. from 9:35 A.M. to 1:55 P.M.

5. from 5:26 P.M. to 9:56 P.M.

Add or subtract. pages 148–149

6. 6 h 25 min
   + 7 h 50 min

7. 4 h 25 min
   + 6 h 35 min

8. 2 h 52 min
   − 1 h 53 min

9. 10 h 36 min
   − 5 h 11 min

Use the graph at the right. pages 152–155

10. In what year was there a reduction in the number of toys sold? How much of a reduction was there?

11. How many more toys were sold in 1979 than in 1983?

12. In what year was the greatest gain in toy sales?

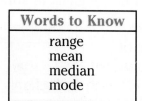

TOYS - FOR - ALL COMPANY SALES

Choose the correct word to complete each sentence.

13. The _____ is the middle number when the data is arranged in order.

14. The _____ is the difference between the highest and lowest numbers.

15. The _____ is the number that occurs most often.

16. The _____ is the average of the numbers.

Words to Know
range
mean
median
mode

Solve. pages 146–148

17. Jessica has 8 h to complete her project. Drawing each picture takes her 45 min and she needs $\frac{1}{2}$ h to put the pages together. How many drawings does she have time to do?

18. Ruth and Maureen divided their pet sitting job. Ruth sat from 5:30 P.M. to 8:15 P.M. and Maureen from 8:15 P.M. to 10:45 P.M. Who sat longer?

Chapter Test

Complete.

1. 49 d = _____ wk
2. 180 s = _____ min
3. 1 h 36 min = _____ min

4. 48 mo = _____ yr
5. 156 wk = _____ yr
6. 240 min = _____ h

Estimate. Then add or subtract.

7.   8 h 15 min
   +3 h 50 min

8.   4 h 10 min
  −   55 min

9.   13 h 46 min
   −10 h 27 min

10.   5 h 25 min
    +9 h 24 min

11.   9 h 59 min
    +1 h 2 min

12.   23 h 5 min
   −17 h 59 min

Answer the questions below each graph.

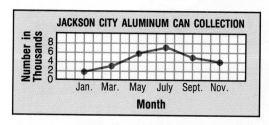

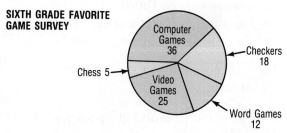

13. How many more aluminum cans were collected in July than January?

14. Which two months had the highest number of aluminum cans collected?

15. What was the favorite game of the children surveyed?

16. How many more children liked checkers than chess?

Find the range, mode, mean, and median for each.

17. 8, 10, 8, 2, 12

18. 7, 4, 10, 4, 5

Solve.

19. Dan drove to school at 6:40 A.M. He arrived at 7:22 A.M. Dan left school at 3:16 P.M. and arrived home at 4:55 P.M. How long did he drive that day?

20. Sandy and Joe collected bottle caps. Together they had 18 bottle caps. Joe had 4 more bottle caps than Sandy. How many caps did Joe have?

THINK   The Hiking Club started walking at 9:25 A.M. and stopped for lunch at 11:40 A.M. They resumed the walk at 12:30 P.M. and took a ten-minute break at 2:05 P.M. They finished their walk at 3:40 P.M. How much time did they spend walking that day?

Time Zones

There are six time zones in the United States. Find your time zone on the map. Decide what time it is now in each of the other time zones.

UNITED STATES TIME ZONES

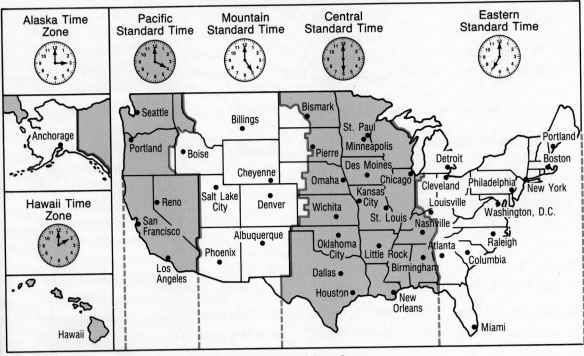

Knowing about time zones can help you decide when to place a telephone call.

1. Suppose you lived in New York and you wanted to call a friend in Hawaii. Would you place the call at 8:00 A.M. Eastern Time? Why?

Knowing about time zones is also important when you travel.

2. If you were placing a call from Anchorage, Alaska at 10:00 A.M., what time would it be in Houston, Texas?

3. When Chicago passengers depart on each of these flights, what time is it in the cities where they are going?

CHICAGO O'HARE AIRPORT	
Destination	**Departure**
Phoenix	11:25 A.M.
Boston	11:50 A.M.
Seattle	12:15 P.M.
Anchorage	12:40 P.M.
Houston	12:45 P.M.

Maintaining Skills

Choose the correct answers. Write A, B, C, or D.

1. 292 ÷ 5

   A 58 R2   **C** 54 R2

   B 56 R2   **D** not given

2. 7)215

   A 3 R5   **C** 30 R5

   B 35   **D** not given

3. Find the average. 622, 331, and 400

   A 45   **C** 451

   B 1,353   **D** not given

4. 360 ÷ 60

   A 60   **C** 16

   B 6   **D** not given

5. 20)848

   A 4 R8   **C** 428

   B 42 R8   **D** not given

6. 5,293 ÷ 56

   A 94 R9   **C** 94 R29

   B 95 R3   **D** not given

7. Find the GCF of 28 and 45.

   A 8   **C** 4

   B 7   **D** not given

Use the graph for 8 and 9.

VISITORS TO SPACE EXPO	
October	🚀 🚀 🚀
November	🚀 🚀
December	🚀 🚀 🚀 🚀

Each 🚀 stands for 150 people.

8. What month had the most visitors?

   A October   **C** December

   B November   **D** not given

9. How many visitors were there in October?

   A 450   **C** 300

   B 400   **D** not given

Use these facts to solve 10 and 11.

14 pennies were placed in a row. Every second penny was changed to a dime. After this change was made, every third coin was changed to a quarter.

10. How many pennies remained unchanged?

   A 4   **C** 3

   B 6   **D** not given

11. How much were the 14 coins worth after the experiment?

   A $1.07   **C** $1.55

   B $1.00   **D** not given

Sharing What You Know

These are signs of our times. Can you identify them? Why do people use signs without words? What things make signs eye-catching? Why are there so many different shapes for signs? What other things have special shapes?

Using Language

A famous United States government building is known by its shape. It is called the **Pentagon**. A **pentagon** is a polygon with five sides. What do you think the Greek word *penta* means?

Words to Know: perpendicular, parallel, closed, polygon, angle, point, ray, vertex, pentagon, triangle, congruent

Be a Problem Solver

How would you arrange the one–way signs for these streets? Explain.

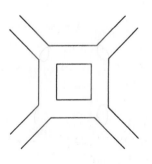

Design a sign of your own. What shape would you use? Explain your choice.

Is a flagpole an example of a line segment?
Name a line segment that cannot be seen.

Geometric Ideas

How does a weather vane suggest such geometric
ideas as point, line, line segment, and ray?

Example	Description	Symbol	Read
Point ● *K*	an exact location in space, named by any capital letter	*K*	point *K*
Line ←●――●→ A D	an endless collection of points along a straight path, named by any two of its points	$\overleftrightarrow{AD}$	line *AD*
Line segment ●――――――● B C	a part of a line, named by its two endpoints	$\overline{BC}$	segment *BC*
Ray ●――●――――→ E F	a part of a line having one endpoint and extending endlessly in one direction, named by the endpoint and any other of its points	$\overrightarrow{EF}$	ray *EF*
Plane ●L ●K ●M	an endless flat surface, named by any three of its points not on the same line	plane *KLM*	plane *KLM*

Check Your Understanding

Copy and use this drawing.

1. How many points are named?

2. Give two different names for the ray that extends
   upward from *Z*.

3. Name the line in as many ways as possible.

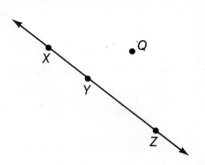

Share Your Ideas   Discuss different ways to name the
plane that was used to make this drawing.

Practice

Draw and label your own example for each.

4. point *E*   5. line *AB*

6. ray *QY*   7. line segment *CD*

8. line segment *ST*   9. plane *AFR*

10. ray *LM*   11. line *XY*

12. **Look back** at **4–11**. Write symbols to name each figure.

Trace only these parts of the drawing.

13. $\overrightarrow{BA}$ and $\overrightarrow{BC}$

14. $\overleftrightarrow{AF}$ and $\overleftrightarrow{GL}$

15. $\overleftrightarrow{DK}$ and $\overleftrightarrow{CI}$

16. $\overline{HJ}$ and $\overline{JD}$

17. $\overline{BH}$ and $\overline{EJ}$

18. $\overrightarrow{JL}$ and $\overrightarrow{JK}$

Use the drawing to complete each sentence.

19. The drawing can be made by tracing 1 line segment and _____ lines.

20. The drawing can be made by tracing 1 line segment, 2 lines, and _____ rays.

Problem Solving

Choose a correct word to complete each sentence.

21. One exact location is called a _____ .

22. A _____ is an endless flat surface.

23. The symbol $\overrightarrow{PQ}$ means _____ .

24. A _____ is part of a line.

Logical Thinking

You deliver newspapers to the houses below.

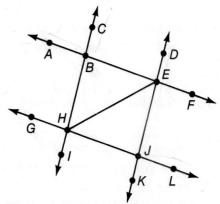

your house

25. Find a route from your house to every other house. Travel each street once. Trace the diagram and mark your route.

List a few examples of points, line segments, and parts of planes found in the classroom. Explain your choices.

SUMMING UP

179

Does a street corner form an angle? Does a door that is ajar look like it forms an angle? Where else have you seen angles?

Measuring and Estimating Angles

Architect Frank Lloyd Wright designed this house with many dramatic angles.

▶ An angle is formed by two rays with a common endpoint called the **vertex**.

write ∠*QPR*

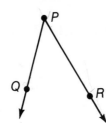

The vertex is always named in the middle. How else can you name ∠*QPR*?

▶ A **protractor** is used to measure or draw angles. The unit of measure is the **degree** (°).

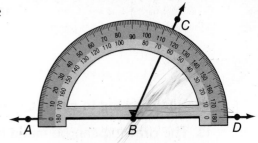

▶ To measure an angle
 • place the center of the protractor at the vertex.
 • place one ray at 0°.
 • read the scale that begins at the 0° mark.

The measure of ∠*ABC* is 115°.
The measure of ∠*CBD* is 65°.

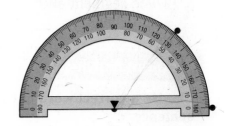

▶ To draw an angle
 • draw points at the center of the protractor, at 0°, and at the desired measure.
 • draw rays to connect the two outer points with the vertex.

Draw a 50° angle.

Check Your Understanding

Trace each angle and extend the rays with a ruler.
Estimate, then find the measure of each angle.

1.
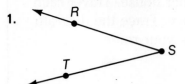

2.

Share Your Ideas Explain how to draw a 120° angle.

Practice

Trace each angle and extend the rays. Estimate, then find the measure of each angle.

3.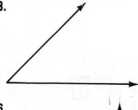

4.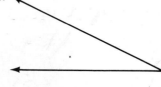

5.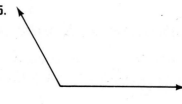

6.

7.

8.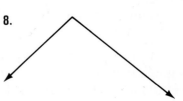

Estimate to choose the most appropriate angle measure.

9.   a. 45° b. 85° c. 105°

10.   a. 90° b. 115° c. 180°

Use a protractor to draw an angle with the measure shown.

11. 45°   12. 75°   13. 90°   14. 150°   15. 180°

CHOICES The sides of angles *BAC* and *DAC* form a straight line. Use mental math, paper and pencil, or a calculator to complete the chart.

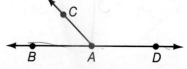

If ∠BAC measures	45°	90°	120°	65°	165°
then ∠DAC measures	**16.**	**17.**	**18.**	**19.**	**20.**

Problem Solving

DATA Trace each route and measure the angle that it forms.

21. Boston to Houston to San Francisco

22. San Francisco to Chicago to Houston

23. Chicago to Boston to Houston

24. Chicago to San Francisco to Houston

Find three angles in the classroom that appear to be less than 90°; about 90°; more then 90°. Write a description or draw a sketch of each.

SUMMING UP

Does it take longer to print your name in capital or lowercase letters? Which letters have more angles, capital or lowercase?

Identifying Angles

How many right angles can be found in this tic-tac-toe design?

▶A **right angle** measures 90°.

Use a pipecleaner, toothpicks, or a geoboard to form a 90° angle. Show the angle in any of these positions. Find them in the tic-tac-toe design.

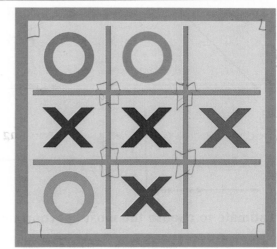

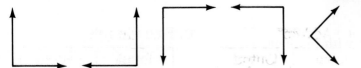

▶An **acute angle** measures less than 90°.

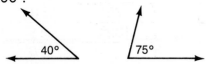

▶An **obtuse angle** measures more than 90° but less than 180°.

Draw acute and obtuse angles of your own in various positions.

▶Two angles with the same measure are said to be **congruent**.

Check Your Understanding

Use a protractor to draw an example of each. Show the measure of each angle.

1. an obtuse angle

2. an acute angle

3. a right angle

4. two congruent angles

Share Your Ideas   What is the greatest possible whole number of degrees in an acute angle? in an obtuse angle?

Practice

Estimate, then measure each angle. Write *acute*, *right*, or *obtuse* for each.

5. ∠*TEK*   6. ∠*KIT*   7. ∠*SET*

8. ∠*SIK*   9. ∠*IKE*   10. ∠*EKS*

11. ∠*KTI*   12. ∠*ITS*   13. ∠*KSE*

14. ∠*ESI*   15. ∠*ESK*   16. ∠*SEK*

Choose the correct measure for each angle.

17. ∠*PQR* is acute.   **a.** 90°   **b.** 89°   **c.** 98°

18. ∠*ABC* is congruent to a right angle.   **a.** 80°   **b.** 180°   **c.** 90°

19. ∠*XYZ* is obtuse.   **a.** 180°   **b.** 109°   **c.** 90°

Complete. Follow each rule.

Rule: Subtract 90°.

	Input	Output
20.	145°	
21.	180°	
22.	98°	
23.	156°	
24.	126.5°	

Rule: Add 45°.

	Input	Output
25.	25°	
26.	78°	
27.	45°	
28.	66°	
29.	34.5°	

30. Find the rule.

Input	Output
13°	26°
28°	56°
59°	118°
75°	150°
132°	264°

Problem Solving

Look back at 25–29.

31. Name the kind of angle shown in each output.

32. How many degrees must be added to each input to form a right angle?

33. What is the least whole number of degrees that must be added to each input to form an obtuse angle?

When Jane saw ∠*HGF* she called it a left angle. Has she misunderstood how angles are named? Explain.

Visual Thinking

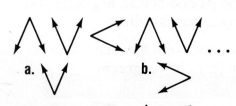

34. Which angle is next in the pattern?

35. What word describes all the angles in the pattern?

Find a pair of line segments in the classroom that appear to be always the same distance apart.

Pairs of Lines

Intersecting, perpendicular, and parallel lines are used to design gates.

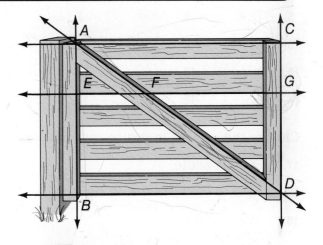

▶ **Intersecting lines** are two lines that meet at a point.

$\overleftrightarrow{AD}$ intersects $\overleftrightarrow{AC}$ at A.
What lines intersect at F?

▶ **Perpendicular lines** are two lines that intersect and form right angles.

$\overleftrightarrow{AB}$ is perpendicular to $\overleftrightarrow{EG}$.

Write $\overleftrightarrow{AB} \perp \overleftrightarrow{EG}$.

Is $\overleftrightarrow{FG} \perp \overleftrightarrow{CD}$?

▶ **Parallel lines** are two lines in the same plane that never intersect.

$\overleftrightarrow{AC}$ is parallel to $\overleftrightarrow{EF}$.

Write $\overleftrightarrow{AC} \parallel \overleftrightarrow{EF}$.

Is $\overleftrightarrow{EB} \parallel \overleftrightarrow{FD}$?

Check Your Understanding

Refer to the first gate design. Write *parallel*, *perpendicular*, or *intersecting* for each.

1. $\overleftrightarrow{AB}$ and $\overleftrightarrow{BD}$

2. $\overleftrightarrow{EF}$ and $\overleftrightarrow{CD}$

3. $\overleftrightarrow{BD}$ and $\overleftrightarrow{AC}$

4. $\overleftrightarrow{FG}$ and $\overleftrightarrow{BD}$

5. $\overleftrightarrow{CG}$ and $\overleftrightarrow{AB}$

6. $\overleftrightarrow{FG}$ and $\overleftrightarrow{AD}$

Share Your Ideas Are all intersecting lines perpendicular? Explain. Are all perpendicular lines intersecting? Explain.

Practice

Write *parallel*, *perpendicular*, or *intersecting* for each.

7. $\overleftrightarrow{AB}$ and $\overleftrightarrow{ED}$ **8.** $\overleftrightarrow{AG}$ and $\overleftrightarrow{FD}$ **9.** $\overleftrightarrow{FA}$ and $\overleftrightarrow{FE}$

10. $\overleftrightarrow{AC}$ and $\overleftrightarrow{CD}$ **11.** $\overleftrightarrow{FE}$ and $\overleftrightarrow{AF}$ **12.** $\overleftrightarrow{AF}$ and $\overleftrightarrow{BD}$

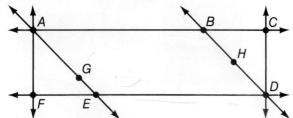

Use the figure above. Write *yes* or *no*.

13. $\overleftrightarrow{AF} \perp \overleftrightarrow{CD}$ **14.** $\overleftrightarrow{AC} \perp \overleftrightarrow{CD}$ **15.** $\overline{GE} \perp \overline{FE}$

16. $\overleftrightarrow{DB} \parallel \overleftrightarrow{AF}$ **17.** $\overleftrightarrow{BD} \perp \overleftrightarrow{AC}$ **18.** $\overline{AB} \parallel \overline{ED}$

Write *true* or *false*. Then explain.

19. Some intersecting lines are perpendicular.

20. All perpendicular lines intersect.

21. Parallel lines rarely intersect.

Problem Solving

Use the gate designs on page 184. Trace an example of each.

22. Horizontal lines that are parallel

23. Vertical lines that are parallel

24. Diagonal lines that are parallel

25. Diagonal lines that are perpendicular

Write a description for the design of each. Use the words *perpendicular*, *intersecting*, *parallel*, *diagonal*, *vertical*, and *horizontal*.

26. corduroy slacks   **27.** a plaid shirt

28. a checkerboard   **29.** a musical staff

> Describe some things that you have seen that are examples of parallel, perpendicular, or intersecting lines.

SUMMING UP

Use exactly ten line segments to draw the sides of the angles in a star.

Classifying Polygons

Geoboards can be used to help us investigate shapes. All the shapes on these geoboards are polygons.

▶ A **polygon** is a closed plane figure made up of line segments. Each line segment is a side. Each point where two sides meet is called a **vertex**.

Find the number of sides and vertices for each polygon. Are the two numbers the same?

Some polygons are named for the number of sides or angles they have.

Polygon	Sides	Angles
Triangle	3	3
Quadrilateral	4	4
Pentagon	5	5
Hexagon	6	6
Octagon	8	8

What special name would you give to each of the geoboard shapes?

Check Your Understanding

Use dot paper or a geoboard. Make your own shape for each.

1. octagon   **2.** pentagon   **3.** hexagon   **4.** quadrilateral

Share Your Ideas   One way of writing this letter forms a polygon. The other way does not. Explain.

Use dot paper or a geoboard to make each shape. If it
is a polygon, write its name. If not, explain why.

5. 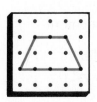   6.   7. 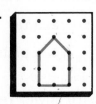   8.

9.   10.   11.   12.

Explain why these figures are not polygons.

13.   14.   15.   16.

Choose the correct answer to complete each sentence.

17. A hexagon has _____ sides.

    a. 4   b. 5   c. 6   d. 8

18. An octagon has _____ vertices.

    a. 6   b. 8   c. 4   d. 5

19. A pentagon has _____ angles.

    a. 3   b. 4   c. 5   d. 6

20. A quadrilateral has _____ angles.

    a. 3   b. 4   c. 6   d. 8

Problem Solving

The shapes of these road signs are
based on polygons. Name each shape.

21. stop

22. caution

23. yield

24. school crossing

The stencil letter ⊤ is an octagon. Draw a
different stencil letter that is also an octagon.

SUMMING UP

idchapter Review

Draw, label, and write symbols for each. pages 178–181

1. a point   **2.** a ray   **3.** a line segment

4. a line   **5.** a plane   **6.** a 55° angle

Estimate, then measure each angle. Tell whether the angle is acute, right, or obtuse. pages 182–183

7.    **8.**    **9.**

Draw an example for each. pages 184–187

10. horizontal lines that are parallel   **11.** two lines that are perpendicular

12. intersecting lines   **13.** $\overleftrightarrow{AB} \parallel \overrightarrow{CD}$

14. $\overleftrightarrow{EF} \perp \overleftrightarrow{GH}$ **15.** a pentagon

16. a quadrilateral   **17.** an octagon

18. a hexagon   **19.** a polygon with 7 sides

Choose the correct word to complete each sentence.

20. The symbol for an _____ is ∠ .

21. The symbol ⊥ means _____ .

22. The symbol ∥ means _____ .

23. A polygon is a _____ figure.

24. A triangle is a type of _____ .

Words to Know
perpendicular
parallel
closed
polygon
angle

Solve.

25. Draw a right angle in four different positions.

26. Give the least and the greatest possible whole number of degrees in an obtuse angle.

Exploring Problem Solving

One-Way Streets

The main streets in Hometown are crowded with traffic. The City Council wants to make all the streets within the town boundaries one-way streets. A person must be able to drive from any corner to any other corner (A, B, C, or D).

US Route 9
(2-way)

State Highway 4
(2-way)

State Highway 4
(2-way)

Hometown
Town Boundary

US Route 9
(2-way)

FROM POINT:			
A to	B to	C to	D to
B ___	A ___	A ___	A ___
C ___	C ___	B ___	B ___
D ___	D ___	D ___	C ___

Thinking Critically

Find the best way to change the streets within the town boundaries to one-way streets. Consider each line segment on the map to be one block in length.

Analyzing and Making Decisions

1. Draw some different one-way patterns. Can you drive away from every corner?

2. Compare your patterns. How many blocks must a person travel to get from point A to point B? to point C? to point D? Make a chart like the one above for each of your patterns to show the distance from each point to every other point.

3. Which pattern do you think is the best choice? Why?

Look Back Make up a problem of your own like this one.

189

Problem Solving Strategies

Finding Patterns

Tom was having a difficult time learning the notes on the piano.

"I just don't get it, Miss Strauss," he said flatly.

"I have noted as much," his teacher replied sharply. "A pattern connects the names of the white keys and the black keys. Here, I have made a drawing. The little symbol that looks like a letter *b* stands for a flat, and the little tic-tac-toe symbol stands for a sharp. What are the names of the numbered keys?

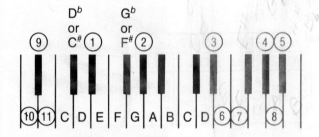

Symbols
b = flat
= sharp
D^b is read D flat

Finding patterns is a strategy that can be used to solve many problems.

Solving the Problem

Think What directions are given in the problem?

Explore What symbol stands for a sharp? What symbol stands for a flat? What is the pattern of the names of the white keys? What is the pattern of the names of the black keys? How does the pattern of the black keys relate to the white keys?

Solve What are the names of the numbered keys 1–8?

Look Back Did you answer and follow the directions? Explain.

Share Your Ideas

1. Use the same pattern to find the names of the keys numbered 9, 10 and 11 on the piano.

Practice

Solve. Use a calculator where appropriate.

CHOICES

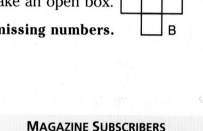

2. You are designing a box. Which of the patterns shown at the right will make an open box?

3. Draw another pattern that will make an open box.

Find the patterns in 4–5. Name the missing numbers.

4. 1, 3, 7, 15, 31, _____ , _____

5. 8, 15, 21, 26, _____ , _____

Mixed Strategy Review

6. The bar graph shows the number of magazine subscribers rounded to the nearest hundred. What was the increase in the number of subscribers from 1983 to 1988?

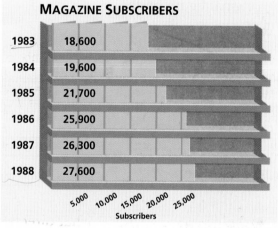

MAGAZINE SUBSCRIBERS

Year	Subscribers
1983	18,600
1984	19,600
1985	21,700
1986	25,900
1987	26,300
1988	27,600

5,000 10,000 15,000 20,000 25,000
Subscribers

DATA
7. Use the bar graph. Between which two consecutive years, was there the greatest increase in the number of subscribers?

8. An art pencil costs $.50 more than an eraser. Together they cost $1.30. How much does the eraser cost?

9. A pen costs $1.50 more than a sheet of posterboard. Two pens and two sheets of posterboard cost $5. How much does a sheet of posterboard cost?

Create
Your Own

Use the information in the graph to write a new problem.

All squares have the same shape. Do all triangles have the same shape? Explain.

Identifying Similar Figures

The rectangles in the first group are similar in shape. Those in the next group are not.

Similar figures have the same shape. They may or may not have the same size.

To create a similar figure,

- multiply or divide the length of each side of the original figure by the same number.

- keep the same angle measures.

Look for patterns. Use the rule for drawing similar figures to explain why rectangles *B*, *C*, and *D* are similar to *A*.

Explain why rectangles *E* and *F* are not similar to each other.

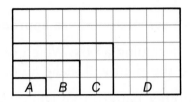

Rectangle	Width in Inches	Length in Inches
A	1	2
B	2	4
C	3	6
D	5	10
E	1	4
F	3	5
G	4	8

Measure the sides of each triangle. Explain why triangle *MNO* is similar to triangle *STU* but is not similar to triangle *PQR*.

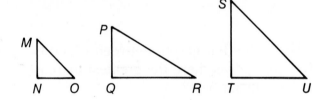

Use dot paper (Workmat 2) to draw a similar figure for each. Double the length of each side.

1.

2.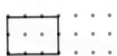

3.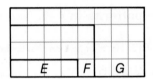

Share Your Ideas Explain why figures **a** and **b** are not similar. Explain why figures **a** and **c** are similar.

a. □   b. ▭   c. □

Practice

Use dot paper to draw a similar figure for each. Double the length of each side.

4.

5.

6.

7.

Choose the two figures that are similar.

8. a.   b. 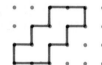   c.

9. a.   b.   c.

10. a.   b.   c.

11. a.   b.   c.

Problem Solving

Use a larger dot pattern to draw similar figures.

12.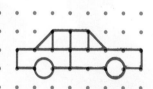

13.

Explain why the large hexagon and the small hexagon are similar figures.

Mixed Review

1. 452 + 36,999

2. 50,000 − 12,435

3. 9 × 12

4. 90 × 120

5. 3,700 ÷ 5

6. 900 ÷ 30

7. 5 × 500

8. 3,000 − 10

9. $26\overline{)494}$

10. $18\overline{)9,842}$

11. $33\overline{)12,880}$

Complete.

12. 3 h = _____ min

13. 72 mo = _____ yr

14. 5 yr = _____ mo

15. 3 yr = _____ d

16. $1\frac{1}{2}$ yr = _____ wk

Write in words.

17. 4,098

18. 100,100

19. 1,000,000

20. 1,000,000,000

21. 1,500,000

22. 1,000,500

23. 1,234,567,809

SUMMING UP

193

Exploring Congruent Figures

Congruent figures are identical in size and shape.

Can you draw congruent figures in different positions?

Working together

Materials: dot or grid paper, or Workmats 2 or 3

Draw a figure that is congruent to each of the drawings shown. Place the longest side of each congruent figure on a horizontal line at the bottom.

Try to picture each congruent figure in your mind. Make your drawing without tracing it and without rotating the book or dot paper.

A.

B.

C.

Sharing Your Results

1. Which congruent figure was easiest to draw? Explain.

2. Which figure was easier to draw in the new position, *B* or *C*? Why?

3. Compare your results with those of others. Do any drawings differ? Could you follow the directions and still have more than one way to show each congruent figure? Explain.

Practice

Designs are often made by repeating congruent figures.
Name the congruent figures that are shaded in each design.

4.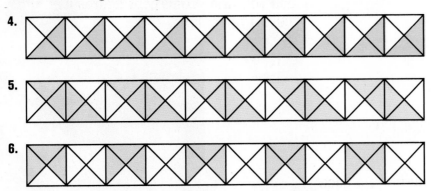

5.

6.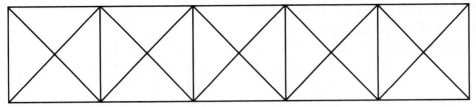

7. *Create your own* designs. Trace this pattern on a
separate sheet of paper. Repeat the pattern to extend
the full length of the paper. Make a design by
coloring repeated, congruent figures on the pattern.

8. Repeat the activity on two more pieces of paper with
a new design on each. Cut out the three designs and
use them for bookmarks.

9. Make a new pattern and create your own design.
Try different geometric shapes.

Summing Up

10. Discuss how you could sort and classify the
designs made by the class.

11. Discuss where designs such as these are used in
everyday life.

12. Write a paragraph describing five pairs of congruent
shapes that you see regularly in your daily life.

Exploring Symmetry

What if you were a fashion designer or a jewelry designer? Why would you use symmetry?

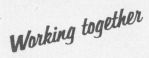

Materials: dot or grid paper, or Workmats 2 or 3, a ruler

A. Copy the drawing of the suit lapel and earring onto dot paper. Include the straight lines exactly as shown.

B. Draw another lapel and earring on the right to match the ones on the left.

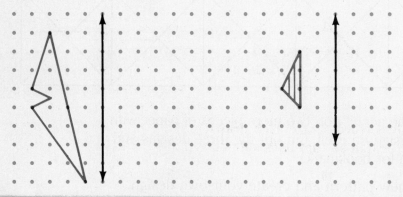

Sharing Your Results

1. How did you decide where to place the line segments to make the shapes match?

2. Can you use folding to prove that the two designs match? Try it.

3. Can you check the accuracy of the match by tracing? Try it.

4. Are the matching designs congruent to the original designs? Explain.

Practice

A figure is **symmetric** if it can be folded so that both
sides match. The fold line is called the **line of symmetry**.

Trace each figure. Then fold it to find a line of symmetry.

5.
6.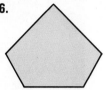
7.
8.

Some figures have more than one line of symmetry.
Trace each figure and draw its lines of symmetry.

9.
10.
11.
12.

Use folding or tracing to decide which lines are lines
of symmetry.

13.
14.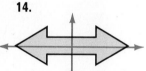
15.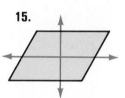
16.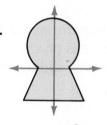

Find the mystery word. Trace each drawing and
complete the design so that both sides match.

17.
18.
19.
20.

Summing Up

21. List the digits 0–9 that can be
divided by a line of symmetry.

22. List the capital letters that can have
a line of symmetry.

23. Which capital letters can have more
than one line of symmetry?

24. Describe five items in the classroom
with one, two, or more than two
lines of symmetry.

A baseball player slides. A dancer turns. A gymnast flips. Describe things that slide, turn, or flip.

Transformations

If a typesetter accidentally turns a *p*, it can look like a *d*. A *q* can look like a *b*. Change the position of other letters in the alphabet. How are they the same? How are they different?

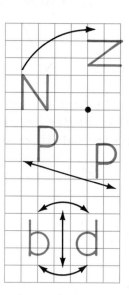

▶ A **turn image** is made by moving a figure around a point.

▶ A **slide image** is made by moving a figure along a line.

▶ A **flip image** is made by using a line of symmetry.

▶ A **transformation** of a figure is produced by turning, sliding, or flipping the figure.

Check Your Understanding

Tell whether each transformation is the result of a flip, a slide, or a turn.

1.
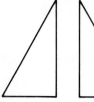

2.

3.

Share Your Ideas Look at **1–3**. Does a transformation change a figure's shape? Explain.

Trace the figure and draw a point alongside it. Then, trace four turn images by holding your pencil on the point and turning the tracing paper.

4.   5.   6.   7.

Trace the figure and the line. With the paper on this page, slide the traced line along the original line. Retrace the figure to make a slide image.

8. 9. 10. 11.

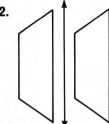

Trace the first figure and the line segment. Flip the tracing so that the line segments are congruent. Decide if the second figure is a flip image.

12. 13.

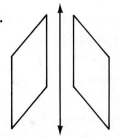

14. 15.

What if a typesetter accidentally turned each of these letters? What letter might you see instead?

16. n   17. M   18. b

Explain why you always get a congruent figure if you turn, slide, or flip a figure.

SUMMING UP

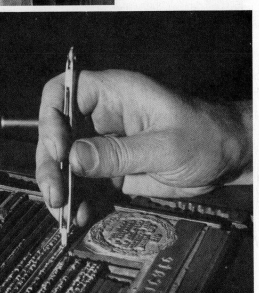

Find examples of triangles in your classroom. Decide whether there are three, two, or no congruent sides in each.

Classifying Triangles

Triangles often appear in patchwork quilt designs. Use these designs to find examples of some of the triangles named below.

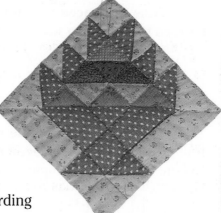

Triangles are named according to their sides and angles.

Triangle	Special Property
equilateral	all sides congruent
isosceles	exactly two congruent sides
scalene	no congruent sides
right	exactly one right angle

Some triangles have more than one name.

This is an **isosceles right** triangle.

How would you draw a **scalene right** triangle?

List all the names that apply to each triangle.

1.

2.

3.

Share Your Ideas   Is this triangle isosceles or equilateral? Explain.

List all the names that apply to each triangle.

4.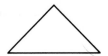

5.

6.

7.

8.

9.

Write *always*, *sometimes*, or *never* for each.

10. An isosceles triangle is a right triangle.

11. A right triangle is a scalene triangle.

12. An isosceles triangle is an equilateral triangle.

13. A right triangle has more than one right angle.

Make paper strips in the lengths below. Use the strips to decide if a scalene triangle can be formed.

14. 3 cm, 4 cm, 5 cm

15. 2 cm, 6 cm, 9 cm

16. 5 cm, 6 cm, 8 cm

17. 2.5 cm, 4 cm, 7 cm

Problem Solving

Make the following drawings. Use a protractor when needed.

18. Divide a square into 2 right triangles.

19. Divide a square into 4 right triangles and 1 smaller square.

20. Draw a triangle with exactly 2 congruent angles. What type of triangle is it?

Visual Thinking

21. How many squares and how many triangles are in this drawing?

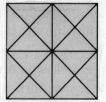

Use any square piece of paper. Fold one side along another side to form two triangles. Name the triangles.

SUMMING UP

Using Problem Solving

Angles in a Triangle

What is the missing angle measure in this triangle?

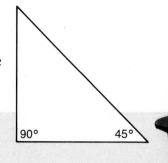

90°   45°

Working together

Materials: grid paper or Workmat 3, ruler, protractor

A. Using a ruler and grid paper, draw a right angle. Mark a point 3 inches from the vertex, along each ray. Connect the points to make a triangle similar to the one above.

B. Use a protractor to measure all three angles. Record the measures.

C. Draw three different right triangles on grid paper. Measure each angle. Record.

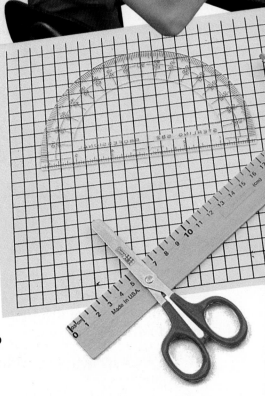

Sharing Your Ideas

1. Find the sum of the angle measures in each right triangle. What do you notice?

2. Compare your answers with those of other groups. Do the angle measures of all right triangles have the same sum?

3. How can you find a missing angle measure in a right triangle without using a protractor?

4. Each triangle below is a right triangle. Find each missing angle measure without using a protractor.

a.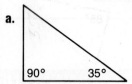
90°   35°

b. 90°
40°

c.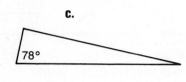
78°

d.
17°

Practice

Work in a small group. You will need paper, ruler, markers, scissors, tape, and a protractor.

5. Draw three triangles of different shapes and sizes.

6. Label angles **a**, **b**, and **c** in each triangle. Shade each a different color.

7. The measure of a **straight angle** is 180°. Cut the angles from each triangle. Tape them together along a straight line so the vertices meet. What conclusion can you draw about the sum of the angle measures?

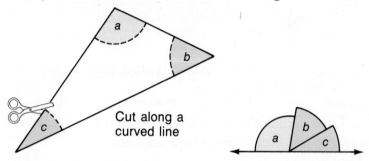

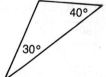
Cut along a curved line

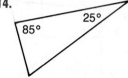

8. Draw another triangle. Use a protractor to measure each angle. Record. Find the sum of the measures of the angles. What do you notice?

Summing Up

9. Were you always able to tape the three angles along a straight line without any holes or gaps?

10. What can you conclude about the sum of the degrees in the angles of any triangle?

Find each missing angle measure. Use mental math, paper and pencil, or a calculator.

11.
60°
75°

12.
40°   40°

13.
40°
30°

14.
85°   25°

Find examples of a square and a rectangle in the classroom. How are they alike? How are they different? Can you find other four-sided polygons?

Quadrilaterals

Which polygon in the stage design is not a quadrilateral?

▶A **quadrilateral** is a polygon with four sides and four angles.

Some quadrilaterals have special names and properties.

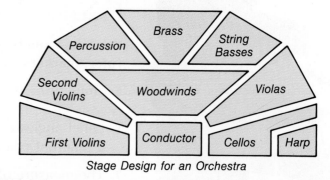
Stage Design for an Orchestra

Quadrilateral	Properties	Example
trapezoid	exactly one pair of opposite sides parallel	
parallelogram	two pairs of opposite sides parallel and congruent	
rhombus	parallelogram with all sides congruent	
rectangle	parallelogram with four right angles	
square	rectangle with all sides congruent	

Which polygons in the design are not **trapezoids**?

Explain each statement.

Figure *E* is the only trapezoid.

Figures *A*, *B*, *C*, *D* are parallelograms.

Figures *A* and *B* are the only rhombuses.

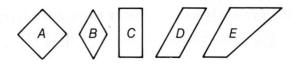

▶A **diagonal** is a segment that joins two vertices of a polygon but is not a side. $\overline{AC}$ and $\overline{BD}$ are diagonals.

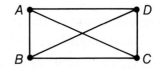

Check Your Understanding

A figure can have more than one name. List those that apply to each polygon.

1.

2.

3.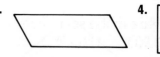

4. (figure: square)

Share Your Ideas   Explain why this shape is a quadrilateral. Explain why it does not have one of the names listed above.

List all the names that apply to each polygon.

5. 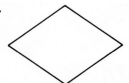 **6.**   **7.** 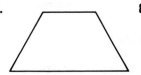 **8.**

Choose the one that does not belong.

9. quadrilaterals a.   b.   c.   d.

10. rectangles a.   b. c. d.

11. parallelograms a.   b. c.   d.

12. rhombuses a.   b. c.  d.

Make drawings to help you answer each question.

13. How many diagonals are there in a rectangle?

14. How many diagonals are there in a triangle?

15. What types of quadrilaterals always have congruent diagonals?

16. Draw an example of a trapezoid with congruent diagonals.

17. Draw the next figure in the sequence.
O   OX   OXO   OXOO   OXOOX...

Logical Thinking

18. Trace this quadrilateral. Draw line segments to separate it into exactly two triangles and a hexagon.

All squares are rectangles. Write three more statements about quadrilaterals, using "All _____ are _____ ."

SUMMING UP

Identify three things in everyday life that are in the shape of a circle.

Circles

The design for a railroad crossing sign can be made by drawing a circle and two of its diameters. How would you describe a diameter?

▶ All of the points on a **circle** are the same distance from a point called the **center**. A circle is named by its center.

▶ A **diameter** is a line segment that passes through the center of a circle and has both endpoints on the circle. $\overline{AB}$ is the diameter.

▶ A **radius** is a line segment with one endpoint on the circle and the other endpoint at the center. The length of a radius is one-half the length of a diameter. $\overline{OC}$ is a radius.

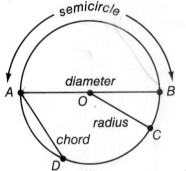

▶ A **chord** is a line segment with both endpoints on the circle. $\overline{AD}$ is a chord.

▶ A **semicircle** is half a circle. $\overset{\frown}{AB}$ is a semicircle.

▶ **Use a compass to construct a circle.**

Step 1	Put the metal tip at a point to be the center.
Step 2	Open the compass to the length of the radius.
Step 3	Rotate the pencil around the center.

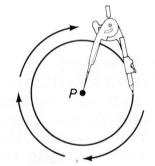

Check Your Understanding

1. Name three radii in circle O.

2. Name two chords in circle O.

3. Draw and label a circle with center P, diameter QR, radius PS, and chord ST.

Share Your Ideas   What is another name for the longest chord in a circle?

Use the figure at the right to name each.

4. the circle

5. two diameters

6. three chords

7. five radii

8. two semicircles

9. the length of the diameter in centimeters

10. the length of the radius in centimeters

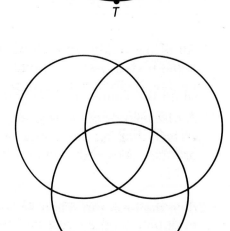

Use a compass.

11. Construct a circle congruent to circle *W*.

12. Construct a circle with a 3-centimeter radius.

13. Construct this 3-ring design. Draw circles with 2-centimeter radii.

Use mental math to complete. The input is a radius of a circle. The output is the diameter. Find the rule. Then find each missing number.

14. Rule:

	Input	Output
15.	4	
16.	8	
17.	12	
18.	7.5	

19. Rule:

	Input	Output
20.		10
21.		18
22.		14
23.		23

Problem Solving

24. **DATA** Artists sometimes use circles to design trademarks or logos. Find examples of logos that use circles. You may want to look in newspapers or the yellow pages of a telephone directory.

25. Use a compass. Design a logo for your fifth grade class.

 If each side of the square is 10 cm, what is the length of a radius of circle *W*?

SUMMING UP

Chapter Review

Name each figure using words. Then make a drawing for each. pages 178–185

1. $\overline{XY}$

2. $\overrightarrow{AB}$

3. $\overleftrightarrow{CD}$

4. $\angle PQR$

5. $\overleftrightarrow{EF} \perp \overleftrightarrow{GH}$

6. $\overleftrightarrow{IJ} \parallel \overleftrightarrow{KL}$

Estimate, then measure each angle. Tell whether each is right, acute, or obtuse. pages 180–183

7.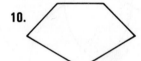

8.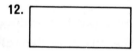

9.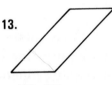

List all the names that apply to each polygon.
pages 186–187, 204–205

10.   **11.**   **12.**   **13.**

Trace the hexagon. Then draw the following figures. pages 192–199

14. a congruent hexagon

15. a similar hexagon

16. a symmetrical figure drawn by using a horizontal line of symmetry

17. a turn image

18. a slide image

19. a flip image

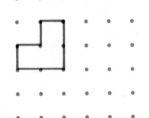

Complete. pages 206–207

20. To draw circle Q, you would use a _____ .

21. In a circle the _____ is half the length of the diameter.

Solve. pages 190–191, 202–203

22. Carl recorded these three angle measures for a triangle: 90°, 45°, and 55°. Did he measure accurately? Explain.

23. Find the pattern. Then write the next three numbers.

1, 4, 10, 22, 46, ▨, ▨, ▨, ...

Chapter Test

Name each figure, using words. Then use symbols to identify each.

1.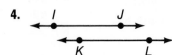

2.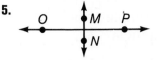

3.

4.

5.

6.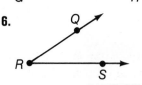

Estimate, then measure each angle. Tell whether each is right, acute, or obtuse.

7.

8.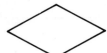

9.

List all the names that apply to each polygon.

10.

11.

12.

13.

Trace the octagon. Then draw the following figures.

14. a congruent octagon

15. a similar octagon

16. a symmetrical figure by using a vertical line of symmetry

17. a slide image

18. a flip image

19. a turn image

Complete.

20. What instrument is used to construct a circle?
21. What instrument would be used to measure ∠DBC?
22. In circle B, what is $\overline{EF}$ called?
23. If $\overline{AC}$ is 4 cm, how long is $\overline{BD}$?

Solve.

24. In a right triangle, what is the sum of the measures of the two angles that are not right angles?

25. Find the pattern. Then write the next three numbers.
1, 3, 7, 15, 31, □, □, □, . . .

THINK   What is the measure of the angle formed by the hands on a clock at 10 o'clock?

Computer Link

Rectangles, What Can You Draw?

A rectangle is a parallelogram with four right angles. What numbers can you use to complete the commands to draw a rectangle?

```
FD 35
RT 90
FD 48
RT _____
FD _____
RT 90
FD _____
RT 90
```

At the Computer

Materials: Logo

A procedure with two inputs can be used to draw rectangles of different sizes. Define the procedure RECTANGLE.

A. Draw a rectangle 50 turtle steps by 90 steps. Enter RECTANGLE 50 90. What figure would RECTANGLE 90 50 draw?

```
TO RECTANGLE :SIDE1 :SIDE2
FD :SIDE1
RT 90
FD :SIDE2
RT 90
FD :SIDE1
RT 90
FD :SIDE2
RT 90
END
```

B. Write commands to draw a figure similar to each figure below. The first one is done for you.

```
HOME
LEFT 45
RECTANGLE 50 15
```

C. Describe the figure drawn by RECTANGLE 43 43. Is it a rectangle? Explain.

Sharing Your Results

1. Explain how RECTANGLE works. What do the commands tell you about the properties of rectangles?

2. Is each figure in **B** a quadrilateral? a parallelogram? a rectangle?

Extending the Activity

3. Can the figures below be drawn by using the RECTANGLE procedure? Write *yes* or *no.*

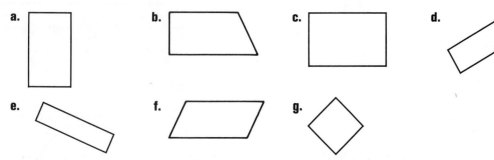

a.   b.   c.   d.

e.   f.   g.

4. Use the turtle to draw each figure that can be drawn by calling RECTANGLE. Record the command(s) you used to draw each.

5. Which figures cannot be drawn by using the RECTANGLE procedure? Give a reason for each.

6. Try this challenge! Write commands to draw the figure in **3f.**

Summing Up

7. Is every rectangle a square? Is every square a rectangle? Explain.

8. What properties can be used to explain why a figure can or cannot be drawn by using the RECTANGLE procedure?

Geometric Modeling

These pictures use geometric ideas to model real-life situations.

Parallel lines help to show events that occur at the same time, but separately. What events are occurring at the same time in this picture?

Circles can be used to show a series of events that repeat. Describe one complete cycle for this situation.

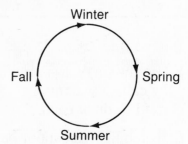

Perpendicular lines are used to mark intersections. What does the sign tell you?

Explain how the lines and circles used in the pictures below model the situations that they represent.

1.

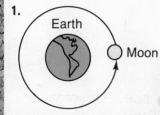

Earth

Moon

2.

3.

4. Draw other models of real-life situations that use lines or circles.

Maintaining Skills

Choose the correct answers. Write A, B, C, or D.

1. 704 ÷ 23

   A 3 R14　　　　**C** 31 R21

   B 30 R14　　　　**D** not given

2. 336 ÷ 3 + 4

   A 48　　　　**C** 28

   B 112　　　　**D** not given

3. Find the GCF of 18 and 45.

   A 9　　　　**C** 3

   B 2　　　　**D** not given

4. 48 h = ■ d

   A 3　　　　**C** 7

   B 2　　　　**D** not given

5.   2 h 31 min
   +   45 min

   A 2 h 16 min　　**C** 3 h 16 min

   B 3 h 6 min　　**D** not given

6. Find the mean for 4, 6, 7, 3, and 5.

   A 5　　　　**C** 3

   B 6　　　　**D** not given

7. Find the mode for 6, 3, 8, 6, 5, and 4.

   A 5.5　　　　**C** 6

   B 4　　　　**D** not given

8. Name $\overline{XY}$.

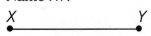

   A line　　　　**C** ray

   B line segment　　**D** not given

9. What is a 6-sided figure called?

   A octagon　　　**C** triangle

   B pentagon　　　**D** not given

10. What kind of triangle is this?

   A scalene　　　**C** isosceles

   B obtuse　　　**D** not given

Use the guess and test method to solve 11 and 12.

11. Pencils are priced 3 for $.35 and erasers cost $.10 each. If Calvin's bill was $1.45, how many pencils did he buy?

   A 12　　　　**C** 9

   B 6　　　　**D** not given

12. Simon and Carl bundle newspaper for collection. Together they made 48 bundles. Carl made twice as many as Simon. How many did Simon make?

   A 32　　　　**C** 14

   B 16　　　　**D** not given

7 Understanding Decimals · Adding and Subtracting

Sharing What You Know

When your parents were your age, car phones didn't exist. People couldn't "Fax" for a pizza. And computers were the size of school buses. Thanks to technology, many things have changed in the last twenty-five years. Everything from computers to ovens keeps getting smaller, faster, and smarter. How might computers and other products of technology use mathematics?

Using Language

A computer can display the answer to a math problem in less than 0.001 second. The digital thermometer registers 98.6 degrees Fahrenheit. The microwave timer shows your food will be ready in 52.3 seconds. What do all these numbers have in common? They are all **decimals!** A **decimal** is a number with one or more places to the right of the decimal point. Where else might you use decimals?

Words to Know: decimal, tenths, hundredths, thousandths

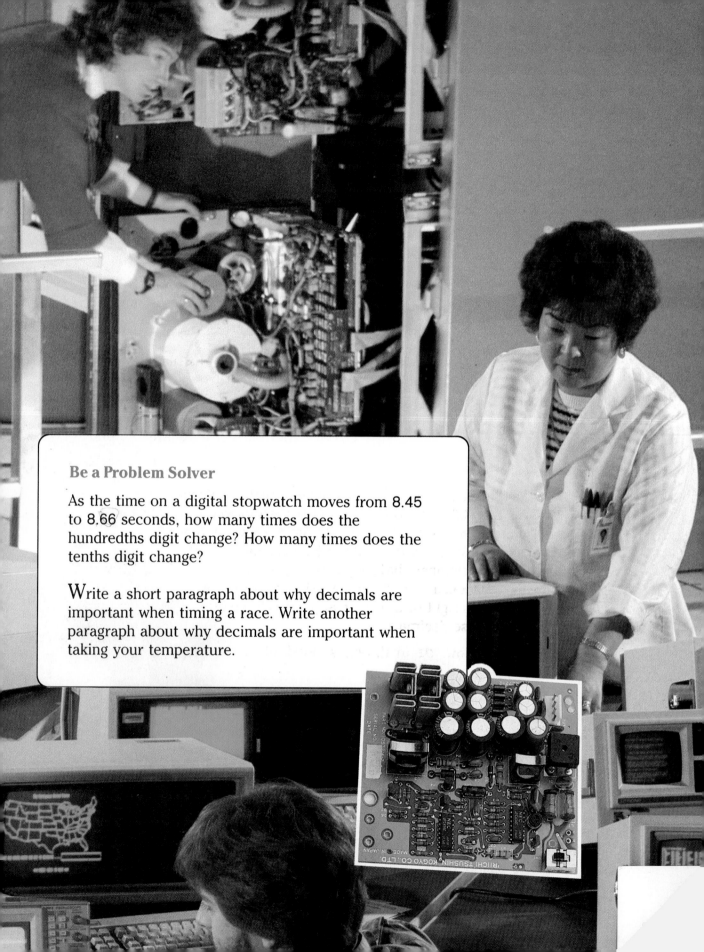

Be a Problem Solver

As the time on a digital stopwatch moves from 8.45 to 8.66 seconds, how many times does the hundredths digit change? How many times does the tenths digit change?

Write a short paragraph about why decimals are important when timing a race. Write another paragraph about why decimals are important when taking your temperature.

Exploring Decimals

If is one whole, what part is shaded red?

Working together

ones	tenths	hundredths

Materials: base-ten blocks, place-value chart or Workmat 28

A. Examine the base-ten blocks. How many tenths are in one whole? How many hundredths are in one whole?

B. Write a number in the place-value chart, using any two digits and a decimal point.

C. Have your partner model the number, using base-ten blocks.

D. Exchange roles and repeat the activity five times, writing different numbers each time.

Sharing Your Results

1. Write a decimal for the part shaded red.

2. Describe two ways to model 0.30. Do these ways also model 0.3?

3. How many different numbers can you make using only the digits 3 and 4? List them. You may include the 0 before a decimal point.

4. What is the greatest number you can write using two digits and a decimal point? What is the least number? You may include the 0 before a decimal point.

Practice

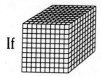 If is one whole, what part is shaded red?

Discuss why you think so.

Write a decimal for each, using **to represent a whole.**

5.   **6.**   **7.**   **8.**

Model each decimal, using **to represent a whole.**

9. 1.07   **10.** 1.026   **11.** 0.126   **12.** 1.111

Use models to complete each sentence.

13. 1 whole = n tenths

14. 1 tenth = n hundredths

15. n thousandths = 1 hundredth

16. 100 thousandths = n hundredths

Summing Up

17. What other decimals are equivalent to 0.4?

18. How are decimals like whole numbers? How are they different?

19. **Look back** at the models you used. Explain why our number system is a base-ten system.

20.  can be used to represent 1 or 0.01 or 0.001. Explain how a model can represent different amounts.

How many tenths of a dollar is $.10? $.50?
How many hundredths of a dollar is $.15? $.75?

Reading and Writing Decimals

Mr. Harvey's computer prints a decimal to show the number of acres in each property.

This drawing shows a decimal that is greater than 1.

```
JOE HARVEY REAL ESTATE    HOUSE
                          LISTINGS
STREET:    25 SEABREEZE LANE
CITY:      ATLANTIC DUNES
STATE:     FL   ZIP: 32233

PRICE: $115,000    SQUARE FEET: 2,000
TAXES: $1,200      BED:          3.0
ACRES:  1.4        BATH:         2.5
```

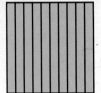

Think of each whole as divided into 10 equal parts. One whole and 4 parts are green.

decimal 1.4
● **read** 1 and 4 tenths
● **word name** one and four tenths

Read the decimal point as *and* in a number greater than 1.

This drawing shows a decimal that is less than 1.

Think of 1 whole as divided into 100 equal parts. 45 parts are green.

decimal 0.45
● **read** 45 hundredths
● **word name** forty-five hundredths

Write 0 before the decimal point in a number less than 1.

The place-value table can help you read decimals.

ones	tenths	hundredths	thousandths
0.	5	7	
1.	2	0	6

57 hundredths
1 and 206 thousandths

The value of a digit depends on its place in a number.

The value of 2 in 1.206 is 2 tenths. What is the value of 6?

Check Your Understanding

Write the decimal for each.

1. 4 and 56 thousandths

2. 5 and 7 hundredths

3. 9 tenths

Share Your Ideas   Read the decimals. Then explain how they are different.   0.2   0.02   0.002

Use a calculator. Display and write the decimal for each.

4. four tenths   **5.** fourteen hundredths   **6.** six thousandths

7. three hundredths   **8.** thirteen thousandths   **9.** one and one tenth

Write the decimal that names the shaded part of each.

10.   **11.**   **12.**

Name the decimal part shown of each thousandths block.

13. 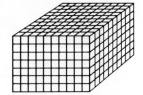   **14.** 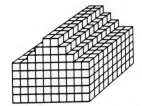   **15.**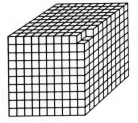

Write the word name for each decimal. Give the value of the underlined digit.

16. <u>3</u>5.6   **17.** <u>9</u>.21   **18.** 0.7<u>5</u>   **19.** 14.1<u>2</u>3   **20.** 0.88<u>4</u>

Problem Solving

Use grid paper to show the amount of property for each.

21. 0.72 acres   **22.** 0.4 acres   **23.** 1.2 acres   **24.** 4.07 acres

Estimate how much of the whole has been shaded.
Give your estimate in tenths.

25.   **26.** 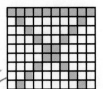   **27.**

Read each decimal. Explain why each shows the
same part of a whole.   0.2   0.20   0.200

SUMMING UP

How do you know if $37.20 is more than or less than $37.60?

Comparing and Ordering Decimals

Patricia's temperature was 37.9° Celsius in the morning and 37.2° Celsius at night. When was her temperature higher?

To compare decimals, follow these steps.

Step 1	Align the decimal points.	**37.9** **37.2**	Normal body temperature is 37°C.
Step 2	Start at the left. Compare digits in the same places.	**37.9** **37.2** same ⌐ ⌐ same	
Step 3	The first greater digit shows the greater decimal.	**37.9** **37.2**	9 > 2 so **37.9 > 37.2**

The morning temperature was higher.

▶ You can order decimals by comparing them two at a time.

List in order from least to greatest.
       0.15   0.20   0.1

0.15 < 0.20
0.10 < 0.15   This zero does not change
         the value of the decimal.

The decimals are in order from least to greatest.   0.1 < 0.15 < 0.20

▶ You can show decimals on a number line.

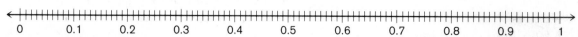

0   0.1   0.2   0.3   0.4   0.5   0.6   0.7   0.8   0.9   1

Check Your Understanding

Compare. Use >, <, or = for ⬤.

1. 0.175 ⬤ 0.17

2. 0.03 ⬤ 0.003

3. 4.516 ⬤ 4.565

Share Your Ideas   Describe how you would draw and label a number line to show these decimals in order from least to greatest.   0.2   0.05   1.2

Practice

Compare. Use >, <, or = for ●.

4. 0.7 ● 0.3

5. 0.5 ● 0.05

6. 0.46 ● 0.64

7. 0.9 ● 0.99

8. 0.15 ● 0.51

9. 0.164 ● 0.16

10. 0.4 ● 0.40

11. 1.07 ● 1.70

12. 0.8 ● 0.88

13. 4.26 ● 4.62

14. 6.02 ● 6.002

15. 0.0007 ● 0.007

List in order from least to greatest.

16. 0.3, 0.1, 0.5

17. 0.8, 0.08, 0.008

18. 3.5, 3.52, 3.057

19. 0.2, 0.25, 0.02, 1.2

20. 0.42, 0.421, 0.425, 0.418

21. 1.05, 1.5, 0.5, 0.05

22. Draw and label a number line that includes the following decimals: 0.8, 0.75, 0.7, and 0.71.

Choose the correct answer.

23. Which decimal is between 0.3 and 0.15?

a. 0.23   **b.** 0.30   **c.** 0.350

24. Which of these numbers is closest to 0.07?

a. 0   **b.** 0.5   **c.** 1

25. Which of these numbers is closest to 0.699?

a. 0   **b.** 0.5   **c.** 1

Problem Solving

Trace the number line. Then estimate where each decimal should be located.

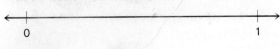

0   1

26. 0.48   **27.** 0.9   **28.** 0.09

29. 0.6   **30.** 0.75   **31.** 0.31

32. We use decimals to record amounts of money or temperature readings. Find examples of other data that are recorded with decimals. Make a collage, a drawing, or write a paragraph to describe the situations.

Common Error

4.8 < ~~4.08~~ < 4.88

WRONG ORDER

33. How can thinking about money help you to avoid this error?

34. Place the decimals in order.

Would it take longer to label a number line from 0 to 1 in tenths or in hundredths? Explain.

SUMMING UP

A whole number is between 150 and 160. It rounds to 150. What could the number be?

Rounding Decimals

The computer rounds actual amounts to the nearest dollar. Which rounded number shows a $28.54 meal?

To round $28.54 to the nearest one dollar, follow these steps.

VACATION EXPENSES		
	Meals	Parking
3-1	$19.00	$ 6.00
3-2	25.00	6.00
3-3	28.00	7.00
3-4	30.00	5.00
3-5	29.00	7.00

Step 1	Find the rounding place.	
Step 2	Look at the digit to the right. If it is less than 5, leave the digit in the rounding place unchanged. If it is 5 or more, increase the digit in the rounding place by 1.	$28.54 ↓ $28.54 5 or more add 1
Step 3	Write the rounded number. Change each digit to the right of the rounding place to zero.	$28.54 —rounds to→ $29.00

The rounded number is $29.00.

More Examples

a. Round to the nearest hundredth.
67.128 rounds to 67.13.
    8 > 5

b. Round to the nearest ten cents.
$8.63 rounds to $8.60.
    3 < 5

1. Round $58.49 to the nearest dollar.

2. Round 3.625 to the nearest tenth.

3. Round 0.348 to the nearest hundredth.

4. Round 0.75 to the nearest one.

Share Your Ideas A decimal is between 0.21 and 0.31. It rounds to 0.2. What could the decimal be?

Round to the nearest one.

5. 7.2   **6.** 16.78   **7.** 4.05

Round to the nearest tenth.

8. 0.38   **9.** 4.35   **10.** 41.052

Round to the nearest hundredth.

11. 0.425   **12.** 7.680   **13.** 26.709

Round to the nearest one dollar.

14. $19.75   **15.** $2.45   **16.** $300.50

Round to the nearest ten cents.

17. $.65   **18.** $3.99   **19.** $2.03

Write each rounded number in standard form.

20. 6.5 thousand

21. 7.8 million

22. 1.4 billion

23. 0.5 million

24. 0.2 million

25. 0.25 billion

Problem Solving

26. Why do you think the Internal Revenue Service allows you to round amounts to the nearest one dollar when you prepare your income taxes?

27. An accountant's income tax spreadsheet shows the rounded number $47.00. What are the greatest and the least amounts that can be rounded to this number?

Draw a number line to explain why 3.6 is closer to 4 than to 3.

Mixed Review

1. 39 + 49

2. 639 + 449

3. 6,390 + 4,490

4. $6.39 + $4.49

5. 87 − 49

6. 870 − 490

7. $8.70 − $4.90

8. 3 × 185

9. 30 × 185

10. 4,550 ÷ 25

11. 4,575 ÷ 25

12. 4,600 ÷ 25

Use the figure to answer each question.

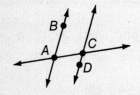

13. Name six rays.

14. Name the plane in which the drawing was made.

15. Name three line segments.

16. Name two parallel lines.

17. Name two lines that intersect.

SUMMING UP

Midchapter Review

Complete. pages 216–217

1. There are _____ tenths in 1 whole.

2. There are _____ hundredths in 1 whole.

3. There are _____ thousandths in 1 whole.

4. There are _____ hundredths in 1 tenth.

Write the decimal and the word name for each of the shaded regions. pages 218–219

5.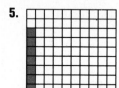

6.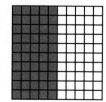

7.

Write the decimal. pages 218–219

8. fourteen thousandths

9. eight tenths

10. one and seven hundredths

Compare. Use >, <, or = for ⬤. pages 220–221

11. 0.75 ⬤ 0.57

12. 0.02 ⬤ 0.20

13. 0.76 ⬤ 0.670

14. 0.345 ⬤ 0.43

15. 0.3 ⬤ 0.30

16. 0.07 ⬤ 0.7

Choose the correct word to complete each sentence.

17. One _____ is less than one hundredth.

18. When you round 35.375 to the nearest _____ , you get 35.4.

19. When a whole is divided into 100 equal parts, each part is called one _____ .

Words to Know
tenth
thousandth
hundredth

Solve.

20. A list of county farms shows their sizes to the nearest acre. How will a farm of 239.49 acres be listed?

21. Sally charges $.52 each for roses but always rounds the total sale to the nearest ten cents. How much will she charge for 12 roses?

Exploring Problem Solving

THINK
EXPLORE
SOLVE
LOOK BACK

How Can the Food Be Divided Equally?

Jane Murphy is helping her mother bag groceries. The grocery tape shows the food she has just bought.

```
CABBAGE      3.82 lb
BANANAS      2.89 lb
APPLES       3.15 lb
QUART OF MILK

LETTUCE
JELLY        16 oz
CHICKEN      1.2 lb
POTATOES     5 lb
BREAD        22 oz
```

Thinking Critically

Use a calculator where appropriate.

CHOICES

How can they group the food they have bought so that each bag has about the same weight?

Analyzing and Making Decisions

1. Does Jane need to know the weights of items to the nearest hundredth of a pound? To what place would you round each weight?

2. What other weights does Jane need to know? How can she estimate them? Would it help if she knew that a pint of milk weighed about a pound and that the lettuce weighed about half as much as the head of cabbage? Estimate the weights that are missing.

3. List some ways of arranging the groceries in two bags. What are some things to keep in mind when packing a grocery bag?

Look Back What if Mrs. Murphy had also purchased 1.37 lb of green beans and 1.97 lb of hamburger meat? Then how might she pack the bags?

Problem Solving Strategies

Multi-Stage Problems

The Moorestown School Science Club is raising money
to buy a computer. Club members need to earn $150
more. They purchased 28 outdoor thermometers for
$6 each and sold all of them for $10 each. They sold
45 rain gauges at $3 each, which they had purchased
for $.50 each. Did they sell enough equipment to
reach their goal? Explain your answer.

Often you must answer several questions before you
can solve a problem.

Solving the Problem

Use a calculator where appropriate.

CHOICES

Think   What is the question?

Explore   How much did members pay for each item?
For how much did they sell each item? How much
money did they make on each item? How many of each
item did they sell?
How much money did they make selling the thermometers?
the rain gauges?
How much money did they make all together?

Solve   Did they reach their goal?
Explain.

Look Back   Did you answer the question?
Why didn't the club keep all of the money
it got from the sales?

Share Your Ideas

1. **What if** the Science Club also sold
   15 barometers for a profit of $2 on
   each? How would that change the
   amount of money the club earned?

Practice

Solve. Use a calculator where appropriate.

CHOICES

2. The school ordered 18 boxes of thermometers, with 4 thermometers in each box. They were to be divided among the three fifth-grade classes. How many thermometers did each class get?

3. An inch of rain is considered equivalent to 1 foot of snow. Last month there were snowstorms in which 6 inches, 12 inches, 5 inches, 7 inches, and 6 inches of snow fell. If the snow had been rain, how much rain would have fallen?

Use the graph to solve 4 and 5.

The graph at the right shows the average high and low temperatures for April in four United States cities.

4. In which of the four cities was the difference the greatest?

5. In which of the four cities was the difference the least?

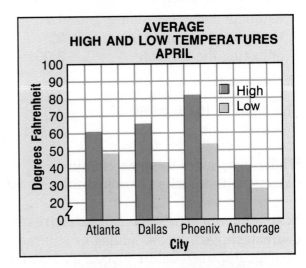

Mixed Strategy Review

6. Lenny bought 2 Ping-Pong paddles and 1 box of Ping-Pong balls for a total of $9. Sarah bought 1 paddle and 2 boxes of Ping-Pong balls for a total of $6. How much does 1 paddle cost? How much does 1 box of Ping-Pong balls cost?

7. In a contest there are 23 box, dragon, and triangular kites entered. There are 13 more triangular kites than dragon kites. There are 3 times as many box kites as dragon kites. How many kites of each kind are in the contest?

8. The air and the water temperatures were the same at 9:00 A.M. The air temperature rose 20 degrees during the day, but the water temperature rose only 6 degrees. How much higher was the highest air temperature than the highest water temperature?

Create
Your **O**wn

Write a problem about changes in air temperature.

We often estimate when an exact answer is not needed. Describe some other reasons for using estimation.

Estimating with Decimals

Tech Gear, Inc. adds a shipping charge if your order weighs more than 4 pounds. If you buy the items shown, must you pay the shipping charge?

Portable Video
1.75 pounds

Portable Phone
2.5 pounds

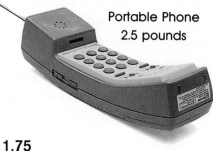

Estimate 1.75 + 2.5.

▶ Estimate a sum by adding the front digits and then adjusting the estimate.

$$1.75$$
$$+2.5$$
$$\overline{3.00} \leftarrow \text{estimate}$$

Adjust the estimate by using the digits to the right of the front digits.

$$1.75 \searrow$$
$$+2.5 \nearrow \text{greater than 1}$$
$$3 + 1 = 4 \text{ adjusted estimate}$$ The sum is more than 4.

There is an extra shipping charge.
Why was it important to adjust the estimate?

▶ An amount can also be estimated by rounding to its greatest place before adding or subtracting.

a.
$$\$28.65 \xrightarrow{\text{rounds to}} \$30.00$$
$$+\ 11.25 \xrightarrow{\hspace{1cm}} +\ 10.00$$
$$\text{estimate} \rightarrow \overline{\$40.00}$$

b.
$$\$18.35 \xrightarrow{\text{rounds to}} \$20.00$$
$$-\ \ 9.89 \xrightarrow{\hspace{1cm}} -\ 10.00$$
$$\text{estimate} \rightarrow \overline{\$10.00}$$

Check Your Understanding

Estimate. Then complete this sentence with the greatest possible whole number: "The sum is greater than _____ ."

1. $3.45
    + 9.63

2. 4.8
    +7.6

3. 24.6
    +34.1

4. $85.24
    + 5.15

5. 3.75
    +7.9

Share Your Ideas Explain why $9.50 − $3.75 is less than $6.

228

Estimate. Then complete this sentence with the greatest possible whole number: "The sum is greater than _____ ."

6. 6.2
   +3.4

7. 8.9
   +3.6

8. 9.5
   +6.7

9. $11.55
   + 12.55

10. 45.4
   + 5.7

11. 3.72
   +4.51

12. 0.6
   +0.6

13. 0.4
   +9.7

14. $2.83
   + 2.65

15. 25.75
   +10.35

16. 4.5 + 6.75 + 19 + 12

17. $34.58 + $6.20 + $50.80

Estimate each by mentally subtracting the value of the front digits. Then tell if the actual difference will be greater than or less than this estimate.

18. $20.00 − $6.45

19. 3.7 − 1.95

20. 10.5 − 3.25

21. 0.95 − 0.21

22. 12.3 − 2.8

23. $7.50 − $4.69

24. 9 − 0.7

25. 4 − 0.25

26. 9.66 − 3.5

Use the chart to estimate each answer.

27. Can you buy one B and one D with $20?

28. Can you buy one A and one D with $25?

29. Can you buy one of each kind with $45?

COMPACT DISCS		
A	Classical	$10.95
B	Popular	$ 9.29
C	Country/Western	$11.75
D	Jazz	$13.99

Problem Solving

30. **Look back** at **27–29.** Explain your thinking for each.

31. **What if** you order one item that weighs 2.5 pounds, one that weighs 0.75 pounds, and two items that weigh 0.6 pounds each? Will this order weigh

   a. more than 2 pounds?
   b. more than 3 pounds?
   c. more than 4 pounds?

Test Taker

32. You can save time when taking a test by ruling out answers that are not sensible. Use estimation to explain why the first three answers do not make sense for 34.75 + 44.75.

   a. 68.5

   b. 78.5

   c. 79.0

   d. 79.5

Explain why adjusting the sum of the front digits gives a better estimate than rounding for $22.33 + $5.35 + $4.30.

SUMMING UP

Exploring Adding and Subtracting Decimals

When is the sum of two decimals greater than 1?

Look at the shaded parts of these decimal squares. How can you tell if their sum is greater than 1?

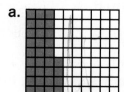

a.

b.

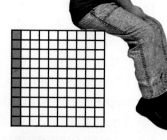

Working together

Materials: color decimal squares; use Workmat 5 to make 18 squares with different shaded areas

Play this game with your partner.

A. Shuffle the color decimal squares. Distribute the same number of cards to each player. Keep the cards face down.

B. The first player (Player 1) turns a card face up. The second player (Player 2) then turns a card face up.

C. If the sum of the cards is greater than 1, Player 1 keeps the cards. If the sum is 1 or less than 1, the cards are kept in the middle, to be won in the next round.

D. Take turns being the first to play a card. Remember, you can win cards only when you play your card first.

Sharing Your Results

1. Describe what method you used to tell if the sum was greater than 1.

2. More than 0.5 is shaded on each of two decimal squares. Can you be sure their sum is greater than one? Explain.

Practice

Let a 10-by-10 grid represent a whole.
Shade 0.24 on the grid.

3. How can you find the amount of the unshaded region?

4. What decimal describes the unshaded region?

5. What is the sum of the shaded and the unshaded regions?

6. Write two addition and two subtraction sentences that describe your grid.

Use the grids to help you find *n*.

7.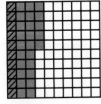

   $0.35 - 0.1 = n$

8.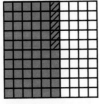

   $0.6 - 0.05 = n$

9.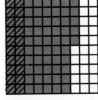

   $0.75 - 0.2 = n$

10.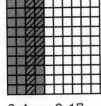

    $0.4 - 0.17 = n$

11.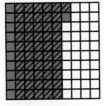

    $0.62 - 0.51 = n$

12.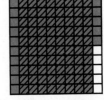

    $0.95 - 0.8 = n$

Summing Up

Model the following on grid paper.

13. $0.65 + 0.3 = 0.95$

14. $0.7 - 0.45 = 0.25$

15. $0.9 + 0.55 = 1.45$

16. $1.5 - 0.9 = 0.6$

> 0.35 is an example of a decimal in hundredths. How would you show 0.4 or 2 as decimals in hundredths?

Adding Decimals

The display screen shows that Janice rode 1.75 kilometers on the first day. She plans to increase her daily workout by 0.75 kilometers each week until she reaches 10 kilometers a day.

What if this was your plan? How would you find the cycling distance for the second week?

$1.75 + 0.75 = n$

Step 1 Line up the decimal points. Use zeros to hold places.	Step 2 Add hundredths. Regroup if necessary.	Step 3 Add tenths. Regroup if necessary.	Step 4 Add ones. Place the decimal point in the answer.
1.75 +0.75	¹ 1.75 +0.75 0	¹ ¹ 1.75 +0.75 50	¹ ¹ 1.75 +0.75 2.50

In the second week, Janice will ride 2.5 kilometers daily.

More Examples

a. $32.4 + 1.86 + 5 = n$

```
    1
  32.40
   1.86    Use zeros to
+  5.00    hold places.
  39.26
```

b. $\$4.20 + \$6 + \$.85 = n$

```
     1
  $4.20
   6.00
+   .85
$ 11.05
```

Add. Estimate to be sure the answer makes sense.

1.	2.	3.	4.	5.
0.34 +0.75	$1.98 + .89	$2.45 + 3.66	0.125 +0.79	12.75 + 0.5

Share Your Ideas Explain how you would find Janice's cycling distance for the third week.

Add. Use mental math or paper and pencil. Explain each choice.

6. 2.3
  +4.8

7. 7.9
  +0.5

8. 0.85
  +0.8

9. 6.25
  +1.95

10. $3.14
  + 9.28

11. 1.45
  +0.75

12. 3.050
  +6.85

13. $12.35
  + 24.75

14. 1.09
  +4.03

15. 14.55
  + 0.65

16. 10.6 + 10.6 = n

17. 17.3 + 16.65 = n

18. $48.09 + $2.91 = n

Follow the rule to find each missing number.
Use mental math.

Rule: Add 0.5.

	Input	Output
19.	1.5	
20.	3.2	
21.	30.5	

Rule: Add 0.75.

	Input	Output
22.	0.25	
23.	0.35	
24.	1.25	

Find the pattern. Give the next number.

25. 0.1, 0.3, 0.5, 0.7, 0.9, _____

26. 0.54, 0.60, 0.66, 0.72, 0.78, _____

27. 5.6, 5.9, 6.2, 6.5, 6.8, _____

28. 0.38, 0.45, 0.52, 0.59, 0.66, _____

Write an addition example to illustrate each statement.

29. The sum of two decimals that are each less than 0.5 can be close to 0.

30. The sum of two decimals that are each less than 1 can be close to 2.

Visual Thinking

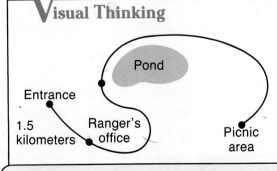

Pond

Entrance

1.5 kilometers

Ranger's office

Picnic area

Estimate the distance

31. from the ranger's office to the pond.

32. from the pond to the picnic area.

Explain how you can tell without computing that the sum of 24.715 and 3.4 is more than 28 and has a 5 in the thousandths place.

SUMMING UP

Name some pairs of decimals in hundredths that have a sum of 1.

Subtracting Decimals

A recent survey shows that 0.72 of the American population has flown in a commercial airplane. What part of the population has not flown commercially?

$1 - 0.72 = n$

Explain why the number 1 is used.

Step 1	Step 2	Step 3	Step 4
Line up the decimal points. Use zeros to hold places.	Subtract hundredths. Regroup if necessary.	Subtract tenths. Regroup if necessary.	Subtract ones. Place the decimal point in the answer.
$\begin{array}{r} 1.00 \\ -0.72 \\ \hline \end{array}$	$\begin{array}{r} \scriptstyle 9 \\ \scriptstyle 0\ 10\ 10 \\ 1.00 \\ -0.72 \\ \hline 8 \end{array}$	$\begin{array}{r} \scriptstyle 9 \\ \scriptstyle 0\ 10\ 10 \\ 1.00 \\ -0.72 \\ \hline 28 \end{array}$	$\begin{array}{r} \scriptstyle 9 \\ \scriptstyle 0\ 10\ 10 \\ 1.00 \\ -0.72 \\ \hline 0.28 \end{array}$

0.28 of the population, or 28 out of 100 people, has not flown commercially.

Another Example

Find $4.13 - 1.26 = n$

Can you tell without computing that the answer will be a little less than 3? Explain.

$$\begin{array}{r} \scriptstyle 10 \\ \scriptstyle 3\ 0\ 13 \\ 4.13 \\ -1.26 \\ \hline 2.87 \end{array}$$

Check
$$\begin{array}{r} \scriptstyle 1\ 1 \\ 2.87 \\ +1.26 \\ \hline 4.13 \end{array}$$

Check Your Understanding

Subtract. Estimate to be sure the answer makes sense.

1. $\begin{array}{r} 2.45 \\ -0.75 \\ \hline \end{array}$

2. $\begin{array}{r} 1 \\ -0.89 \\ \hline \end{array}$

3. $\begin{array}{r} 4.6 \\ -0.8 \\ \hline \end{array}$

4. $\begin{array}{r} 12.505 \\ -\ 0.125 \\ \hline \end{array}$

5. $\begin{array}{r} \$20 \\ -\ 3.45 \\ \hline \end{array}$

Share Your Ideas Why is it important to line up decimal points and use zeros as place holders when subtracting decimals?

Practice

Subtract. Then estimate to be sure the answer makes sense.

6. 0.7
    − 0.4

7. 1.3
    − 0.6

8. 2
    − 0.8

9. 1.05
    − 0.69

10. $10
    −   5.59

11. 1.625
    − 0.125

12. 3.6 − 0.7

13. 1.15 − 0.99

14. $5 − $2.39

15. $20 − $12.56

16. 10 − 1.7 − 2.5

17. 1 − 0.36 − 0.24

 Find the missing numbers. The sum of each row, column, and diagonal must be the same. Use a calculator if you wish.

18.

0.9	0.2	
	0.6	0.8
0.5	1	

19.

	0.18	0.33
0.24	0.3	
	0.42	0.21

Problem Solving

20. Amanda needs $55 for a plane ticket. She has saved $5.25, $7.50, and $4.75 from babysitting. How much more money does she need?

Rewrite these survey results. Show what part of the American population does *not* do each of these things.

21. 0.11 of the American population speaks a language other than English at home.

22. 0.23 of all Americans own a cat.

23. 0.49 of all Americans want to live to be 100.

24. 0.64 of Americans live in the state where they were born.

> Explain why knowing the number of tenths in 1 whole and the number of hundredths in 1 tenth is important when you subtract decimals.

Mixed Review

1. 648 + 212

2. 10,000 − 999

3. 1,680 ÷ 3

4. 4 × 5,050

5. 500 − 98

6. 85 ÷ 9

7. 499 + 501

8. 12 × 250

9. 12)4,836

10. 40 × 50

11. 2 × 700

12. 9)6,300

Name the parts of circle G.

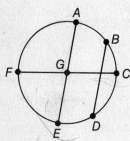

13. the center

14. three chords

15. four radii

16. two diameters

17. four semicircles

SUMMING UP

235

Using Problem Solving

Interview: Calculators at Home

Pamela Yoka teaches kindergarten in Cincinnati, Ohio. Calculators help her to keep track of her money.

Ms. Yoka said, "Using a calculator helps me save money because I make fewer mistakes. The bank charges a service fee if I write checks for more money than I have in my account."

Here is a page from Ms. Yoka's checking account.

CHECK NUMBER	DATE	DESCRIPTION	PAYMENT (−)		DEPOSIT (+)		BALANCE	
							$ 125	65
—	1/20				550	00	675	65
851	1/21	Page's Book Shop	12	51			663	14
852	1/21	De Hart Pharmacy	9	48			653	66
853	1/27	Royal Food Market	65	70			587	96
854	1/28	Cincinnati Water Works	40	12				
855	1/28	Cincinnati Bell Telephone	29	13				
856	1/28	Home Finance, Inc.	425	00				
857	1/28	Charge-a-Card	17	81				

Each time Ms. Yoka writes a check, she subtracts to find out how much money she has left in her account.

old balance − expense = new balance

$675.65 − $12.51 = $663.14

Sharing Your Ideas

Use the information in the checking account above to answer each question.

1. What is the total of all the expenses shown from January 21 through January 28?

2. How much money is left in Ms. Yoka's checking account after all the bills have been paid?

CHECK NUMBER	DATE	DESCRIPTION	PAYMENT (-)	DEPOSIT (+)	BALANCE $

Practice

THINK
EXPLORE
SOLVE
LOOK BACK

Make a copy of the checking account form or use Workmat 6. Use mental math, paper and pencil, or a calculator to solve **3–7**.

Your opening balance is $870.70. This week's bills are shown below.

3. List all your checks and show the balance after each is paid.

4. What is the total of the expenses paid by check this week?

5. What balance was left in the account after the bills were paid?

6. What if you wrote all the checks the same evening? Would you find a new balance after each check? How else could you keep track of the balance?

7. What if you had an unexpected visit to the doctor after your bills were paid? Could you write a check to pay the doctor $50?

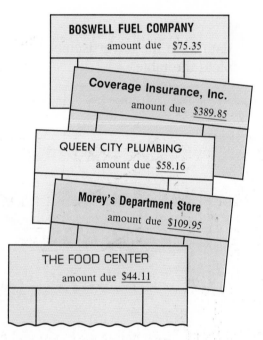

BOSWELL FUEL COMPANY
amount due $75.35

Coverage Insurance, Inc.
amount due $389.85

QUEEN CITY PLUMBING
amount due $58.16

Morey's Department Store
amount due $109.95

THE FOOD CENTER
amount due $44.11

Summing Up

What if you are paid $675 each week? Your expenses are about $525 each week and you put $135 into a savings account each week.

8. How much money is left each week to be saved for a major purchase?

9. How many weeks will it take to save $400 for an entertainment center?

10. How does keeping an accurate checking account help you to keep track of your money?

Using Problem Solving

Collecting Data

The advertisement shows the prices of several computers and their specifications. How could you use data in the advertisement to choose the best computer to buy?

Working together

A. Use data from the advertisement to complete the table.

Brand Name	Price ($)	Hard Drive (MB)	RAM (K)

MEMORY

1 megabyte (MB) = 1,000 kilobytes (K)

B. Give some examples of data that are in the advertisement that are not needed to complete the table.

C. Which spaces in the table cannot be completed because the data is not in the advertisement?

Sharing Your Ideas

1. Does your data indicate that a computer's price is related to either its hard drive or RAM? Give examples to justify your answer.

2. Which computer in the advertisement would you buy? Why?

Practice

THINK
EXPLORE
SOLVE
LOOK BACK

COMPUTER STAR

- 30 MB Hard Drive
- VGA Card & VGA Mono Monitor

Your Final Cost!

$1499

PRO COM

Lap Top
- 1 MB RAM
- Rechargeable Battery Pack (up to 48 hours)

20 MB $2995   40 MB $3295

3. Look in a newspaper or catalog for prices and features of stereo systems.

4. Make a table like the one on page 238 to display the data you collect about stereos.

5. Which data seems most related to the cost of the stereo system? How would you describe this relationship?

6. Decide which stereo system is the best buy based on the data you collected. Explain your decision.

Summing Up

7. How does collecting data about a consumer product help you make a decision about your best buy?

8. Describe a situation other than consumer buying where data collection would be helpful.

Chapter Review

Complete. pages 216–217

1. There are _____ hundredths in 1 whole.

Write the decimal and the word name for the shaded part. pages 218–219

2.   **3.**   **4.**

Write the decimal. pages 218–219

5. twelve thousandths **6.** one and six tenths **7.** fifty-six hundredths

Compare. Use >, <, or = for ●. pages 220–221

8. 0.36 ● 0.63 **9.** 0.04 ● 0.40 **10.** 0.27 ● 0.270

Round. pages 222–223

11. Round 6.28 to the nearest tenth. **12.** Round $8.49 to the nearest one dollar.

Estimate to complete each sentence. pages 228–229

13. The sum of 38.7 and 10.4 is _____ than 49.

14. The difference between $45.50 and $15.75 is _____ than $30.

Add or subtract. pages 232–235

15.	16.	17.	18.	19.
0.8 +0.7	0.35 +0.35	1.3 −0.9	10 − 4.75	$10.50 − 3.89

20. 11.5 + 9.7 = n **21.** $56.18 − $24.25 = n **22.** 3.5 + 0.28 + 1.57 = n

Solve. pages 225–227

23. How much change will you get from a $20-bill if you buy two items for $6.59 and $9.95?

24. Is 0.36 or 0.65 closer to 0.5? Explain how you decided.

Chapter Test

Write the decimal and the word name for the shaded part.

1.   2. 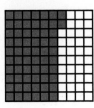   3.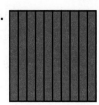

Write the decimal.

4. three thousandths

5. one and two tenths

6. one hundredth

Compare. Use >, <, or = for ●.

7. 0.21 ● 0.125

8. 0.6 ● 0.60

9. 0.45 ● 0.54

Round.

10. Round 1.286 to the nearest hundredth.

11. Round $2.65 to the nearest dime.

Estimate mentally to complete each sentence.

12. The sum of 4.45 and 10.5 is _____ than 15.

13. The difference between $10.30 and $6.25 is _____ than $4.

Add or subtract.

14.
```
  0.9
+ 0.8
```

15.
```
  0.27
+ 0.87
```

16.
```
  1.5
- 0.7
```

17.
```
  10
-  2.85
```

18.
```
  $20.40
-  13.69
```

19.
```
  0.682
+ 2.37
```

20.
```
  11.13
+ 49.27
```

21.
```
  6
- 1.18
```

22.
```
  4.234
- 0.353
```

23.
```
  2.197
+ 0.065
```

24. How much change will you get from a $10-bill if you buy two items that cost $.79 each?

25. Is 0.48 or 0.53 closer to 0.5? Explain how you decided.

THINK   Find the missing digits. The second addend must use the same two digits as the first but in reverse order.

```
  0.□□
+ 0.□□
─────
  1.1 0
```

Puzzle Patterns

Find the missing decimals.

Rule: Each missing decimal is equal to the difference between the decimals on either side.

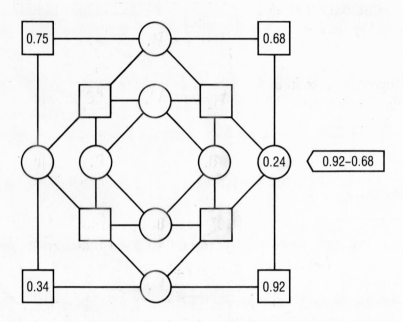

1. Trace the pattern or use Workmat 6. Then use the rule to complete the puzzle. If you solve the puzzle correctly, the four inner circles will all contain the same number.

2. Solve a new puzzle. Trace the pattern again. Enter these decimals in the four corner boxes beginning at the upper right and moving clockwise: 0.36, 0.63, 0.55, and 0.29.

3. **Create your own** puzzle. Begin with any four corner decimals that you wish. Your puzzle may require more or less steps but you will always end with four identical numbers.

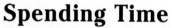

Family Math

In Chapters 4-7 we studied division of whole numbers, time, adding and subtracting decimals, geometry, and graphing.

Spending Time

As a family, choose one activity that all members spend time doing during the day.

For one week, work together to keep a record of the time family members spend on the chosen activity.

At the end of the week, find the total number of hours for each member. Round the time to the nearest hour.

Totals	Actual	Rounded
Mom	5 h 15 min	5 h
Dad	5 h 37 min	6 h
John	1 h 30 min	2 h
Sara	4 h 25 min	4 h

Using grid paper, construct a graph to show the total time spent by each family member. Use the rounded times.

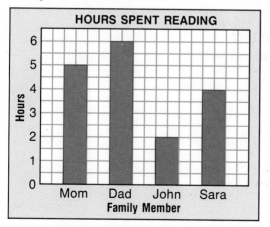

Mom

Monday   15 min
          20 min
        + 35 min
         ────────
          70 min = 1 h 10 min

Tuesday   5 min
        + 14 min
         ────────
          19 min =   19 min

Wednesday

Who spent the most time on the activity? Who spent the least time? Calculate the difference between their times. Use the actual times.

Cumulative Review

Choose the correct answers. Write A, B, C, or D.

1. 600 sec = ☐ min

  A 60   **C** 10

  B 6   **D** not given

2. Find the elapsed time from 7:45 to midnight.

  A 3 h 15 min   **C** 4 h 45 min

  B 3 h 45 min   **D** not given

3.   2 h 10 min
      − 1 h 40 min

  A 30 min   **C** 20 min

  B 1 h 30 min   **D** not given

Use the line graph for 4 and 5.

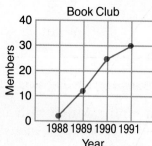

4. What year had the fewest members?

  A 1988   **C** 1991

  B 1989   **D** not given

5. How many members in 1991?

  A 25   **C** 13

  B 30   **D** not given

6. Find the median for 16, 37, 42, 18, and 21.

  A 21   **C** there is none

  B 27   **D** not given

7. Name $\overrightarrow{EF}$.

  A line   **C** ray

  B line segment   **D** not given

8. Estimate the measure of the angle.

  A 82°   **C** 111°

  B 135°   **D** not given

9. How many sides does an octagon have?

  A 6   **C** 5

  B 8   **D** not given

10. What kind of triangle has 3 congruent sides?

  A scalene   **C** equilateral

  B isosceles   **D** not given

11. Name the figure.

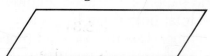

  A parallelogram   **C** square

  B trapezoid   **D** not given

12. What is $\overline{AB}$?

  A diameter   **C** center

  B radius   **D** not given

Choose the correct answers. Write A, B, C, or D.

13. Write the decimal for 6 and 1 tenth.

   A 60.1   **C** 6.01

   B 6.1   **D** not given

14. Compare. 0.8 ⬭ 0.4

   A <   **C** =

   B >   **D** not given

15. Round 4.68 to the nearest one.

   A 5   **C** 4.7

   B 4   **D** not given

16. Round 3.046 to the nearest hundredth.

   A 3.04   **C** 3.1

   B 3.0   **D** not given

17.   3.46
     + 4.85

   A 7.21   **C** 8.31

   B 8.21   **D** not given

18. 8.27 + 4.35

   A 12.62   **C** 3.92

   B 12.52   **D** not given

19. 0.47 − 0.35

   A 1.2   **C** 0.12

   B 0.012   **D** not given

Solve.

20. A pattern was made with bottle caps. The top row had 3 in it. If each row down had 2 more in it, how many were in the 5th row?

   A 11   **C** 10

   B 9   **D** not given

Solve.

21. Paula and Keri sold some old records at a garage sale. Together they sold 50 records, but Paula sold 8 more than Keri. How many did Keri sell?

   A 20   **C** 29

   B 25   **D** not given

Find the pattern to solve 22 and 23.

22. Brad started his design with 1 white tile. The next three were black. After that came 5 blue tiles. If this pattern continued, how many tiles should the next color be?

   A 6   **C** 8

   B 7   **D** not given

23. Katie was cutting string for art projects. The first was 15 cm long. Each one after that needed to be 5 cm longer than the one before. How long was the 5th piece of string?

   A 35 cm   **C** 40 cm

   B 20 cm   **D** not given

8 Multiplying and Dividing Decimals ·

Metric Measurement THEME Fascinating Places

Sharing What You Know

Would you like to explore a world where rocks grow and rivers run under the ground? A spelunker does this every day! Spelunkers are people who explore and map underground caves and tunnels. What kinds of data might they collect? What measurement tools might they use?

Using Language

Spelunkers often use metric measurements in collecting data. What are some metric measurements that you know? Did you think of a millimeter? A **millimeter** is a measure of length equal to one thousandth of a meter. It is formed by the prefix *milli-,* which comes from the Latin word *mille,* meaning thousand. Discuss the meanings of the words milligram and milliliter.

Words to Know: product, quotient, factor, millimeter, centimeter, decimeter, meter, kilometer, milligram, gram, kilogram, milliliter, liter

Be a Problem Solver

On your desk are a 1-centimeter stick, a 2-centimeter stick, and so on. What are the fewest number of sticks you need in order to measure objects, side by side, that range in length from 1 to 10 centimeters? Which sticks are they?

Write about what your life would be like if you could use only the metric system to measure things.

If one item costs $1.50, how can you use mental math to find the cost for 10 items? for 100 items?

Mental Math: Multiplication and Division Patterns

The world's oldest and tallest trees stand in Redwood National Park, California. A redwood tree grows an average of 0.25 foot a year. At that rate, how tall will the redwood grow in 1,000 years?

You can use multiplication patterns to find the answer.

0.25 × 1 = 0.25
0.25 × 10 = 2.5   What pattern
0.25 × 100 = 25   do you see?
0.25 × 1,000 = 250

The redwood tree will grow 250 feet tall in 1,000 years.

What pattern do you see when dividing by 10, 100, or 1,000?

475 ÷ 1 = 475	34 ÷ 1 = 34
475 ÷ 10 = 47.5	34 ÷ 10 = 3.4
475 ÷ 100 = 4.75	34 ÷ 100 = 0.34
475 ÷ 1,000 = 0.475	34 ÷ 1,000 = 0.034

Why is there a zero after the decimal point?

Check Your Understanding

Use a pattern to find each product or quotient.

1. 2.75 × 1
   2.75 × 10
   2.75 × 100
   2.75 × 1,000

2. 380 ÷ 1
   380 ÷ 10
   380 ÷ 100
   380 ÷ 1,000

3. 0.675 × 1
   0.675 × 10
   0.675 × 100
   0.675 × 1,000

Share Your Ideas   Describe how the decimal point is placed in each.   3.6 × 10   4.5 ÷ 100

Practice

Use a pattern to find each product or quotient.

4. 6.05 × 1
6.05 × 10
6.05 × 100
6.05 × 1,000

5. 7 ÷ 1
7 ÷ 10
7 ÷ 100
7 ÷ 1,000

6. 0.389 × 1
0.389 × 10
0.389 × 100
0.389 × 1,000

7. 230 ÷ 1
230 ÷ 10
230 ÷ 100
230 ÷ 1,000

8. 32.75 × 1

9. 32.75 × 10

10. 32.75 × 100

11. 32.75 × 1,000

12. 450 ÷ 10

13. 450 ÷ 100

14. 450 ÷ 1,000

15. 0.5 × 10

16. 0.5 × 100

17. 0.5 × 1,000

18. 10)68

19. 100)68

Follow the rule. Use mental math, paper and pencil, or a calculator to complete.

Rule: Multiply by 100.

	Input	Output
20.	8.3	
21.	3.17	
22.	4.5	
23.	62.9	

Rule: Divide by 10.

	Input	Output
24.	5	
25.	40.8	
26.	16.5	
27.	35	

Rule: Multiply by 1,000.

	Input	Output
28.	2,500	
29.	350	
30.		3.89
31.		0.125

Find *n*.

32. 69.5 × *n* = 6,950

33. $55.90 ÷ *n* = $5.59

34. 389.6 × *n* = 38.960

35. 7.5 ÷ *n* = 0.75

36. 6.2 × *n* = 6,200

37. 4.5 ÷ *n* = 0.045

Problem Solving

38. If you travel an average of 45 mph, how many miles can you travel in 10 hours?

39. At 45 mph, would it take you more or less than 100 hours to drive from Miami to Redwood National Park?

40. If you pay $3.89 for 100 picnic plates, about how much does each one cost?

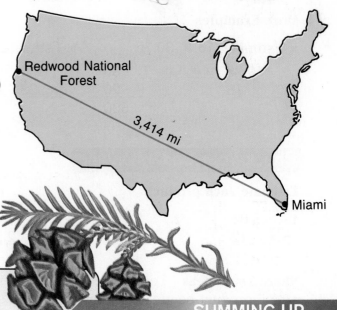

Redwood National Forest

3,414 mi

Miami

Write a rule for multiplying and dividing decimals by 10, 100, and 1,000.

SUMMING UP

249

Use mental math to help you decide.
Is 4 × $19.40 greater than $40?
greater than $76? greater than $77? Explain.

Estimating Products

Postcards of historic
Williamsburg cost $.35
each. Would $5 be
enough money to buy
12 postcards?

You can estimate to find the answer.

One way to estimate a product is to
round each factor to its greatest
nonzero place. Then multiply.

$.35   rounds to $.40
× 12 ————→ × 10
                    $4.00 ← estimated product

The 12 postcards would cost about $4,
so $5 is enough money.

Do you think the actual cost will be
greater or less than $4? Explain.

More Examples

a. Estimate. 16 × 30.75

30.75 rounds to 30
× 16 ————→ × 20
                   600

b. Estimate. 6.6 × 23

6.6 rounds to 7
× 23 ————→ × 20
             140

Check Your Understanding

Estimate each product.

1. $.85 × 12
2. $.35 × 19
3. 10.5 × 2.5
4. 30.4 × 1.6
5. 6.6 × 10.5

Share Your Ideas Look back at **a** and **b**. Will the
actual product be greater or less than the
estimate? Why?

Estimate each product.

6. $3.45
   × 14

7. $1.65
   × 12

8. $.95
   × 15

9. 20
   × 2.6

10. 40
    × 3.4

11. 4.4
    × 10.5

12. 29
    × 3.2

13. 145
    × 6.7

14. 213
    × 12.9

15. 5.8
    × 41

16. $1.63
    × 18

17. $84.50
    × 9.5

18. 2.4 × 300

19. 13 × 10.55

20. 17 × 2.4 × 0.8

21. 69 × 14.375 × 2.19

Estimate to find the correct answer.

22. 6.4 × 5.9

   a. 3,776
   b. 377.6
   c. 37.76
   d. 3.776

23. 13.5 × 8.26

   a. 11,151
   b. 1,115.1
   c. 111.51
   d. 11.151

Problem Solving

24. The driving time to Williamsburg from the Graham family's home is 21 hours. Can they get there in three days by driving 6.5 hours each day? Explain.

25. Will four paperback books at $5.95 each cost you more or less than $25 if there is no tax? Explain.

26. What is the greatest number of $1.29 souvenirs you can buy if you have $5?

> Describe how you would estimate the cost of 18 travel books at $22.50 each.

1. 340 + 920 + 45

2. 605 − 412

3. 8 × 4,502

4. 28 × 927

5. 18.3 + 19.75

6. $4.50 − $2.89

7. 3)$\overline{207}$

8. 12)$\overline{4,850}$

9. 36)$\overline{450}$

10. 38 + 46 + 2

11. 2 × 87 × 50

12. 35 + 65 + 59

13. 25 × 92 × 4

14. 4,200 ÷ 70

15. 25 + 95 + 75

16. 30 × 800

17. 400 × 900

18. 36 + 79 + 64

19. 100 − 58 − 12

20. 70)$\overline{6,300}$

SUMMING UP

Exploring Multiplication of Decimals

One tenth of the area for rides is used for water rides. How much of the total area of the park is used for water rides?

Find 0.1 of 0.4

Working together

Material: grid paper or Workmat 3

A. Draw a 10 by 10 grid. Shade 0.4 of the grid to show the section of the park used for rides.

B. The water rides take up 0.1 of the rides section. Put an **X** in 0.1 of the rides section. What part of the total park area is used for water rides?

C. How much of the total area of the park does the parking area occupy? Only buses use 0.3 of this area. Mark this area on your grid. How much of the total area of the park is used for bus parking?

AMUSEMENT PARK

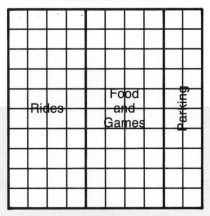

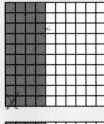

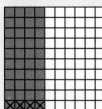

Sharing Your Results

1. **Look back** at your grid paper. Explain how you found the answers for **B** and **C**. The answer to **B** can be solved by multiplying. $0.1 \times 0.4 = 0.04$ Write a multiplication for **C**.

2. How is the number of decimal places in both factors related to the number of decimal places in the product?

Practice

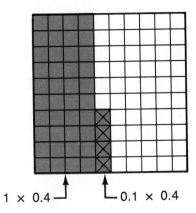

1×0.4 ⌐   ⌐ 0.1×0.4

Find 1.1 × 0.4

3. Use the identity property of multiplication. Look back at 1. What is 0.1 × 0.4? Use these two answers to find 1.1 × 0.4. Explain.

4. Explain how the top grid shows 1.1 × 0.4.

5. How is the number of decimal places in both factors related to the number of decimal places in the product?

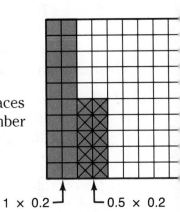

6. **Find 1.5 × 0.2**

1×0.2 ⌐   ⌐ 0.5×0.2

Explain how the bottom grid shows 1.5 × 0.2.

Use a grid to find each product.

7. 0.3 × 0.4   8. 1.3 × 0.4   9. 1.6 × 0.3

Summing Up

Use a grid to explain each statement.

10. When you multiply a whole number by a decimal between 0 and 1, the product is less than the original number.

11. The number of decimal places in both factors determines the number of decimal places in the answer.

A student lives 0.8 of a kilometer from school. What can the student find out by multiplying this decimal by the whole number 2?

Multiplying a Decimal by a Whole Number

White-water rafting on the Colorado River is exciting and fun! Your guide tells you that you will complete 3 sections of the river today. Each section is 6.75 km long. How many kilometers will you raft today?

Estimate first.

3×6.75 rounds to $3 \times 7 = 21$

The product will be about 21.

Then multiply.

Step 1	Step 2	Step 3
Multiply as with whole numbers. $\begin{array}{r} 6.75 \\ \times\quad 3 \\ \hline 2025 \end{array}$	Count the number of decimal places in both factors. $\begin{array}{r} 6.75 \\ \times\quad 3 \\ \hline 2025 \end{array}$ ← 2 decimal places	Place the decimal point in the product. $\begin{array}{r} 6.75 \\ \times\quad 3 \\ \hline 20.25 \end{array}$ ← 2 decimal places ← 2 decimal places

You will raft 20.25 km.

▶ When you multiply with paper and pencil, the number of decimal places in the product is the total number of decimal places in the factors.

Check Your Understanding

Estimate first. Then multiply.

1. $\begin{array}{r} 4.6 \\ \times\quad 8 \\ \hline \end{array}$

2. $\begin{array}{r} 13.5 \\ \times\quad 5 \\ \hline \end{array}$

3. $\begin{array}{r} \$0.39 \\ \times\quad 25 \\ \hline \end{array}$

4. $\begin{array}{r} \$1.45 \\ \times\quad 12 \\ \hline \end{array}$

5. $\begin{array}{r} 0.875 \\ \times\quad 9 \\ \hline \end{array}$

Share Your Ideas Explain how estimation helps you know where to place the decimal point in the product.

254

Estimate first. Then multiply.

6.	2.7	7.	4.8	8.	3.9	9.	$3.08	10.	1.4
	× 3		× 10		× 6		× 7		× 8

11.	1.2	12.	9.02	13.	$.49	14.	0.25	15.	0.08
	× 4		× 5		× 12		× 2		× 19

16.	19.5	17.	$7.89	18.	$42.50	19.	$29.95	20.	0.375
	× 6		× 25		× 7		× 30		× 4

21. 6.5 × 100

22. 2 × 12.5

23. 10 × $.99

24. 72 × 8.5

25. 3 × 0.69

26. 29 × $1.76

Compare. Use mental math, paper and pencil, calculator, or estimation. Write >, <, or = for each ●.

CHOICES

27. 0.95 × 27 ● 27

28. 1.05 × 32 ● 32

29. 0.89 × 64 ● 64

30. 0.425 × 1 ● 0.425

31. 0.6 × 24 ● 12

32. 0.5 × 40 ● 0.9 × 20

Find the pattern. Give the next number.

33. 0.2, 0.6, 1.8, 5.4, 16.2, _____

34. 1.7, 3.4, 6.8, 13.6, 27.2, _____

35. 8.5, 42.5, 212.5, 1,062.5, _____

36. 4.9, 19.6, 78.4, 313.6, _____

Problem Solving

37. The Stevens family paid $21.75 each to go rafting. There are 4 members of the family. What is the total cost?

38. Mrs. Stevens bought lunch meat for $3.86, 6 rolls at $.29 each, and 10 apples at $.18 each. How much did she spend on food?

Test Taker

Sometimes you can save time by estimating answers for a multiple choice test.

Use estimation and ending digits to help you choose the correct answer.

39.	0.592 × 6	40.	3.2 × 4
	a. 3.552		a. 12.4
	b. 3.660		b. 1.28
	c. 35.52		c. 12.8

Make up your own multiplication exercise with one factor that is a whole number and a product that has two decimal places.

SUMMING UP

What part of $40.50 would you get if someone gave you 0.5 of this amount? Explain.

Multiplying Decimals

On the planet Mars, there is less gravity than there is on the earth. Multiply the earth weight by 0.38 to find the weight on Mars. What would a 12.5-pound dog weigh on Mars?

$0.38 \times 12.5 = n$

Use these steps to multiply.

Step 1 Multiply as with whole numbers.	Step 2 Count the number of decimal places in both factors.	Step 3 Place the decimal point in the product.
12.5 × 0.38 1000 3750 4750	12.5 ← 1 decimal place × 0.38 ← 2 decimal places 1000 3750 4750	12.5 ← 1 decimal place × 0.38 ← 2 decimal places 1000 3750 4.750 ← 3 decimal places

If you used a calculator, the product would be [4.75] Explain why 3 decimal places are not displayed.

A 12.5-pound dog would weigh 4.75 pounds on Mars.

Estimate to be sure the answer makes sense.

Check Your Understanding

Multiply. Estimate to be sure each answer makes sense.

| 1. | 2.5
× 0.4 | 2. | 0.6
× 0.7 | 3. | $26.50
× 0.9 | 4. | 1.86
× 0.25 | 5. | 84
× 1.5 |

Share Your Ideas Write two decimals that will have a product with 4 decimal places. Explain how you chose the decimals.

Practice

Multiply. Estimate to be sure each answer makes sense.

6. 1.7
    × 0.2

7. 0.8
    × 0.7

8. 6.5
    × 0.4

9. 13.5
    × 0.3

10. $15.50
    ×   2.5

11. 10.8
    × 4.9

12. 0.2
    × 3.5

13. $.36
    × 0.75

14. $.96
    × 0.25

15. 1.54
    × 0.9

16. 3.05
    × 0.6

17. 18.5
    × 12

18. 10.3
    × 0.1

19. 20.8
    × 0.2

20. $420.50
    ×   0.5

21. 1.5 × 1.2

22. 3.8 × 2.6

23. 16.5 × 30.4

24. 0.5 × 68 × 0.5

25. 0.1 × 90 × 0.5

26. 0.01 × 500 × 0.1

Find each product. Use mental math, paper and pencil, or a calculator. Explain your choices.

CHOICES

27. 2 × $38.75

28. 10 × $38.75

29. 9.6 × 12.35

30. 0.9 × 0.12

31. 0.5 × 2,416

32. 0.003 × 100

33. 0.1 × 0.3

34. 1.3 × 1.3

35. 0.45 × 0.32

The decimal point on this calculator does not function. Estimate to decide where to place the decimal point.

36. 0.5 × 216.4

    | 1082 |

37. 0.8 × 95.75

    | 766 |

38. 1.5 × 2,044

    | 3066 |

Problem Solving

39. Jan weighs 70 pounds. On Mercury, she would weigh 0.36 times this amount. How much would she weigh on Mercury?

40. On Jupiter, objects weigh 2.64 times as much as they weigh on Earth. How much would a 5.6-pound radio weigh on Jupiter?

Common Error

41. How can estimation help you avoid this common error? Explain.

        1.8
      × 0.5
      ─────
        9.0 ← Incorrect!

Explain how you know where to place the decimal point in the product of two decimals.

SUMMING UP

Look for a pattern: 200 × 0.3 = 60;
20 × 0.3 = 6; 2 × 0.3 = 0.6. What do
you expect the product of 0.2 × 0.3 to be?

Zeros in the Product

The Saguaro cactus is the tallest cactus
in the world. It measures 17 meters
high. Saguaros grow slowly, reaching
0.005 of this height after ten years.

How tall is the cactus after ten years?

0.005 × 17 = **n**

Step 1	Step 2	Step 3
Multiply as with whole numbers.	Count the number of decimal places in both factors.	Write zeros in the product to place the decimal point.
17 × 0.005 85	17 × 0.005 ← 3 decimal places 85	17 × 0.005 0.085 ← 3 decimal places

After ten years the cactus is only
0.085 meter, or 8.5 cm tall.

More Examples

a.   0.03 ← 2 decimal places
   ×   0.2 ← 1 decimal place
   0.006 ← 3 decimal places
      ↑↑ Write zeros for these places

b.   0.15
   ×   0.6
   0.090   How would a
            calculator display
            this product?

Check Your Understanding

Multiply.

1.   0.2
   × 0.2

2.   0.8
   × 0.1

3.   0.04
   ×   0.3

4.   0.25
   ×   0.6

5.   1.04
   × 0.05

6.   17.1
   ×   2.4

Share Your Ideas   Should the product of
0.23 × 0.4 be written as tenths, hundredths,
or thousandths? Explain.

Multiply.

7. 0.3
    × 0.2

8. 0.7
    × 0.1

9. 0.4
    × 0.1

10. 0.01
    ×   2

11. 0.04
    × 0.2

12. 0.01
    ×   8

13. 0.3
    × 0.3

14. $1.02
    ×   5

15. 32.21
    ×   4

16. $.03
    × 96

17. 0.09
    × .3

18. 0.08
    ×   6

19. 0.07
    × .5

20. $.40
    ×   5

21. .003
    ×   9

Find *n*.

22. $0.3 \times 0.02 = n$

23. $0.5 \times 0.1 = n$

24. $0.01 \times 6 = n$

25. $0.8 \times \$2.50 = n$

26. $6 \times 0.3 = 2 \times n$

27. $0.1 \times 10 = 0.01 \times n$

CHOICES **Find the product. Use mental math, paper and pencil, or a calculator. Explain your choices.**

28. 1.5×900

29. 100×0.35

30. 0.5×27

31. 10×5.3

32. 0.5×7

33. 0.8×628.75

34. 3×1.71

35. 3×17

36. 0.9×150

Problem Solving

37. Joey visited Saguaro National Monument. He was surprised to find a cactus that was 12.4 times as tall as he was. Joey is 0.97 meter tall. How tall is the cactus?

38. The John Hancock Center in Chicago is 100 stories tall. The World Trade Center in New York has 1.1 times that number of stories. How many stories does the World Trade Center have?

39. The Transamerica Pyramid in San Francisco is 48 stories tall. First Canadian Place in Toronto has 1.5 times that many stories. How many stories does it have?

Write a few sentences explaining how you know when to write zeros in a product before placing the decimal point. Give examples.

SUMMING UP

Use a 10 by 10 grid to divide 0.5 into two equal parts. What is the answer to 0.5 ÷ 2?

Dividing a Decimal by a Whole Number

The St. Gotthard Tunnel in Switzerland is the longest vehicular tunnel in the world. It measures 10.2 miles in length. This is four times the length of the Lincoln Tunnel, which connects New York and New Jersey.

How long is the Lincoln Tunnel?

$10.2 \div 4 = n$

Step 1	Step 2	Step 3
Place the decimal point in the quotient above the decimal point in the dividend. $4\overline{)10.2}$	Divide as with whole numbers. $\begin{array}{r} 2.5 \\ 4\overline{)10.2} \\ -8\downarrow \\ \hline 2\,2 \\ -2\,0 \\ \hline 2 \end{array}$	Use zeros for additional places in the dividend. Continue to divide until the remainder is zero. $\begin{array}{r} 2.55 \\ 4\overline{)10.20} \\ -8\downarrow \\ \hline 2\,2 \\ -2\,0\downarrow \\ \hline 20 \\ -20 \\ \hline 0 \end{array}$ 10.2 and 10.20 are equivalent decimals.

The Lincoln Tunnel is 2.55 miles long.

More Examples

a. $6.5 \div 5$

$\begin{array}{r} 1.3 \\ 5\overline{)6.5} \\ -5\downarrow \\ \hline 1\,5 \\ -1\,5 \\ \hline 0 \end{array}$ Check $\begin{array}{r} 1.3 \\ \times\; 5 \\ \hline 6.5 \end{array}$

b. $\$53.50 \div 25$

$\begin{array}{r} \$2.14 \\ 25\overline{)\$53.50} \\ -50\downarrow \\ \hline 3 \\ -2\downarrow \\ \hline 1\,00 \\ -1\,00 \\ \hline 0 \end{array}$ Check $\begin{array}{r} \$\,2.14 \\ \times\quad 25 \\ \hline 10\,70 \\ +42\,8 \\ \hline \$53.50 \end{array}$

Divide.

1. $6\overline{)17.4}$
2. $12\overline{)\$59.76}$
3. $37.5 \div 30$
4. $75.5 \div 25$

Share Your Ideas Why is the answer in hundredths when you divide 0.5 by 2?

Practice

Divide. Check by multiplying.

5. 2)3.4　　　　　　**6.** 6)53.4　　　　　　**7.** 3)32.1　　　　　　**8.** 7)9.8

9. 3)20.4　　　　　**10.** 8)24.4　　　　　**11.** 5)9.5　　　　　**12.** 9)157.5

13. 5)17　　　　　**14.** 4)$.60　　　　　**15.** 9)14.4　　　　　**16.** 10)282

17. 12)$114　　　　　**18.** 25)33.75　　　　　**19.** 36)1,177.2　　　　　**20.** 14)$33.04

21. $63 ÷ 42　　　　　**22.** $137.50 ÷ 50　　　　　**23.** 278.8 ÷ 82　　　　　**24.** $19 ÷ 20

Use grid paper. Make a drawing to show each division and its quotient.

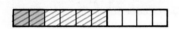

0.6 ÷ 3

25. 0.6 ÷ 3　　　　　**26.** 0.24 ÷ 8　　　　　**27.** 1.2 ÷ 4

28. 0.08 ÷ 4　　　　　**29.** 0.7 ÷ 2　　　　　**30.** 1 ÷ 2

Follow the rule to complete.

Rule: Divide by 3.

	Input	Output
31.	24.6	
32.	28.56	
33.	2.4	
34.	0.375	

Rule: Divide by 12.

	Input	Output
35.	2.4	
36.	9.48	
37.	40.8	
38.	17.88	

Rule: Divide by 100.

	Input	Output
39.	670	
40.	201	
41.		18.5
42.		0.005

Problem Solving

43. At 10.2 miles long, the St. Gotthard Tunnel is 8 times the length of the Queens Midtown Tunnel in New York City. How long is the Queens Midtown Tunnel?

44. John bought 16 gallons of gasoline. It cost $19.68. What was the price per gallon?

45. It took John 2 hours to drive 23.5 miles in heavy traffic. What was his average speed in miles per hour?

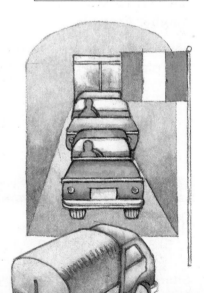

Explain in your own words how to divide a decimal by a whole number.

SUMMING UP

What is half of 0.16? Explain why there is a zero in the tenths place.

Zeros in Division

Because the earth's crust is constantly moving, coral steps are rising out of the ocean near the coast of New Guinea. The steps have risen 4.8 centimeters in the last fifteen years.

What if you were a scientist writing a report about this fascinating fact? How would you find the annual growth rate of the steps?

One way to find out is to divide. $4.8 \div 15 = n$

Step 1	Step 2	
Place the decimal point. Write a zero in the ones place.	Continue to divide.	Multiply to check.

Step 1
Place the decimal point. Write a zero in the ones place.

$$\begin{array}{r} 0. \\ 15\overline{)4.8} \end{array}$$

Think
There are not enough ones to divide. Divide tenths.

Step 2
Continue to divide.

$$\begin{array}{r} 0.32 \\ 15\overline{)4.80} \\ \underline{4\ 5} \\ 30 \\ \underline{-30} \\ 0 \end{array}$$

Write this zero to continue dividing.

Multiply to check.

$$\begin{array}{r} 0.32 \\ \times\ \ \ 15 \\ \hline 160 \\ 32 \\ \hline 4.80 \end{array}$$

The steps are growing at a rate of 0.32 centimeters per year.

Another Example

Sometimes you need zeros in more than one place of the quotient.

$$\begin{array}{r} 0.09 \\ 2\overline{)0.18} \\ \underline{-18} \\ 0 \end{array}$$

There are not enough tenths to divide. Divide hundredths.

Check

$$\begin{array}{r} 0.09 \\ \times\ \ \ 2 \\ \hline 0.18 \end{array}$$

Check Your Understanding

Divide.

1. $5\overline{)3.5}$ 2. $4\overline{)2}$ 3. $0.56 \div 7$ 4. $1.48 \div 4$

Share Your Ideas Look back at **4**. Explain how you found the quotient.

Divide. Check by multiplying.

5. 4.8 ÷ 8

6. 6 ÷ 5

7. 71.1 ÷ 9

8. 3.5 ÷ 7

9. 2 ÷ 100

10. 2.25 ÷ 3

11. 23.4 ÷ 6

12. 0.96 ÷ 2

13. $4.68 ÷ 12

14. $1.25 ÷ 25

15. 4 ÷ 10

16. $253.50 ÷ 39

17. 3 ÷ 1,000

18. 5 ÷ 40

19. 4 ÷ 200

20. 3 ÷ 3,000

Find the pattern. Give the next number.

21. 1.62, 0.54, 0.18, 0.06, _____

22. 322.4, 161.2, 80.6, 40.3, _____

23. 26.88, 6.72, 1.68, 0.42, _____

Solve each division for 24–33. Then trace the pattern. Create a design by drawing line segments to match each division with its quotient.

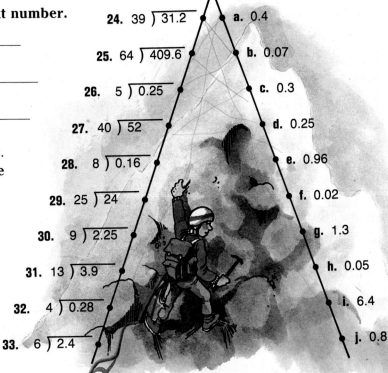

24. $39 \overline{)31.2}$

25. $64 \overline{)409.6}$

26. $5 \overline{)0.25}$

27. $40 \overline{)52}$

28. $8 \overline{)0.16}$

29. $25 \overline{)24}$

30. $9 \overline{)2.25}$

31. $13 \overline{)3.9}$

32. $4 \overline{)0.28}$

33. $6 \overline{)2.4}$

a. 0.4

b. 0.07

c. 0.3

d. 0.25

e. 0.96

f. 0.02

g. 1.3

h. 0.05

i. 6.4

j. 0.8

Problem Solving

34. Mauna Loa in Hawaii is the largest volcanic mountain in the world. The length of the crater is 4.2 kilometers. If the length is twice the width, how wide is the crater?

35. The Jones children paid $2.25 for a package of 25 sinkers for their fishing trip. How much did each sinker cost?

Explain how to divide $8 \overline{)0.12}$

Midchapter Review

Write each product or quotient. pages 248–249

1. 8.7 ÷ 100   **2.** 0.8 × 1,000   **3.** $89.50 ÷ 10   **4.** 50.5 ÷ 100

Estimate. Then find the correct answer. pages 250–251

5. 18 × $.59   **a.** $1,062   **b.** $106.20   **c.** $10.62   **d.** $1.62

6. 16 × 20.75   **a.** 0.332   **b.** 3.32   **c.** 33.2   **d.** 332

7. 61 × 6.75   **a.** 41.175   **b.** 411.75   **c.** 4,117.5   **d.** 41,175

Multiply. pages 252–259

8. 7.2 × 9	**9.** $9.07 × 5	**10.** 18.2 × 0.5	**11.** 30.6 × 0.01	**12.** 0.2 × 0.4

13. 0.3 × 0.04 = n   **14.** 3.1 × 17.25 = n

Divide. pages 260–263

15. 3)4.2   **16.** 6)6.24   **17.** 12)$37.68   **18.** 60)25.8

19. 0.28 ÷ 7 = n   **20.** 100.05 ÷ 29 = n

Choose the best word at the right to complete each sentence.

21. When 100 is a _____, you can use patterns and mental math to multiply.

22. The _____ of two decimals that are each between 0 and 1 is always less than 1.

23. When you solve 1.5 ÷ 3, you must remember to place a zero in the _____.

Words to Know
product
quotient
factor

Solve.

24. The driest place in the United States, Death Valley, averages 1.6 inches of rain per year. In 1982, the rainiest place, Kukui in Hawaii, had 440 times this amount of rain. How many inches of rain fell in Kukui in 1982?

25. Angel Falls in Venezuela is 0.6 mile high. Niagara Falls is 0.05 of the height of Angel Falls. How high is Niagara Falls?

Exploring Problem Solving

Toronto by Taxi

Taxi fares in Toronto are $2 for the first 305 meters (or 0.305 kilometer). They are $.25 for each additional 305 meters or fractional part thereof.

Taxi Distances in Kilometers

	Metro Toronto Zoo	Casa Loma	Eaton Centre	Royal Ontario Museum
CN Tower	4.2	4.6	2.1	3.2
Metro Toronto Zoo		6.8	3.8	4.4
Casa Loma	6.8		4.8	2.4
Eaton Centre	3.8	4.8		3.8
Royal Ontario Museum	4.7	2.4	3.8	

Thinking Critically

Use a calculator where appropriate.

CHOICES

Starting at the CN Tower, in which order might you visit all the sites so that you spend the least amount of money on taxi fare? How much will it cost? Work in a group as you solve this problem.

Analyzing and Making Decisions

1. How much does it cost to go by taxi from the CN Tower to Eaton Centre? from the CN Tower to the Metro Zoo? It is twice as far to the Metro Zoo. Does it cost twice as much? Explain.

2. Make a table showing taxi fares. How will that help you solve the problem?

3. How can you use the map to help you solve the problem? Explain.

4. Try some different routes. Find the costs. Which route would you take? Explain.

Look Back   What if you did not have to visit one of the places that day? Which would you leave out so that you could save the most money on your taxi fare? Explain.

Problem Solving Strategies

Making and Using Drawings

Brad and Sandy are climbing the steps of an ancient pyramid. Beginning at the bottom, they do the following:

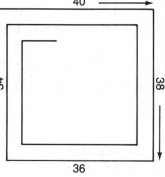

1. Walk 40 steps, turn right
2. Walk 38 steps, turn right
3. Walk 36 steps, turn right
4. Walk 34 steps, turn right
5. And so on.

They keep walking around the four sides of the pyramid, climbing until they reach the top. How many times will they walk around the pyramid during the climb?

Making and using drawings can sometimes help solve problems that are difficult to solve in any other way.

Solving the Problem

Think   What question do they need to answer?

Explore   Describe the first 4 stages of their walk. What would it look like? What patterns do you see? Make a drawing of their walk to the top. How do you know when they reach the top?

Solve   How many times did they walk around the pyramid in their climb?

Look Back   How did you count the number of trips around the pyramid?

Share Your Ideas

1. **What if** there were 54 steps on the first set of stairs? How many trips would they have made?

2. Could you have solved this problem without a drawing? Explain.

Practice

Solve. Use a calculator where appropriate.

CHOICES

3. A rope 80 meters long forms the boundaries of the swimming area at the lake. A buoy is placed at the beginning of the rope. There is a buoy every 10 meters. How many buoys are there?

4. A circular fence is 110 meters long. There is a post every 10 meters. How many posts support the fence?

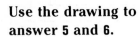

Use the drawing to answer 5 and 6.

A   B

5. Look at the four views of the same cube. Which cube, **A** or **B**, is the same as the one above?

6. What are the colors of the hidden sides?

Mixed Strategy Review

7. The normal height of a wave is about 6 feet. During a storm the wave is nearly 4 times as high. How many feet high is the wave during a storm?

8. The weather station reported that as of the 13th of the month, 20.7 cm of rain had fallen. As of the 14th, it reported that 22.9 cm of rain had fallen that month. On the 15th, 24.3 cm had fallen. Did it rain more on the 14th or on the 15th?

9. "My coins are quarters and dimes. I have 8 coins in all, with a total value of $1.25," said Steve. How many quarters and how many dimes does Steve have?

10. "My coins are quarters and nickels. I have 10 coins in all, with a total value of $1.30," said Denise. How many quarters and nickels does Denise have?

Create **Y**our **O**wn
Look back at **9** and **10**. Write a problem about coins.

Exploring Length

You can tell about how big an animal is by measuring its tracks. **What if** you were camping and did not have a ruler? How could you measure the animal tracks around your campsite?

Working together

Materials: string

A. In your backpack you have a book that you know is 18 cm wide and a matchbox that is 4 cm wide. You also have a long piece of string. Discuss how you could use these items to measure.

B. Estimate the length and width of each animal track on these two pages. Record your estimates.

C. Decide how to use your string as a ruler. Then use it to measure each track at its longest and widest point. Record your measurements.

18 cm

Sharing Your Results

1. Describe how you made your estimates. What item could you have used to estimate 10 centimeters? How did your estimates compare with the actual measurements?

2. Describe how you used the string as a ruler. Did you have a mark for 18 cm? for 20 cm? for 1 cm? Explain how you could find these measurements.

Practice

Continue to work in your group.

3. Look at a meterstick. Compare it with your string ruler. How are they the same? different?

4. Each group member should copy and complete this table. Describe things that you see around you.

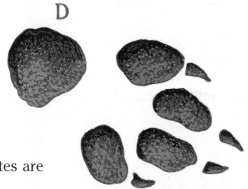

C

ESTIMATE	DESCRIPTION OF ITEM
about 3 mm	Thickness of math textbook cover
about 30 cm	
about 7 dm	
about 0.5 m	
about 0.5 cm	
about 0.25 m	
about 2.5 cm	

D

5. Compare your tables. Discuss which estimates are the best for each item.

6. Find the actual measurement for each of the objects listed in the tables.

7. There are 1,000 meters in a kilometer. It takes a fast walker about 10 minutes to walk 1 kilometer. Have each person in your group write the name of a place that could be about 1 kilometer from your school. Share and discuss your estimates.

E

Summing Up

8. Name three lengths or distances that would be likely to be measured in millimeters.

9. Name three lengths or distances that would be likely to be measured in meters.

 **10.** Use the table and the record of your work to identify the animal tracks.

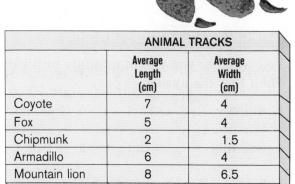

ANIMAL TRACKS		
	Average Length (cm)	Average Width (cm)
Coyote	7	4
Fox	5	4
Chipmunk	2	1.5
Armadillo	6	4
Mountain lion	8	6.5

Estimate. Draw a line segment that is 10 centimeters long. Measure it. Is your estimate close to the actual measurement? Try again.

Relating Units of Length

Tourists who visit Paris, France, can still see some marble metersticks displayed on public buildings. They were placed there in the late 1790s to help people learn the metric system.

The information below shows how metric units are related.

1,000 meters (m) = 1 kilometer (km)
10 decimeters (dm) = 1 meter
10 centimeters (cm) = 1 decimeter
100 centimeters (cm) = 1 meter
10 millimeters (mm) = 1 centimeter
1,000 millimeters (mm) = 1 meter

× 1,000	× 10	× 10	× 10

km	m	dm	cm	mm

÷ 1,000   ÷ 10   ÷ 10   ÷ 10

▶ To change to a smaller unit, multiply.

4.5 m = _____ cm

Think 1 m = 100 cm

$4.5 \times 100 = 450$

4.5 m = 450 cm

▶ To change to a larger unit, divide.

35 mm = _____ cm

Think 10 mm = 1 cm

$35 \div 10 = 3.5$

35 mm = 3.5 cm

Check Your Understanding

Tell whether you would multiply or divide to complete each sentence. Then find the answer.

1. 4 dm = _____ cm

2. 3500 mm = _____ m

3. 2000 m = _____ km

4. 250 mm = _____ dm

5. 0.1 m = _____ cm

6. 2.3 cm = _____ mm

Share Your Ideas Explain how to change 2.75 kilometers to meters.

Complete.

7. 25 cm = _____ dm

8. 1.5 m = _____ mm

9. 3 km = _____ m

10. 6 dm = _____ mm

11. 75 cm = _____ m

12. 15 mm = _____ cm

13. 125 mm = _____ m

14. 0.1 dm = _____ cm

15. 0.01 m = _____ cm

16. 900 m = _____ km

17. 50 mm = _____ dm

18. 4 cm = _____ mm

19. 0.35 m = _____ cm

20. 0.8 m = _____ mm

21. 0.95 m = _____ dm

Find the missing unit. Use mental math, paper and pencil, or a calculator for each. Explain your choices.

CHOICES

22. 2.5 m = 250 _____

23. 200 m = 0.2 _____

24. 8 mm = 0.008 _____

25. 3.4 cm = 34 _____

26. 7 dm = 700 _____

27. 6 cm = 0.06 _____

Compare. Write >, <, or = for ●.

28. 4.2 m ● 420 cm

29. 0.75 m ● 75 dm

30. 2.9 dm ● 290 cm

Problem Solving

Explain your choice for each.

31. Is the height of an adult more likely to be 0.18 m or 1.8 m?

32. Would 0.3 cm or 30 mm be better to describe the thickness of your math textbook cover?

33. You have a piece of wood that is 1 meter square. Make a drawing to show how 4 shelves can be cut from it. Each shelf must be 30 cm wide and 60 cm long.

34. Is the distance from your elbow to your wrist closer to 15 mm or 1.5 dm?

Visual Thinking

35. Examine each line segment. Estimate what decimal part of a meter is its length. The first one is done for you.

a. ▬▬ 0.01 m

b. ▬▬▬▬▬

c. ▬▬▬▬▬▬▬▬▬

d. ▬▬▬▬▬▬▬▬

Explain how you can use mental math to change meters to centimeters.

SUMMING UP

Exploring Capacity

- How many buckets of warm water will it take to fill the tub?

- Is there enough juice left to give each friend a full glass?

When you answer questions like these, you are estimating capacity. Since containers come in many shapes and sizes, estimating capacity accurately takes practice.

Working together

Materials: empty film canisters or small paper cups; 3 or 4 empty containers of various sizes and shapes; water, sand, or dried beans; metric measuring cup; Workmat 7

A. Use the film canister or a small cup as your unit of measure. Estimate how many times you would have to fill it with water in order to fill the other containers you collected. Record your estimate.

Unit of Measure: film canister		
Number of times filled		
Container	Estimate	Actual
Thermos		

B. Use the film canister or paper cup and water, sand, or beans to measure the actual capacity of the container. Record this information also.

C. Repeat **A** and **B** for each of the different containers. Compare actual measurements and order the containers from least to greatest capacity.

Sharing Your Results

1. How did your estimates and the actual measurements compare for the first container? for the last? Did your estimating improve?

2. How did the shape of the container affect how well you estimated its capacity?

Practice

Standard units for capacity in the metric system are the **liter (L)** and the **milliliter (mL)**.

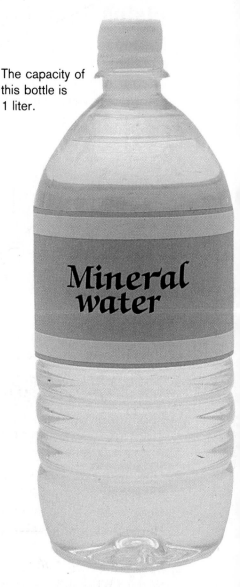

The capacity of this bottle is 1 liter.

UNITS OF CAPACITY
1000 mL = 1 L
1 mL = 0.001 L

The capacity of a pen cap is about 1 mL.

3. Use a metric measuring cup to find how many milliliters your unit of measure in the previous experiment holds. Then write the capacity in milliliters for each container you measured. Use a calculator if you wish.

4. There are 1000 milliliters in 1 liter. How much more or less than 1 liter did your largest container hold?

5. One milliliter is one thousandth of a liter, or 0.001 L. Refer to your list of containers. Write a decimal to show each capacity as part of a liter.

Summing Up

Use what you have learned about measuring in liters and milliliters to answer each question.

Would mL or L be best to give an estimate for each amount?

6. water in a bathtub
7. milk in a baby's bottle
8. juice that you drink for breakfast
9. capacity of a car's fuel tank
10. liquid in a test tube

Complete.

11. 4000 mL = _____ L   **12.** 0.008 L = _____ mL
13. 2500 mL = _____ L   **14.** 35 mL = _____ L
15. 0.5 L = _____ mL   **16.** 25 L = _____ mL

Using Problem Solving

Celsius Temperature

A fifth grade class in Seattle, Washington is planning a 7-day field trip through western Canada during spring vacation. They found a chart which listed the distances in kilometers between some western Canadian cities.

TRAVELING DISTANCES IN KILOMETERS							
	Calgary	Edmonton	Jasper	Prince George	Seattle	Vancouver	Victoria
Calgary		294	418	796	1,175	1,049	1,232
Edmonton	294		357	735	1,504	1,231	1,445
Prince George	796	735	378		1,023	785	969
Vancouver	1,049	1,231	904	785	231		183
Victoria	1,232	1,445	1,088	969	183	183	

Use the information in the chart to solve these problems.

A. The bus will average 80 kilometers an hour. If the class travels 8 hours each day, how many kilometers will they travel in a day? List any two cities they could travel between in a day.

B. One group of students thought that a trip from Seattle to Vancouver to Calgary to Jasper to Prince George and back to Seattle would be a good one. How many kilometers is this trip?

C. Plan your own 7-day trip through western Canada. Record where you will be each day, how far you will have to travel between cities, and how long you will stay in each place.

Sharing Your Ideas

1. Look at your answer for B. What is your opinion of the students' trip? Do you think they had enough time to sightsee? Were they riding the bus too much?

2. Share the trip that you planned with other students. How did it compare to the one the other students planned?

276

Practice

While planning their trip to Canada, students studied the **Celsius scale** for temperature. If the average high temperature for this time of year is 11°C, what clothing should they take for the daytime? If the average low temperature was 0°C, what clothing should they take for early morning and late at night?

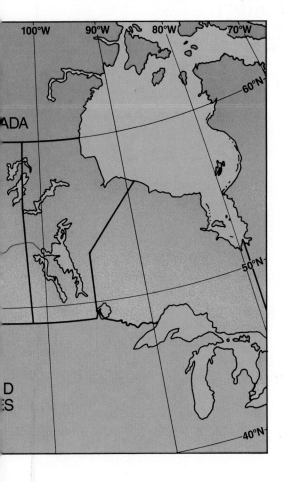

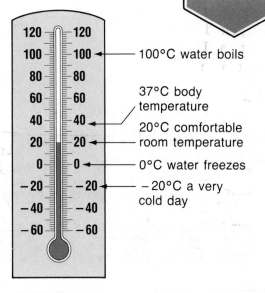

100°C water boils

37°C body temperature

20°C comfortable room temperature

0°C water freezes

−20°C a very cold day

4. The group wants to know whether or not they can do these activities. What do you think? Explain your answer.

   a. ice skating   **c.** soccer

   b. sledding   **d.** sightseeing

Summing Up

5. What activities might you do when the temperature range is 0° to 10°C? Explain your reasons for choosing these.

6. Place a Celsius scale thermometer outside the window of your classroom. On each hour, between 9:00 A.M. and 3:00 P.M. record the temperature. What is the highest and lowest temperature for the time period? What accounts for the differences in temperature?

Chapter Review

Estimate to find the correct answer. pages 250–251

1. 16 × $.85	**a.** $1.36	**b.** $13.60	**c.** $136
2. 8.9 × 98	**a.** 8.722	**b.** 87.22	**c.** 872.2
3. 7.2 × $8.55	**a.** $6,156	**b.** $615.60	**c.** $61.56
4. 5.4 × 11.75	**a.** 6.345	**b.** 634.5	**c.** 63.45

Multiply or divide. pages 256–257, 260–261

5. $82.90 ÷ 10	**6.** 4.6 × 100	**7.** 9 × 0.6	**8.** 25 ÷ 100
9. 38 × $.29	**10.** 2.3 × 0.75	**11.** 0.6 × 0.7	**12.** 0.1 × 0.8
13. 7.5 ÷ 15	**14.** $.80 ÷ 10	**15.** $4)\overline{31.2}$	**16.** $15)\overline{0.6}$

Complete. pages 268–275

17. 1 km = _____ m

18. 1 g = _____ mg

19. 1000 mL = _____ L

Write the name of the metric unit that best completes each sentence. pages 268–277

20. The width of a watch band is about 1 _____ .

21. The weight of 2 pennies is about 6 _____ .

22. The capacity of a drinking glass is about 250 _____ .

23. Water freezes at 0° _____ .

Solve. pages 248–249; 266–267

24. The John Hancock Center in Chicago has 100 stories. The John Hancock Center in Boston has 0.6 of that number of stories. Make a drawing to show how to find the number of stories the John Hancock Center in Boston has.

25. **What if** you pay $2.19 for a notebook with 100 sheets of graph paper? About how much does each sheet of paper cost?

Chapter Test

Estimate to find the correct answer.

1. 18 × $.95   a. $1.71   b. $17.10   c. $171

2. 3.2 × 34   a. 1.088   b. 10.88   c. 108.8

3. 9.5 × $6.74   a. $6,043   b. $64.03   c. $640.30

4. 6.4 × 13.25   a. 0.848   b. 8.48   c. 84.8

Multiply or divide.

5. 3.8 × 100   6. $56.10 ÷ 10   7. 14 ÷ 100   8. 3 × 0.7

9. 29 × $.59   10. 6.5 × 0.28   11. 0.9 × 0.8   12. 0.1 × 0.5

13. 3)$\overline{57.6}$ 14. 15)$\overline{0.45}$ 15. $175.50 ÷ 39   16. 0.6 ÷ 12

Complete.

17. 0.75 m = _____ cm   18. 4500 g = _____ kg   19. 0.001 L = _____ mL

Write the name of the metric unit that best completes each sentence.

20. The thickness of this page is less than 1 _____ .

21. The best unit to use for the weight of this page is the _____ .

22. There are 500 _____ in half a liter.

23. Water boils at 100° _____ .

Solve.

24. A farmer plans to grow squash on 0.2 of his farm. He will use 0.7 of the squash field for yellow squash. Make a drawing to show how much of the farm will be planted with yellow squash.

25. What is the greatest number of $.45-postcards you can buy if you have $2.89?

THINK **What if** you have a lot of lightweight plastic beads? The only available scale measures to the nearest hundred grams. Describe how you would find the weight of one bead.

Introduction to Spreadsheets

A spreadsheet consists of rows and columns of numbers. A computer spreadsheet records data electronically and performs calculations rapidly. It is convenient to use, especially if any data change. "What if" questions can be answered easily.

Materials: computer spreadsheet

The smallest unit of a spreadsheet is called a cell. It is identified by its column and row.

SPREADSHEET DEFINITION

row →

↑ column

	A	B	C	D
1	CURRENCY	VALUE	NUMBER	AMOUNT
2				
3	PENNY	0.01		B3*C3
4	NICKEL	0.05		B4*C4
5	DIME	0.10		B5*C5
6	QUARTER	0.25		B6*C6
7	$1–bill	1.00		B7*C7
8	$5–bill	5.00		B8*C8
9	TOTAL			D3+D4+D5+D6+D7+D8

A. Cell D3 contains a formula B3 * C3. What information is in cell B3? in cell B4?

SPREADSHEET DISPLAY

	A	B	C	D
1	CURRENCY	VALUE	NUMBER	AMOUNT
2				
3	PENNY	0.01	7	0.07
4	NICKEL	0.05	2	0.10
5	DIME	0.10		
6	QUARTER	0.25		
7	$1–bill	1.00		
8	$5–bill	5.00		
9	TOTAL			0.17

B. Enter the data shown above in your spreadsheet. Then enter 7 in cell C3 and 2 in cell C4. What value is displayed in cell D3? in cell D9?

C. Use the spreadsheet. Find the total value of each of these amounts of money.
- 25 nickels, 3 quarters, and 2 $5–bills
- 15,000 pennies and 1,000 nickels
- 6 pennies, 10 dimes, 15 quarters, and 2 $1–bills

D. What combination of coins could give a sum of 55 cents? Use the spreadsheet to find as many different combinations as you can. Use 0 as the number of $1–, and $5–bills.

Sharing Your Results

1. Explain what the formulas in column D calculate.

2. What strategies did you use to find combinations of coins in **D**?

Extending the Activity

What if you had $17.76. What combinations of coins and bills could you have?

3. Work with a partner. Use a spreadsheet to find combinations of coins and bills that total $17.76. Use estimation to help you find as many different combinations as you can. Record each combination in a chart.

PENNY								
NICKEL								
DIME								
QUARTER								
$ 1-bill								
$ 5-bill								
$10-bill								
TOTAL								

4. Compare your results with those of other teams. How many combinations did you find?

5. What is the greatest number of coins or bills that are worth $17.76? What is the least number of coins and bills worth that amount?

Summing Up

6. Explain some advantages of using a computer spreadsheet.

7. **Look back** at your results for **4**. Did you find all possible combinations? Why or why not?

Flowcharts

A flowchart is a way to show a plan or procedure. These geometric figures are used in a flowchart.

means stop or start

means follow an instruction

means make a decision

means go to the next step

1. Use this flowchart for each decimal in the box. 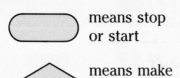 1.2   8.5   3.01

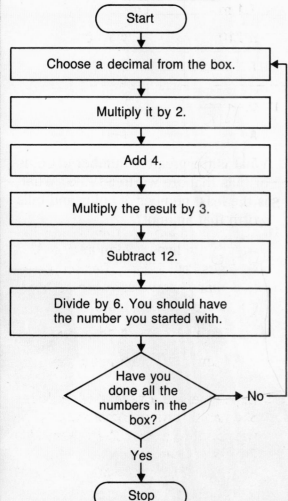

2. Use this flowchart as many times as you like.

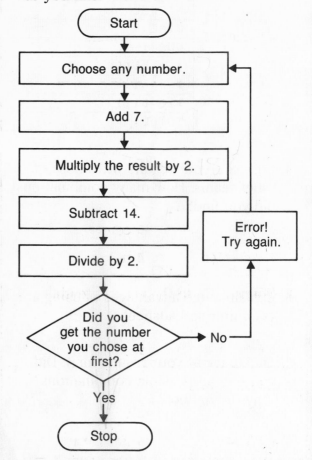

3. Write a flowchart to show how to change meters to centimeters.

4. Write a flowchart to show how to use a pay telephone.

Maintaining Skills

Choose the correct answers. Write A, B, C, or D.

1. Name the angle.

90°

A acute   **C** obtuse

B right   **D** not given

2. What is a quadrilateral with 4 right angles called?

A trapezoid   **C** scalene

B rectangle   **D** not given

3. What is $\overline{MN}$?

A radius   **C** center

B diameter   **D** not given

4. Round 0.63 to the nearest tenth.

A 0.7   **C** 0.6

B 0.64   **D** not given

5. 64.92 − 14.08

A 50.84   **C** 50.83

B 50.94   **D** not given

6.   2.48
  + 7.07

A 9.45   **C** 9.55

B 9.53   **D** not given

7. 100 × 0.492

A 4.92   **C** 492

B 0.0492   **D** not given

8. 4.5 × 0.03

A 0.115   **C** 1.35

B 0.135   **D** not given

9. 7.1 m = _____ cm

A 710   **C** 7,100

B 71   **D** not given

10. 0.4 dm = _____ cm

A 0.4   **C** 4

B 40   **D** not given

Solve.

11. Carlos lives 3.5 km from school. His friend Paul lives 0.2 km further. If he visits Paul 2 days after school, how many kilometers does he travel on these two days in all?

A 3.7 km   **C** 14.8 km

B 7.4 km   **D** not given

12. Carrie planted a vegetable garden. She had 3 rows of tomato plants with 6 in each row. There were also 2 rows of bean plants with 11 in each row. How many plants were there altogether?

A 28   **C** 20

B 40   **D** not given

Understanding Fractions

THEME   Classroom Happenings

Sharing What You Know

Do you want to be a doctor? A pilot? A dancer? Would you want to go to a school where you could work toward that career for several hours a day? Dance students at the Kirov School in the Soviet Union spend about 4 hours in dance classes every day. What part of their day is spent dancing? Think about a typical day at your school. How would you use fractions to describe how your school day is organized?

Using Language

Dance classes fill a large part of a student's day at the Kirov School. Out of a 24-hour day, a student may spend $\frac{4}{24}$, or $\frac{1}{6}$, of the day in dance class. $\frac{4}{24}$ and $\frac{1}{6}$ are equivalent fractions. **Equivalent** means equal in value. In mathematics, **equivalent** fractions are fractions that name the same number. How could you use fractions to prepare a class schedule where equal parts of the school day are spent in dance class and in other studies?

Words to Know: denominator, least common denominator, equivalent, numerator, proper fraction, improper fraction, mixed number

Be a Problem Solver

Cheryl figured she had spent an entire half week dancing during the past month. Rudy figured he spent $3\frac{1}{2}$ days dancing during the same month. Who spent more time dancing?

List things you enjoy doing during your school day. Write the fraction that tells what part of your day you spend doing your favorite activity.

Use a dollar sign and a decimal point to write each amount of money.

one quarter   one half-dollar

Fractions and Decimals

Mark needs to complete a multiplication chart for homework. He has filled in answers for 75 out of the 100 boxes on the grid.

What part of the assignment has Mark completed?

The answer can be written as a decimal or a fraction.

$$0.75 = \frac{75}{100} = \frac{3}{4}$$

Mark has completed 0.75, or $\frac{3}{4}$, of the assignment. 0.75 and $\frac{3}{4}$ are different names for the same number.

▶ A **fraction** names part of a whole. The **numerator** and the **denominator** are called the **terms** of the fraction.

numerator ⟶ **3** ⟵ number of equal parts being named
denominator ⟶ **4** ⟵ number of equal parts in the whole

More Examples

a. three tenths
$0.3 = \frac{3}{10}$

b. thirty-seven hundredths
$0.37 = \frac{37}{100}$

Write a fraction and a decimal for each shaded part.

1.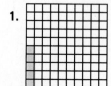

2.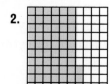

3.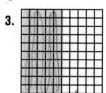

Share Your Ideas **Look back** at **1–2**. How can you tell whether a decimal is greater than or less than $\frac{1}{2}$?

Write a fraction and a decimal for each shaded part.

4.   5.   6.

Write a decimal for each fraction. Use this number line
to help you.

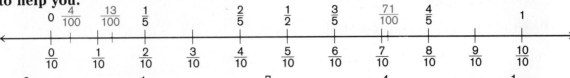

7. $\frac{2}{5}$ 8. $\frac{1}{5}$ 9. $\frac{7}{10}$ 10. $\frac{4}{5}$ 11. $\frac{1}{2}$

12. $\frac{13}{100}$ 13. $\frac{3}{5}$ 14. $\frac{71}{100}$ 15. $\frac{1}{10}$ 16. $\frac{4}{100}$

Write a fraction for each decimal.

17. 0.7   18. 0.49   19. 0.5   20. 0.3   21. 0.53

22. 0.1   23. 0.03   24. 0.19   25. 0.007   26. 0.011

Draw a picture or a number line to show each fraction.

27. $\frac{1}{3}$ 28. $\frac{2}{7}$ 29. $\frac{3}{8}$ 30. $\frac{2}{3}$ 31. $\frac{1}{6}$

Problem Solving

32. How many times would you add 0.25
to get 1? How does this help you
show that $0.25 = \frac{1}{4}$? Use this method
to show the fraction equivalent for
0.2.

33. Prove or disprove the following
statements by using a calculator.

$1 \div 2 = \frac{1}{2}$ $3 \div 4 = \frac{3}{4}$

Can you find a decimal equivalent
for any fraction by dividing the
numerator by the denominator?
Explain.

Visual Thinking

34. If •————• represents 0.4 of a
line segment, which line segment
would represent the whole?

a. •————————————————•

b. •————————————•

c. •————•

Draw a picture to show how $\frac{4}{5}$ and 0.8 name the
same number.

SUMMING UP

287

Exploring Patterns and Fractions

You are challenged to find the least fraction
in the world.

fifth grade

DISCOVERY DAYS

WIN PRIZES!

for the oldest! the smallest!

the coldest! the tallest!...

Contest rules:
- Decide on a category
- Do research
- Write a paragraph to justify your conclusion

Working together

Materials: calculator, grid paper or Workmat 3, fraction strips or Workmat 29

A. Investigate numerators.
Shade grid paper to show each.

$$\frac{1}{22} \quad \frac{5}{22} \quad \frac{13}{22} \quad \frac{17}{22}$$

B. Choose another fraction. Use this fraction to write 3 more fractions. Keep the same denominator but increase the numerator each time. Draw a picture for each. What pattern do you see?

C. Try increasing the numerator with some other fractions. What do you notice? Is the pattern the same?

Sharing Your Results

1. Describe the pattern you found when you increased the numerator.

2. What can you conclude if the numerator and denominator of a fraction are the same?

3. If you could find the least fraction in the world, what would its numerator be? Explain.

Practice

Continue to work in your group.

4. Investigate denominators. Place fraction strips above a number line. Mark the number line to show $\frac{1}{2}$, $\frac{1}{3}$, $\frac{1}{4}$, and $\frac{1}{5}$. What pattern do you see?

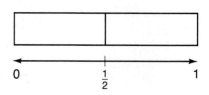

0         $\frac{1}{2}$ 1

5. Find four fractions with 1 as the numerator. Make each of the fractions less than $\frac{1}{5}$. What do you notice about their denominators?

6. Use a calculator to compare these fractions.

$$\frac{1}{10} \quad \frac{1}{11} \quad \frac{1}{12} \quad \frac{1}{13} \quad \frac{1}{14} \quad \frac{1}{20}$$

Divide each numerator by the denominator, then compare the resulting decimals. Record your work.

Fraction	Decimal
$\frac{1}{10}$	0.1
$\frac{1}{11}$	
$\frac{1}{12}$	

a. Which is the greatest fraction?
b. Which is the least fraction?

7. Name some fractions that you think are less than $\frac{1}{20}$. Use a calculator to find out. Record your work.

Summing Up

8. Describe the pattern you found when you increased the denominator.

9. One group says that $\frac{1}{27,587}$ is the least fraction in the world. Is that correct? Explain.

10. Write a few sentences about the least fraction in the world. Justify your conclusion.

What does the word *equivalent* mean? Why are these amounts equivalent?

3.5 and $3\frac{1}{2}$ \$.62 and 62¢

Equivalent Fractions

Each classroom window is being decorated for spring. Each window is the same size but has been divided into a different number of equal parts. What part of each window is finished?

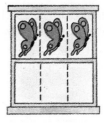

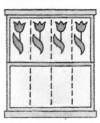

$\frac{1}{2}$ $\frac{1}{2} = \frac{2}{4}$ $\frac{1}{2} = \frac{3}{6}$ $\frac{1}{2} = \frac{4}{8}$

Each window is $\frac{1}{2}$ finished.

$\frac{1}{2}, \frac{2}{4}, \frac{3}{6}$, and $\frac{4}{8}$ are **equivalent fractions.**

▶ To find equivalent fractions, multiply or divide the numerator and denominator of a fraction by the same number, but not by zero.

$$\frac{1}{2} \times \boxed{\frac{4}{4}} = \frac{4}{8} \qquad \frac{4}{8} \div \boxed{\frac{2}{2}} = \frac{2}{4}$$

Check Your Understanding

Write two equivalent fractions for each shaded part.

1.

2.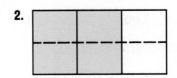

3.

Share Your Ideas Name three pairs of equivalent fractions. Draw a picture for each pair.

Write two equivalent fractions for each shaded part.

4.

5.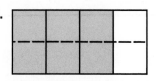

6.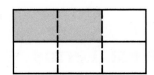

Make a drawing for each. Find the missing numerator.

7. $\frac{1}{2} = \frac{\square}{12}$

8. $\frac{1}{4} = \frac{\square}{8}$

9. $\frac{3}{3} = \frac{\square}{8}$

10. $\frac{1}{5} = \frac{\square}{10}$

11. $\frac{3}{5} = \frac{\square}{10}$

12. $\frac{2}{3} = \frac{\square}{9}$

13. $\frac{1}{2} = \frac{\square}{10}$

14. $\frac{1}{4} = \frac{\square}{12}$

Find the missing number. Use mental math, paper and pencil, or a calculator.

15. $\frac{1}{3} = \frac{\square}{6}$

16. $\frac{\square}{3} = \frac{4}{6}$

17. $\frac{2}{3} = \frac{\square}{312}$

18. $\frac{1}{3} = \frac{\square}{12}$

19. $\frac{8}{12} = \frac{\square}{3}$

20. $\frac{1}{4} = \frac{\square}{468}$

21. $\frac{\square}{36} = \frac{3}{4}$

22. $\frac{1}{3} = \frac{\square}{180}$

23. $\frac{1}{8} = \frac{\square}{24}$

24. $\frac{\square}{5} = \frac{12}{5}$

25. $\frac{1}{2} = \frac{\square}{1,018}$

26. $\frac{1}{2} = \frac{575}{\square}$

Problem Solving

27. Which fractions are not equivalent to $\frac{3}{4}$? Explain.

$\frac{6}{8}$ $\frac{9}{12}$ $\frac{13}{16}$ $\frac{15}{20}$ $\frac{20}{24}$

 Use the graph to answer the following questions.

28. Look at the scale 0-500. How many equal segments are there?

29. How many of these segments equal $\frac{1}{2}$ of the scale?

30. How could you find the total number of points scored by Sally and Mary?

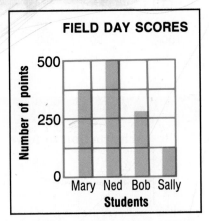

Explain how you could use a number line to find two pairs of equivalent fractions.

Why do you think recipes ask for $\frac{1}{2}$ cup instead of $\frac{2}{4}$ or $\frac{4}{8}$?

Lowest Terms

A fifth–grade class conducted a consumer experiment to see which brand of popcorn pops the best. Help them write the results in lowest terms.

▶ A fraction is in **lowest terms** when the greatest common factor (GCF) of the numerator and denominator is 1.

$\frac{4}{25}$ is in lowest terms.

Brand	Pop it Fresh	Tasty Kernels	Hot Corn
Number of kernels used	50	100	25
Fraction that did not pop	$\frac{6}{50}$	$\frac{24}{100}$	$\frac{4}{25}$

To find $\frac{6}{50}$ in lowest terms, follow these steps.

Step 1 Find the greatest common factor of 6 and 50. Factors of 6: 1, 2, 3, 6 Factors of 50: 1, 2, 5, 10, 25, 50	**Step 2** Divide the numerator and the denominator by their GCF. $\frac{6}{50} \div \frac{2}{2} = \frac{3}{25}$

Are $\frac{6}{50}$ and $\frac{3}{25}$ equivalent fractions? Explain.

▶ Sometimes it is easier to divide the numerator and denominator by any common factor. Keep dividing until lowest terms are reached.

$$\frac{24}{100} \div \frac{2}{2} = \frac{12}{50} \longrightarrow \frac{12}{50} \div \frac{2}{2} = \frac{6}{25}$$

Check Your Understanding

Write each fraction in lowest terms.

1. $\frac{4}{6}$ 2. $\frac{9}{12}$ 3. $\frac{24}{36}$ 4. $\frac{8}{10}$ 5. $\frac{4}{20}$

Share Your Ideas   True or false? In any pair of equivalent fractions, one will be in lowest terms. Justify your answer.

Write each fraction in lowest terms.

6. $\frac{4}{8}$ 7. $\frac{5}{20}$ 8. $\frac{6}{8}$ 9. $\frac{3}{9}$ 10. $\frac{6}{12}$ 11. $\frac{4}{16}$

12. $\frac{18}{36}$ 13. $\frac{8}{12}$ 14. $\frac{8}{24}$ 15. $\frac{15}{20}$ 16. $\frac{10}{15}$ 17. $\frac{6}{18}$

18. $\frac{30}{50}$ 19. $\frac{8}{50}$ 20. $\frac{25}{100}$ 21. $\frac{75}{100}$ 22. $\frac{25}{200}$ 23. $\frac{50}{150}$

Choose the fraction that is not in lowest terms.

24. a. $\frac{9}{10}$ b. $\frac{5}{10}$ c. $\frac{7}{10}$ d. $\frac{1}{10}$

25. a. $\frac{1}{8}$ b. $\frac{2}{8}$ c. $\frac{3}{8}$ d. $\frac{5}{8}$

26. a. $\frac{6}{9}$ b. $\frac{2}{9}$ c. $\frac{7}{9}$ d. $\frac{4}{9}$

27. a. $\frac{7}{12}$ b. $\frac{5}{12}$ c. $\frac{3}{12}$ d. $\frac{1}{12}$

Write a fraction in lowest terms to show each number of days as part of a 30-day month.

28. 5 days   29. 3 days   30. 6 days   31. 9 days

32. 15 days   33. 20 days   34. 12 days   35. 24 days

Problem Solving

36. In the consumer experiment on page 292, is it necessary to write each fraction in lowest terms to compare the results? Explain.

37. There are 26 students in the class. Twelve students conducted experiments. The rest wrote reports. What fraction of the students conducted experiments? What fraction of the students wrote reports?

Give three examples of fractions that are not in lowest terms. Then rewrite each in lowest terms.

SUMMING UP

Name three numbers that are multiples of both 3 and 4.

Using the Least Common Denominator

Two after-school activities are very popular. Play rehearsal is $\frac{3}{4}$ of an hour and soccer practice is $\frac{2}{3}$ of an hour.

Fractions with different denominators are called **unlike fractions.**
Fractions with the same denominator are called **like fractions.**

▶ To change unlike fractions to like fractions, find the least common denominator.

▶ The **least common denominator (LCD)** of unlike fractions is the least common multiple of their denominators.

Find like fractions for $\frac{3}{4}$ and $\frac{2}{3}$.

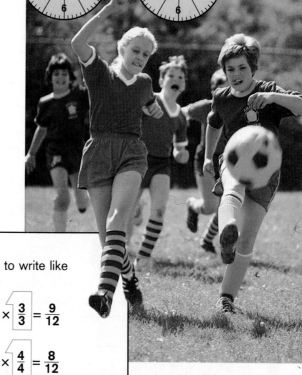

Step 1	**Step 2**
Find the LCM of the denominators. This multiple is the LCD.	Use the LCD to write like fractions.

Step 1
Find the LCM of the denominators.
This multiple is the LCD.

Multiples of 4: **0, 4, 8, 12, 16,** . . .

Multiples of 3: **0, 3, 6, 9, 12,** . . .

Least common multiple: 12

Step 2
Use the LCD to write like fractions.

$\frac{3}{4} = \frac{n}{12} \rightarrow \frac{3}{4} \times \frac{3}{3} = \frac{9}{12}$

$\frac{2}{3} = \frac{n}{12} \rightarrow \frac{2}{3} \times \frac{4}{4} = \frac{8}{12}$

$\frac{9}{12}$ and $\frac{8}{12}$ are like fractions for $\frac{3}{4}$ and $\frac{2}{3}$.

Check Your Understanding

Find the least common denominator. Then write like fractions.

1. $\frac{1}{3}, \frac{3}{5}$ **2.** $\frac{1}{2}, \frac{3}{8}$ **3.** $\frac{1}{5}, \frac{1}{6}$ **4.** $\frac{3}{8}, \frac{5}{16}$ **5.** $\frac{1}{4}, \frac{3}{8}$

Share Your Ideas Describe how to write two unlike fractions as like fractions.

Find the least common denominator. Then write like fractions.

6. $\frac{2}{3}, \frac{2}{5}$

7. $\frac{3}{4}, \frac{2}{5}$

8. $\frac{5}{6}, \frac{3}{4}$

9. $\frac{1}{2}, \frac{7}{12}$

10. $\frac{1}{3}, \frac{6}{7}$

11. $\frac{5}{12}, \frac{1}{3}$

12. $\frac{5}{12}, \frac{5}{6}$

13. $\frac{3}{5}, \frac{7}{10}$

14. $\frac{1}{2}, \frac{3}{8}$

15. $\frac{2}{9}, \frac{1}{3}$

16. $\frac{4}{7}, \frac{1}{2}$

17. $\frac{4}{9}, \frac{2}{5}$

18. $\frac{4}{5}, \frac{9}{10}$

19. $\frac{1}{4}, \frac{5}{8}$

20. $\frac{7}{16}, \frac{3}{8}$

21. $\frac{1}{3}, \frac{3}{10}$

22. $\frac{5}{8}, \frac{9}{16}, \frac{1}{2}$

23. $\frac{3}{4}, \frac{2}{3}, \frac{1}{5}$

24. Look back at **6–20.** For which pairs did you have to rewrite both fractions? Explain.

Problem Solving

25. Laura spends $\frac{1}{6}$ of each year with her grandparents. She spends $\frac{1}{12}$ of a year at camp. Write these fractions as like fractions.

26. Winston has study hall for $\frac{5}{6}$ of an hour each day. He plans to use $\frac{1}{3}$ of an hour to study spelling. Write these fractions as like fractions.

27. Sometimes the LCD is the same as the product of the denominators. Give two examples. Explain when this statement is true.

Write a few sentences explaining how the least common denominator is used to write like fractions.

Mixed Review

1. 27,563
    + 4,279

2. 109,037
    − 62,408

3. 206
    × 42

4. 8)2,786

5. 20)5,420

6. $175.95
    − 28.52

7. 25.2 + 1.83

8. 16.25 − 7.8

9. 0.563 + 0.82

10. 56.2 × 3

11. 6.17 × 0.9

12. 2.05 × 0.36

13. $12.87 ÷ 3

14. $39.55 ÷ 5

Give the time 50 minutes later.

15. 4:52 P.M.

16. 9:12 A.M.

17. 7:45 P.M.

18. 11:36 A.M.

SUMMING UP

Midchapter Review

Write a decimal for each fraction. pages 286–287

1. $\frac{1}{2}$ 2. $\frac{1}{4}$ 3. $\frac{3}{5}$ 4. $\frac{7}{10}$ 5. $\frac{41}{100}$

Write a fraction for each decimal. pages 286–287

6. 0.03   7. 0.9   8. 0.17   9. 1.1   10. 3.25

Find the missing number. pages 288–291

11. $\frac{3}{4} = \frac{\square}{12}$ 12. $\frac{5}{25} = \frac{1}{\square}$ 13. $\frac{\square}{6} = \frac{9}{18}$ 14. $\frac{2}{5} = \frac{\square}{40}$ 15. $\frac{14}{49} = \frac{2}{\square}$

Write each fraction in lowest terms. pages 292–293

16. $\frac{9}{54}$ 17. $\frac{6}{8}$ 18. $\frac{16}{20}$ 19. $\frac{16}{64}$ 20. $\frac{5}{45}$

21. $\frac{9}{12}$ 22. $\frac{54}{81}$ 23. $\frac{10}{30}$ 24. $\frac{15}{18}$ 25. $\frac{12}{36}$

Find the least common denominator. Then write the fractions as like fractions. pages 294–295

26. $\frac{1}{6}, \frac{1}{3}$ 27. $\frac{2}{5}, \frac{1}{6}$ 28. $\frac{3}{4}, \frac{2}{8}$ 29. $\frac{1}{9}, \frac{2}{12}$ 30. $\frac{4}{9}, \frac{2}{81}$

Choose the correct word to complete each sentence.

31. Fractions that are equal in value are called _____ fractions.

32. The _____ and _____ are terms of the fraction.

33. The _____ of two or more fractions is the least common multiple of their denominators.

Words to Know
denominator
LCD
equivalent
numerator

Solve.

34. Make a drawing to show that $\frac{3}{4} = \frac{6}{8}$.

35. Jane answered 84 out of 100 questions correctly. John answered 17 out of 25 correctly. Who received the higher score?

Exploring Problem Solving

THINK
EXPLORE
SOLVE
LOOK BACK

What Are the Missing Numbers?

New technology in medicine is helping us. An X-ray can help to measure the density of an object. X-rays are sent through an object, and a computer assists in reading the measure. Below is a simple mathematical model or explanation of how this works.

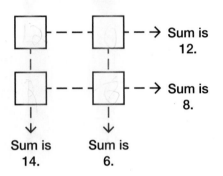

The line represents the path of the X-rays.
The sums represent the information received.
The boxes represent the information needed.

Thinking Critically

Copy the diagram above and find the missing numbers. Use the information shown to help you.

Analyzing and Making Decisions

1. Write a number in the upper left hand box. What number would be a good first guess? Explain.

2. In what box would you try your next guess? Explain.

3. Fill in all the other boxes. Be sure that your numbers add up to the correct sums. Did you have to change some of your first guesses? Why?

4. Find several solutions. What are they?

Look Back. To make the model more complex, the diagonal sum is 8. Now which numbers should go in the boxes? Make a problem of your own to give to a partner.

Problem Solving Strategies

Simulation

R-2-Dee-Liver, a robot, delivers newspapers at the doors of ten classrooms, 201–210. The hallway is 10 feet wide. The doors of each pair of rooms, which are across from each other, are 40 feet apart. The robot is kept in room 201.

R-2-Dee-Liver goes from one side of the hall to the other. It returns to the middle of the hall and walks until it is centered on the next doorway. How far does it travel from Room 201 and back when it delivers all of its papers?

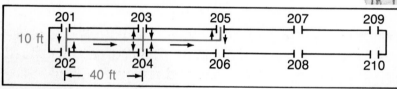

Some problems are hard to act out. You can often simulate the action with a drawing or table.

Solving the Problem

Think What is the question? What are the facts?

Explore Make a drawing of the hallway. Label the distances. In what direction does R-2-Dee-Liver walk its route? Act out its route on your drawing. What is one way to keep track of how far it walks?

Solve How far does R-2-Dee-Liver walk to deliver all the newspapers?

Look Back How did you keep track of the distance? How can you use your drawing to check your work?

Share Your Ideas

1. **What if** R-2-Dee-Liver walked down one side of the hallway and delivered papers to those rooms? Then it crossed the hallway and delivered papers to those rooms. Would its trip be shorter? Explain the difference.

Practice

Solve. Use a calculator where appropriate.

CHOICES

2. Lasers are being installed on an assembly line. The line is 75 ft long. Lasers are put every 15 feet, beginning with the start of the line. How many lasers are on the line?

3. Lasers inspect radios at 3 points on an assembly line. Today, 2,000 radios were inspected. The first laser removed 0.05 of the radios. The second laser found 0.1 of the remaining radios defective. The last one removed 0.1 of the remaining radios. How many radios were found defective?

4. The Dry Gulch Mine used robots to operate water pumps in the mine. The first day they found 1,000 gallons of water and removed 0.25 of it. Overnight, 50 more gallons seeped in, and they removed 0.25 of all the water. That night, 40 gallons of water seeped in, and they removed 0.25 of the total amount. How much water was left in the mine?

5. The leaks in the mine were fixed. Each day the robots removed 0.25 of what was left. How long did it take the robots to remove all the water from the mine?

Mixed Strategy Review

The rocket club is selling buttons to raise $183. The manufacturer charges $.20 for each of the first 100 buttons, $.15 for each of the next 200, and $.12 for the rest.

6. The rocket club ordered 575 buttons. How much did they cost?

7. How much money must the club take in to make $183?

8. Can they sell all the buttons for $.35 each and achieve their goal? Explain.

Create
Your Own

Write a problem for which the action can be simulated.

How can you divide your class into two groups so that about $\frac{1}{2}$ of your class is in each group?

Estimation with Fractions

Eighteen students are in the orchestra. Eleven of them play the violin. Is $\frac{1}{2}$ a good estimate for the fraction of the group that plays the violin?

Use a number line. Is $\frac{11}{18}$ closer to **0**, $\frac{1}{2}$, or **1**?

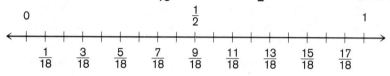

$\frac{11}{18}$ is closer to $\frac{1}{2}$. $\frac{1}{2}$ is a good estimate.

▶ A fraction is close to $\frac{1}{2}$ when the numerator is about half of the denominator.

$\frac{6}{10}$ is close to $\frac{1}{2}$.

▶ A fraction is close to 0 when the numerator is much less than half the denominator.

$\frac{1}{8}$ is close to 0.

▶ A fraction is close to 1 when the values of the numerator and the denominator are about the same.

$\frac{7}{8}$ is close to 1.

Another Example

0.3, or $\frac{3}{10}$, is closer to $\frac{1}{2}$ than to **0**.

How would you continue to shade the grid to show 0.67? Why is 0.67, or $\frac{67}{100}$, closer to $\frac{1}{2}$ than to 1?

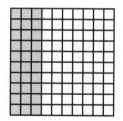

Check Your Understanding

Is the fraction that names the shaded part of each whole closer to 0, $\frac{1}{2}$, or 1?

1.

2.

3.

Share Your Ideas How would you complete the fraction $\frac{\square}{12}$ to show a fraction close to 0? a fraction close to $\frac{1}{2}$? a fraction close to 1?

Is the fraction that names the shaded part of each
whole closer to 0, $\frac{1}{2}$, or 1?

4.

5.

6.

Tell whether each number is closer to 0, $\frac{1}{2}$, or 1.
Use mental math, drawings, or number lines.

CHOICES

7. $\frac{6}{10}$ 8. $\frac{1}{6}$ 9. $\frac{2}{3}$ 10. $\frac{11}{12}$ 11. $\frac{2}{5}$ 12. $\frac{10}{12}$

13. $\frac{2}{10}$ 14. $\frac{4}{5}$ 15. $\frac{9}{10}$ 16. $\frac{1}{12}$ 17. $\frac{5}{6}$ 18. $\frac{8}{10}$

19. 0.27   20. 0.4   21. 0.62   22. 0.09   23. $\frac{13}{1,000}$ 24. $\frac{625}{1,000}$

Decide if each number is closer to 0, $\frac{1}{2}$, or 1.

25. 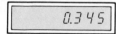   0.345

26.    0.4

27.    0.19

28. 0.825

29.    0.61

30. 0.3333333

31. Mrs. Clarke wants a new bookshelf
for her classroom that is at least
$\frac{1}{2}$ yd long. The custodian has a board
that is $\frac{9}{16}$ yd long. Is it long enough?
Explain.

32. The class aquarium was $\frac{5}{8}$ full after
vacation. George said it was about $\frac{1}{2}$
full. Martha said it was almost full.
Who is right? Explain.

Logical Thinking

33. A contestant on a television
game show saw 8 letters of a
song title, or about $\frac{1}{2}$ of the title.
How many letters could the
song title have? Give several
possible answers.

Write a fraction with a denominator of 100 that
is close to 0; close to $\frac{1}{2}$; close to 1.

Tell whether each fraction is greater than or less than $\frac{1}{2}$: $\frac{2}{5}$ $\frac{3}{8}$ $\frac{3}{4}$ $\frac{5}{8}$

Comparing and Ordering Fractions

For a geography project, $\frac{2}{5}$ of the fifth graders chose to study countries in Africa. South American countries were chosen by $\frac{3}{10}$ of the students. Did more fifth graders study Africa or South America?

You can compare $\frac{2}{5}$ and $\frac{3}{10}$ by drawing number lines or examining fraction strips.

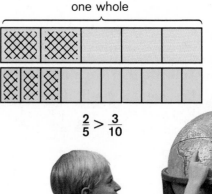

one whole

$\frac{2}{5} > \frac{3}{10}$

▶ Here is another way to compare unlike fractions.

Step 1	Step 2
Use the least common denominator to write like fractions.	Compare the numerators.
$\frac{2}{5} \times \frac{2}{2} = \frac{4}{10}$ LCD = 10 $\frac{3}{10} = \frac{3}{10}$	$4 > 3$ $\frac{4}{10} > \frac{3}{10}$ so $\frac{2}{5} > \frac{3}{10}$

More fifth graders studied Africa than South America.

▶ To order fractions, write them as like fractions. Then compare them two at a time.

Order $\frac{1}{2}, \frac{5}{6}$, and $\frac{2}{3}$ from least to greatest.

The LCD is 6. $\frac{1}{2} = \frac{3}{6}$ $\frac{5}{6} = \frac{5}{6}$ $\frac{2}{3} = \frac{4}{6}$

$\frac{3}{6} < \frac{4}{6} < \frac{5}{6}$, so $\frac{1}{2} < \frac{2}{3} < \frac{5}{6}$.

Explain how you could compare 0.5 and $\frac{3}{4}$.

Check Your Understanding

Compare. Write >, <, or = for 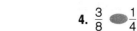.

1. $\frac{2}{5}$ ⬤ $\frac{3}{5}$

2. $\frac{1}{2}$ ⬤ $\frac{7}{14}$

3. $\frac{2}{3}$ ⬤ $\frac{3}{5}$

4. $\frac{3}{8}$ ⬤ $\frac{1}{4}$

Share Your Ideas   How can you use estimation to determine whether $\frac{5}{8}$ is greater than or less than $\frac{8}{16}$?

Practice

Compare. Write >, <, or = for .

5. $\frac{3}{4}$ ● $\frac{1}{4}$ 6. $\frac{1}{8}$ ● $\frac{3}{8}$

7. $\frac{2}{3}$ ● $\frac{1}{3}$ 8. $\frac{3}{10}$ ● $\frac{9}{10}$

9. $\frac{2}{4}$ ● $\frac{3}{6}$ 10. $\frac{1}{3}$ ● $\frac{4}{5}$

11. $\frac{3}{4}$ ● $\frac{7}{8}$ 12. $\frac{1}{2}$ ● $\frac{5}{6}$

13. $\frac{1}{4}$ ● $\frac{1}{5}$ 14. $\frac{1}{6}$ ● $\frac{1}{3}$

15. $\frac{1}{4}$ ● $\frac{1}{8}$ 16. $\frac{1}{3}$ ● $\frac{1}{5}$

17. $\frac{2}{3}$ ● $\frac{2}{5}$ 18. $\frac{2}{5}$ ● $\frac{2}{7}$

19. $\frac{2}{3}$ ● $\frac{2}{7}$ 20. $\frac{2}{9}$ ● $\frac{2}{3}$

Order each from least to greatest.

21. $\frac{1}{2}, \frac{1}{4}, \frac{1}{3}$ 22. $\frac{2}{5}, \frac{2}{3}, \frac{2}{6}$

23. $\frac{2}{3}, \frac{4}{8}, \frac{2}{5}$ 24. $\frac{1}{10}, \frac{1}{2}, \frac{1}{6}$

25. $\frac{3}{8}, \frac{5}{6}, 0.5$ 26. $\frac{4}{5}, 0.5, \frac{2}{3}$

Estimate to compare. Write >, <, or = for ●.

27. $\frac{1}{5}$ ● $\frac{3}{4}$ 28. $\frac{3}{9}$ ● $\frac{5}{10}$ 29. $\frac{5}{6}$ ● $\frac{2}{5}$ 30. $\frac{2}{4}$ ● $\frac{3}{6}$

Problem Solving

31. An art project calls for $\frac{3}{8}$ yd of fabric. Do you have enough if you have $\frac{1}{2}$ yd? How do you know?

DATA 32. On which test does Ralph have the best results? Explain.

33. On which test does Ralph have the poorest results? Explain.

34. Find a different way to justify your answers to **32** and **33**.

Name Ralph
SPELLING TEST
$\frac{80}{100}$

Name Ralph
GEOGRAPHY TEST
$\frac{36}{50}$

Name Ralph
SCIENCE TEST
$\frac{19}{25}$

Describe how you would order $\frac{5}{8}$, 0.5, and $\frac{3}{5}$.

SUMMING UP

303

Exploring Fractions and Mixed Numbers

A whole pizza at Vinnie's is divided into 8 equal slices. Suppose you and your friends want to order pizzas for a party. How would you decide how many whole pizzas to buy?

Working together

Materials: circle models or Workmat 9, ruler, colored markers

A. Use the models to draw a few circles on a sheet of paper. Use a ruler to draw lines dividing the circles into eighths.

B. Each student in turn should color in one eighth for each slice of pizza that he or she would like to eat. Continue until all the group members have had a turn.

C. How many whole pizzas should your group order? Will there be any extra pieces?

D. Write the amount of pizza your group plans to eat as a fraction, a whole number, or a whole number and a fraction.

Sharing Your Results

1. Explain how you recorded the amount of pizza for your group. Compare your results with those of other groups.

2. Make a table like the one below to record each group's pizza order. Draw pictures if you wish.

Number of slices of pizza	Fraction	Number of whole pizzas	Fraction of another pizza
8	$\frac{8}{8}$	1	none
10	$\frac{10}{8}$	1	$\frac{2}{8}$
17	$\frac{17}{8}$	2	$\frac{1}{8}$

Practice

▶ In a **proper fraction** the numerator is less than the denominator.

$\frac{5}{8}$ and $\frac{7}{8}$ are examples of proper fractions.

▶ In an **improper fraction** the numerator is equal to or greater than the denominator.

$\frac{8}{8}$ and $\frac{16}{8}$ are examples of improper fractions.

Some improper fractions can be named by using whole numbers.

Some are named by using **mixed numbers.** A mixed number is a number written as a whole number and a fraction.

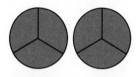
$\frac{6}{3} = 2$

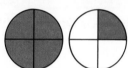
$\frac{5}{4} = 1\frac{1}{4}$

Continue working in your group. Draw a picture for each fraction. Then write each as a whole number or as a mixed number.

3. $\frac{4}{2}$ **4.** $\frac{7}{2}$ **5.** $\frac{8}{3}$ **6.** $\frac{12}{4}$ **7.** $\frac{11}{5}$

Write each as an improper fraction.

8. 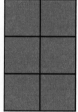 **9.** 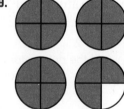 **10.**

11. $2\frac{1}{3}$ **12.** $1\frac{1}{6}$ **13.** $2\frac{1}{2}$ **14.** $1\frac{3}{8}$ **15.** $2\frac{3}{4}$

Summing Up

16. Explain how you can decide if a fraction is a proper or an improper fraction.

17. Explain how you can decide if an improper fraction can be expressed as a whole number or a mixed number.

18. Draw a number line to show that $\frac{7}{2} = 3\frac{1}{2}$.

Recipes sometimes use mixed numbers such as $1\frac{1}{2}$ cups of milk or $1\frac{3}{4}$ cups of flour. Give other examples of mixed numbers you have seen.

Writing Fractions and Mixed Numbers

For his science project, Jeremy used $\frac{1}{2}$ inch of toothpaste each time he brushed his teeth. He recorded his results to show how long a tube of toothpaste lasts. How many inches of toothpaste is $\frac{7}{2}$ in.?

TOOTHPASTE EXPERIMENT							
Brushings	1	2	3	4	5	6	7
Inches Used	$\frac{1}{2}$	$\frac{2}{2}$	$\frac{3}{2}$	$\frac{4}{2}$	$\frac{5}{2}$	$\frac{6}{2}$	$\frac{7}{2}$

Follow these steps to write an improper fraction as a mixed number or whole number.

Step 1	Step 2
Divide the numerator by the denominator.	Write the remainder as the numerator of the fraction. The divisor is the denominator.
$\frac{7}{2}$ $\quad 2\overline{)7} \atop \!\!\begin{array}{r}3\\-6\\\hline 1\end{array}$	$\begin{array}{r}3\frac{1}{2}\\ 2\overline{)7}\\ -6\\ \hline 1\end{array}$

Explain why the denominator for the remainder is 2.

$\frac{7}{2}$ in. of toothpaste is the same as $3\frac{1}{2}$ in.

Follow these steps to write $4\frac{2}{3}$ as an improper fraction.

Step 1	Step 2	Step 3
Multiply the whole number by the denominator of the fraction.	Add the numerator of the fraction to the product.	Write the sum as the numerator of the fraction. The denominator is the same.
$4\frac{2}{3}$ $\quad 4 \times 3 = 12$	$4\frac{2}{3}$ $\quad (4 \times 3) + 2 = 14$ $12 + 2 = 14$	$4\frac{2}{3} = \frac{14}{3}$

Check Your Understanding

Write each mixed number as an improper fraction.
Write each improper fraction as a whole number or mixed number.

1. $\frac{8}{5}$ 2. $2\frac{3}{4}$ 3. $1\frac{7}{8}$ 4. $\frac{9}{3}$ 5. $4\frac{2}{5}$ 6. $\frac{13}{2}$

Share Your Ideas Draw a picture to show that $\frac{7}{4} = 1\frac{3}{4}$. Then explain how you can use division to write the improper fraction as a mixed number.

Write each improper fraction as a whole number or mixed number.

7. $\frac{3}{2}$ **8.** $\frac{4}{3}$ **9.** $\frac{7}{4}$ **10.** $\frac{8}{2}$

Write each mixed number as an improper fraction.

11. $2\frac{3}{8}$ **12.** $1\frac{3}{4}$ **13.** $4\frac{5}{6}$ **14.** $25\frac{4}{5}$

Choose mental math, paper and pencil, or a calculator. Write each as a mixed number or a whole number. Explain your choice.

15. $\frac{9}{4}$ **16.** $\frac{79}{4}$ **17.** $\frac{16}{5}$ **18.** $\frac{19}{2}$

19. $\frac{85}{3}$ **20.** $\frac{10}{3}$ **21.** $\frac{60}{3}$ **22.** $\frac{100}{25}$

Choose the correct answer.

23. Which mixed number is between 2 and $2\frac{1}{2}$?

     a. $2\frac{5}{8}$ **b.** $2\frac{7}{8}$ **c.** $2\frac{3}{8}$ **d.** $2\frac{3}{4}$

24. Which improper fraction is not equal to 3?

     a. $\frac{6}{2}$ **b.** $\frac{12}{4}$ **c.** $\frac{9}{3}$ **d.** $\frac{6}{3}$

Problem Solving

What if you continue each pattern until you reach 12? How many numbers will be in each list?

25. $\frac{1}{3}$, $\frac{2}{3}$, 1, $1\frac{1}{3}$, $1\frac{2}{3}$, 2, $2\frac{1}{3}$, $2\frac{2}{3}$,...

26. $\frac{1}{5}$, $\frac{2}{5}$, $\frac{3}{5}$, $\frac{4}{5}$, 1, $1\frac{1}{5}$, $1\frac{2}{5}$,...

27. $\frac{2}{5}$, $\frac{4}{5}$, $1\frac{1}{5}$, $1\frac{3}{5}$, 2, $2\frac{2}{5}$, $2\frac{4}{5}$, $3\frac{1}{5}$,...

28. Jeremy finished his tube of toothpaste. There were $62\frac{1}{2}$ in. of toothpaste in the tube. How long did the tube last if he brushed his teeth twice a day?

Describe how to change a mixed number to a fraction and a fraction to a mixed number. Give an example of each.

Mixed Review

1. $1.5 + 1.5 = n$

2. $2 \times 1.5 = n$

3. $3 \times 1.5 = n$

4. $4.5 \div 3 = n$

5. $6 \times 1.5 = n$

6. $9 \div 6 = n$

7. $9 \times 1.5 = n$

8. $13.5 \div 9 = n$

9. $10 \times 1.5 = n$

10. $15 \div 10 = n$

Estimate.

11.   495
     $\times$ 3

12.   99
     $\times$ 98

13. $4\overline{)356}$

14. $8\overline{)73}$

Change each to centimeters.

15. 3.45 m

16. 0.72 m

17. 3 dm

18. 20 mm

19. 100 mm

Using Problem Solving

Interview: Calculators in the Classroom

Mr. Procaccino said, "One day my class took a test that had 16 questions. As in the past, I used my calculator to find how many points to give for each correct answer."

Mr. Procaccino follows these steps to score a test.

- Each test has 100 points. Divide to find the number of points for each right answer.

$$100 \div 16 = 6.25$$

- One student got 15 questions correct. Multiply to find the total number of points.

$$6.25 \times 15 = 93.75$$

- Round to the nearest one to find the score on the test.

$$93.75 \longrightarrow 94$$

This time Mr. Procaccino made a table that he can use next time he gives a test with 16 questions.

Number Correct	Number of Points	Score on the Test
16	100	100
15	93.75	94
14	87.5	
13		

Sharing Your Ideas

1. Copy and complete Mr. Procaccino's table for 0 through 16 correct answers.

2. Describe a method for completing the chart that uses subtraction rather than multiplication.

Practice

THINK
EXPLORE
SOLVE
LOOK BACK

Use a calculator where appropriate. Each test has 100 points.

CHOICES

3. How many points would each test item be worth if the test had the following number of items? Give each answer as a fraction or a whole number.

    a. 40   **b.** 10   **c.** 12   **d.** 20   **e.** 32   **f.** 25

4. Look back at **3**. Why might a teacher want a test to have 10, 20, or 25 questions?

5. Make a table for scoring a test with 15 questions. Copy the table on page 308 or use Workmat 10.

Find the final grade for each student. Use a calculator to compute the average test grade. Then round to the nearest one.

	Name	Test 1	Test 2	Test 3	Test 4	Average Grade	Final Grade
6.	Anne	87	78	80	82		
7.	Elena	78	76	81	80		
8.	George	100	98	100	95		
9.	Manuel	92	89	88	94		
10.	Rob	65	73	79	68		
11.	Tish	79	84	87	89		

Summing Up

12. Form a committee to make a set of test grade tables for your teacher.

    a. Identify which tables would be useful to your teacher.

    b. Ask for volunteers to make the tables.

    c. Put the tables together in booklet form and present it to your teacher.

Chapter Review

Write a fraction and a decimal for each shaded part. pages 286–287

1.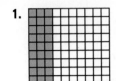

2.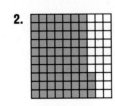

3.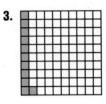

Find the missing number. pages 290–291

4. $\frac{1}{2} = \frac{\square}{10}$

5. $\frac{6}{9} = \frac{\square}{3}$

6. $\frac{\square}{15} = \frac{4}{5}$

7. $\frac{9}{12} = \frac{\square}{4}$

Write each fraction in lowest terms. pages 292–293

8. $\frac{6}{8}$

9. $\frac{9}{27}$

10. $\frac{16}{48}$

11. $\frac{4}{28}$

Find the LCD. Then write as like fractions. pages 294–295

12. $\frac{1}{2}, \frac{1}{3}$

13. $\frac{3}{4}, \frac{5}{6}$

14. $\frac{3}{5}, \frac{1}{4}$

15. $\frac{3}{8}, \frac{1}{6}$

Tell whether each fraction is closer to 0, $\frac{1}{2}$, or 1. pages 300–301

16. $\frac{3}{5}$

17. $\frac{18}{20}$

18. $\frac{2}{10}$

19. $\frac{9}{16}$

Compare. Write >, <, or = for ⬤. pages 302–303.

20. $\frac{4}{5}$ ⬤ $\frac{3}{10}$

21. $\frac{7}{8}$ ⬤ $\frac{3}{4}$

22. $\frac{5}{9}$ ⬤ $\frac{7}{12}$

23. $\frac{2}{3}$ ⬤ $\frac{24}{36}$

Write each improper fraction as a mixed number and each mixed number as an improper fraction. pages 304–307

24. $\frac{13}{9}$

25. $\frac{25}{6}$

26. $3\frac{2}{6}$

27. $1\frac{5}{8}$

Choose the correct word to name each.

28. $5\frac{2}{7}$ _____.

29. $\frac{3}{8}$ _____.

30. $\frac{10}{3}$ _____.

Words to Know
proper fraction improper fraction mixed number

Solve. pages 297–299

31. Twelve of the 50 members of the school band play drums. Write this amount as a fraction in lowest terms.

32. Three pizza pies were each cut into 8 equal slices. Half of the 12 friends ate 2 slices each. How many pies were left for the others?

Chapter Test

Write a fraction and a decimal for each shaded part.

1.

2.

3.

Find the missing number.

4. $\frac{1}{3} = \frac{\square}{9}$

5. $\frac{\square}{5} = \frac{6}{10}$

6. $\frac{5}{6} = \frac{\square}{12}$

7. $\frac{4}{16} = \frac{\square}{4}$

Write each fraction in lowest terms.

8. $\frac{4}{8}$

9. $\frac{9}{12}$

10. $\frac{10}{15}$

11. $\frac{14}{49}$

Find the LCD. Then write as like fractions.

12. $\frac{2}{5}, \frac{3}{10}$

13. $\frac{2}{3}, \frac{5}{8}$

14. $\frac{4}{9}, \frac{1}{6}$

15. $\frac{1}{3}, \frac{3}{18}$

Compare. Write >, <, or = for ●.

16. $\frac{1}{8}$ ● $\frac{1}{7}$

17. $\frac{3}{5}$ ● $\frac{6}{10}$

18. $\frac{3}{4}$ ● $\frac{5}{8}$

19. $\frac{5}{6}$ ● $\frac{3}{4}$

Write each improper fraction as a mixed number and each mixed number as an improper fraction.

20. $\frac{28}{20}$

21. $\frac{9}{4}$

22. $6\frac{2}{8}$

23. $2\frac{5}{6}$

Solve.

24. Michael packed 3 books in Box A, 5 books in Box B, 7 books in Box C, and so on. He used 5 boxes. Which box held $\frac{1}{7}$ of the total number of books?

25. Mrs. Harbold ordered $7\frac{3}{4}$ pounds of cheese. If she planned $\frac{1}{4}$ pound per person, how many people can she serve?

THINK   Carl has 13 nickels. Kim has 7 dimes. Write each amount as a decimal. Who has more money?

Magic Squares

Albrecht Dürer made the engraving, *Melancholy,* in the sixteenth century. Magic squares were popular at the time and the famous German artist included one in this work.

In a magic square the sums of the numbers along every row, column, and diagonal are equal.

The sum of the magic square in this picture is 34.

16	3	2	13
5	10	11	8
9	6		12
4	15	14	

Use a calculator to explore magic squares.

1. Find the missing addends for the magic square in the picture.

2. What is the magic sum of this square?

0.32	0.72	0.16
0.24	0.4	0.56
0.64	0.08	0.48

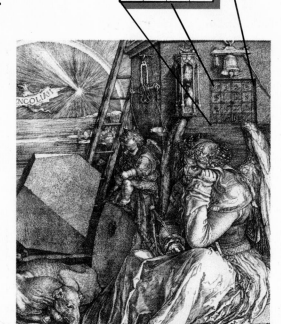

a. Try adding 0.18 to each number. Is the square still a magic square?

b. Try subtracting 0.07 from each number. Is the square still a magic square?

3. Is this a magic square? How could you use decimals to help you find out? Justify your answer.

$\frac{2}{5}$	$\frac{9}{10}$	$\frac{1}{5}$
$\frac{3}{10}$	$\frac{1}{2}$	$\frac{7}{10}$
$\frac{4}{5}$	$\frac{1}{10}$	$\frac{3}{5}$

Maintaining Skills

Choose the correct answers. Write A, B, C, or D.

1. Compare. 0.06 ⬤ 0.6

   A <   C =

   B >   D not given

2. Round 4.77 to the nearest tenth.

   A 4.7   C 5

   B 4.77   D not given

3.   22.06
   +   0.95

   A 21.11   C 23.01

   B 22.91   D not given

4. 2 − 0.48

   A 1.62   C 1.52

   B 0.28   D not given

5. Estimate. 282 × 4.7

   A 1,500   C 15,000

   B 150   D not given

6. $21.40 × 5.5

   A $214.00   C $115.50

   B $117.70   D not given

7. 9)61.2

   A 68   C 7.8

   B 6.8   D not given

8. 3.1 km = _____ m

   A 3,100   C 0.0031

   B 310   D not given

9. What fraction is 0.39?

   A $3\frac{9}{10}$ C $\frac{39}{100}$

   B $\frac{39}{1,000}$ D not given

10. Write $\frac{6}{8}$ in lowest terms.

    A $\frac{4}{5}$ C $\frac{3}{5}$

    B $\frac{2}{4}$ D not given

11. Choose the mixed number for $\frac{11}{3}$.

    A $1\frac{1}{3}$ C $4\frac{1}{3}$

    B $3\frac{2}{3}$ D not given

Use a drawing to solve.

12. Marsha lives 15 blocks from school. Burt is 3 blocks closer. Jean lives 10 blocks from school in the opposite direction. How far apart do Burt and Jean live?

    A 25   C 28

    B 22   D not given

13. Mike has a board 31 inches long. He cuts off a 9-inch piece. How many 3-inch pieces can he cut from what is left?

    A 7   C 10

    B 8   D not given

THEME   Arts and Crafts: Handmade Treasures

Sharing What You Know

Among the things we treasure most are those things that are made by hand. A handknit sweater or a young child's first clay pot are always special. Talk about something you own that is special. Are any of your treasures handmade? What kind of arts and crafts do you like to do? How is mathematics used in these projects?

Using Language

From ancient times, pottery has been an important craft. There are many steps involved in this craft. A potter forms the clay to within fractions of an inch. A fraction has a numerator and a denominator. The numerator is the number above the fraction bar. It tells the number of parts being compared to the whole. The denominator is the number below the fraction bar. It tells into how many parts the whole is divided. How are the meanings of these words alike? different?

Words to Know: fraction, mixed number, numerator, denominator, proper and improper fractions, terms, lowest terms, unlike denominators, like denominators, equivalent fractions

Be a Problem Solver

Carlos is making a change purse for his mother. He needs two $5\frac{1}{2}$-inch pieces of leather. Can he cut both pieces from one $11\frac{1}{2}$-inch piece? Can he cut both pieces from a 4-inch piece and a $7\frac{1}{2}$-inch piece?

Design a poster advertising an arts and crafts show at your school. Make sure to include important information about the show.

Exploring Addition of Fractions

Amanda mixed $\frac{2}{4}$ can of white paint with $\frac{1}{4}$ can of red paint. To find what part of the can Amanda filled with pink paint, find the sum of $\frac{2}{4}$ and $\frac{1}{4}$.

Working together

Materials: fraction pieces

A. To find the sum of $\frac{2}{4}$ and $\frac{1}{4}$, find fraction pieces that show each addend. Then lay the fraction pieces end-to-end on one whole.

B. What is the sum? Is the sum in lowest terms?

C. Write the addition sentence for the fraction pieces. Give the answer in lowest terms.

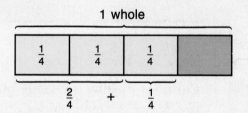

D. Use the fraction pieces to show each sum for the examples below. Write an addition sentence with the sum in lowest terms.

$$\frac{1}{3} + \frac{1}{3} \qquad \frac{1}{6} + \frac{4}{6} \qquad \frac{5}{12} + \frac{2}{12}$$

$$\frac{2}{6} + \frac{3}{6} \qquad \frac{1}{2} + \frac{1}{2} \qquad \frac{4}{12} + \frac{3}{12}$$

E. Like fractions are fractions with the same denominator. Create your own addition problems, using like fractions. Use fraction pieces to show each sum.

Sharing Your Results

1. What part of the can did Amanda fill with pink paint?

2. When adding two like fractions, how do you find the numerator of the sum? the denominator of the sum?

3. Is the sum of two fractions always greater than each addend? Justify your answer.

Practice

Fractions with different denominators are **unlike fractions.** Use fraction pieces to add $\frac{1}{3} + \frac{1}{4}$.

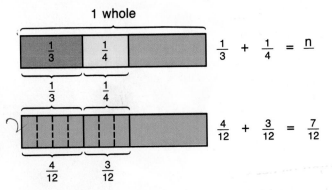

1 whole

$\frac{1}{3} + \frac{1}{4} = \frac{n}{}$

$\frac{4}{12} + \frac{3}{12} = \frac{7}{12}$

Use your fraction pieces. Estimate. Then give each answer in lowest terms.

4. $\frac{1}{3} + \frac{1}{2}$

5. $\frac{1}{12} + \frac{2}{3}$

6. $\frac{1}{4} + \frac{5}{6}$

▶ You can add unlike fractions by first writing the addends with like denominators and then adding.

7. Find fraction pieces that show $\frac{1}{3}$ and $\frac{1}{2}$ with like denominators. Write an addition sentence with the like fractions and find the sum. Give the sum in lowest terms.

8. Compare the sum you found in **4** with the sum you found in **7**. Are they equal? Explain.

Use fraction pieces to show fractions with like denominators. Write the fractions, than add. Write each sum in lowest terms.

9. $\frac{5}{12} + \frac{1}{3}$

10. $\frac{1}{4} + \frac{1}{6}$

11. $\frac{1}{2} + \frac{7}{12}$

Summing Up

12. Describe how adding like fractions is different from adding unlike fractions.

13. Use the fraction pieces to write an addition sentence with a sum less than 1; equal to 1; greater than 1.

Use a ruler to draw a segment $\frac{7}{8}$ inch long. Extend the segment $\frac{1}{2}$ inch. How long is the new segment?

Adding Fractions

Luis and Sharon made their own music video. They completed $\frac{2}{6}$ in the morning and $\frac{3}{6}$ in the afternoon. How much of the video was completed?

Use fraction pieces.

Explain how to find the sum.

1 whole or $\frac{6}{6}$

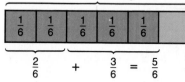

$$\frac{2}{6} + \frac{3}{6} = \frac{5}{6}$$

$\frac{5}{6}$ of the video was completed.

▶ To add like fractions, add the numerators. Use the common denominator. Write the sum in lowest terms.

▶ To add unlike fractions, follow these steps.

Find $\frac{3}{4} + \frac{2}{3}$.

Step 1	Step 2	Step 3
Find the least common denominator. $\begin{array}{r}\frac{3}{4}\\+\frac{2}{3}\end{array}$ LCD = 12	Write equivalent fractions, using the LCD. $\frac{3}{4} \times \frac{3}{3} = \frac{9}{12}$ $+\frac{2}{3} \times \frac{4}{4} = \frac{8}{12}$	Add. Write the sum in lowest terms. $\frac{3}{4} = \frac{9}{12}$ $+\frac{2}{3} = \frac{8}{12}$ $\frac{17}{12} = 1\frac{5}{12}$

Check Your Understanding

Add. Use fraction pieces, if you wish. Write the sum in lowest terms.

1. $\frac{1}{3} + \frac{1}{3}$
2. $\frac{1}{4} + \frac{3}{4}$
3. $\frac{2}{3} + \frac{2}{3}$
4. $\frac{5}{6} + \frac{3}{6}$

5. $\frac{1}{2} + \frac{2}{3}$
6. $\frac{1}{4} + \frac{1}{2}$
7. $\frac{3}{4} + \frac{1}{3}$
8. $\frac{2}{3} + \frac{5}{6}$

Share Your Ideas Look back at Step 2. Why do you multiply $\frac{3}{4}$ by $\frac{3}{3}$? Does this change the value of the fraction? Explain.

Use fraction pieces to show each. Then find each sum.

9. $\frac{1}{4} + \frac{2}{4}$ 10. $\frac{3}{6} + \frac{1}{6}$

11. $\frac{1}{3} + \frac{3}{6}$ 12. $\frac{1}{2} + \frac{1}{4}$

13. $\frac{1}{4} + \frac{5}{12}$ 14. $\frac{1}{2} + \frac{2}{12}$

Add. Write each sum in lowest terms.

15. $\begin{array}{r} \frac{1}{5} \\ + \frac{3}{5} \\ \hline \end{array}$ 16. $\begin{array}{r} \frac{1}{8} \\ + \frac{5}{8} \\ \hline \end{array}$ 17. $\begin{array}{r} \frac{4}{5} \\ + \frac{1}{2} \\ \hline \end{array}$ 18. $\begin{array}{r} \frac{1}{2} \\ + \frac{1}{10} \\ \hline \end{array}$

19. $\begin{array}{r} \frac{5}{6} \\ + \frac{1}{2} \\ \hline \end{array}$ 20. $\begin{array}{r} \frac{4}{9} \\ + \frac{5}{9} \\ \hline \end{array}$ 21. $\begin{array}{r} \frac{3}{8} \\ + \frac{1}{4} \\ \hline \end{array}$ 22. $\begin{array}{r} \frac{1}{2} \\ + \frac{1}{3} \\ \hline \end{array}$

23. $\begin{array}{r} \frac{3}{10} \\ + \frac{2}{5} \\ \hline \end{array}$ 24. $\begin{array}{r} \frac{3}{4} \\ + \frac{3}{4} \\ \hline \end{array}$ 25. $\begin{array}{r} \frac{1}{3} \\ + \frac{5}{6} \\ \hline \end{array}$ 26. $\begin{array}{r} \frac{2}{3} \\ + \frac{2}{9} \\ \hline \end{array}$

27. $\frac{1}{10} + \frac{3}{10} + \frac{1}{10}$ 28. $\frac{1}{4} + \frac{3}{4} + \frac{1}{4}$

29. $\frac{1}{8} + \frac{3}{8} + \frac{7}{8}$ 30. $\frac{3}{5} + \frac{7}{10} + \frac{1}{10}$

Problem Solving

31. Half of a music video is singing. Another $\frac{1}{3}$ of the video is dancing. How much of the video is singing or dancing?

32. Luis and Sharon spent $\frac{1}{2}$ hour practicing their first song. They spent $\frac{3}{4}$ hour practicing their second song. How much time was spent practicing both songs?

How do equivalent fractions help you add unlike fractions?

SUMMING UP

Exploring Subtraction of Fractions

What if you had $\frac{3}{4}$ yard of blue ribbon and $\frac{1}{3}$ yard of yellow ribbon? You can use fraction pieces to find out how much more blue ribbon you had than yellow ribbon.

Working together

Materials: fraction pieces

A. Follow these steps to find $\frac{3}{4} - \frac{1}{3}$.

Place pieces showing the greater fraction on the 1 whole.

Cover the pieces showing the greater fraction with pieces showing the lesser fraction.

Compare the lengths. Then find one or more fraction pieces, of one color, that will cover the rest of the greater fraction.

1 whole

| $\frac{1}{4}$ | $\frac{1}{4}$ | $\frac{1}{4}$ | | $\frac{3}{4}$ |

$\frac{1}{3}$ $\frac{1}{12}$ $\frac{1}{12}$ $\frac{1}{12}$ $\frac{1}{12}$ $\frac{1}{12}$

$$\begin{array}{r} \frac{3}{4} \\ -\frac{1}{3} \\ \hline \frac{5}{12} \end{array}$$

B. Use fraction strips to find each difference. Write each in lowest terms.

$$\frac{11}{12} - \frac{6}{12} \qquad \frac{5}{6} - \frac{1}{6} \qquad \frac{3}{4} - \frac{1}{2} \qquad \frac{2}{3} - \frac{7}{12}$$

C. Create your own subtraction examples that can be answered using fraction strips. Trade your examples with a classmate. Use fraction strips to find the answers.

Sharing Your Results

1. How much more blue ribbon did you have than yellow ribbon?

2. **Look back** at the model of fraction pieces. Why did you need to use $\frac{1}{12}$ pieces to cover the space between the $\frac{1}{4}$ pieces and the $\frac{1}{3}$ piece?

Practice

Addition of like fractions and subtraction of like fractions are done in similar ways.

Find each difference. Give each in lowest terms.

3. $\frac{7}{8} - \frac{4}{8}$

4. $\frac{9}{10} - \frac{5}{10}$

5. $\frac{2}{3} - \frac{1}{3}$

When subtracting unlike fractions, first write them as equivalent fractions with like denominators and then subtract.

Use fraction pieces. Write equivalent fractions with like denominators for each. Then find the difference. Give each answer in lowest terms.

6. $\frac{2}{3} - \frac{1}{2}$

7. $\frac{5}{12} - \frac{1}{3}$

8. $\frac{1}{2} - \frac{1}{6}$

Use fraction pieces to help you complete each number sentence.

9. $\frac{3}{4} - \square = \frac{1}{12}$

10. $\square - \frac{5}{12} = \frac{1}{6}$

11. $\square - \square = \frac{1}{2}$

12. $\frac{1}{2} - \square = \frac{1}{3}$

13. $\square - \frac{1}{4} = \frac{1}{2}$

14. $\square - \square = \frac{1}{3}$

Summing Up

15. How are addition of unlike fractions and subtraction of unlike fractions alike? How are they different?

16. Describe how you would write unlike fractions as like fractions without using fraction pieces.

Subtracting Fractions

Bryan and Frank used tin cans to make lanterns. Bryan finished $\frac{3}{4}$ of his lantern, while Frank finished $\frac{2}{4}$ of his lantern. How much more did Bryan finish?

$$\frac{3}{4}$$

| $\frac{1}{4}$ | $\frac{1}{4}$ | $\frac{1}{4}$ | |
| $\frac{1}{4}$ | $\frac{1}{4}$ | $\frac{1}{4}$ | |

$$\frac{2}{4} \qquad \frac{1}{4}$$

$$\begin{array}{r} \frac{3}{4} \\ -\frac{2}{4} \\ \hline \frac{1}{4} \end{array}$$

Explain how to find the difference.

▶ To subtract like fractions, subtract the numerators. Use the common denominator. Write the difference in lowest terms.

▶ To subtract unlike fractions, follow these steps.

Find $\frac{2}{3} - \frac{1}{2}$.

Step 1 Find the least common denominator.	**Step 2** Write equivalent fractions, using the LCD.	**Step 3** Subtract.
$\begin{array}{r} \frac{2}{3} \\ -\frac{1}{2} \\ \hline \end{array}$ LCD = 6	$\dfrac{2}{3} \times \dfrac{2}{2} = \dfrac{4}{6}$ $-\dfrac{1}{2} \times \dfrac{3}{3} = \dfrac{3}{6}$	$\begin{array}{r} \frac{2}{3} = \frac{4}{6} \\ -\frac{1}{2} = \frac{3}{6} \\ \hline \frac{1}{6} \end{array}$ Is the difference in lowest terms?

Check Your Understanding

Subtract. Use fraction pieces if you wish. Write the difference in lowest terms.

1. $\frac{3}{4} - \frac{1}{4}$

2. $\frac{5}{8} - \frac{3}{8}$

3. $\frac{7}{10} - \frac{3}{10}$

4. $\frac{4}{5} - \frac{2}{5}$

5. $\frac{1}{2} - \frac{1}{8}$

6. $\frac{2}{3} - \frac{1}{2}$

7. $\frac{5}{6} - \frac{1}{6}$

8. $\frac{3}{4} - \frac{1}{3}$

Share Your Ideas Describe how the steps for subtracting unlike fractions relate to the above model for subtracting like fractions.

Practice

Subtract. Write each difference in lowest terms.

9. $\frac{2}{3}$
   $-\frac{1}{3}$

10. $\frac{1}{6}$
    $-\frac{1}{6}$

11. $\frac{7}{8}$
    $-\frac{3}{8}$

12. $\frac{1}{2}$
    $-\frac{1}{5}$

13. $\frac{3}{5}$
    $-\frac{1}{10}$

14. $\frac{7}{10}$
    $-\frac{3}{10}$

15. $\frac{7}{10}$
    $-\frac{1}{2}$

16. $\frac{3}{4}$
    $-\frac{1}{2}$

17. $\frac{3}{4}$
    $-\frac{3}{8}$

18. $\frac{5}{8}$
    $-\frac{5}{8}$

19. $\frac{7}{10}$
    $-\frac{2}{5}$

20. $\frac{5}{6}$
    $-\frac{1}{2}$

21. $\frac{5}{8} - \frac{1}{8} - \frac{3}{8}$

22. $\frac{7}{10} - \frac{3}{10} - \frac{1}{10}$

23. $\left(\frac{3}{8} + \frac{7}{8}\right) - \frac{1}{8}$

24. $\left(\frac{3}{4} + \frac{1}{2}\right) - \frac{3}{8}$

Explain how you would use a calculator to find each difference.

25. $1 - \frac{3}{10}$

26. $\frac{7}{10} - \frac{3}{10}$

27. $\frac{1}{2} - \frac{1}{4}$

Use what you know about fractions and decimals. Follow the rule to find the output.

Rule: Add 0.5.

	Input	Output
28.	$\frac{1}{4}$	
29.	$\frac{1}{5}$	
30.	$\frac{7}{8}$	

Rule: Subtract 0.25.

	Input	Output
31.	$\frac{1}{2}$	
32.	$\frac{3}{4}$	
33.	$\frac{5}{8}$	

Problem Solving

34. Bryan's lanterns are either red or blue. If $\frac{5}{8}$ of his lanterns are red, what fractional part are blue?

Can the difference of two like fractions have a different denominator? Explain.

Mixed Review

1. $1,000 - 299$
2. $380 + 477$
3. $630 \div 9$
4. 20×15
5. 3×147
6. $751 - 363$
7. $448 \div 8$
8. $5 + 8 - 2$
9. $15 \times 2 \div 3$
10. $16 \div 2 \div 2$

Write in lowest terms.

11. $\frac{9}{12}$
12. $\frac{7}{14}$
13. $\frac{4}{6}$
14. $\frac{7}{21}$
15. $\frac{9}{24}$
16. $\frac{18}{2}$

Solve.

17. How many minutes are in $2\frac{1}{2}$ hours?

18. How many hours are between 10 A.M. and 5 P.M.?

19. Would the number of days in March, April, and May be closer to 80, 90, or 100?

20. About how many days are in 5 years?

SUMMING UP

323

Estimating with Fractions

A wire squirrel sculpture requires $\frac{3}{8}$ yard of wire. A giraffe sculpture requires $\frac{5}{6}$ yard. About how much wire is required for both?

To estimate a sum or difference, you can round each fraction to 0, $\frac{1}{2}$, or 1.

$\frac{3}{8}$ is closest to $\frac{1}{2}$.

$\frac{5}{6}$ is closest to 1.

$\frac{3}{8} + \frac{5}{6}$ is about $\frac{1}{2} + 1$, or $1\frac{1}{2}$.

About $1\frac{1}{2}$ yards of wire are required for both.

More Examples

a. $\frac{7}{16}$ $\xrightarrow{\text{rounds to}}$ $\frac{1}{2}$

$+ \frac{1}{5}$ $\xrightarrow{}$ 0

about $\frac{1}{2}$ ← estimate

b. $\frac{7}{8}$ $\xrightarrow{\text{rounds to}}$ 1

$- \frac{3}{5}$ $\xrightarrow{}$ $\frac{1}{2}$

about $\frac{1}{2}$ ← estimate

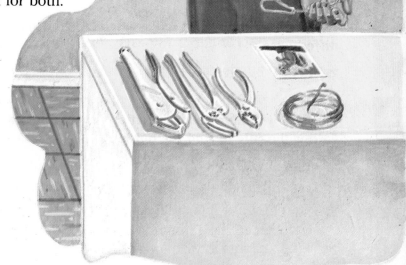

Estimate each sum or difference.

1. $\frac{3}{4} + \frac{2}{5}$

2. $\frac{4}{5} + \frac{5}{8}$

3. $\frac{5}{6} - \frac{3}{8}$

4. $\frac{4}{9} - \frac{6}{13}$

Share Your Ideas Look back at the opening problem. Is the exact answer more than or less than $1\frac{1}{2}$? Explain.

Estimate each sum or difference.

5. $\frac{1}{10} + \frac{2}{5}$ **6.** $\frac{7}{12} + \frac{7}{100}$ **7.** $\frac{2}{5} + \frac{6}{7}$ **8.** $\frac{5}{8} + \frac{7}{15}$

9. $\frac{9}{10} - \frac{3}{100}$ **10.** $\frac{49}{100} - \frac{1}{15}$ **11.** $\frac{2}{5} - \frac{1}{8}$ **12.** $\frac{3}{7} - \frac{2}{5}$

13. $\frac{15}{16} + \frac{7}{8}$ **14.** $\frac{8}{9} - \frac{2}{3}$ **15.** $\frac{3}{7} + \frac{4}{5}$ **16.** $\frac{7}{8} - \frac{2}{11}$

Estimate to compare. Use > or < for each ●.

17. $\frac{99}{100} - \frac{4}{9}$ ● $1\frac{1}{10} - \frac{9}{10}$ **18.** $\frac{47}{100}$ ● $\frac{5}{11} + \frac{12}{25}$ **19.** $\frac{3}{7} + \frac{5}{11}$ ● $\frac{4}{7} - \frac{1}{10}$

20. $\frac{7}{16} - \frac{1}{11}$ ● $1\frac{1}{8} - 1\frac{1}{9}$ **21.** $\frac{5}{6} + \frac{5}{8}$ ● $\frac{99}{100}$ **22.** $\frac{9}{10} + \frac{2}{5}$ ● $\frac{3}{5} + \frac{9}{20}$

Estimate to choose the actual sum or difference.

23. $\frac{4}{9} + \frac{2}{3}$ **24.** $\frac{9}{10} - \frac{2}{6}$ **25.** $\frac{1}{10} + \frac{2}{5}$ **26.** $\frac{4}{5} - \frac{4}{10}$

a. $\frac{6}{9}$ **a.** $\frac{17}{30}$ **a.** $\frac{3}{15}$ **a.** $\frac{1}{10}$

b. $1\frac{1}{9}$ **b.** $\frac{11}{60}$ **b.** $\frac{1}{2}$ **b.** $\frac{8}{10}$

c. $1\frac{3}{4}$ **c.** $\frac{7}{8}$ **c.** $\frac{9}{10}$ **c.** $\frac{2}{5}$

Write possible addends for each. Then estimate each sum.

27. two fractions that round to 1

28. two fractions that round to $\frac{1}{2}$

29. a fraction that rounds to 0 and a fraction close to 1

30. a fraction that rounds to $\frac{1}{2}$ and a fraction that rounds to 0

Problem Solving

31. Cliff needs one piece of wire that is $\frac{3}{8}$ yard and one piece that is $\frac{5}{11}$ yard. Can he cut these from a piece of wire that is one yard long?

32. Cliff worked $\frac{5}{6}$ hour on his robot on Monday and $\frac{3}{4}$ hour on Tuesday. On Wednesday he spent $\frac{1}{2}$ hour working on a giraffe. About how much time did he work on his robot?

Logical Thinking

Use each digit 1 through 8 once. Write two fractions that have

33. a sum close to 1.

34. a difference close to 0.

Describe a way to estimate the sum or difference of two fractions.

SUMMING UP

Midchapter Review

Add or subtract. Write each answer in lowest terms.
pages 316–323

1. $\dfrac{1}{6}$ $+\dfrac{5}{6}$

2. $\dfrac{2}{5}$ $+\dfrac{2}{5}$

3. $\dfrac{4}{5}$ $-\dfrac{1}{5}$

4. $\dfrac{7}{10}$ $-\dfrac{1}{10}$

5. $\dfrac{1}{4}$ $+\dfrac{1}{4}$

6. $\dfrac{2}{3}$ $-\dfrac{1}{3}$

7. $\dfrac{1}{2}$ $+\dfrac{1}{3}$

8. $\dfrac{2}{3}$ $+\dfrac{1}{4}$

9. $\dfrac{1}{5}$ $+\dfrac{1}{3}$

10. $\dfrac{2}{3}$ $-\dfrac{1}{9}$

11. $\dfrac{4}{5}$ $-\dfrac{3}{10}$

12. $\dfrac{5}{6}$ $-\dfrac{2}{3}$

13. $\dfrac{5}{6} + \dfrac{1}{4}$

14. $\dfrac{1}{3} + \dfrac{1}{4}$

15. $\dfrac{3}{4} - \dfrac{1}{6}$

16. $\dfrac{9}{10} - \dfrac{3}{5}$

Estimate each sum or difference. pages 324–325

17. $\dfrac{1}{2}$ $+\dfrac{1}{12}$

18. $\dfrac{8}{9}$ $+\dfrac{3}{4}$

19. $\dfrac{9}{10}$ $+\dfrac{3}{8}$

20. $\dfrac{4}{5}$ $+\dfrac{1}{10}$

21. $\dfrac{3}{5}$ $+\dfrac{1}{8}$

22. $\dfrac{11}{12}$ $-\dfrac{3}{4}$

23. $\dfrac{1}{4} + \dfrac{3}{8}$

24. $\dfrac{7}{10} - \dfrac{1}{5}$

25. $\dfrac{9}{10} - \dfrac{6}{7}$

26. $\dfrac{4}{5} + \dfrac{1}{3}$

Choose the correct word to complete each sentence.

27. The fractions $\dfrac{3}{10}$ and $\dfrac{7}{10}$ have _____ denominators.

28. The fractions $\dfrac{2}{3}$ and $\dfrac{1}{6}$ have _____ denominators.

29. $\dfrac{1}{4}$ and $\dfrac{2}{8}$ are called _____ fractions.

30. $\dfrac{10}{12}$ written in _____ is $\dfrac{5}{6}$.

Words to Know
unlike
equivalent
like
lowest terms

Solve.

31. Velma is making a patchwork quilt. She has $\dfrac{3}{4}$ yard of blue calico and $\dfrac{7}{8}$ yard of red gingham. How many yards of material does she have in all?

32. José had a piece of birchwood that was $\dfrac{2}{3}$ foot long. He cut off $\dfrac{1}{6}$ foot to use as the pedestal for a model airplane. How much is left?

33. Lynn recycled $\dfrac{3}{4}$ pound of newspapers, $\dfrac{1}{2}$ pound of aluminum cans, and $\dfrac{7}{8}$ pound of clear glass. How many pounds of material did she recycle?

34. Peter is making a paper collage. He has covered $\dfrac{1}{3}$ of his sheet of paper with leftover wallpaper and another $\dfrac{1}{2}$ of the sheet of paper with magazine pictures. How much of the sheet of paper is left to cover?

Exploring Problem Solving

How Much Wire to Move an Inch?

You want to hang the picture shown in **A** on a wall. The picture hooks are 8 inches apart. You need an extra inch of wire on each side to tie to the hooks which are on each side of the frame.

A   B

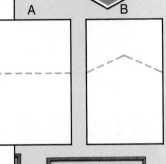

Thinking Critically

How much wire do you need to hang the picture? Use string, paper, and a ruler to help you solve this problem.

Analyzing and Making Decisions

1. How much wire do you need to stretch across the back of the picture? Do not forget the extra inch you need on each side.

2. **What if** you wanted the wire to pull up 1 inch as shown in **B**? How much longer should the wire be? Make an estimate. Check it with your string.

3. **What if** you wanted the wire to pull up $1\frac{1}{2}$ inches? 2 inches? $2\frac{1}{2}$ inches? Estimate the amount of wire you would need for each situation. Check it with your string.

4. How much wire would *you* use to hang the picture? Explain.

Look Back To make the wire pull up 1 inch, do you need an inch of wire? Explain.

Problem Solving Strategies

Alternate Solutions

Mr. Rodrigues is making leather belts. He has a design that is $1\frac{3}{4}$ inches long and one that is $2\frac{1}{2}$ inches long. Will both designs fit in a space on the belt that is 4 inches long?

Many problems can be solved in more than one way. Try to find two different ways to solve this problem.

Solving the Problem

Think What is the question? What facts are given?

Explore If you add the lengths of the two designs, what is the total?
How can you simulate the action? Draw a line segment that is $1\frac{3}{4}$ inches long. Draw one next to it that is $2\frac{1}{2}$ inches long. What is the total length?

Solve Will the two designs fit in the 4-inch space?

Look Back How are the two solutions alike? How are they different?

Share Your Ideas

1. **What if** you want to combine a third design that is $1\frac{1}{4}$ inches long with the two other designs? Now the space on the belt is 5 inches. Will the combined designs fit in the space? Explain.

Practice

Solve. Use a calculator where appropriate.

CHOICES Solve each problem in more than one way. Check to be sure that your answers are the same.

2. Tommy ran a fruit stand at a craft fair. He brought 12 pineapples to the fair. He cut each one into quarters and sold each quarter as one portion. He sold 25 portions before lunch and 17 portions after lunch. How many portions did he have left?

3. At the craft fair Lou spent $4.75 for 12 designs. Some designs cost $.25 each and the others cost $.50 each. How many designs of each kind did he buy?

4. Ms. Tang made posters for the fair. One third of the posters were for the pottery booths, and one fourth were for the painting booths. The others were for the needlework booths. What fractional part of the posters was for the needlework booths?

5. At the fair, Janet sold mugs for $3 and plates for $2. She had brought the same number of mugs and plates. When she closed her booth, she noticed that she had taken in $48. She had twice as many plates as mugs left. How many of each did she sell?

Mixed Strategy Review

Use this information to solve 6–7.

The book stand at the fair sold the following books: 53 books in the morning and 79 books in the afternoon.

6. How many books did they sell that day?

7. How many people bought books?

> **C**reate **Your Own**
>
> Write a problem that can be solved by using two different methods.

Give two examples of each:
a mixed number close to 2, but less than 2;
a mixed number close to 2, but greater than 2.

Estimating with Mixed Numbers

When you make
musical chimes
with a spoon, you
get a lower tone
with more water.

The glasses with the most water have about $3\frac{3}{4}$ inches and $2\frac{7}{8}$ inches of water in them. If each glass is the same size and shape, would the water in these two glasses fit into the empty 6-inch water glass? How could you estimate to decide?

▶ When estimating with mixed numbers, round each mixed number to the nearest whole number.

$$3\frac{3}{4} \xrightarrow{\text{rounds to}} 4$$
$$+ 2\frac{7}{8} \xrightarrow{\phantom{\text{rounds to}}} + 3$$
$$\overline{7} \quad \text{The sum will be close to 7.}$$

All the water will not fit into the empty glass.

More Examples

a. Estimate.

$$4\frac{1}{16} + 5\frac{1}{2}$$

$$4\frac{1}{16} \xrightarrow{\text{rounds to}} 4$$
$$+ 5\frac{1}{2} \xrightarrow{\phantom{\text{rounds to}}} + 6$$
$$\overline{10}$$

The estimate is 10.

b. Estimate.

$$4\frac{1}{2} - 1\frac{2}{5}$$

$$4\frac{1}{2} \xrightarrow{\text{rounds to}} 5$$
$$- 1\frac{2}{5} \xrightarrow{\phantom{\text{rounds to}}} - 1$$
$$\overline{4}$$

The estimate is 4.

Check Your Understanding

Estimate each sum or difference.

1. $1\frac{3}{4} + 2\frac{4}{5}$ **2.** $4\frac{7}{8} - 1\frac{3}{16}$ **3.** $6\frac{3}{4} - 1\frac{1}{8}$ **4.** $5\frac{2}{3} + 3\frac{1}{6}$ **5.** $10\frac{3}{16} - 5$

Share Your Ideas Find a pair of mixed numbers whose sum rounds to 10 and whose difference rounds to 1.

Estimate each sum or difference.

6. $6\frac{1}{8}$
   $+ 6\frac{1}{8}$

7. $8\frac{1}{4}$
   $- 5\frac{1}{8}$

8. $7\frac{1}{5}$
   $+ 1\frac{9}{10}$

9. $4\frac{3}{4}$
   $- 1\frac{2}{3}$

10. $5\frac{1}{2}$
    $- 2\frac{3}{8}$

11. $1\frac{5}{6}$
    $+ 1\frac{1}{2}$

12. $2\frac{7}{8}$
    $+ 1\frac{3}{4}$

13. $1\frac{1}{2}$
    $- \frac{3}{8}$

14. $6\frac{1}{2}$
    $- \frac{4}{10}$

15. $3\frac{1}{6}$
    $+ 4\frac{1}{5}$

16. $3\frac{7}{8} - 1$

17. $4\frac{2}{5} + \frac{4}{5}$

18. $3\frac{1}{2} - 2\frac{1}{2}$

19. $3\frac{9}{10} + 4\frac{1}{2}$

20. $2\frac{1}{3} + 8\frac{3}{4}$

21. $16\frac{9}{10} - 1\frac{1}{5}$

22. $13 + 1\frac{13}{16}$

23. $100\frac{3}{8} - 49\frac{1}{4}$

24. $6\frac{1}{2} + 9\frac{3}{8} + 7\frac{1}{16}$

25. $1\frac{1}{8} + 2\frac{1}{8} + 3\frac{7}{8}$

Estimate.

26. Which sum is not close to 7?

    a. $3\frac{3}{4} + 3\frac{7}{8}$

    b. $3\frac{3}{4} + 2\frac{7}{8}$

    c. $4\frac{7}{8} + 1\frac{3}{4}$

27. Which difference is not close to 3?

    a. $10\frac{1}{2} - 7\frac{5}{8}$

    b. $10\frac{1}{8} - 6\frac{7}{8}$

    c. $10\frac{1}{8} - 7\frac{7}{8}$

Problem Solving

28. A meatloaf recipe calls for 3 pounds of ground beef. Would a $1\frac{1}{2}$–pound package and a $1\frac{5}{8}$–pound package be enough? Explain.

29. **What if** one wall of an art gallery is $22\frac{1}{3}$ feet wide? Can the curator hang two paintings that are $9\frac{3}{4}$ feet wide and $12\frac{3}{4}$ feet wide?

Visual Thinking

30. **What if** you want the glass to be about two-thirds full? About how many inches of water would you add? Explain.

6 in.

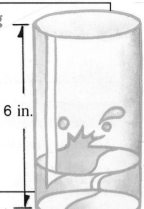

How does knowing whether a fraction is closer to 0, $\frac{1}{2}$, or 1 help you estimate with mixed numbers?

SUMMING UP

How is combining one dollar and three quarters with three dollars and three quarters like adding $1\frac{3}{4}$ with $3\frac{3}{4}$?

Adding Mixed Numbers

To weave a finished piece of fabric that is about $5\frac{3}{4}$ feet long, a weaver needs to add $1\frac{3}{4}$ feet to allow for waste and shrinkage. How long does the weaver need to make the piece of fabric?

$$5\frac{3}{4} + 1\frac{3}{4} = n$$

Use, draw, or think about fraction pieces.

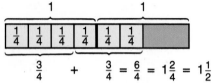

$$\frac{3}{4} \quad + \quad \frac{3}{4} = \frac{6}{4} = 1\frac{2}{4} = 1\frac{1}{2}$$

The weaver needs a piece of fabric $7\frac{1}{2}$ feet long.

▶ To add unlike mixed numbers, follow the steps below. Find $2\frac{1}{2} + 5\frac{1}{3}$.

Step 1 Find the LCD.	**Step 2** Write equivalent fractions.	**Step 3** Add.
$\begin{array}{r}2\frac{1}{2}\\+5\frac{1}{3}\\\hline\end{array}$ LCD = 6	$\frac{1}{2} \times \frac{3}{3} = \frac{3}{6}$ $+\frac{1}{3} \times \frac{2}{2} = \frac{2}{6}$	$\begin{array}{r}2\frac{1}{2} = 2\frac{3}{6}\\+5\frac{1}{3} = 5\frac{2}{6}\\\hline 7\frac{5}{6}\end{array}$ Is the sum in lowest terms?

1 whole

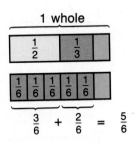

$$\frac{3}{6} + \frac{2}{6} = \frac{5}{6}$$

Check Your Understanding

Add. Use fraction pieces or fraction strips if you like.

1. $2\frac{1}{2} + 3\frac{1}{2}$ **2.** $7\frac{1}{4} + 3\frac{1}{2}$ **3.** $5\frac{2}{3} + 1\frac{1}{2}$ **4.** $4\frac{1}{2} + 6\frac{1}{6}$

Share Your Ideas Describe when and how equivalent fractions are used to add two mixed numbers. Give an example.

Practice

Add. Use mental math, fraction pieces, fraction strips, or drawings to help you. Write each sum in lowest terms.

5. $1\frac{3}{4}$
$+ 2\frac{1}{4}$

6. $6\frac{1}{2}$
$+ 8\frac{1}{2}$

7. $9\frac{1}{5}$
$+ 7\frac{2}{5}$

8. $8\frac{1}{3}$
$+ 10\frac{2}{3}$

9. $2\frac{1}{5}$
$+ 3\frac{7}{10}$

10. $3\frac{3}{4}$
$+ 1\frac{1}{2}$

11. $1\frac{8}{10}$
$+ 1\frac{1}{5}$

12. $6\frac{2}{3}$
$+ 9$

13. $4\frac{2}{3}$
$+ 4\frac{2}{3}$

14. $5\frac{3}{4}$
$+ 2\frac{3}{4}$

15. $1\frac{7}{8}$
$+ 2\frac{1}{2}$

16. 10
$+ 4\frac{3}{10}$

17. $4\frac{1}{2}$
$+ \frac{3}{8}$

18. $6\frac{1}{4}$
$+ \frac{7}{8}$

19. $\frac{1}{5}$
$+ 1\frac{7}{10}$

Estimate to choose the correct answer.

20. $5\frac{9}{10} + 5\frac{3}{4}$ is closer to   a. 10   b. 11   c. 12

21. $2\frac{1}{10} + 3\frac{2}{5}$ is closer to   a. 5   b. $5\frac{1}{2}$ c. 6

22. $4\frac{1}{8} + 1\frac{1}{16}$ is closer to   a. 5   b. $5\frac{1}{2}$ c. 6

Follow the rule to find the output.

Rule: Add $1\frac{1}{2}$.

	Input	Output
23.	$2\frac{1}{2}$	
24.	$5\frac{1}{8}$	
25.	$9\frac{1}{4}$	

Rule: Add $\frac{1}{4}$.

	Input	Output
26.	$6\frac{1}{4}$	
27.	$3\frac{5}{8}$	
28.	$1\frac{3}{16}$	

Rule: Add $5\frac{1}{8}$.

	Input	Output
29.	$15\frac{3}{8}$	
30.	$45\frac{1}{2}$	
31.	$85\frac{3}{4}$	

Problem Solving

32. How many $1\frac{3}{4}$-inch line segments would you have to draw end to end to get a line segment $5\frac{1}{4}$ inches long?

33. A weaver wants her finished fabric to be 19 inches long. If she adds $4\frac{3}{4}$ inches to the length for waste, how long will the total fabric be?

In your own words, write the steps you use to add mixed numbers.

SUMMING UP

Use a ruler to draw a line segment $1\frac{1}{2}$ inches long. Erase $\frac{1}{4}$ inch. How long is the segment now?

Subtracting Mixed Numbers

Joseph made his bowl $3\frac{5}{6}$ inches high. He made a second bowl that was $\frac{1}{2}$ inch shorter. How high was the second bowl?

$$3\frac{5}{6} - \frac{1}{2} = n$$

Step 1 Find the LCD.	**Step 2** Write equivalent fractions.	**Step 3** Subtract. Write the difference in lowest terms.
$\begin{array}{r}3\frac{5}{6}\\[2pt]-\ \frac{1}{2}\end{array}$ LCD = 6	$\dfrac{5}{6} = \dfrac{5}{6}$ $\dfrac{1}{2} \times \boxed{\dfrac{3}{3}} = \dfrac{3}{6}$	$\begin{array}{r}3\frac{5}{6}\\[2pt]-\ \frac{1}{2}\end{array}$ $\begin{array}{r}3\frac{5}{6}\\[2pt]-\ \frac{3}{6}\end{array}$ $3\frac{2}{6} = 3\frac{1}{3}$

The second bowl was $3\frac{1}{3}$ inches high.

Another Example

$$\begin{array}{r}2\frac{7}{8}\\[2pt]-\ 1\frac{1}{8}\\\hline 1\frac{6}{8} = 1\frac{3}{4}\end{array}$$

Write your answer in lowest terms.

Check Your Understanding

Use mental math, fraction pieces, or drawings to solve.

1. $8\frac{1}{2} - 2$ 　　 2. $6\frac{3}{8} - 1\frac{1}{8}$ 　　 3. $4\frac{5}{8} - 3\frac{1}{4}$ 　　 4. $10\frac{1}{4} - \frac{1}{8}$ 　　 5. $5\frac{1}{2} - 1\frac{3}{8}$

Share Your Ideas In your own words, explain how to subtract $3\frac{1}{2} - 1\frac{1}{4}$.

Practice

Use mental math, fraction pieces, or drawings to solve.

 CHOICES

6. $4\frac{5}{8}$
$-1\frac{1}{8}$

7. $3\frac{4}{5}$
$-1\frac{3}{5}$

8. $5\frac{1}{2}$
$-\frac{1}{8}$

9. $2\frac{1}{2}$
$-1\frac{1}{4}$

10. $6\frac{1}{2}$
$-2\frac{1}{3}$

11. $7\frac{1}{2}$
$-2\frac{3}{8}$

12. $10\frac{4}{5}$
$-\ \ 5$

13. $9\frac{5}{6}$
$-1\frac{1}{6}$

14. $4\frac{2}{5}$
$-2\frac{3}{10}$

15. $5\frac{3}{5}$
$-2\frac{1}{2}$

16. $10\frac{2}{3}$
$-\ 8\frac{2}{6}$

17. $15\frac{3}{5}$
$-\ 9\frac{6}{15}$

18. $1\frac{3}{5}$
$-\ \ \frac{1}{10}$

19. 3
$-1\frac{1}{6}$

20. 4
$-3\frac{2}{5}$

Estimate each difference to the nearest whole number.

21. $16\frac{7}{8} - 6\frac{1}{16}$

22. $4\frac{4}{5} - 1\frac{1}{10}$

23. $3\frac{7}{8} - 1\frac{3}{4}$

24. $6\frac{1}{8} - 3\frac{1}{16}$

25. $7\frac{1}{2} - 2\frac{3}{8}$

26. $18\frac{7}{10} - 10\frac{1}{2}$

Problem Solving

27. What if Joseph had made his second bowl $\frac{3}{8}$ inch shorter than the first bowl? How high would the second bowl have been?

 DATA
28. Write a story problem in which you have to subtract two mixed numbers. Exchange problems with a classmate and solve.

Draw a picture that shows how to subtract $1\frac{1}{2}$ from $3\frac{2}{3}$.

Mixed Review

Compute.

1. $0.3 + 0.7$

2. $0.75 + 0.75$

3. $0.24 + 0.6$

4. $0.6 - 0.2$

5. $0.8 - 0.5$

6. $0.7 - 0.25$

7. $\$3.45 - \$.95$

8. 30×60

9. 6×700

10. $40\overline{)2,400}$

11. $6\overline{)630}$

12. $3\overline{)1,290}$

13. $4\overline{)4,020}$

Give each answer.

14. How many sides does a quadrilateral have?

15. How many quarters do you have if you have $\$15.25$ in quarters?

16. How many nickels do you have if you have $\$1.90$ in nickels?

17. Are there more or less than 8 hours between 10:30 P.M. and 7 A.M.?

SUMMING UP

What would happen if you tried to subtract $\frac{7}{8}$ from $1\frac{3}{8}$?

Renaming Before Subtracting

You have $2\frac{1}{2}$ hours to complete five Japanese paper-folding projects. **What if** you have already worked for $\frac{3}{4}$ hour? How much time is left?

$2\frac{1}{2} - \frac{3}{4} = n$

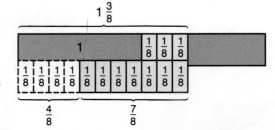

Step 1	Step 2	Step 3
Find the LCD. Write equivalent fractions.	Try to subtract. Rename if necessary.	Subtract.
$2\frac{1}{2} = 2\frac{2}{4}$ $-\ \frac{3}{4} = \frac{3}{4}$	$2\frac{2}{4} = 1\frac{6}{4}$ $-\ \frac{3}{4} = \frac{3}{4}$ Think $2\frac{2}{4} = 1 + 1 + \frac{2}{4}$ $= 1 + \frac{4}{4} + \frac{2}{4}$ $= 1 + \frac{6}{4}$	$2\frac{3}{4} = 1\frac{6}{4}$ $-\ \frac{3}{4} = \frac{3}{4}$ $1\frac{3}{4}$

There are $1\frac{3}{4}$ hours left.

Explain how the steps relate to the model shown.

Another Example

$1\frac{3}{8} - \frac{7}{8} = n$

$1\frac{3}{8} = \frac{11}{8}$

$-\ \frac{7}{8} = \frac{7}{8}$

$\frac{4}{8} = \frac{1}{2}$

Write the difference in lowest terms.

$1\frac{3}{8}$

$-\ \frac{7}{8}$

$\frac{4}{8} = \frac{1}{2}$

Check Your Understanding

Use fraction pieces or drawings to show each. Then subtract.

1. $2\frac{1}{2}$
   $-1\frac{1}{8}$

2. $3\frac{3}{8}$
   $-1\frac{1}{2}$

3. $2\frac{1}{6}$
   $-\ \frac{2}{3}$

Share Your Ideas Make a drawing that shows how you would solve $5\frac{1}{8} - 3\frac{3}{4}$.

Practice

Use fraction pieces or drawings to show each. Then subtract.

4. $2\frac{1}{4}$
   $-1\frac{1}{2}$

5. $2\frac{1}{4}$
   $-\frac{1}{2}$

6. $2\frac{1}{2}$
   $-1\frac{3}{4}$

7. $1\frac{1}{2}$
   $-\frac{5}{8}$

8. $1\frac{1}{2}$
   $-\frac{3}{4}$

9. $3\frac{1}{8}$
   $-1\frac{1}{2}$

10. $1\frac{1}{6}$
    $-\frac{2}{3}$

11. $2\frac{1}{8}$
    $-1\frac{1}{4}$

12. $1\frac{3}{4}$
    $-\frac{3}{8}$

13. $1\frac{1}{2}$
    $-1\frac{1}{8}$

Subtract. Write each difference in lowest terms.

14. $4\frac{1}{2}$
    $-1\frac{3}{4}$

15. $2\frac{1}{8}$
    $-1\frac{5}{8}$

16. $5\frac{1}{2}$
    $-1\frac{3}{8}$

17. $6\frac{1}{4}$
    $-1\frac{3}{8}$

18. $2\frac{1}{2}$
    $-\frac{7}{8}$

19. $3\frac{1}{6}$
    $-2\frac{1}{3}$

20. $9\frac{1}{2}$
    $-2\frac{1}{6}$

21. $4\frac{3}{4}$
    $-1\frac{5}{8}$

22. 45
    $-3\frac{3}{4}$

23. 100
    $-6\frac{1}{2}$

24. **Look back** at **4** to **13**. Is it possible to solve some of the above exercises without renaming before subtracting?

Choose the example that needs renaming. Explain how you decided.

25. a. $2\frac{1}{2} - \frac{1}{4}$
    b. $2\frac{1}{2} - \frac{5}{16}$
    c. $2\frac{1}{2} - \frac{5}{8}$

26. a. $3\frac{1}{4} - 1\frac{1}{16}$
    b. $3\frac{1}{4} - 1\frac{1}{8}$
    c. $3\frac{1}{4} - 1\frac{1}{3}$

27. a. $5\frac{5}{8} - 1\frac{3}{4}$
    b. $5\frac{5}{8} - 1\frac{3}{8}$
    c. $5\frac{5}{8} - 1\frac{1}{2}$

Problem Solving

28. Janet had a block of wood that was 6 inches high. She cut off $3\frac{3}{4}$ inches from its height to carve a sculpture. How high was the block that was left?

29. Bill wants to put a border around his painting. He needs $5\frac{1}{4}$ yards of wood molding. He has $2\frac{7}{8}$ yards. How much more molding does he need?

Pretend you are writing to an absent classmate. Explain how to subtract mixed numbers. Include an example that needs renaming.

Using Problem Solving

Strategy Game

The goal of this game is to force your opponent to complete a fraction strip that represents one whole. Think about a strategy for winning as you play the game.

Working together

Materials: fraction pieces: 1 whole, 2 halves, 3 thirds, 4 fourths, 6 sixths, and 12 twelfths

Follow these rules.

A. Player 1 starts the game and puts the one whole on the table.

B. Player 2 chooses a fraction piece and places it on the one whole.

C. Player 1 chooses a fraction piece and places it on the one whole next to Player 1's piece.

D. Players take turns choosing and playing. The person who plays the last fraction piece to cover the one whole loses.

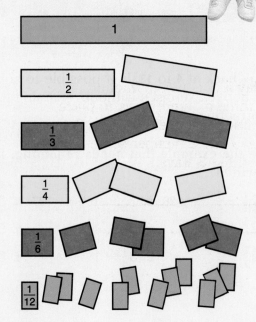

Sharing Your Ideas

1. How often did the last player cover up the one whole exactly? How often did the last player cover up more than the one whole?

2. What strategy did you use to make sure you won the game?

Practice

3. Play the strategy game again. This time, try to be the player who places the fraction piece that covers the one whole exactly.

4. Bill is playing the game. What fraction piece should he play to win? Choose from the game pieces below.

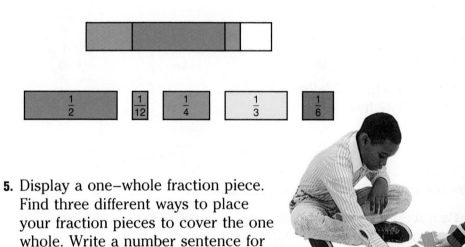

$\frac{1}{2}$ $\frac{1}{12}$ $\frac{1}{4}$ $\frac{1}{3}$ $\frac{1}{6}$

5. Display a one–whole fraction piece. Find three different ways to place your fraction pieces to cover the one whole. Write a number sentence for each of the 3 ways.

Summing Up

6. What did you do differently to try to win at this game?

7. Were you always able to cover the one whole exactly? Why or why not?

Chapter Review

Add or subtract. Write each answer in lowest terms. pages 316–323

1. $\frac{3}{8}$
$+\frac{3}{8}$

2. $\frac{2}{3}$
$+\frac{2}{3}$

3. $\frac{7}{9}$
$-\frac{2}{9}$

4. $\frac{9}{10}$
$-\frac{1}{10}$

5. $\frac{3}{4}$
$-\frac{1}{4}$

6. $\frac{2}{3}$
$+\frac{5}{6}$

7. $\frac{6}{7}$
$+\frac{1}{2}$

8. $\frac{3}{8}$
$-\frac{1}{4}$

9. $\frac{3}{4}$
$-\frac{1}{3}$

10. $\frac{7}{10}$
$+\frac{2}{5}$

Estimate each sum or difference. pages 324–325, 330–331

11. $\frac{4}{5}$
$+\frac{5}{6}$

12. $\frac{5}{8}$
$+\frac{1}{2}$

13. $\frac{1}{6}$
$+\frac{1}{3}$

14. $\frac{7}{8}$
$-\frac{1}{6}$

15. $\frac{9}{10}$
$-\frac{3}{8}$

16. $3\frac{1}{4} + 2\frac{7}{8}$

17. $6\frac{3}{8} + 5\frac{2}{5}$

18. $11\frac{2}{3} - 2\frac{3}{10}$

19. $6\frac{5}{6} - 2\frac{9}{10}$

Add. Write each answer in lowest terms. pages 332–333

20. $7\frac{1}{4}$
$+6\frac{5}{8}$

21. $9\frac{9}{10}$
$+1\frac{3}{5}$

22. $8\frac{2}{3}$
$+3\frac{4}{5}$

23. $6\frac{3}{8}$
$+7\frac{1}{4}$

24. $2\frac{2}{3}$
$+5\frac{1}{4}$

Subtract. Write each answer in lowest terms. pages 334–337

25. $7\frac{5}{6}$
$-3\frac{1}{3}$

26. $8\frac{1}{4}$
$-2\frac{5}{8}$

27. $4\frac{4}{5}$
$-2\frac{1}{10}$

28. $9\frac{2}{3}$
$-6\frac{1}{4}$

29. $12\frac{1}{8}$
$-5\frac{3}{4}$

Solve. pages 328–329, 336–337

30. George had $3\frac{3}{4}$ yards of wire for a metal sculpture. He cut off $1\frac{7}{8}$ yards. How much wire does he have left?

31. Sarah has a 48-inch length of plywood. She will cut a 12-inch length from it to use as a sign for her family's new house. Her dad will cut the rest into 2 equal parts to use for shelves in their new den. How long will each shelf be? Show two ways to solve this problem.

Chapter Test

Add or subtract. Write each answer in lowest terms.

1. $\begin{array}{r} \frac{2}{9} \\ + \frac{3}{9} \\ \hline \end{array}$

2. $\begin{array}{r} \frac{1}{8} \\ + \frac{5}{8} \\ \hline \end{array}$

3. $\begin{array}{r} \frac{7}{10} \\ - \frac{2}{10} \\ \hline \end{array}$

4. $\begin{array}{r} \frac{5}{6} \\ - \frac{1}{6} \\ \hline \end{array}$

5. $\begin{array}{r} \frac{1}{2} \\ + \frac{1}{4} \\ \hline \end{array}$

6. $\begin{array}{r} \frac{3}{4} \\ + \frac{1}{6} \\ \hline \end{array}$

7. $\begin{array}{r} \frac{9}{10} \\ - \frac{1}{2} \\ \hline \end{array}$

8. $\begin{array}{r} \frac{5}{8} \\ - \frac{1}{6} \\ \hline \end{array}$

Estimate each sum or difference.

9. $\begin{array}{r} \frac{1}{8} \\ + \frac{3}{4} \\ \hline \end{array}$

10. $\begin{array}{r} \frac{1}{2} \\ + \frac{1}{10} \\ \hline \end{array}$

11. $\begin{array}{r} \frac{8}{9} \\ - \frac{1}{3} \\ \hline \end{array}$

12. $\begin{array}{r} \frac{7}{8} \\ - \frac{1}{6} \\ \hline \end{array}$

13. $4\frac{1}{3} + 3\frac{1}{9}$

14. $8\frac{7}{10} + 1\frac{1}{5}$

15. $6\frac{7}{8} - 3\frac{1}{2}$

Add. Write each answer in lowest terms.

16. $\begin{array}{r} 1\frac{1}{6} \\ + 6\frac{3}{8} \\ \hline \end{array}$

17. $\begin{array}{r} 7\frac{2}{3} \\ + 4\frac{1}{6} \\ \hline \end{array}$

18. $\begin{array}{r} 5\frac{1}{2} \\ + 8\frac{3}{4} \\ \hline \end{array}$

19. $\begin{array}{r} 3\frac{5}{6} \\ + 4\frac{3}{10} \\ \hline \end{array}$

Subtract. Write each answer in lowest terms.

20. $\begin{array}{r} 5\frac{3}{4} \\ - 2\frac{1}{4} \\ \hline \end{array}$

21. $\begin{array}{r} 7\frac{5}{6} \\ - 1\frac{1}{2} \\ \hline \end{array}$

22. $\begin{array}{r} 8\frac{1}{10} \\ - 5\frac{1}{2} \\ \hline \end{array}$

23. $\begin{array}{r} 3\frac{3}{8} \\ - 1\frac{3}{4} \\ \hline \end{array}$

Solve.

24. Whitney had $4\frac{1}{2}$ yards of film. He cut off $1\frac{5}{6}$ yards. How much film does he have left?

25. Lila has 6 coins. Their total value is $.48. What coins does she have? Show two ways to solve this problem.

THINK Fill in the circles to make each sentence true. Use each fraction only once.

$\frac{1}{6}, \frac{5}{6}, \frac{1}{4}, \frac{3}{4}, \frac{1}{12}, \frac{7}{12}$

$\bigcirc + \bigcirc + \bigcirc = 1$

$\bigcirc + \bigcirc + \bigcirc = 1\frac{2}{3}$

EXTENSION

Musical Notes

Fractions are used to name symbols in music.

whole note ○ $\frac{1}{2}$ note ♩ or ♩

$\frac{1}{4}$ note ♩ or ♩ $\frac{1}{8}$ note ♪ or ♪

$\frac{1}{4}$ rest 𝄽 $\frac{1}{8}$ rest 𝄾

All the notes and rests in each measure of a song must have a sum of 1.

Look at the notes used by the composer in the first measure of this song.

Does the sum of the notes equal 1?

Math and Music

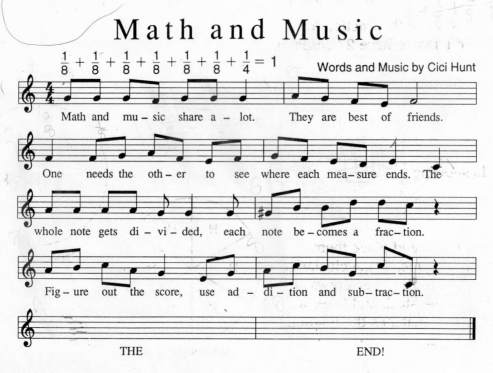

$$\frac{1}{8} + \frac{1}{8} + \frac{1}{8} + \frac{1}{8} + \frac{1}{8} + \frac{1}{8} + \frac{1}{4} = 1$$

Words and Music by Cici Hunt

Math and mu – sic share a – lot.   They are best of friends.

One   needs the oth – er   to   see where each mea – sure ends. The

whole note gets di – vi – ded,   each   note be – comes a   frac – tion.

Fig – ure out the score,   use ad – di – tion and sub – trac – tion.

THE   END!

1. Name the types of notes and rests for the remainder of the song.

2. Record the sum for each measure.

3. Create your own score for the last two measures.

342

Family Math

In Chapters 8-10 we studied how to multiply and divide decimals. We explored the meaning of fractions, and we learned how to add and subtract fractions.

Try this game with your family.

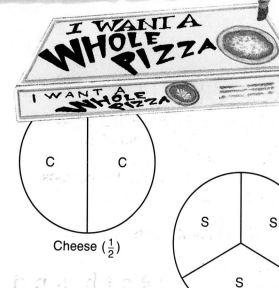

Object of Game

Each player tries to make a whole pizza with **three or more** different toppings. The player with the first whole pizza wins the game.

Materials

Trace each pizza and label them as shown. Cut out the slices of each pizza.

On index cards, write the fraction for each piece. You should have **27 cards** in all.

Cheese ($\frac{1}{2}$)

Sausage ($\frac{1}{3}$)

2 cards showing $\frac{1}{2}$

3 cards showing $\frac{1}{3}$

4 cards showing $\frac{1}{4}$

6 cards showing $\frac{1}{6}$

12 cards showing $\frac{1}{12}$

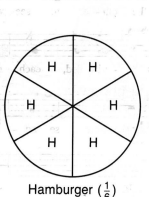

Pepperoni ($\frac{1}{4}$)

Rules

Mix the index cards and place them face down on the table. Going clockwise around the table, each player draws an index card from the stack and takes a piece of pizza that matches the fraction shown on the card.

Hamburger ($\frac{1}{6}$)

Take turns drawing cards. If you cannot use a card or do not want to use it, return the card to the stack. When a player makes a whole pizza, the game is over.

Remember, the pizza must have three or more different toppings.

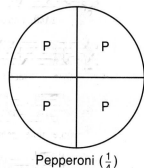

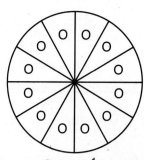

Onion ($\frac{1}{12}$)

Cumulative Review

Choose the correct answers. Write A, B, C, or D.

1. $462 \div 1{,}000$

    A 46,000   **C** 0.0462

    B 4.62   **D** not given

2. 4.2×6

    A 2.42   **C** 2.52

    B 25.2   **D** not given

3. 16.4
     $\times \ 6.2$

    A 68.68   **C** 101.68

    B 131.2   **D** not given

4. 6×0.02

    A 0.12   **C** 1.2

    B 0.012   **D** not given

5. $6.51 \div 7$

    A 0.93   **C** 97

    B 0.97   **D** not given

6. $7\overline{)21.14}$

    A 3.2   **C** 3.02

    B 3.05   **D** not given

7. $0.65 \text{ m} = \underline{\hspace{2em}} \text{ cm}$

    A 6.5   **C** 65

    B 0.065   **D** not given

8. Write a decimal for $\frac{3}{5}$.

    A 0.4   **C** 0.6

    B 0.35   **D** not given

9. $\frac{4}{5} = \frac{\square}{25}$

    A 20   **C** 22

    B 16   **D** not given

10. Write $\frac{7}{21}$ in lowest terms.

    A $\frac{1}{7}$ **C** $\frac{1}{4}$

    B $\frac{1}{3}$ **D** not given

11. Find the LCD of $\frac{2}{6}$ and $\frac{5}{8}$.

    A 16   **C** 48

    B 12   **D** not given

12. Choose the fraction closest to 1.

    A $\frac{8}{16}$ **C** $\frac{8}{9}$

    B $\frac{1}{2}$ **D** $\frac{2}{5}$

13. Compare. $\frac{6}{8}$ ⬤ $\frac{3}{4}$

    A $<$ **C** $=$

    B $>$ **D** not given

14. Write the improper fraction for $1\frac{7}{8}$.

    A $\frac{13}{8}$ **C** $\frac{17}{8}$

    B $\frac{15}{8}$ **D** not given

Choose the correct answers. Write A, B, C, or D.

15. $\frac{3}{8}$
$+ \frac{2}{8}$
_____

   A $\frac{7}{8}$ **B** $\frac{5}{16}$

   B $\frac{5}{8}$ **D** not given

16. $\frac{7}{9} - \frac{2}{3}$

   A $\frac{1}{9}$ **C** $\frac{5}{9}$

   B $\frac{5}{6}$ **D** not given

17. Estimate. $\frac{8}{9} + \frac{11}{13}$

   A $\frac{1}{2}$ **C** 2

   B 1   **D** not given

18. Estimate. $18\frac{5}{6} - 5\frac{1}{6}$

   A 15   **C** 8

   B 13   **D** 23

19. $15\frac{2}{3} + 12\frac{5}{6}$

   A $27\frac{7}{9}$ **C** $28\frac{1}{2}$

   B $27\frac{3}{4}$ **D** not given

20. $5\frac{1}{4} - 1\frac{2}{4}$

   A $4\frac{1}{4}$ **C** $4\frac{3}{4}$

   B $3\frac{1}{2}$ **D** not given

Solve.

21. Mr. Sands commutes to the city each day. The highway toll costs $1.25 each way and the bridge toll is $2.00 each way. How much does he spend on tolls in 5 days?

   A $16.25   **C** $3.25

   B $32.50   **D** not given

22. Marcia is cutting art letters for a bulletin board. She cuts 8 large letters on each of 4 sheets and 12 small letters on each of 2 sheets. How many letters did she cut out?

   A 20   **C** 56

   B 32   **D** not given

Use a drawing to solve.

23. Brendan's backyard fence is 172 feet from the house. The edge of the patio is $\frac{1}{8}$ the distance to the fence. The rock garden is 6 feet from the patio. How far is the rock garden from the house?

   A 21.5 ft   **C** 27.5 ft

   B 15.5   **D** not given

Solve.

24. Fran went to visit her mother at work. The elevator went up 5 floors, down 2, up 15, and down 3 floors. If Fran gets off here, what floor is this?

   A 15th   **C** 12th

   B 20th   **D** not given

Sharing What You Know

How do you weigh a wild dolphin? Scientist Randy Wells knows how. Randy has been studying one group of dolphins for 17 years. He uses nets, scales, tape measures, and photographs to gather data. What kind of measurements do you think he records? How would Randy compare data gathered year to year?

Using Language

Animals come in various sizes. A wild dolphin can weigh up to 1,400 pounds. A hummingbird may weigh only a few ounces. Pounds and ounces are both **customary units of measurement.** What other measurements would differ between a dolphin and a hummingbird? What other animals would have great differences in their measurements?

Words to Know: fraction, mixed number, numerator, denominator, customary units of measurement, inch, foot, yard, ounce, pound, ton, gallon

Be a Problem Solver

What if you owned a small dog that wouldn't sit on a scale? How could you weigh the dog?

Write about how you would measure the difference in weight between two small dogs.

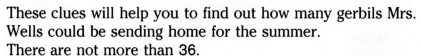

Exploring a Fraction of a Whole Number

These clues will help you to find out how many gerbils Mrs. Wells could be sending home for the summer.
There are not more than 36.

Susan will take $\frac{1}{2}$ of the gerbils.

Carlos will take $\frac{1}{3}$ of what is left.

Maria will take the rest.

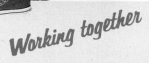
Working together

Experiment with counters.
Find different ways to solve the riddle.

Materials: counters

A. Suppose Mrs. Wells has 12 gerbils. Take 12 counters. Show $\frac{1}{2}$ of 12. How many gerbils will Susan take? Show $\frac{1}{3}$ of the remaining counters. How many gerbils will Carlos take? How many remain for Maria to take?

B. Use 18 counters. Find the number of gerbils each student would take home.

C. Experiment with 15 counters. Could Mrs. Wells have 15 gerbils? Explain.

D. Find other possible solutions for the number of gerbils in the class.

Sharing Your Results

1. How many gerbils could Mrs. Wells be sending home? Share several possible answers. Explain why each one is possible.

2. Give some numbers of gerbils that Mrs. Wells could not be sending home. Explain why each amount is impossible.

3. Explain how you would find $\frac{1}{2}$ of 24, and $\frac{1}{3}$ of 12 with counters.

4. Can you take $\frac{1}{2}$ of 17 gerbils? $\frac{1}{2}$ of 17 inches? $\frac{1}{2}$ of 17 apples? Explain.

Practice

To solve the riddle you needed to find a fraction of a whole number.

▶ Finding a fraction of a whole number is like multiplying a whole number by a fraction.

★★★★★★ ★★★★★★	★★★★ ★★★★ ★★★★ ★★★★	★★★ ★★★ ★★★ ★★★ ★★★
$\frac{1}{2}$ of 12 is 6.	$\frac{1}{4}$ of 16 is 4.	$\frac{2}{5}$ of 15 is 6.
$\frac{1}{2} \times 12 = 6$	$\frac{1}{4} \times 16 = 4$	$\frac{2}{5} \times 15 = 6$

Solve. Use counters or draw pictures.

5. $\frac{1}{2}$ of 16

6. $\frac{3}{4}$ of 16

7. $\frac{1}{3}$ of 12

8. $\frac{2}{3}$ of 24

9. $\frac{3}{5}$ of 15

10. $\frac{2}{3}$ of 21

11. $\frac{3}{4}$ of 24

12. $\frac{1}{5}$ of 25

Decide whether $\frac{1}{2}$ of each amount would be a whole number. Write yes or no.

13. 8

14. 9

15. 18

16. 13

Decide whether or not $\frac{1}{4}$ of each amount would be a whole number. Write yes or no.

17. 4

18. 10

19. 12

20. 9

Summing Up

21. Explain what it means to find a fraction of a whole number.

22. **What if** you want to take one fifth of a number and you want the result to be a whole number? What are some numbers you could choose and why?

If a pizza is cut into 8 equal slices, how many slices are in $\frac{1}{2}$ of the pizza? $\frac{1}{4}$ of the pizza? $\frac{1}{8}$ of the pizza?

Multiplying Fractions and Whole Numbers

Rabbits eat about $\frac{1}{4}$ of their weight in food every day. Would 20 ounces of food be enough to feed this rabbit?

You can multiply to find $\frac{1}{4}$ of 72 ounces.

$\frac{1}{4} \times 72 = n$

Step 1	Step 2	Step 3
Write the whole number as a fraction.	Multiply numerators. Multiply denominators.	Write the product in lowest terms.
$\frac{1}{4} \times \frac{72}{1}$	$\frac{1}{4} \times \frac{72}{1} = \frac{72}{4}$	$\frac{72}{4} = 18$

The rabbit eats about 18 ounces of food daily. So 20 ounces of food would be enough.

Another Example

$\frac{1}{2} \times 37 = n$

Step 1

Write the whole number as a fraction.

$\frac{1}{2} \times \frac{37}{1}$

Step 2

Multiply numerators. Multiply denominators.

$\frac{1}{2} \times \frac{37}{1} = \frac{37}{2}$

Step 3

Write the product in lowest terms.

$\frac{37}{2} = 18\frac{1}{2}$

Check Your Understanding

Multiply. Write each product in lowest terms. Use models or drawings if you wish.

1. $\frac{2}{3} \times 18$ 2. $\frac{3}{8} \times 8$ 3. $16 \times \frac{5}{8}$ 4. $\frac{3}{4} \times 24$ 5. $\frac{1}{4} \times 13$

Share Your Ideas   When multiplying a fraction and a whole number, how can you tell whether the answer will be a whole number or a mixed number?

Practice

Multiply. Write each product in lowest terms. Use models or drawings if you wish.

6. $\frac{1}{3} \times 27$

7. $\frac{1}{2} \times 19$

8. $\frac{3}{4} \times 28$

9. $25 \times \frac{2}{5}$

10. $\frac{3}{4} \times 0$

11. $27 \times \frac{1}{2}$

12. $\frac{1}{6} \times 20$

13. $1 \times \frac{3}{5}$

14. $\frac{5}{6} \times 27$

15. $\frac{5}{8} \times \$32$

16. $\frac{1}{2} \times 40 \times \frac{1}{2}$

17. $\frac{1}{2} \times 20 \times \frac{1}{4}$

Multiply. Use mental math or paper and pencil. Write each product in lowest terms.

18. $\frac{1}{2} \times 19 = n$

19. $\frac{2}{3} \times 20 = n$

20. $45 \times \frac{3}{5} = n$

21. $\frac{3}{4} \times 15 = n$

22. $\frac{1}{6} \times 20 = n$

23. $\frac{1}{3} \times 170 = n$

24. $\frac{3}{4} \times 16 = n$

25. $\frac{1}{8} \times 72 = n$

Problem Solving

Give the number of months in each fraction of a year.

26. $\frac{1}{6}$

27. $\frac{2}{3}$

28. $\frac{7}{12}$

29. $\frac{3}{4}$

Give the number of minutes in each fraction of an hour.

30. $\frac{1}{3}$

31. $\frac{1}{4}$

32. $\frac{2}{3}$

33. $\frac{3}{10}$

Solve.

34. Sally has 35 pet rabbits for sale. One fifth of them are spotted. The rest are red. How many are red?

Describe a situation in everyday life where someone might need to find a fraction of a whole number.

Mixed Review

1. $\begin{array}{r} 8.4 \\ +0.7 \end{array}$

2. $\begin{array}{r} 34.5 \\ +\ 9.15 \end{array}$

3. $\begin{array}{r} 56.254 \\ -30.065 \end{array}$

4. $\begin{array}{r} 22.6 \\ -19.142 \end{array}$

5. 5.89×100

6. $5.6 \div 16$

7. 9×0.7

8. 1.6×0.3

9. $4.5 \div 10$

10. $\frac{3}{4} + \frac{1}{6}$

11. $\frac{1}{2} + \frac{2}{5}$

12. $\frac{5}{6} - \frac{1}{2}$

13. $\frac{7}{12} - \frac{1}{4}$

Tell whether each fraction is closer to 0, $\frac{1}{2}$, or 1.

14. $\frac{5}{8}$

15. $\frac{5}{12}$

16. $\frac{3}{8}$

17. $\frac{1}{12}$

Write each fraction in lowest terms.

18. $\frac{12}{15}$

19. $\frac{6}{8}$

20. $\frac{9}{12}$

21. $\frac{10}{15}$

SUMMING UP

Exploring Multiplication of Fractions

A pet store manager uses $\frac{1}{2}$ of the counter to display cages with singing birds. She uses $\frac{3}{4}$ of that space for canaries. How much of the total counter space is used for canaries?

Working together

You can find $\frac{3}{4}$ of $\frac{1}{2}$ by folding paper.

Materials: paper, grid paper, ruler

A. Show $\frac{1}{2}$ by folding your paper in half, as shown. Open the paper and shade $\frac{1}{2}$ of it.

B. To find $\frac{3}{4}$ of $\frac{1}{2}$, take the folded paper and fold it in half in the opposite direction. Then fold it in half lengthwise.

C. Open the paper. Find 4 parts in the shaded half. Outline this section. Draw lines on 3 of the 4 parts.

Your paper should look like this.

Sharing Your Results

1. What is the total number of sections formed by the folds?

2. What part of the whole paper is shaded?

3. What part of the shaded area has lines drawn on it?

4. What part of the whole paper has lines on it?

5. Think of the whole piece of paper as the whole counter. Explain how you can use this model to show what part of the whole counter is used for canaries.

Practice

Use grid paper to show $\frac{4}{5}$ of $\frac{1}{3}$.

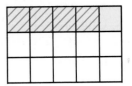

6. Draw a rectangle with a length of 5 units and a width of 3 units.

7. Shade $\frac{1}{3}$ of the rectangle.

8. Draw lines on $\frac{4}{5}$ of the shaded area.

9. Find what fractional part of the whole rectangle has lines drawn on it.

▶ You can use multiplication to find a fraction of a fraction.

Fraction of a fraction	Multiplication	Result	
$\frac{4}{5}$ of $\frac{1}{3}$	$\frac{4}{5} \times \frac{1}{3}$	$\frac{4}{15}$	Compare this result with your drawing.

Use paper folding or a drawing to show each multiplication. Complete the table.

	Fraction of a fraction	Multiplication	Result
10.	$\frac{1}{4}$ of $\frac{1}{2}$		
11.	$\frac{1}{2}$ of $\frac{3}{5}$		
12.	$\frac{1}{2}$ of $\frac{5}{6}$		
13.	$\frac{2}{3}$ of $\frac{1}{5}$		

Summing Up

14. How are the numerators of the two original fractions related to the numerator in the product?

15. How are the denominators of the two original fractions related to the denominator in the product?

16. Describe a rule that you could use to multiply two fractions. Does your rule work for $\frac{1}{3} \times \frac{2}{3}$?

Suppose you get $\frac{1}{2}$ of a pizza and you eat $\frac{3}{4}$ of the $\frac{1}{2}$. Make a drawing to show what part of the whole pizza you eat.

Multiplying Fractions

One half of the barnyard is used for cows. One fourth of the remaining barnyard is used for pigs.

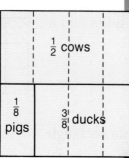

	$\frac{1}{2}$ cows	
$\frac{1}{8}$ pigs	$\frac{3}{8}$ ducks	

Use the drawing to explain why $\frac{1}{4}$ of $\frac{1}{2} = \frac{1}{8}$ of the whole barnyard.

You can multiply to find $\frac{1}{4}$ of $\frac{1}{2}$.

Step 1	**Step 2**
Multiply the numerators.	Multiply the denominators.
$\frac{1}{4} \times \frac{1}{2} = \frac{1}{}$	$\frac{1}{4} \times \frac{1}{2} = \frac{1}{8}$

$\frac{1}{8}$ of the whole barnyard is used for pigs.

What two fractions would you multiply to show the part of the barnyard used for ducks? Explain.

Another Example

$\frac{3}{8} \times \frac{2}{3} = \frac{6}{24}$

$\frac{6}{24} = \frac{1}{4}$ Write the product in lowest terms.

Check Your Understanding

Multiply. Write each product in lowest terms. Use models or drawings if you wish.

1. $\frac{2}{3} \times \frac{1}{2}$ 2. $\frac{1}{2} \times \frac{7}{8}$ 3. $\frac{1}{3} \times \frac{2}{3}$ 4. $\frac{1}{2} \times \frac{3}{5}$ 5. $\frac{2}{3} \times \frac{3}{5}$

Share Your Ideas   Is the product of two fractions that are both less than 1 always less than one and greater than zero?

Multiply. Write each product in lowest terms. Use models or drawings if you wish.

6. $\frac{1}{2} \times \frac{3}{8}$ 7. $\frac{3}{4} \times \frac{1}{6}$ 8. $\frac{1}{6} \times \frac{1}{2}$ 9. $\frac{2}{3} \times \frac{1}{6}$ 10. $\frac{3}{4} \times \frac{1}{3}$

11. $\frac{1}{2} \times \frac{1}{5}$ 12. $\frac{2}{3} \times \frac{5}{6}$ 13. $\frac{1}{2} \times \frac{5}{8}$ 14. $\frac{1}{2} \times \frac{2}{5}$ 15. $\frac{2}{7} \times \frac{1}{8}$

16. $\frac{3}{4} \times \frac{1}{4}$ 17. $\frac{5}{6} \times \frac{1}{2}$ 18. $\frac{3}{8} \times \frac{1}{6}$ 19. $\frac{1}{5} \times \frac{2}{5}$ 20. $\frac{7}{8} \times \frac{3}{4}$

21. $\frac{1}{8} \times \frac{1}{5}$ 22. $\frac{2}{5} \times \frac{1}{6}$ 23. $\frac{1}{4} \times \frac{1}{5}$ 24. $\frac{6}{7} \times \frac{1}{9}$ 25. $\frac{3}{7} \times \frac{3}{5}$

26. $\frac{3}{4} \times \frac{5}{6}$ 27. $\frac{1}{2} \times \frac{4}{5}$ 28. $\frac{1}{3} \times \frac{3}{8}$ 29. $\frac{2}{3} \times \frac{3}{4}$ 30. $\frac{1}{3} \times \frac{1}{3} \times \frac{1}{3}$

Find each missing fraction.

31. $\frac{\square}{\square} \times \frac{1}{2} = \frac{1}{8}$ 32. $\frac{\square}{\square} \times \frac{3}{5} = \frac{9}{25}$ 33. $\frac{\square}{\square} \times \frac{3}{5} = \frac{1}{5}$

Problem Solving

34. **What if** $\frac{1}{2}$ of the barnyard is used for horses and $\frac{2}{3}$ of the remaining half is used for chickens? Make a drawing to show this situation. What part of the barnyard is used for chickens?

35. Suppose you and your friends eat half of a $\frac{3}{4}$-pound bag of peanuts. What part of a pound of peanuts have you eaten? Make a drawing to explain your answer.

Visual Thinking

Each drawing shows $\frac{1}{2}$ of an original shape. Make drawings of two possible original shapes for each.

36.   37.   38.

What if each drawing shows $\frac{2}{3}$ of an original shape? What could be the original shape?

How is multiplying $\frac{1}{5} \times \frac{1}{2}$ like multiplying 0.2×0.5? How is it different?

SUMMING UP

Midchapter Review

Find *n*. Write each product in lowest terms. pages 348–349; 352–353

1.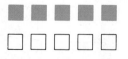

$\frac{1}{3}$ of 15 = n

2.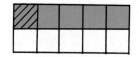

$\frac{1}{5}$ of $\frac{1}{2}$ = n

3.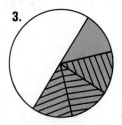

$\frac{3}{4}$ of $\frac{1}{2}$ = n

Find *n*. Write each product in lowest terms. pages 348–355

4. $\frac{4}{6}$ of \$24 = n **5.** $\frac{1}{2}$ of $\frac{2}{3}$ = n **6.** $\frac{3}{8}$ of 12 = n **7.** $\frac{2}{3}$ of $\frac{3}{4}$ = n

8. $\frac{3}{4}$ of $\frac{5}{8}$ = n **9.** $\frac{1}{5}$ of 25 = n **10.** $\frac{2}{5}$ of $\frac{1}{4}$ = n **11.** $\frac{2}{5}$ of \$40 = n

Multiply. Write each product in lowest terms. pages 348–355

12. $\frac{3}{5} \times 10$ **13.** $\frac{1}{2} \times \frac{5}{7}$ **14.** $\frac{3}{4} \times \frac{8}{9}$ **15.** $\frac{1}{5} \times \frac{2}{3}$

16. $\frac{2}{20} \times 60$ **17.** $\frac{3}{7} \times 5$ **18.** $53 \times \frac{1}{2}$ **19.** $\frac{4}{6} \times \frac{6}{7}$

20. $33 \times \frac{3}{8}$ **21.** $\frac{1}{7} \times 30$ **22.** $\frac{4}{5} \times \frac{5}{9}$ **23.** $\frac{2}{9} \times 60$

Give the number of months in each fraction of a year. pages 350–351

24. $\frac{4}{12}$ **25.** $\frac{1}{6}$ **26.** $\frac{1}{4}$ **27.** $\frac{2}{3}$

Give the number of minutes in each fraction of an hour. pages 350–351

28. $\frac{2}{5}$ **29.** $\frac{4}{10}$ **30.** $\frac{1}{4}$ **31.** $\frac{1}{3}$

Solve.

32. Nadia has 20 pets. Of the pets, $\frac{2}{5}$ are rabbits, $\frac{1}{2}$ are fish, and $\frac{1}{10}$ are dogs. How many of each does she have?

33. Nadia earned \$40. She saved $\frac{1}{4}$ of it. She plans to donate $\frac{1}{2}$ of what she saved to a charity. How much will she donate?

Exploring Problem Solving

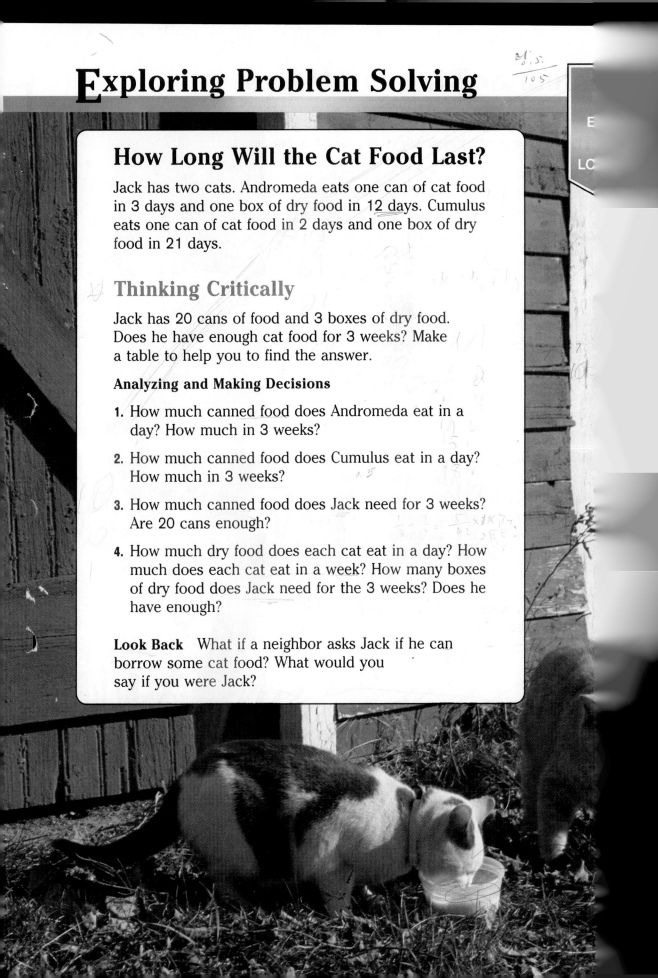

How Long Will the Cat Food Last?

Jack has two cats. Andromeda eats one can of cat food in 3 days and one box of dry food in 12 days. Cumulus eats one can of cat food in 2 days and one box of dry food in 21 days.

Thinking Critically

Jack has 20 cans of food and 3 boxes of dry food. Does he have enough cat food for 3 weeks? Make a table to help you to find the answer.

Analyzing and Making Decisions

1. How much canned food does Andromeda eat in a day? How much in 3 weeks?

2. How much canned food does Cumulus eat in a day? How much in 3 weeks?

3. How much canned food does Jack need for 3 weeks? Are 20 cans enough?

4. How much dry food does each cat eat in a day? How much does each cat eat in a week? How many boxes of dry food does Jack need for the 3 weeks? Does he have enough?

Look Back What if a neighbor asks Jack if he can borrow some cat food? What would you say if you were Jack?

Problem Solving Strategies

Working Backwards

Lincoln School held a tag sale to raise money for the animal shelter, the wildlife fund, and the park fund. The wildlife fund was to receive $\frac{1}{3}$ of the money, the park fund was to receive $\frac{1}{6}$ of the money, and the animal shelter was to receive the rest. The animal shelter received $90. How much did the wildlife fund receive?

A good plan for solving some problems is to start with some given information and then work backwards.

Solving the Problem

Think   What is the question?

Explore   What fraction of the money was the park fund to receive? the wildlife fund? How can you figure out what fraction of the money the animal shelter was to receive? What fraction of the money did the animal shelter receive? How much money was raised altogether? How can you find out how much money the wildlife fund received?

Solve   How much money did the wildlife fund receive?

Look Back   How can you check your answer?

Share Your Ideas

1. **What if** we did not know how much the wildlife fund or the animal shelter received, but we did know that the park fund received $20? How much would each group have received?

Practice

Solve. Use a calculator where appropriate.

2. Janice sold her old bowling ball at the tag sale. Two dollars of the money she received went to the wildlife fund. Since the wildlife fund received $\frac{1}{3}$ of the money, what was the price of the bowling ball?

3. Janice could not sell her old doll house, so she took $9 off the price. That was $\frac{1}{3}$ off. What was the original price?

4. Bill spent $3 at the tag sale. This was $\frac{1}{2}$ the amount that his old book raised for the wildlife fund. How much did his old book sell for? Remember that the wildlife fund received $\frac{1}{3}$ of the money.

5. Mike sold animal paintings at the tag sale. He sold half as many bird paintings as dog paintings. He sold 6 fewer dog paintings than cat paintings. He sold 16 cat paintings. How many of each kind did he sell?

Mixed Strategy Review

6. The class needed to set up five tables for the tag sale. The classroom was 20 feet by 30 feet. Each table was 6 feet long and 3 feet wide. Draw a picture to show how the tables might have been arranged so that each table had plenty of room around it.

7. There were postcards at one booth. They were priced at $.30 each or two for $.50. How much would 7 postcards cost?

8. The school wants to raise at least $20 for the park fund. Since $\frac{1}{3}$ of all the money goes to the park fund, how much money will they have to raise to make that goal?

9. The tag sale lasted from 10:00 A.M. to 6:00 P.M. Last year it was only $\frac{3}{4}$ as long. If it started at 10:00 A.M. last year, when was it over?

Create **Your Own**

Write a problem about raising money for the animal shelter, wildlife fund, and park fund.

Place 2 chairs near each other. Move them until everyone agrees that they are about 6 feet apart. Then check your estimate by measuring.

Estimating and Measuring Length

When a kangaroo moves slowly, it hops about 6 feet at a time. When it moves quickly, a kangaroo can cover 10 yards in one jump.

Could a speeding kangaroo jump across your classroom in a single bound?

The **inch (in.)**, the **foot (ft)**, the **yard (yd)**, and the **mile (mi)** are standard units of length in the customary system of measurement.

Estimate each of the following and then use a ruler to measure.

A. height of your desk, to the nearest inch

B. width of your desk, to the nearest $\frac{1}{2}$ inch

C. length of your shoe, to the nearest $\frac{1}{4}$ inch

D. width of your math book, to the nearest $\frac{1}{8}$ inch

E. diameter of a nickel, to the nearest $\frac{1}{16}$ inch

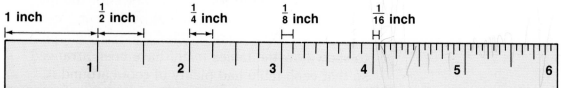

Choose inch, foot, yard, or mile to measure each.

1. width of a window

2. distance from New York City to Chicago

3. width of your classroom

4. length of a soccer field

Share Your Ideas   Compare your answers to **D** and **E** above with those of your classmates. Did your estimates vary greatly? Did your measurements agree? Discuss.

Choose inch, foot, yard, or mile to measure each.

5. length of a cat's tail   6. height of the ceiling

7. jogging distance   8. width of a picture frame

9. length of the playground   10. distance to Mexico City

Choose the most reasonable measurement.

11. height of a house	a. 24 in.	b. 24 ft	c. 24 yd
12. diameter of a frying pan	a. 10 in.	b. 10 ft	c. 10 yd
13. length of an ant	a. $\frac{1}{2}$ in.	b. $\frac{1}{2}$ ft	c. $\frac{1}{2}$ yd
14. height of a TV screen	a. 12 in.	b. 12 ft	c. 12 yd
15. distance to the moon	a. 239,000 ft	b. 239,000 yd	c. 239,000 mi
16. length of a car	a. 16 in.	b. 16 ft	c. 16 yd

Estimate, then measure the distance around each polygon.

17.

18.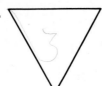

19.

20.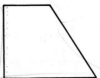

Problem Solving

 Be a detective. Find an item in your classroom for each item below. List the items. Then find and record their actual measurements.

21. 10 in.   22. $1\frac{1}{2}$ ft   23. 4 ft

24. 1 in.   25. 7 ft   26. 1 yd

Describe how you would estimate the length of the classroom in feet.

SUMMING UP

> Would measuring an object in feet or in yards give you the greater number? Why?

Relating Units of Length

The zoo moves animals in a special cage. It is 192 inches long. Will a 15–foot rhinoceros fit in the cage?

12 inches (in.) = 1 foot (ft)
3 feet = 1 yard (yd)
36 inches = 1 yard
5,280 feet = 1 mile (mi)

The Rhinoceros

The Rhino is a homely beast,
For human eyes he's not a feast.
But you and I will never know
Why Nature chose to make him so.
Farewell, farewell, you old rhinoceros,
I'll stare at something less prepoceros.

Ogden Nash

To change units of length, use the table.

▶ To change to a smaller unit, multiply. Why?

15 ft = _____ in.
Think 1 ft = 12 in.
$$15 \times 12 = 180$$
$$15 \text{ ft} = 180 \text{ in.}$$

▶ To change to a larger unit, divide. Why?

15 ft = _____ yd
Think 3 ft = 1 yd
$$15 \div 3 = 5$$
$$15 \text{ ft} = 5 \text{ yd}$$

The rhinoceros will fit. 180 in. < 192 in.

More Examples

a. 51 ft = _____ yd
3 ft = 1 yd
$$51 \div 3 = 17$$
$$51 \text{ ft} = 17 \text{ yd}$$

b. $\frac{1}{2}$ yd = _____ in.
1 yd = 36 in.
$$\frac{1}{2} \times 36 = 18$$
$$\frac{1}{2} \text{ yd} = 18 \text{ in.}$$

c. 2 mi = _____ ft
1 mi = 5,280 ft
$$2 \times 5,280 = 10,560$$
$$2 \text{ mi} = 10,560 \text{ ft}$$

Check Your Understanding

Complete.

1. _____ in. = 4 ft
2. 3 yd = _____ in.
3. $\frac{1}{4}$ mi = _____ ft
4. 48 ft = _____ yd
5. _____ ft = 30 in.
6. 54 in. = _____ yd

Share Your Ideas What unit of measure is based on a multiple of 12 in.? What unit of measure describes a multiple of 3 ft?

Practice

Complete.

7. _____ in. = 2 ft

8. 12 ft = _____ yd

9. _____ ft = 7 yd

10. 3 mi = _____ ft

11. _____ yd = 90 in.

12. 6 in. = _____ ft

13. _____ in. = 4 yd

14. 18 in. = _____ ft

15. _____ ft = $\frac{2}{3}$ mi

16. $\frac{1}{3}$ ft = _____ in.

17. _____ ft = 8 in.

18. $\frac{2}{3}$ yd = _____ ft

19. _____ in. = 1 ft 3 in.

20. 1 yd 2 ft = _____ ft

21. _____ in. = 1 yd 7 in.

22. _____ in. = $1\frac{3}{4}$ ft

23. $3\frac{1}{2}$ yd = _____ in.

24. _____ yd = 1 mi

Complete. Follow the rule to find each output.

Rule: Change to yards.

	Input	Output
25.	24 ft	
26.	9 ft	
27.	5 ft	

Rule: Change to feet.

	Input	Output
28.	6 yd	
29.	3 yd	
30.	$2\frac{1}{3}$ yd	

Rule: Change to inches.

	Input	Output
31.	5 ft	
32.	3 yd	
33.	$10\frac{1}{2}$ ft	

Is each measurement a whole number of feet? Write yes or no. Use mental math, paper and pencil, or calculator. Explain your choices.

34. 2 yd

35. 30 in.

36. 17 yd

37. 324 in.

38. $\frac{1}{2}$ yd

39. 360 in.

40. 180 in.

41. 60 in.

42. $\frac{1}{3}$ yd

43. 600 in.

44. $\frac{2}{3}$ yd

45. 54 in.

46. 148 in.

47. 216 in.

48. 250 in.

Problem Solving

49. If you could safely watch a rhinoceros from one of these distances, which would offer the closest view?

    a. $\frac{1}{8}$ mi   b. 220 yd   c. 300 ft

50. The zoo has half as many rhinos as elephants. There are 6 more elephants than giraffes. If there are 8 giraffes, how many rhinos are there?

Logical Thinking

51. The longest recorded jump for a horse is 5 feet less than that for a kangaroo and $34\frac{1}{2}$ feet more than that for a grasshopper.

    The grasshopper's longest recorded jump is 30 inches.

    How many yards is the kangaroo's longest jump?

Describe in your own words how you would change $3\frac{1}{2}$ yards to inches.

SUMMING UP

Estimating and Measuring Weight

About how many pennies weigh a pound?
Find out. Then use your findings to estimate
the weights of other objects.

Working together

Materials: balance scale, 4 rolls of pennies

A. Ten pennies weigh about 1 ounce. Hold 10 pennies in your hand and feel their weight. Find other classroom objects that weigh about an ounce.

B. Place the 10 pennies on one side of a balance scale. Then place each object that you found, one at a time, on the other side of the scale. Record your findings in a chart like the one shown.

C. 16 ounces equal 1 pound. Combine your pennies so you have enough to weigh about 1 pound.

D. Find some objects that seem to weigh about a pound. Weigh each on the balance scale using the pennies. Record your findings.

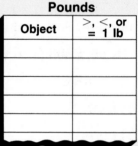

| Ounces | | Pounds | |
Object	>, <, or = 1 oz	Object	>, <, or = 1 lb
Pencil	<		

Sharing Your Results

Compare your findings with those of other groups.

1. How many ounces are in a pound? About how many pennies are in a pound?

2. Make class lists of things that weigh close to an ounce and close to a pound.

Practice

The **ounce (oz), pound (lb),** and **ton (T)** are customary units of weight.

16 ounces (oz) = 1 pound (lb)
2,000 pounds = 1 ton (T)

To change units of weight, use the table.

▶ To change to a smaller unit, multiply.

3 lb = _____ oz

Think 1 lb = 16 oz

$3 \times 16 = 48$

3 lb = 48 oz

▶ To change to a larger unit, divide.

6,000 lb = _____ T

Think 2,000 lb = 1 T

$6,000 \div 2,000 = 3$

6,000 lb = 3 T

More Examples

a. 3 lb 2 oz = _____ oz

1 lb = 16 oz

$(3 \times 16) + 2 = 50$

3 lb 2 oz = 50 oz

b. _____ oz = $\frac{3}{4}$ lb

16 oz = 1 lb

$\frac{3}{4} \times 16 = \frac{48}{4} = 12$

12 oz = $\frac{3}{4}$ lb

c. $\frac{1}{2}$ T = _____ lb

1 T = 2,000 lb

$\frac{1}{2} \times 2,000 = 1,000$

$\frac{1}{2}$ T = 1,000 lb

Complete.

3. _____ oz = $\frac{1}{4}$ lb

4. 3 lb = _____ oz

5. _____ lb = $\frac{1}{4}$ T

6. $\frac{3}{4}$ T = _____ lb

7. _____ lb = 24 oz

8. _____ lb = 2 T 500 lb

9. 1 lb 8 oz = _____ oz

10. $1\frac{3}{4}$ lb = _____ oz

11. $2\frac{1}{5}$ T = _____ lb

Summing Up

Choose the most reasonable estimate for the weight of each. Compare choices with others and discuss any differences.

12. a letter
   a. 1.5 ounces
   b. 1.5 pounds
   c. 1.5 tons

13. a dog
   a. 20 ounces
   b. 20 pounds
   c. 20 tons

14. a gorilla
   a. 500 ounces
   b. 500 pounds
   c. 500 tons

15. an elephant
   a. 2,000 ounces
   b. 2,000 pounds
   c. 2,000 tons

16. Write an activity similar to **12–15** above. Use four of the objects that you weighed earlier. Display the activity on the bulletin board.

Estimate the size of some containers in your classroom. Can you find containers that look like they may hold 1, 2, 3, or 4 cups? Label them.

Estimating and Measuring Capacity

Bob knows that it takes $7\frac{1}{2}$ pints of varnish to cover the seal's diving platform. What size container of varnish should he buy?

1 cup

1 pint

1 quart

1 half gallon

1 gallon

The **fluid ounce (fl oz), cup (c), pint (pt), quart (qt),** and **gallon (gal)** are customary units of capacity.

8 fluid ounces	= 1 cup (c)
2 cups	= 1 pint (pt)
2 pints	= 1 quart (qt)
2 quarts	= 1 half gallon ($\frac{1}{2}$ gal)
4 quarts	= 1 gallon (gal)

Bob needs $7\frac{1}{2}$ pints of varnish. He could buy 8 pints, 4 quarts, 2 half gallons, or 1 gallon. Explain which size container you think Bob should choose.

To change units of capacity, use the table.

▶ To change to a smaller unit, multiply.

3 gal = _____ qt

Think 1 gal = 4 qt

3 × 4 = 12

3 gal = 12 qt

▶ To change to a larger unit, divide.

16 c = _____ qt

Think 4 c = 1 qt

16 ÷ 4 = 4

16 c = 4 qt

Complete.

1. 13 gal = _____ qt   **2.** _____ qt = 3 c   **3.** 8 pt = _____ $\frac{1}{2}$ gal

Share Your Ideas Sally bought a quart of detergent and used some for cleaning the food pails. Study the picture and estimate how many cups she has left.

Complete.

4. _____ c = 10 pt

5. 16 fl oz = _____ c

6. _____ pt = 9 qt

7. 12 c = _____ pt

8. _____ pt = 5 c

9. 3 c = _____ fl oz

10. _____ qt = 24 pt

11. 36 pt = _____ gal

12. _____ gal = 6 qt

13. $3\frac{1}{2}$ gal = _____ qt

14. $3\frac{1}{2}$ c = _____ fl oz

15. $24\frac{1}{2}$ qt = _____ gal

Choose cup, pint, quart, or gallon to measure each.

16. paint for a house

17. gas to fill a car's tank

18. milk for four

19. juice for eight

Find the number of quarts for each. Use mental math, paper and pencil, or calculator. Explain your choices.

CHOICES

20. $2\frac{1}{2}$ gal

21. 3,000 gal

22. 3,765 gal

23. 20 pt

24. 36 pt

25. 480 pt

26. 8 gal

27. $\frac{3}{4}$ gal

28. 10 gal

Problem Solving

29. Sally and Bob feed 12 harbor seals. They bring them 3 gallons of small fish. How many quarts of fish are there for each seal?

30. **What if** Sally bought 18 gallons of fish for the seals? How many quarts is this for each seal?

31. What capacity can be doubled to get a quart? a $\frac{1}{2}$ gallon? a gallon? What pattern do you find?

Guess Your Best Work in a small group to estimate and measure. You will need 3 milk or juice cartons in cup ($\frac{1}{2}$ pint), pint, and quart sizes with tops removed; several small jars, bottles, or cans; water or dried beans for measuring.

DATA

32. Choose a small container and estimate its capacity. Then measure and record its capacity using the standard cartons. Was your estimate close? Repeat this activity with 3 more containers.

Describe in your own words how you would change 33 pints to gallons.

SUMMING UP

Exploring Fahrenheit Temperature

How hot is water from the hot–water faucet?
How cold is water from the cold–water faucet?
How cold can you make ice water? Let's find out.

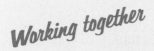
Working together

Materials: Fahrenheit thermometer, plastic container, ice cubes, water

A. First experiment with hot water. Let the faucet run for a few seconds before filling the container.

B. Place the base of the thermometer in the center of the container. Read the thermometer when the temperature has stopped rising. Record your finding.

C. Empty the container and repeat the activity with cold water from the faucet. Record your finding.

D. Empty the container again and half fill it with ice. Fill it the rest of the way with cold water.

E. Stir the contents for a few minutes. Read the thermometer when the temperature has stopped falling. Record your finding.

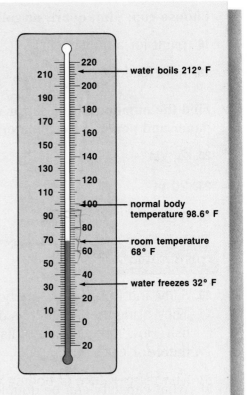

water boils 212° F

normal body temperature 98.6° F

room temperature 68° F

water freezes 32° F

Sharing Your Results

1. Compare your results with those of other groups. Explain why there may be some differences.

Choose the most likely temperature for each.

2. a hot shower   **a.** 115°F   **b.** 70°F   **c.** 50°F

3. frozen yogurt   **a.** 32°F   **b.** 15°F   **c.** ⁻10°F

Practice

Copy and complete the chart. You may use the thermometer on page 368.

	Starting Temperature	Change	Final Temperature
4.	55°F	+ 10°F	
5.	95°F	− 25°F	
6.	22°F		79°F
7.	10°F		⁻2°F
8.	⁻4°F		6°F
9.		+ 15°F	5°F

Tell whether each temperature is cold, comfortable, or hot.

10. 30°F   **11.** 98°F   **12.** 32°F   **13.** 68°F

14. 0°F   **15.** − 15°F   **16.** 75°F   **17.** 105°F

Complete.

18. The temperature of boiling water is _____.

19. Pat's temperature is 2°F above normal. It is _____.

20. When Ralph's temperature returns to normal from 101.2°F, it will have dropped _____ .

Summing Up

What is the normal range of temperatures for your home town in January? in July? Discuss and come to an agreement about the high and low temperatures that you expect to occur in those months. Check the class estimates with an almanac or a local weather authority.

Using Problem Solving

Which Way Should He Go?

Bill Burrell has a string of lobster traps offshore. The diagram shows where the traps are located.

Bill runs his boat from the shore to trap **A**. From there he goes to the rest of the traps and returns to trap **A** before returning to the shore.

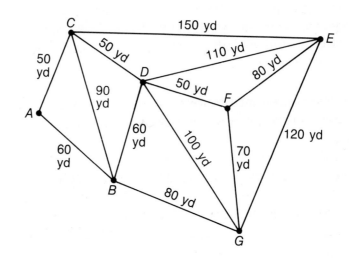

Working together

Materials: paper for making diagrams

Try several routes for checking all the traps. Find the route which has the shortest total distance.

Sharing Your Ideas

1. Compare different routes to visit all the traps. What similarities do you notice?

2. What did you find to be the shortest route?

370

Practice

3. Sometimes the route between traps D and F is dangerous because of strong currents. Determine the best route for visiting the traps while avoiding the route between D and F.

4. Pick one route that cannot be used. Challenge a partner to find the best route without using that route.

5. **What if** there was a dock where Bill could sell his lobsters close to the trap at point E? Now Bill would need to visit point A first and point E last. Show how he could do that. How long would that trip be? Make a diagram.

Summing Up

6. In 3, what changes did you have to make on your route to avoid the route D to F? How much distance did it add to your total trip?

7. How did you change your route when you ended up at point E? Was this route shorter or longer than the route from A to all the traps and then back to A? Explain why you think this happened.

Chapter Review

Find _n_. Write each product in lowest terms. pages 348–355

1. $\frac{2}{3}$ of $\frac{3}{4} = n$

2. $16 \times \frac{3}{8} = n$

3. $\frac{3}{16} \times \frac{2}{4} = n$

4. $\frac{1}{4} \times \frac{3}{4} = n$

5. $\frac{1}{6}$ of $36 = n$

6. $10 \times \frac{1}{2} = n$

7. $\frac{1}{4}$ of $32 = n$

8. $\frac{2}{3} \times \frac{4}{5} = n$

9. $40 \times \frac{2}{8} = n$

10. $\frac{1}{6}$ of $24 = n$

11. $\frac{2}{7}$ of $\frac{9}{10} = n$

12. $\frac{1}{2} \times \frac{3}{5} = n$

Multiply. Write each product in lowest terms. pages 348–355

13. $\frac{1}{2}$ of 20

14. $\frac{1}{6} \times 30$

15. $\frac{1}{5} \times 45$

16. 32×4

17. $5 \times \frac{1}{5}$

18. $\frac{3}{5} \times 15

19. $\frac{1}{2}$ of 47

20. $\frac{2}{7} \times \frac{4}{5}$

21. $\frac{2}{3} \times \frac{3}{4}$

22. $\frac{6}{7} \times \frac{8}{9}$

23. $\frac{2}{3}$ of 50

24. $\frac{2}{8} \times \frac{6}{9}$

25. $\frac{1}{5} \times 75

26. $\frac{5}{6} \times 60$

27. $\frac{3}{4} \times \frac{5}{7}$

Complete. pages 362–367

28. _____ in. = 5 ft

29. 99 yd = _____ ft

30. $\frac{1}{2}$ mile = _____ ft

31. $\frac{1}{4}$ ton = _____ lb

32. 5 lb 4 oz = _____ oz

33. $\frac{5}{8}$ lb = _____ oz

34. _____ qt = 8 gal

35. 2 qt = _____ c

36. 32 fl oz = _____ gal

Tell whether each temperature is cold, comfortable, or hot. pages 368–369

37. 32°F

38. 70°F

39. 0°F

40. 200°F

Choose the correct word to complete each sentence.

41. In customary measurement, length can be measured in _____ . Weight can be measured in _____ . Capacity can be measured in _____ .

Words to Know
pounds
feet
gallons

Solve. pages 358–359

42. After $\frac{1}{3}$ of the water in the fish tank evaporated, there were only 12 gallons in the tank. How many gallons had been in the tank?

43. To build a new rabbit hutch Paul needs eight 24–in. pieces of wood for legs and two 48–in. pieces for crosspieces. How many 8–ft pieces should he buy?

Chapter Test

Find *n*. Write each product in lowest terms.

1. $\frac{4}{5} \times \frac{7}{8} = n$

2. $25 \times \frac{4}{5} = n$

3. $\frac{2}{3}$ of $\frac{4}{5} = n$

4. $\frac{5}{6} \times 28 = n$

5. $\frac{3}{8} \times 32 = n$

6. $\frac{2}{5}$ of $25 = n$

7. $35 \times \frac{2}{7} = n$

8. $\frac{1}{5} \times \frac{3}{4} = n$

Multiply. Write each product in lowest terms.

9. $\frac{2}{3} \times 9$

10. $\frac{7}{9} \times \frac{2}{8}$

11. $67 \times \frac{2}{3}$

12. $\frac{3}{7} \times 32$

13. $\frac{1}{2} \times \frac{5}{8}$

14. $\frac{3}{5}$ of $75

15. $\frac{3}{8} \times \frac{5}{6}$

16. $\frac{1}{4} \times \frac{6}{7}$

Complete.

17. 8 ft = _____ in.

18. 84 in. = _____ ft

19. 54 in. = _____ yd

20. 10,560 ft = _____ mi

21. $\frac{7}{8}$ mi = _____ ft

22. 5,280 ft = _____ yd

Complete.

23. 6 lb = _____ oz

24. 40 oz = _____ lb

25. 3,500 lb = _____ T

Complete.

26. 16 fl oz = _____ c

27. 12 qt = _____ gal

28. 8 pt = _____ qt

Complete.

29. 62°F + 15°F = _____ degrees: hot/comfortable/freezing?

30. 1°F + 30°F = _____ degrees: hot/comfortable/freezing?

31. 90°F + 15°F = _____ degrees: hot/comfortable/freezing?

Solve.

32. Agnes has 36 tropical fish. She put $\frac{1}{4}$ in the red tank and $\frac{4}{9}$ in the blue tank. How many will she have left to put in the green tank?

33. Waldorf, the whale, swims along the edges of his aquarium. The edges are 48 ft long and 20 yd wide. How many feet will he swim if the tank is a rectangle?

THINK   If Waldorf's trainer has 2 rolls of tape with 30 yd of tape on each roll, will he have enough to mark the edge of the tank?

Dividing Fractions

Use a compass to draw a circle, or trace this one, to represent a whole pizza. Divide the pizza into eight equal pieces.

Work with a partner. Experiment with your pizza pieces. Find out how many eighths there are in the following portions of the pizza.

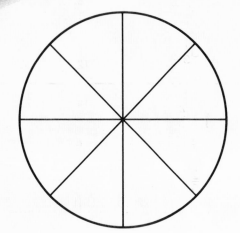

1. 1 whole   **2.** $\frac{1}{2}$ **3.** $\frac{1}{4}$

4. $\frac{3}{4}$ **5.** $\frac{5}{8}$ **6.** $\frac{3}{8}$

To solve $1 \div \frac{1}{8} = n$, answer this question: "How many eighths are there in 1 whole?" Since there are 8 eighths in 1 whole, $1 \div \frac{1}{8} = 8$.

Work with a partner. Write the question that you would answer to solve for n. Then use your fraction pieces to find n.

7. $\frac{7}{8} \div \frac{1}{8} = n$ **8.** $\frac{1}{8} \div \frac{1}{8} = n$ **9.** $\frac{1}{2} \div \frac{1}{8} = n$

10. $1\frac{1}{4} \div \frac{1}{8} = n$ **11.** $1\frac{1}{2} \div \frac{1}{8} = n$ **12.** $1\frac{3}{4} \div \frac{1}{8} = n$

13. $1 \div \frac{1}{2} = n$ **14.** $1 \div \frac{1}{4} = n$ **15.** $\frac{3}{4} \div \frac{1}{4} = n$

16. $2 \div \frac{1}{2} = n$ **17.** $2 \div \frac{1}{4} = n$ **18.** $2\frac{1}{2} \div \frac{1}{2} = n$

Write a summary to explain in your own words what the numbers mean when you divide by a fraction.

Maintaining Skills

Choose the correct answers. Write A, B, C, or D.

1. $\frac{5}{6} = \frac{\Box}{36}$

  A 25   C 30

  B 32   D not given

2. Write $\frac{10}{15}$ in lowest terms.

  A $\frac{2}{5}$ C $\frac{2}{3}$

  B $\frac{5}{3}$ D not given

3. Compare. $\frac{5}{6}$ ⬤ $\frac{8}{10}$

  A $<$ C $=$

  B $>$ D not given

4. Write the mixed number for $\frac{12}{5}$.

  A $2\frac{3}{5}$ C $5\frac{2}{5}$

  B $2\frac{2}{5}$ D not given

5. $\begin{array}{r} \frac{2}{7} \\ + \frac{5}{7} \\ \hline \end{array}$

  A 1   C $1\frac{1}{7}$

  B $\frac{6}{7}$ D not given

6. $\frac{2}{5} + \frac{3}{10}$

  A $\frac{1}{3}$ C $\frac{7}{20}$

  B $\frac{7}{10}$ D not given

7. $5\frac{1}{2} - 2\frac{5}{6}$

  A $2\frac{2}{3}$ C $3\frac{2}{3}$

  B $3\frac{1}{3}$ D not given

8. $\frac{2}{3} \times \frac{4}{5}$

  A $\frac{3}{4}$ C $\frac{8}{15}$

  B $\frac{2}{5}$ D not given

9. $1\frac{1}{2}$ qt = _____ pt

  A 5   C $2\frac{1}{2}$

  B 3   D not given

Solve.

10. The ceiling in Bob's den is 20 feet long by 15 feet wide. The ceiling will be covered by tiles that are 3 ft long by 1 ft wide. What is the fewest number of tiles he will need?

  A 100   C 60

  B 300   D not given

11. Mrs. Carson used her food coupons on a day they were worth double their value. She had 3 at \$.25, 2 at \$.40, and 4 at \$.50. If her bill was \$67.50, what was it after the coupons were deducted?

  A \$63.95   C \$7.10

  B \$60.40   D not given

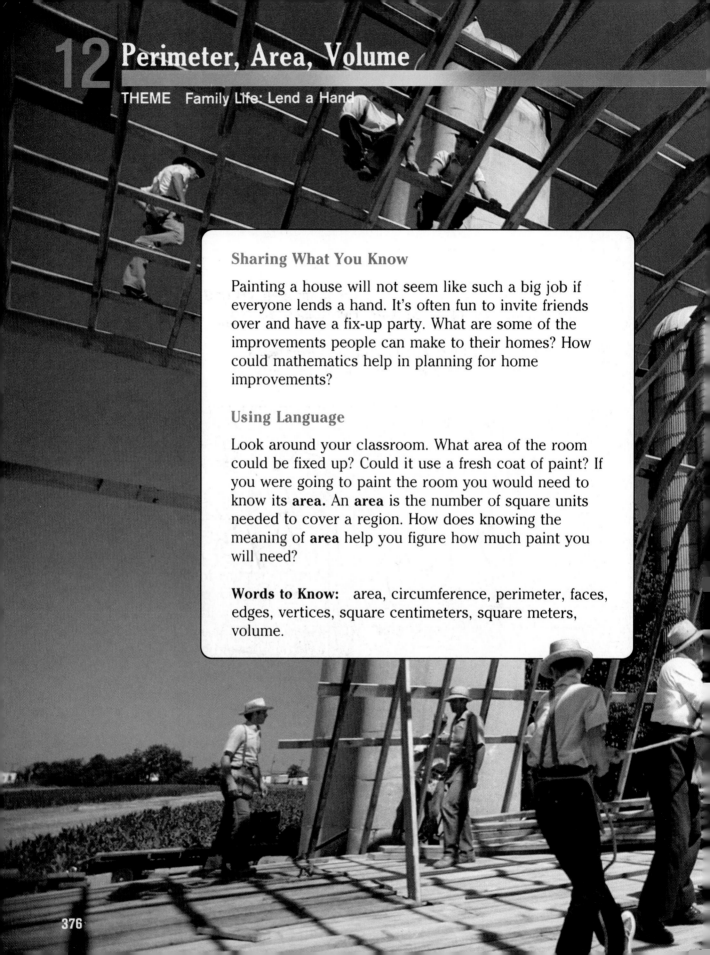

Sharing What You Know

Painting a house will not seem like such a big job if everyone lends a hand. It's often fun to invite friends over and have a fix-up party. What are some of the improvements people can make to their homes? How could mathematics help in planning for home improvements?

Using Language

Look around your classroom. What area of the room could be fixed up? Could it use a fresh coat of paint? If you were going to paint the room you would need to know its **area.** An **area** is the number of square units needed to cover a region. How does knowing the meaning of **area** help you figure how much paint you will need?

Words to Know: area, circumference, perimeter, faces, edges, vertices, square centimeters, square meters, volume.

Be a Problem Solver

Two walls of a classroom have the same area, yet one needs only half as much paint. How might this be?

Draw a floor plan of any room in your house or apartment. Include the measurements of the room.

What words do you use when referring to the distance around a country, a blanket, a table? What word can be used for all of them?

Estimating and Measuring Perimeter

Sarah wants to put a lace border around her picture. Would 75 cm of lace be enough? Estimate to find out.

Sarah needs to find the distance around the picture.

The distance around a polygon is called the **perimeter.**

▶ To find the perimeter of a polygon, add the lengths of its sides.

$$P = 22 + 22 + 27 + 27$$

Estimate. **20 + 20 + 30 + 30 = 100**

75 cm would not be enough lace.

22 cm

27 cm

The formula for the perimeter of a rectangle can be written as
$P = (2 \times \text{length}) + (2 \times \text{width})$
or
$P = (2 \times l) + (2 \times w)$

The formula for the perimeter of a square can be written as
$P = 4 \times \text{side}$
or
$P = 4 \times s$

Check Your Understanding

Use a ruler to measure the sides of each polygon to the nearest centimeter. Then give an estimate of the perimeter for each.

1.
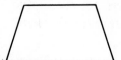

2.

3.

Share Your Ideas   How would you write the formula for the perimeter of a pentagon, if all its sides are congruent?

Use a ruler to measure the sides of each polygon to the nearest centimeter. Then give an estimate of the perimeter for each.

4.  **5.**  **6.** 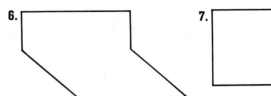 **7.**

Find the perimeter of each rectangle.

8. l = 25 cm
w = 10 cm

9. l = 1,000 mm
w = 750 mm

10. l = 75 cm
w = 15 cm

11. l = 16.2 m
w = 6.3 m

12. l = 1.25 m
w = 0.95 m

13. l = 85.4 m
w = 42.7 m

14. l = 5 cm
w = 30 mm

15. l = 1 km
w = 800 m

Estimate to find which answer makes sense.

16. A rectangle is 47 m long and 24 m wide. What is the perimeter?
a. about 70 m   **b.** about 140 m   **c.** less than 100 m

17. The perimeter of a square is 144 cm. What is the length of each side?
a. about 12 cm   **b.** about 35 cm   **c.** more than 40 cm

18. Each side of a hexagon is about 11 m long. What is its perimeter?
a. about 60 m   **b.** less than 60 m   **c.** more than 70 m

19. Estimate the perimeter of your classroom floor. Explain your method.

20. Draw on grid paper 3 different rectangles that have a perimeter of 40 centimeters each.

21. List all the different rectangles that have a perimeter of 40 centimeters. Use only whole numbers for the length and width.

Visual Thinking

22. Do any of these squares have the same perimeter? Explain.

What if you change the shape of a polygon? Must the perimeter change? Explain.

SUMMING UP

ACTIVITY

Exploring Circumference

The perimeter of a circle is called its **circumference.** The length of a circle's circumference is related to the length of its diameter. Explore this relationship.

CIRCUMFERENCE ?

DIAMETER
8 cm

Working together

Materials: centimeter ruler (Workmat 11); about 30 cm of string; 3 circular objects of different sizes, such as a soup can, a paper cup, a roll of tape

A. Trace and cut out the base of a circular object. Then fold the circle in half to show the diameter. Measure the length of the diameter to the nearest centimeter. Record your measurement on your drawing.
  • How many diameters do you think equal the circumference? Record your prediction.

B. Place a string around the object and mark the circumference. Measure and record the length of the circumference.

C. Repeat **A** and **B** for two more circular objects. Record your data.

D. Compare the length of the diameter with the length of the circumference in each of the experiments.

Sharing Your Results

1. Describe the relationship of the diameter to the circumference of each circle. Is the relationship the same? Explain.

2. Which is more difficult to measure, diameter or circumference? How can you estimate a circumference if you know the diameter?

3. Approximately how many times the diameter is the circumference?

Practice

The circumference of a circle is about 3 times its diameter. The Greek letter *pi* (π) is used to express the relationship between circumference and diameter. π is approximately equal to (≈) 3.14.

Work with a partner.

You can use this formula to find circumference.

$C = π \times d$
$C ≈ 3.14 \times 6$
$C ≈ 18.84$ cm

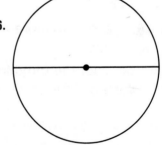

6 cm

Now use a ruler and string to find the circumference. Is your answer about 19 cm?

Find the circumference of each circle in two ways. Take turns using a calculator and the formula, and measuring with string and a ruler. Round each answer to the nearest one and compare.

4.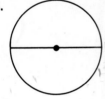

5.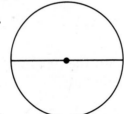

6.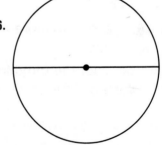

Use the formula to find the circumference of each.
Round each answer to the nearest one.

7. $d = 150$ mm

8. $d = 23$ cm

9. $d = 15$ m

10. $d = 6.5$ cm

Summing Up

11. When we say π is *approximately* 3.14, do we mean that π changes? Explain.

12. If you know the circumference of a circle, how can you find the diameter?

One garden measures 5 yd by 3 yd. Another is 7 yd by 1 yd. Are their fences the same length? Do they hold the same number of plants?

Area of Rectangles and Squares

Hall Floor Plan

Why does the plan show an area of 24 square units?

The Cohen family tiled the floor in their front hall. They used square tiles that measure 1 foot on each side. How many tiles did they use?

▶ The number of square units needed to cover a region is its **area.**

Some commonly used units of area are: **square inch** ($in.^2$), **square foot** (ft^2), **square yard** (yd^2), and **square mile** (mi^2).

One way to find area is to count squares. You can count 24 tiles in the floor plan. The area of the hall is 24 square feet.

Another way to find the area of a rectangle is to multiply the length times the width.

A = $l \times w$ A = 6 × 4 = 24 ft^2

How would you write the formula for the area of a square?

Find each area.

1.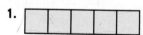

2.

3.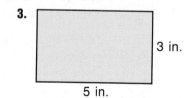
3 in.
5 in.

Look back at **1–2**. Can different rectangles with the same perimeters have different areas? Explain.

Find each area.

4.

5.

6.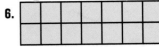

7.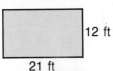
12 ft
21 ft

8.
9 yd
9 yd

9.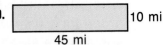
10 mi
45 mi

10. 4 in.
12 in.
8 in.
4 in.
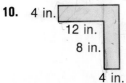

11. 4 mi
4 mi 1 mi 1 mi
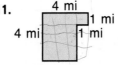

12. 42 ft
7 ft 14 ft
14 ft 14 ft
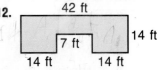

Find the area of each rectangle. Use mental math, paper and pencil, or a calculator. Explain your choices.

CHOICES

13. l = 8 yd
w = 9 yd

14. l = 18 in.
w = 9 in.

15. l = 89 ft
w = 67 ft

16. l = 13 in.
w = 12 in.

17. l = 13.5 ft
w = 2 ft

18. l = 1.5 mi
w = 2 mi

19. l = 9.2 mi
w = 7.5 mi

20. l = 48.25 mi
w = 35.5 mi

Tell whether you would find perimeter or area in each situation.

21. You need wood to frame a picture.

22. You need paint to cover four walls.

23. You need a hose to go around the house.

24. You need wall-to-wall carpeting.

Problem Solving

25. How many different rectangles can you draw with an area of 24 square units? Use whole numbers and list them by length and width. Compare your list to those of others.

26. **What if** an area was measured in square feet and you need it in square yards? Use grid paper to help you find how many square feet are in a square yard.

How does a unit that is used to measure perimeter differ from a unit that is used to measure area?

Test Taker

Be careful! Sometimes you need to change the units that are given before you answer a question.

27. What is the area of this rectangle?

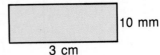
10 mm
3 cm

a. 30 cm^2 **b.** 300 mm^2
c. 30 mm^2 **d.** 300 cm^2

SUMMING UP

Which do you think we use most in our daily lives, estimates or exact amounts? Explain your choice.

Estimating Area of Irregular Regions

The Okadas outlined a region in their garden for a fish pool. Then they estimated its area in order to buy enough concrete. In Mr. Okada's drawing, each square unit represents 1 square foot.

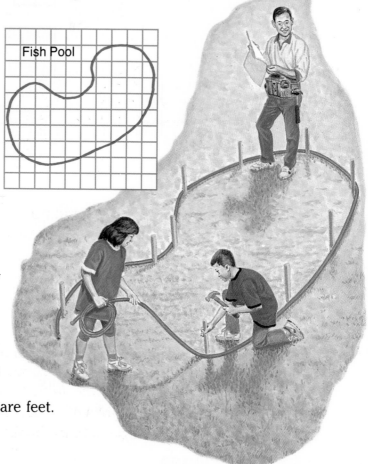

Fish Pool

Here is one way to estimate the area.

Count the number of whole squares inside the region. **29**

Count the number of partial squares inside the region. **28**

Find about how many whole squares can be made by partial squares. Multiply the number of partial squares by $\frac{1}{2}$.

$\frac{1}{2} \times 28 = 14$

Add the number of whole squares and the number of whole squares made from partial squares. **29 + 14 = 43**

The area of the fish pool is about 43 square feet. Is this a reasonable estimate? Explain.

Check Your Understanding

Estimate the number of square units in each irregular region.

1.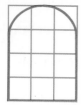

2.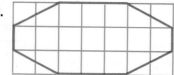

3.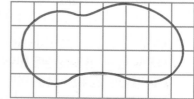

Share Your Ideas What if you counted each partial square as $\frac{1}{2}$ and then added this sum to the number of whole squares? Would the estimate be the same? Explain.

Practice

Estimate the number of square units in each irregular region.

4.

5.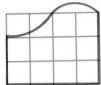

6.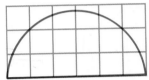

7.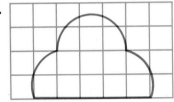

8. Outline your shoe on 1-inch grid paper. About how many square inches of material were used to make the sole of your shoe?

9. Is the following method a reasonable way to estimate the area of the Okada's fish pond? Explain why or why not.

Place a piece of string over the outline of the pond in Mr. Okada's drawing. Tape the string together where the ends meet. Use the string to outline any rectangular shape on $\frac{1}{4}$-inch grid paper. Calculate the area of the rectangle outlined by the string.

Problem Solving

10. Explain how a scientist might estimate the number of cells in a beehive.

11. **What if** a scientist wants to know how many bacteria cells are scattered on a microscope slide? The slide has a grid with squares on it. How can the scientist estimate the total number of bacteria cells in all the squares?

Explain what you would do to estimate the area of your hand in square inches.

Mixed Review

1. 38×450

2. 15×15

3. $27\overline{)5,400}$

4. $1,000 \div 35$

5. $582 + 618$

6. $2,500 - 385$

7. $4 \times \$17.50$

8. $\$20 - \$12.58$

9. 7×3.5

10. $9\frac{1}{4} + 4\frac{1}{2}$

11. $12 - 2\frac{3}{4}$

12. 2.5×6.5

13. $16.5 \div 2$

14. $\frac{1}{2} \times \frac{3}{4}$

Complete.

15. _____ ft = 3 yd

16. 18 in. = _____ yd

17. 12 c = _____ qt

18. _____ qt = 2 gal

19. _____ oz = 3 lb

20. 1 T = _____ lb

Exploring Area of Parallelograms and Triangles

What you know about the area of a rectangle can be used to explore the area of other shapes.

Figure	Parallelogram		Rectangle	
	base	height	base	height
red				
blue				
green				
brown				

Working together

Materials: centimeter ruler, paper, scissors, tangram pieces

A. Measure and record the length of the **base** (*b*) and the **height** (*h*) of each parallelogram.

B. Trace and cut out each parallelogram. Cut along each dotted line. Place the two pieces of each parallelogram together in a different way to form a rectangle.

C. Measure and record the length of the base and the height of each rectangle.

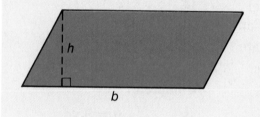

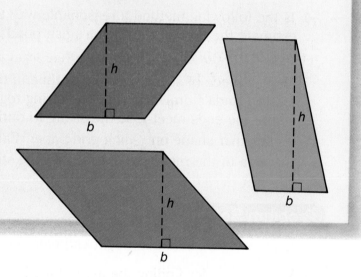

Sharing Your Results

1. Were you always able to form a rectangle from a parallelogram? How would you measure the height of a parallelogram if it were not marked with a dotted line?

2. How does the area of the parallelogram compare to the area of the corresponding rectangle?

3. How do the base and height of the parallelogram relate to the base and height of the corresponding rectangle?

4. Use what you know to write a formula for the area of a parallelogram, using the base (*b*) and height (*h*).

Practice

Work on your own. Use tangram pieces or trace and cut the figures on the right.

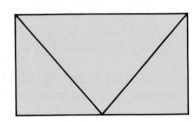

5. How many of the triangles can fit on the parallelogram?

6. Is the base of the triangle equal to the base of the parallelogram?

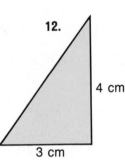

7. Is the height of the triangle equal to the height of the parallelogram?

8. What fraction of the area of the parallelogram is the area of the triangle? How could you find the area of the triangle?

Trace the following triangles. Then draw a parallelogram with the same base and height of each triangle. Find the area of each parallelogram and then find the area of the triangle.

9.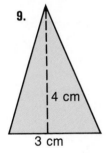
4 cm
3 cm

10.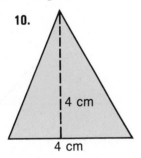
4 cm
4 cm

11.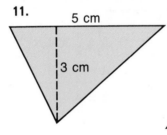
5 cm
3 cm

12.
4 cm
3 cm

13. Write a rule for finding the area of a triangle.

Summing Up

14. What two measurements do you need for finding the areas of parallelograms and triangles?

15. How does the area of the larger triangle relate to the area of the rectangle? Justify your answer.

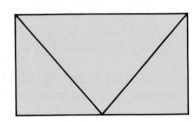

What is a parallelogram? Are all rectangles parallelograms? Are all parallelograms rectangles?

Area of Parallelograms and Triangles

Susan and her father drew a plan for a deck. To fit the available space, they shaped the deck like a parallelogram. Now they must find the area of the deck so that they can order enough stain.

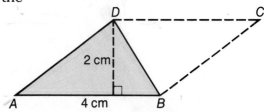

▶ To find the area of a parallelogram, multiply the base (b) times the height (h).

$$A = b \times h$$
$$A = 6 \times 4$$
$$A = 24$$

The area of the deck is 24 m^2.

The area of a triangle is $\frac{1}{2}$ the area of a parallelogram that has the same base and height.

▶ To find the area of a triangle, multiply $\frac{1}{2}$ times the base times the height.

$$A = \frac{1}{2} \times b \times h \qquad A = \frac{1}{2} \times 4 \times 2$$
$$A = \frac{1}{2} \times 8$$
$$A = 4$$

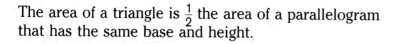

The area of triangle *ABD* is 4 cm^2.

What is the area of parallelogram *ABCD*?

Measure the base and height. Find the area in square centimeters.

1.
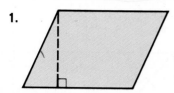

2.
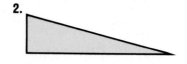

3.
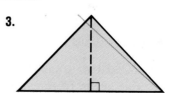

Share Your Ideas Explain why we can use the same formula to find the area of rectangles and parallelograms.

Practice

Measure the base and the height. Find the area in square centimeters.

4.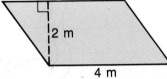

5.

6.

Find the area of each figure using the dimensions given.

7.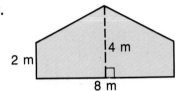
2 m
4 m

8.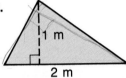
1 m
2 m

9.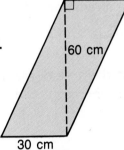
60 cm
30 cm

10.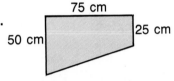
2 m
4 m
8 m

11.
75 cm
50 cm
25 cm

12.
6 km
8 km
10 km

13. triangle:
$b = 16$ m
$h = 4$ m

14. triangle:
$b = 8$ cm
$h = 15$ cm

15. parallelogram:
$b = 90$ km
$h = 50$ km

Problem Solving

Use centimeter grid paper. Draw a parallelogram for each area. Give the base and height for a triangle that is $\frac{1}{2}$ each area.

16. 4 cm^2

17. 10 cm^2

18. 6 cm^2

19. 8 cm^2

20. 14 cm^2

21. 12 cm^2

Common Error

22. Explain the error. What information do you need to find the correct area?

$A = \frac{1}{2} \times b \times h$

$A = \frac{1}{2} \times 4 \times 4$ ←Incorrect

$A = 8$ cm^2

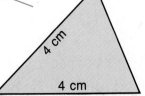
4 cm
4 cm

Explain how the formula for the area of a triangle is related to the formula for the area of a parallelogram.

SUMMING UP

Midchapter Review

Find the perimeter of each. pages 378–379

1.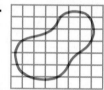
1.6 cm
1.6 cm

2.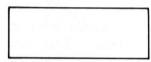

3.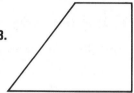

Find the circumference of a circle with the given diameter. pages 380–381

4. $d = 5$ cm

5. $d = 8.1$ m

6. $d = 123$ mm

7. $d = 34$ m

Find the area. pages 382–383

8.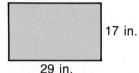
17 in.
29 in.

9.
3 ft
3 ft

10.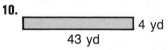
4 yd
43 yd

11.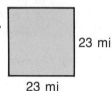
23 mi
23 mi

Estimate the area of the irregular region. pages 384–385

12.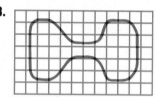

13.

14.

Find the area of each. pages 386–389

15. triangle:
   $b = 3$ m
   $h = 6$ m

16. triangle:
   $b = 24$ cm
   $h = 32$ cm

17. parallelogram:
   $b = 64$ m
   $h = 39$ m

Choose the correct word to complete each sentence.

18. The number of square units needed to cover a region is the _____.

19. The perimeter of a circle is the _____.

20. The distance around a polygon is the _____.

Words to Know
area
perimeter
circumference

Solve.

21. A sheet of paper is 28 cm long and 21 cm wide. What is the area of the paper?

22. Ana's backyard is 36 m long and 24 m wide. How much fencing does she need to enclose it?

Exploring Problem Solving

THINK
EXPLORE
SOLVE
LOOK BACK

Which Way Do We Go?

Aunt Shirley owns a ranch. Often she sends two riders out to check the fence which surrounds it. They ride along the fence until they meet, and then head for home.

Thinking Critically

Look at the diagram. In what directions should Aunt Shirley send the riders? Make a map like the one shown or use Workmat 12 to help you.

Analyzing and Making Decisions

1. **What if** the house is at Point 1 and the riders travel at the same speed? In what directions should they go? Explain. Draw arrows on your map to show your directions. Put an X where they will meet, and then draw another pair of arrows to show the shortest route home. Do they have to ride along the fence to get home?

2. **What if** one rider is faster than the other? Use another copy of the map to show the directions in which the riders should travel. Then mark the point where you think they might meet. Show the route to go home.

3. **What if** the house is at Point 2? In what directions should the riders of equal speed go? Show the routes and mark the meeting point. Then show the routes for returning to Point 2.

4. In what directions should riders of unequal speed ride if they leave from Point 2? Show the routes for going and returning on a separate map.

5. **What if** the house is at Point 3? How would you direct the riders? Use a map to show this.

Look Back   **What if** the boundary of the ranch was a circle? What directions would you give to the two riders? What directions would you give to three riders?

Problem Solving Strategies

Logic

The families in Rockville separate their trash into three different kinds of recycling cans. The cans are yellow, black, and blue. Each can is for a different kind of trash: glass, plastic, or metal. If plastic is put into the yellow can, the collection team will not take it away. If metal or plastic is put into the black can, they will also leave it uncollected. What kind of trash goes into each of the recycling cans?

Not all problems can be solved by arithmetic. To solve some problems, you must think like a detective. You need to put the clues together to find the answer.

Solving the Problem

Think   What is the problem?

Explore   What are the three types of trash? What are the three colors of the cans? What cannot go into the black can? What is left to go into the black can? What cannot go into the yellow can? What is left to go into the yellow can?

Solve   What kind of trash goes into each container?

Look Back   How can rereading the problem help you check your answer?

Share Your Ideas

1. **What if** plastic or metal could not go into the blue can instead of the black can? What kind of trash would go into each can?

Practice

THINK EXPLORE SOLVE LOOK BACK

Solve. Use a calculator where appropriate.

CHOICES

2. Juan, Sal, Bob, and Mike are on a relay team at the family reunion picnic. They run in a special order. The fastest runner runs last. Sal runs faster than Bob. Mike runs first. Juan runs slower than Bob. The slowest runner runs second. In what order do they run?

3. Fran, Tara, Julia, Shirley, and Ruth are from three different families. There are two Smiths, two Joneses, and one Thompson. The tallest is a Thompson. The two girls who run the fastest are Smiths. Julia runs faster than Fran or Tara. Fran is taller than Tara or Ruth. Julia and Shirley have the same last name. What is the last name of each girl?

Use this information to solve 4–5.

Mr. and Mrs. Cooper and their children, John, Barbara, and Helene all brought pictures to put in the family album. Helene brought 5 more than her sister. John brought 5 more than Helene. Mrs. Cooper brought 6 more than John. Mr. Cooper brought 20 pictures. This is two more than Mrs. Cooper brought.

4. How many pictures did each person bring?

5. They have enough pages for 50 pictures. Will they need more pages? Explain.

Mixed Strategy Review

Use this information to solve 6–7.

Mr. Davis has 200 ft of chicken wire for building a fence around a four-sided garden. He wants the garden to have as large an area as possible.

6. How long and how wide should he make the garden?

7. What will the area of the largest four-sided garden be?

Create **Your Own**

Sarah is the grandmother. May is the mother. Beth is the daughter. Write some clues so that these facts can be found out.

Compare a cube and a square.
How are they the same?
How are they different?

Identifying Space Figures

The Scotts are busy doing spring chores. Each family member is working with an object shaped like one of the space figures on this page.

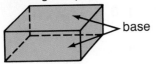
rectangular prism — base

triangular prism

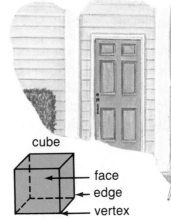
cube — face, edge, vertex

▶ A **prism** has two parallel, congruent **bases**. It is named by the shape of its base.

▶ A **cube** is a prism with 6 congruent, square **faces**. It has 12 **edges** and 8 **vertices**.

square pyramid

rectangular pyramid

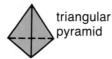
triangular pyramid

▶ These figures are **pyramids.** The faces are triangles with a common vertex. Each base is a polygon.

Some space figures have no straight edges.

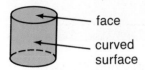
face — curved surface

▶ A **cylinder** has two parallel circular faces that are congruent.

▶ A **cone** has one circular face and one vertex.

▶ A **sphere** has no flat surface.

Look back at the picture. Match the objects with a corresponding space figure.

Check Your Understanding

Name some everyday objects that are shaped like each space figure.

1. cube   **2.** rectangular prism   **3.** cone   **4.** sphere

Share Your Ideas   Is a triangle a space figure? Explain.

Name a space figure suggested by each object.

5. a grapefruit   **6.** a brick   **7.** a new piece of chalk

8. a soup can   **9.** an alphabet block   **10.** a basketball

Choose the number of flat surfaces each space figure has.

11. rectangular prism   **a.** 3   **b.** 4   **c.** 5   **d.** 6

12. triangular prism   **a.** 3   **b.** 4   **c.** 5   **d.** 6

13. cone   **a.** 0   **b.** 1   **c.** 2   **d.** 3

14. cylinder   **a.** 0   **b.** 1   **c.** 2   **d.** 3

15. sphere   **a.** 0   **b.** 1   **c.** 2   **d.** 3

Name a space figure to complete each sentence.

16. A _____ has two flat circular faces.   **17.** A _____ has 6 vertices.

18. A _____ has 9 edges.   **19.** A _____ has 12 edges.

20. Draw a hexagonal prism. It has two congruent hexagons for bases. How many faces, vertices, and edges does it have?

21. Stan wants to buy enough paint to cover a cube that measures 25 cm on each edge. What is the area of each face? How many square centimeters will be covered with paint?

Mathematics and History

A famous German mathematician named Euler counted the vertices (V), the faces (F), and the edges (E) in space figures like these.

He wrote the formula $V + F - E = 2$

22. Show that Euler's formula is true for a cube.

Describe each of the following: a triangular prism, a cylinder, a cone.

SUMMING UP

Exploring Building Space Figures

Sam says that he will need 6 cubes to build this space figure. Joni thinks that 10 cubes are needed. How many cubes do you think are needed?

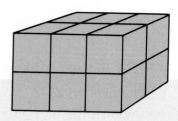

Working together

Materials: 15 cubes, space figure models, Workmat 13

Follow these steps for each space figure on the page.

A. Use cubes to build the figure.

B. Copy the table and record the number of cubes that you used.

C. Compare the number of cubes that you used with those shown in the drawing. Record the number of cubes that are hidden in each drawing.

Space Figure	Number of Cubes Used	Number of Cubes Hidden in the Drawing
Red		
Blue		
Green		
Yellow		
Brown		

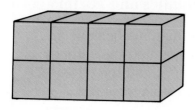

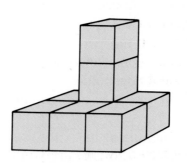

Sharing Your Results

1. The drawings show the front, the top, and the right side of each space figure. Which sides of the space figures cannot be seen?

2. Did each space figure require more cubes than the ones that can be seen in the drawing? Explain.

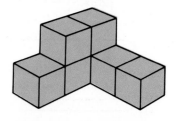

Practice

Work with a partner. Experiment.

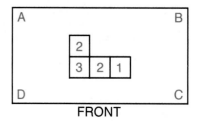

A   B

D   C
FRONT

- Use letters to label the corners of a piece of paper. Place the paper in front of you, as shown.

- Use cubes to build towers on the paper. Make the height of each tower match the number shown.

Carefully turn the paper until you see each of the views drawn below. From which corner do you see each view?

3.

4.

5.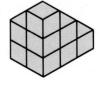

6. Draw the view that you see from the remaining corner. The special dot pattern will help you to draw the blocks in three dimensions. Trace the pattern or use Workmat 13.

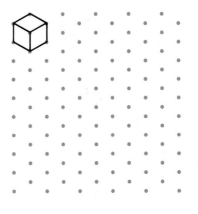

7. Use space figure models. Choose either a cube, triangular prism, or pyramid. Draw the figure from different views. For each view, describe the faces that you cannot see.

Summing Up

8. Look back at **3–5**. In which drawings are you unable to see all of the cubes? How many cubes are hidden in each figure?

9. Each of these drawings is of a space figure viewed from one direction. Name the figure or figures that each could be. From what view is each shown?

a.

b.

c.

Exploring Volume

The **volume** of a container is the number of cubic units it contains. Fill some containers with cubes to find their volumes.

a.

b.

c.

Working together

Materials: centimeter grid paper (Workmat 3), scissors, tape, 20 centimeter cubes

Draw each pattern on centimeter grid paper. Follow this procedure for each of your patterns.

A. Cut out the pattern.

B. Fold and tape the pattern to form an open box. Have the grid show on the outside of the box.

C. Predict the number of cubes it will take to fill the box.

D. Fit centimeter cubes into the box until it is full.

E. Record the length, width, and height of the box. Record the number of cubes it contains. Use a chart like the one shown.

F. Discuss how the length, width, and height of the box are related to its volume.

	length	width	height	volume
a.				
b.				
c.				

Sharing Your Results

1. Without counting, how can you tell how many cubes will fit in the bottom layer of a box?

2. How do you know how many layers of cubes a box will hold? How can you find the volume of a box without counting cubes?

Practice

Trace and cut out this pattern. Fold and tape it to make a model of a cubic centimeter.

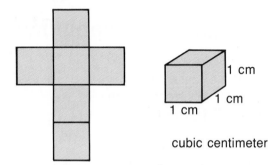

cubic centimeter

▶ The **cubic centimeter (cm³)** is a unit used to measure volume.

3. Use the symbol cm³ to give the volume of each of the rectangular prisms you made on page 398.

4. The capacity of 1 cm³ is 1 milliliter. What is the capacity of each of your rectangular prisms?

5. Cut out 5 cardboard squares that are each 1 decimeter on a side. Tape them together to form a **cubic decimeter (dm³).** What is its volume in cm³?

6. Use a plastic bag to line your dm³ box. Measure 1 L of water into a pitcher. Pour it into the box. Does the box hold all of the water?

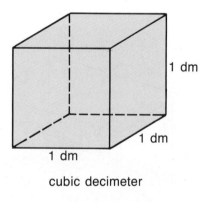

cubic decimeter

Summing Up

7. How many milliliters of water are there in a cubic decimeter of water? Does the result of your activity show this? Explain.

8. Study the results of your work on page 398. Describe a formula or a rule that can be used to find the volume of a rectangular prism.

Name some everyday objects that are shaped like rectangular prisms. Which ones have useful space inside them?

Volume of Rectangular Prisms

Mrs. Bradley is not sure which suitcase to buy since their prices are the same. Her grandson, Tim, says she should buy the one with the greatest volume. Which one does Tim recommend?

Color: Green
Price: $45
l = 20 in.
w = 6 in.
h = 14 in.

Color: Blue
Price: $45
l = 18 in.
w = 9 in.
h = 11 in.

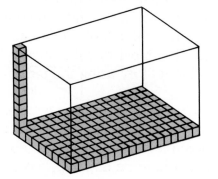

▶ The **volume** of a space figure is the number of cubic units that fit inside the figure. The **cubic inch (in.^{3})** and the **cubic foot (ft^3)** are commonly used units of volume.

To find the volume of a rectangular prism, multiply the length, the width, and the height.

$$V = l \times w \times h$$

Green suitcase

$V = 20 \times 6 \times 14$

$V = 120 \times 14$

$V = 1{,}680 \text{ in.}^3$

Blue suitcase

$V = 18 \times 9 \times 11$

$V = 162 \times 11$

$V = 1{,}782 \text{ in.}^3$

Why does Tim recommend the blue suitcase?

Check Your Understanding

Find the volume of each rectangular prism.

1. 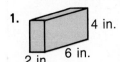 4 in. 6 in. 2 in.

2. 4 ft. 3 ft. 5 ft.

3. l = 24 in.
   w = 8 in.
   h = 16 in.

Share Your Ideas Give some possible dimensions for a rectangular prism with 8 in.^{3} of volume.

Practice

Find the volume of each rectangular prism.

4.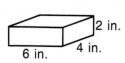
6 in. 4 in. 2 in.

5.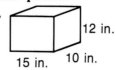
15 in. 10 in. 12 in.

6.
2 ft 2 ft 2 ft

7. $l = 12$ in.

$w = 8$ in.

$h = 10$ in.

8. $l = 18$ in.

$w = 12$ in.

$h = 6$ in.

9. $l = 17$ ft

$w = 10$ ft

$h = 20$ ft

Use cubic units to build each rectangular prism. Find the missing numbers.

	Volume in cubic units	length	width	height
10.	16	2	4	
11.	12	4	1	
12.	18	3	3	
13.	18			6
14.	20		5	

Problem Solving

15. Make oaktag models of a cubic inch and a cubic foot. Study the models and guess how many cubic inches are in a cubic foot. Then find the exact number of cubic inches in a cubic foot by using the formula.

16. What cubic unit might be used to measure the volume of a rectangular prism the size of a cereal box? What unit would be most appropriate to measure the volume of a refrigerator?

17. Mr. Jones ordered 28 ft^3 of sand to fill a sandbox. What could the length, width, and height of the sandbox be if the sand fills it completely?

Visual Thinking

18. All the cubes on the top, bottom, and four sides are red.

All the cubes that are hidden from sight on the inside are blue.

How many cubes of each color are in this rectangular prism?

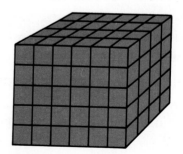

Design a box that would hold your math book. Round each dimension to the nearest inch. What is the volume of your box?

GETTING STARTED

Describe how letters and numbers are used to locate points on highway maps.

Ordered Pairs

Melissa designed a game called Get the Point that uses ordered pairs.

▶ An **ordered pair** of numbers is used to locate a point in a plane.

Follow these steps to locate point B

- Start at 0.
- Move 4 spaces to the right.
- Move 3 spaces up.

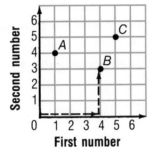

Ordered pair (4,3) locates point B. What ordered pair locates point A? point C?

In the game, Get the Point, each player is given a **coordinate grid** like the one shown. (Workmat 14).

- The first player marks a secret point on the grid and draws zones around it, as shown. The grid is hidden from the other players.

- The other players take turns guessing ordered pairs until someone names the secret point.

- Each time a point is named, the first player tells if it is in the cold, warm, or hot zone.

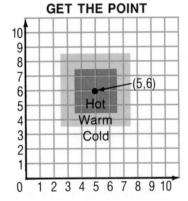

GET THE POINT

The secret point in the model is (5,6). What should the first player say if you guess (4,8)?

Check Your Understanding

Name the point at each location.

1. (4,5)　　　　2. (4,0)　　　　3. (3,4)

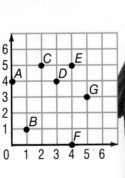

Name the ordered pair for each point.

4. C　　　　5. B　　　　6. A

Share Your Ideas Explain the steps that you would use to locate point G.

402

Practice

Name the point at each location.

7. (8,7) **8.** (6,2) **9.** (0,9) **10.** (3,2)

Name the ordered pair for each point.

11. T **12.** X **13.** Q **14.** Z

Find the rule that relates the second number to the first number in each ordered pair. Then find the missing information. Use mental math, paper and pencil, or calculator.

CHOICES

15. Rule:

	First Number	Second Number	Ordered Pair
	2	6	(2,6)
	15	45	(15,45)
16.	8		
17.		90	
18.	37		
19.		48	

20. Rule:

	First Number	Second Number	Ordered Pair
	8	15	(8,15)
	21	28	(21,28)
21.	52		
22.		49	
23.	316		
24.		200	

Choose the correct answer.

25. Which point is to the right of (0,0)? **a.** (0,1) **b.** (1,0)

26. Which point is above (1,3)? **a.** (3,1) **b.** (1,6)

27. Which point is to the right of (2,5)? **a.** (15,5) **b.** (2,15)

28. Which point is below (14,15)? **a.** (14,16) **b.** (14,14)

Problem Solving

DATA **29.** How many points are in the warm zone on the Get the Point coordinate grid on page 402?

30. Name the ordered pairs for all the points in the hot zone on the coordinate grid.

31. Play Get the Point. Build a winning strategy by keeping track of the guesses. The winner chooses the next secret point.

What can be said about all the ordered pairs that have the same first number? the same second number?

SUMMING UP

Describe what you will see if you plot these points and connect them: (1,1), (1,2), (1,3), (1,4).

Graphing Ordered Pairs

Jimmy is making a sign for the family farm. He reproduces the pine tree symbol by graphing ordered pairs onto a larger grid. He locates this set of points on a coordinate grid and connects them.

(1,2), (4,2), (4,1), (6,1), (6,2), (9,2), (5,10)

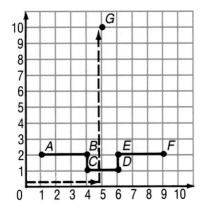

Tall Tree Farm

To find the location of point G, graph the ordered pair (5,10).

- Start at 0.
- Count 5 spaces to the right.
- Count 10 spaces up.
- Plot the point and label it G.

Which ordered pairs mark the spot where the tree would touch the ground?

Check Your Understanding

Copy the grid or use Workmat 14.

1. Graph the point (3,5) and label it A. Graph a point 4 spaces to the right of A. Label it B. Connect the two points.

2. What ordered pair names the midpoint of $\overline{AB}$? Label it point C. Graph point D 4 spaces below C. Connect C and D. What letter have you formed?

Share Your Ideas How could graphing ordered pairs help you to enlarge a drawing?

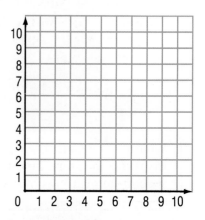

Graph and label the given ordered pair and an ordered
pair three spaces directly above it. Draw a line
segment connecting the two points.

3. (1,2)   **4.** (0,1)   **5.** (2,0)

6. (3,4)   **7.** (4,3)   **8.** (5,5)

Plot each point. Then connect the points in order.
Name the polygon that is formed.

9. (1,4)   **10.** (3,2)   **11.** (4,7)
   (3,2)   (6,2)   (4,11)
   (8,7)   (8,4)   (6,9)
   (6,9)   (1,4)   (8,7)

12. Copy the partial drawing on grid paper. Plot the
points needed to complete the picture. Then finish
the drawing and list
the ordered pairs
that you used.

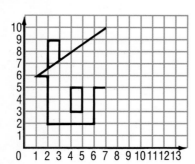

DATA
13. Create your own design by plotting and connecting
points on a coordinate grid like Workmat 14. List
the ordered pairs for the points in your design and
exchange lists with a classmate. See if you can
reproduce each other's designs, using only the lists
of ordered pairs.

14. How can you enlarge your design, using the same
size grid paper?

Explain how graphing ordered pairs can help
you make drawings on a computer screen.

1. 29×37

2. $8\frac{1}{2} + 2\frac{1}{2}$

3. 38×604

4. $4.5 + 8.9$

5. $2 \times 3\frac{1}{2}$

6. $455 \div 7$

7. $13 - 4.2$

8. $\$100 - \$30.25$

9. 4.5×12

10. $16 - 7\frac{3}{8}$

11. $\frac{3}{4} \times \frac{1}{2}$

12. $\frac{1}{3} \times 96$

13. $\frac{3}{4} \times 20$

**Give the Fahrenheit
temperature for
each.**

14. water boils

15. water freezes

16. normal body
temperature

**Name a fraction in
lowest terms to match
each decimal.**

17. 0.5

18. 0.25

19. 0.2

20. 0.75

SUMMING UP

405

Using Problem Solving

Ordered Pairs

The Morenos like to barbecue hamburgers outdoors. They buy hamburger for $2 a pound. Make a graph to show the prices of different amounts of hamburger.

A. Before you start your graph, think about these questions.

- What should each axis represent?
- If you want to be able to find out how much each $\frac{1}{4}$ pound of hamburger costs, how much space should you leave between the marks for the pounds?

B. The Morenos sometimes buy as much as 10 pounds of hamburger. How long should you make each axis on your graph?

C. Use your graph to find the cost of these amounts.

7 lb of hamburger
$2\frac{1}{2}$ lb of hamburger
$4\frac{1}{2}$ lb of hamburger
8 lb of hamburger

D. Sometimes the Morenos recieve a coupon for $.50 off each pound of hamburger. Add a new line to your graph to show the different prices of hamburger when purchased with the coupon. Draw the line in a different color. What is the cost of each amount of hamburger in problem **C** when purchased with the coupon?

Sharing Your Ideas

1. How many points did you plot to make your graph?

2. Was it easy to tell the price of hamburger on your graph? Why or why not?

Practice

3. When the Morenos start their grill they use $2.50 worth of charcoal. Make a new graph that shows both the cost of buying and cooking the hamburgers. Include the cost of starting the grill. (If you cook no hamburgers, you will still start up the grill.) How much does it cost to make and cook the following amounts of hamburger at $2 a pound?

a. 5 lb

b. $3\frac{1}{2}$ lb

c. $7\frac{1}{2}$ lb

d. 8 lb

4. When the Morenos have a party, they plan so that each child can have two $\frac{1}{4}$-pound hamburgers and each adult can have one $\frac{1}{4}$-pound hamburger. Find the cost of buying and cooking hamburgers for these groups of people.

a. 6 children and 6 adults

b. 4 children and 10 adults

c. 10 children and 4 adults

d. 8 children and 6 adults

Summing Up

5. Compare your graph for buying and cooking the hamburgers to your graph for just buying the hamburgers at $2 a pound. How are they different? How are they alike?

6. Hamburger is often sold with labels such as ground round, ground chuck, and ground sirloin. Find the cost of these different types of hamburger in more than one store in two different weeks. What might account for the differences in prices between the stores and between the weeks?

Chapter Review

Use the figures drawn below. pages 378–379, 382–389

1. Find the perimeter of the rectangle.

2. Find the area of the triangle.

3. Find the perimeter of the parallelogram.

4. Estimate the area of the irregular region.

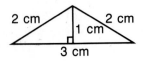

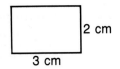

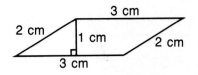

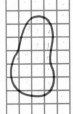

Find the circumference of a circle with the given diameter. pages 380–381

5. $d = 3$ cm

6. $d = 20$ m

7. $d = 2.5$ cm

Name each space figure. pages 394–395

8.

9.

10.

Give the volume of each space figure. pages 398–401

11. 3 in.
3 in.
2 in.

12. 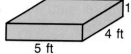 1 ft
4 ft
5 ft

13. 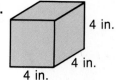 4 in.
4 in.
4 in.

Graph and label each ordered pair. pages 402–405

14. P at (3,4)

15. Q at (0,2)

16. R at (5,1)

Choose the correct word to complete each sentence.

17. A cube has 12 _____.

18. A triangular prism has 6 _____.

Words to Know
faces
edges
vertices

Solve. pages 391–393, 400–401

19. What is the volume of a lunch box that is 8 inches long, 7 inches wide and 4 inches high?

20. A certain whole number is greater than 5. Twice the number is less than 20. Three times the number is greater than 24. What is the number?

Chapter Test

Use the figures drawn below.

1. Find the area of the rectangle.

2. Find the perimeter of the triangle.

3. Find the area of the parallelogram.

4. Estimate the area of the irregular region.

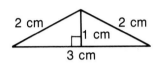

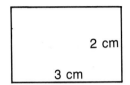

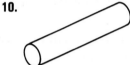

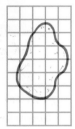

Find the circumference of a circle with the given diameter.

5. $d = 4$ cm

6. $d = 10$ cm

7. $d = 1.5$ km

Name each space figure.

8.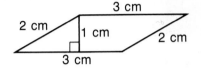

9.

10.

Give the volume of each space figure.

11.

12.

13.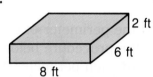

Graph and label each ordered pair.

14. A at $(4,3)$

15. B at $(3,0)$

16. C at $(1,5)$

17. D at $(5,1)$

18. E at $(0,2)$

Solve.

19. What is the volume of a tool box that is 13 in. long, 8 in. wide, and 7 in. high?

20. Carla's garden is three times the area of Ben's and half the area of Art's. Who has the smallest garden?

THINK Two vertices of a right triangle are at $(3,6)$ and $(7,10)$. What ordered pair could name the remaining vertex?

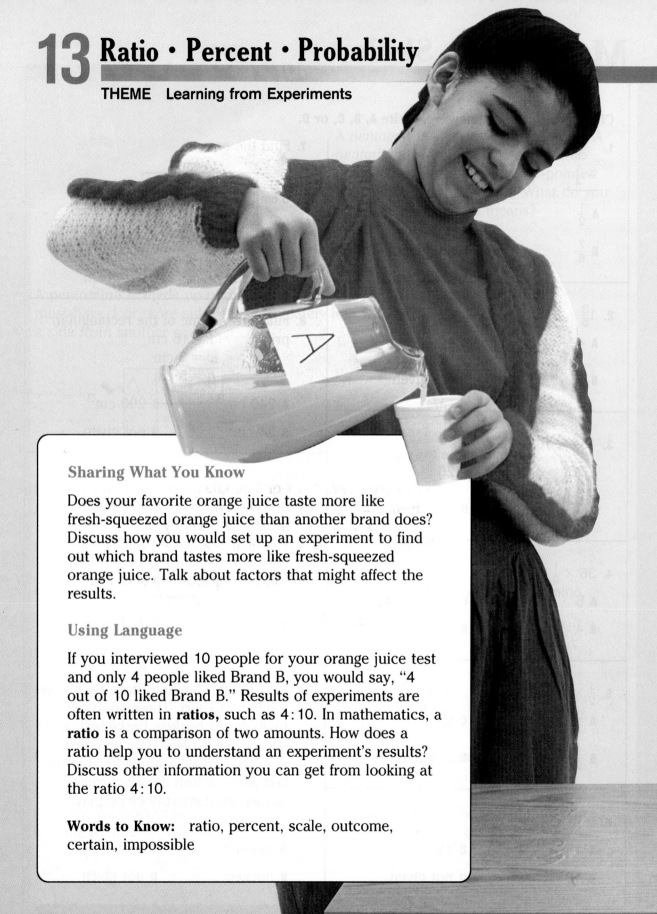

13 Ratio • Percent • Probability

THEME Learning from Experiments

Sharing What You Know

Does your favorite orange juice taste more like
fresh-squeezed orange juice than another brand does?
Discuss how you would set up an experiment to find
out which brand tastes more like fresh-squeezed
orange juice. Talk about factors that might affect the
results.

Using Language

If you interviewed 10 people for your orange juice test
and only 4 people liked Brand B, you would say, "4
out of 10 liked Brand B." Results of experiments are
often written in **ratios,** such as 4:10. In mathematics, a
ratio is a comparison of two amounts. How does a
ratio help you to understand an experiment's results?
Discuss other information you can get from looking at
the ratio 4:10.

Words to Know: ratio, percent, scale, outcome,
certain, impossible

Be a Problem Solver

In one taste test, 4 out of 5 people preferred Brand Y to Brand Z. In a second taste test, 8 out of 10 people preferred Brand Y to Brand Z. In which group was Brand Y more popular? Explain your answer.

Write about why you think companies conduct taste test experiments. Discuss why you think taste tests are or are not a good idea.

Write several six-letter words. Compare the number of consonants with the number of vowels in each word.

Ratios

Jamie is experimenting with blue paint and yellow paint to find out which shades of green he can make.

▶ A **ratio** is a comparison of two quantities.

The ratio of blue paint to yellow paint is 5 to 1.

- **write**   **5 to 1**   **5:1** $\frac{5}{1}$

- **read**   five to one

The ratio of blue paint to yellow paint is 1 to 5.

1 to 5   **1:5** $\frac{1}{5}$

one to five

Explain why 5:1 and 1:5 are not the same ratio.

More Examples

a. Compare the number of items to the price. Write 3 to 2, 3:2, or $\frac{3}{2}$

SALE
3 for $2

b. Compare the distance to the time. Write 40 to 1, 40:1, or
$\frac{40}{1}$ ⟵ What does this 1 mean?

40
MILES PER HOUR

Write each ratio in three ways.

1.

   red to blue

2.

   blue to red

3.

   blue to all circles

Write each ratio in two more ways.

4. 9 to 3

5. 1:6

6. $\frac{85}{100}$

Share Your Ideas   Explain why the order of the numbers is important when you read and write a ratio.

Write each ratio in three ways.

7.

8.

9.

red to blue   red to blue   red to yellow

Use ratios to compare the number of consonants with the number of vowels. Write each in three ways.

10. geometric

11. circle

12. arithmetic

13. average

14. multiplication

15. factor

16. decimal

17. fraction

18. division

Choose the ratio that is the same as the given ratio.

19. $35:1$

a. $\frac{1}{35}$

b 1 to 35

c. 35 to 1

20. $\frac{2}{5}$

a. 5 to 2

b. 2 to 5

c. $5:2$

21. 3 to 4

a. $4:3$

b. $\frac{4}{3}$

c. $\frac{3}{4}$

Write a ratio for each.

22. Compare the number of school days in a week with the number of days in a weekend.

23. Compare the number of days in a weekend with the number of days in a week.

24. Compare the number of letters in your first name with the number of letters in your last name.

25. Compare the number of letters in your whole name with the number of letters in the name of your school.

DATA
26. Compare the distance to the speed limit sign closest to your school with the time it takes to get there.

27. Compare the distance you travel to school with the amount of time it takes you to travel to school.

Describe an everyday situation where amounts like these might be compared.

$80:100$ $12:1$ $24:1$ $60:1$

SUMMING UP

Exploring Equal Ratios

Nicki's art teacher gave her this recipe for modeling clay. She wants to experiment to find an **equal ratio** of ingredients that calls for less flour.

What if Nicki uses 4 cups of flour? How much salt should she use?

Modeling Clay
12 cups flour
3 cups salt
4 cups water

Working together

Materials: 20 red counters, 5 blue counters

A. Use 12 red counters to stand for the flour and 3 blue counters to stand for the salt. Write the ratio of flour to salt.

> flour ⟶ •••• •••• •••
> salt ⟶ • • •

B. How many cups of salt would you use with 8 cups of flour? Show the ratio with your counters. Write the ratio of flour to salt.

C. The ratios $\frac{12}{3}$ and $\frac{8}{2}$ are equal ratios.

$$\frac{12}{3} = \frac{8}{2}$$

D. Use the counters to find other ratios equal to $\frac{12}{3}$. Copy and complete this chart to record the equal ratios.

Flour (c)	4	8	12	16	20
Salt (c)		2	3		

Sharing Your Results

1. What pattern do you notice in the amounts of flour?

2. Use the word **_multiple_** to describe the numbers in the top row.

3. Describe how finding these equal ratios might involve multiplication.

$$\frac{4}{1} = \frac{8}{2} \qquad \frac{4}{1} = \frac{12}{3}$$

4. Describe how finding these equal ratios might involve division.

$$\frac{16}{4} = \frac{8}{2} \qquad \frac{20}{5} = \frac{4}{1}$$

Practice

Here are two ways to find equal ratios.

Multiply each term by the same nonzero number.

first term → $\dfrac{4}{1} \times \boxed{\dfrac{2}{2}} = \dfrac{8}{2}$
second term →

Divide each term by the same nonzero number.

first term → $\dfrac{20}{5} \div \boxed{\dfrac{5}{5}} = \dfrac{4}{1}$
second term →

5. How much water should Nicki use with the flour? Complete the chart using counters, a drawing, or multiplication and division.

Flour (c)	3	6	9	12	15	18
Water (c)				4		

6. How is the chart for flour and water different from the chart for flour and salt?

7. What problem might Nicki have if she uses both equal ratio charts to write a recipe for clay that calls for less flour?

Summing Up

This is a recipe for papier-mâché paste.

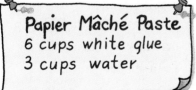

Papier Mâché Paste
6 cups white glue
3 cups water

8. Make a chart of equal ratios to show the amount of glue to use with 1, 2, 3, 4, 5, and 6 cups of water.

Use multiplication and division to give three equal ratios for 10:15.

Finding Equal Ratios

Joshua is experimenting with enlarging a photograph that is 5 inches long and 4 inches wide. **What if** its length is enlarged to 15 inches? What is the width of the enlarged photo?

One way to find the width is to use equal ratios.

$$\text{length} \longrightarrow \frac{5}{4} = \frac{15}{n} \qquad \text{Think } 5 \times 3 = 15$$

$$\frac{5}{4} \times \boxed{\frac{3}{3}} = \frac{15}{12}$$

The width is 12 inches.

More Examples

a. $\frac{4}{24} = \frac{1}{n}$

$$\frac{4}{24} \div \boxed{\frac{4}{4}} = \frac{1}{6}$$

$$\frac{4}{24} = \frac{1}{6}$$

b. $\frac{2}{3} = \frac{n}{9}$

$$\frac{2}{3} \times \boxed{\frac{3}{3}} = \frac{6}{9}$$

$$\frac{2}{3} = \frac{6}{9}$$

Check Your Understanding

Write three equal ratios for each.

1. 45 miles in 1 hour

2. 6 items for $10

3. 5 to 3

Find n.

4. $\frac{1}{3} = \frac{7}{n}$

5. $\frac{3}{4} = \frac{n}{24}$

6. $\frac{8}{18} = \frac{n}{9}$

7. $\frac{12}{32} = \frac{3}{n}$

Share Your Ideas Look back at **4–7**. Tell what number you used to find the missing number.

Practice

Write three equal ratios for each.

8. 2 items for $5

9. 4 students in 1 group

10. a dozen for 96¢

11. 3 to 4

12. 5:6

13. $\frac{3}{10}$

14. $\frac{24}{32}$

15. 10 to 9

 **Compare. Use = or ≠ (is not equal to) for each ⬤.
Choose mental math or a calculator. Explain your
choices.**

16. $\frac{1}{2}$ ⬤ $\frac{14}{7}$

17. $\frac{5}{7}$ ⬤ $\frac{500}{700}$

18. $\frac{3}{4}$ ⬤ $\frac{114}{136}$

19. $\frac{1}{4}$ ⬤ $\frac{5}{20}$

20. $\frac{1}{3}$ ⬤ $\frac{42}{136}$

21. $\frac{1}{2}$ ⬤ $\frac{16}{32}$

22. $\frac{1}{30}$ ⬤ $\frac{6}{180}$

23. $\frac{3}{8}$ ⬤ $\frac{18}{50}$

Multiply or divide to find the value of *n*.

24. $\frac{1}{2} = \frac{6}{n}$

25. $\frac{1}{3} = \frac{n}{12}$

26. $\frac{2}{3} = \frac{100}{n}$

27. $\frac{4}{5} = \frac{n}{150}$

28. $\frac{48}{50} = \frac{n}{25}$

29. $\frac{9}{12} = \frac{3}{n}$

30. $\frac{48}{51} = \frac{n}{17}$

31. $\frac{200}{600} = \frac{1}{n}$

32. $\frac{3}{8} = \frac{15}{n}$

33. $\frac{35}{42} = \frac{n}{6}$

34. $\frac{3}{10} = \frac{n}{40}$

35. $\frac{12}{8} = \frac{n}{2}$

Problem Solving

36. Joshua buys 3 packs of film for $8.99.
How much will 9 packs of film cost?

37. A camera bag holds 1 camera, 2
extra lenses, 4 packs of film. How
many cameras, lenses, and packs of
film will 3 bags hold?

38. A writer knows that it takes about 2
minutes to perform each page of a
play. How many pages would she
have to write for a $\frac{1}{2}$-hour play?

Visual Thinking

39. This is an enlargement of a
picture of an object from
outdoors. What is the object?

Explain how you could use multiplication or
division to find the missing number. $\frac{2}{3} = \frac{n}{18}$

SUMMING UP

Have you or any of your classmates ever built a scale model of a ship or an airplane? What does it mean to build a scale model?

Using Ratios in Scale Drawings

This is a scale drawing of a house. How would you find the actual length of the living room?

▶ A **scale drawing** shows the actual shape of something, but not the actual size.

▶ A **scale** gives the ratio of the measurements in the drawing to the measurements of the actual object.

The scale of this drawing is 1 cm = 2 m. Each centimeter in the drawing stands for 2 meters in the actual house.

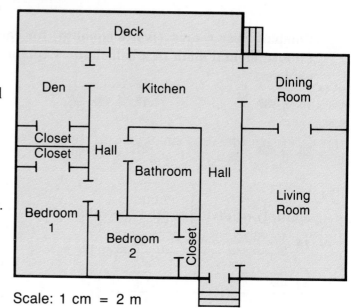

Scale: 1 cm = 2 m

To find the actual length of the living room, follow these steps.

Step 1 Write the scale as a ratio.	Step 2 Measure the length of the living room in the drawing.	Step 3 Write a ratio equal to the scale ratio.
cm → $\dfrac{1}{2}$ ← m	4 cm	cm → $\dfrac{1}{2} = \dfrac{4}{n}$ ← m $\dfrac{1}{2} \times \boxed{\dfrac{4}{4}} = \dfrac{4}{8}$

The actual length of the living room is 8 meters.

Check Your Understanding

Measure the drawing. Then find the actual length and width of each room.

1. dining room   **2.** kitchen   **3.** living room

Share Your Ideas Explain how you would use equal ratios to make a scale drawing of your classroom floor.

Use the scale drawing on page 422 for each.

4. What is the actual length and width of Bedroom 1?

5. What is the actual length and width of Bedroom 2?

6. What is the actual length and width of the bathroom?

7. What is the actual length and width of the deck?

8. Does each closet have the same length and width? Explain.

9. What is the actual length of the den?

10. What is the actual perimeter of the den?

11. Will a rug 800 cm long and 400 cm wide fit into the dining room?

Use each scale to complete.

Scale: 1 cm = 3 m

	Length in Drawing	Actual Length
12.	2 cm	
13.	9 cm	
14.		12 m
15.		300 cm
16.		4.5 m

Scale: 2 cm = 1 m

	Length in Drawing	Actual Length
17.	24 cm	
18.	96 cm	
19.		15 m
20.		200 cm
21.		3.5 m

Problem Solving

22. A basement playroom is 9 meters long. Using the scale 2 cm = 3 m, find the length of the playroom in a scale drawing.

23. **What if** a drawing of a rabbit is 3 cm long? Its actual length is 30 cm. The actual height of a bush is 200 cm. How tall should the bush be drawn to be in the same scale as the rabbit?

Use a ruler to make a scale drawing of each. Use the scale 1 cm = 4 m.

24. An office 8 m long and 4 m wide

25. A library 12 m long and 8 m wide

26. A room 4 m long and 2 m wide

27. A room 12 m long and 6 m wide

Explain the steps a builder would use to interpret an architect's scale drawing of a house.

SUMMING UP

Study the interstate highway numbers on a
United States map. Do north-south and east-west
highway numbers follow a pattern? Explain.

Using Ratios in Road Maps

What if you had to travel from Dallas to Fort Worth?
How would you find out in which direction to travel?
the route to travel? the distance?

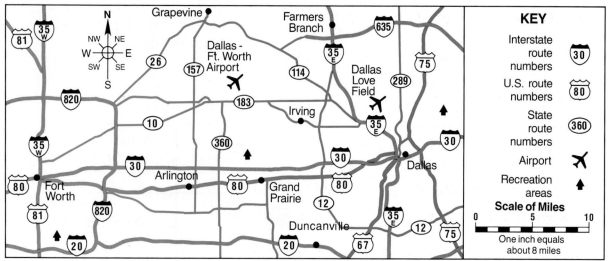

▶ The **key** explains map symbols. The **scale** shows distance
as measured on the map. The **compass** shows direction.

Drive west on Route 30 from Dallas to Fort Worth.

To estimate the actual distance, follow these steps.

• Write the scale as a ratio: $\dfrac{\text{inches} \longrightarrow 1}{\text{miles} \longrightarrow 8}$

• Estimate the distance on the map: about **4** inches
• Write a ratio equal to the scale ratio: $\dfrac{\text{inches} \longrightarrow 1}{\text{miles} \longrightarrow 8} = \dfrac{4}{32}$

Dallas is about 32 miles from Fort Worth.

Check Your Understanding

Use the map above to answer each question.

1. In which direction do you travel from
Arlington to Dallas?

2. Estimate the distance from Arlington
to Dallas.

Share Your Ideas Explain how to use a key, a scale,
and a compass when you map your school neighborhood.

Use the map on page 424 to answer each question.

3. In what direction would you travel to go from Grand Prairie to Dallas?

4. What kind of highway is Route 75?

5. Is Irving north or south of Farmer's Branch?

6. Estimate the distance from Grand Prairie to Dallas.

7. Estimate the distance from Grapevine to Arlington.

Choose the best answer.

8. Which highway goes from east to west?

   a. Route 75   **b.** Route 80   **c.** Route 35

9. Which highway does not go from north to south?

   a. Route 289   **b.** Route 35   **c.** Route 20

10. Which is the best estimate of the distance from Duncanville to Fort Worth?

   a. 18 miles   **b.** 28 miles   **c.** 60 miles

Problem Solving

 Draw one map for 11–14. Show the distance from Pete's house for each place. Use the scale 1 inch = 2 miles.

11. The library is 4 miles north and 2 miles east of Pete's house.

12. The school is 2 miles south of Pete's house.

13. The post office is 2 miles south and 1 mile east of the library.

14. The fire station is 3 miles southwest of the school.

How is a map like a scale drawing?

Mixed Review

1. $\begin{array}{r} 275 \\ \times\ 39 \\ \hline \end{array}$

2. $\begin{array}{r} 4.5 \\ \times\ 19 \\ \hline \end{array}$

3. $\begin{array}{r} 8.25 \\ +\ 9.5 \\ \hline \end{array}$

4. $\begin{array}{r} 1{,}000 \\ -\ \ 458 \\ \hline \end{array}$

5. $\begin{array}{r} 9\frac{2}{3} \\ +\ 11\frac{1}{3} \\ \hline \end{array}$

6. $6 \times 2\frac{1}{2}$

7. $\frac{2}{3} \times 9$

8. $10 - 3\frac{1}{2}$

9. $\$200 - \$13.69$

10. $\frac{3}{4} \times 96$

Find the perimeter and area of each rectangle.

11. $l = 3$ in.
    $w = 2$ in.

12. $l = 4\frac{1}{2}$ in.
    $w = 2$ in.

13. $l = 5$ ft
    $w = 3$ ft

14. $l = 7$ in.
    $w = 2\frac{1}{4}$ in.

15. $l = 6\frac{1}{2}$ ft
    $w = 3$ ft

SUMMING UP

Exploring Percent

A ratio whose second term is 100 is called a **percent.** Percent means "per hundred." Write % for percent.

What percent of the grid is shaded?

Working together

Materials: seven 10 by 10 grids, or Workmat 3

A. Shade 20 squares in a grid. Write a ratio of shaded squares to the total number of squares.

B. Another way to describe the amount shaded is with a percent. Twenty percent of the grid is shaded. Write the percent.

C. Shade a different number of squares in each of your remaining grids. Write a ratio and a percent for each grid.

Sharing Your Results

1. Look back at the grid at the top of the page. Write a percent to describe the shaded part.

Tell how many squares would be shaded on a 10 by 10 grid to show each percent.

2. 45%   **3.** 67%   **4.** 12%   **5.** 50%

Practice

Write a ratio and a percent that tell what part is shaded.

6.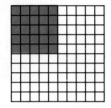

7.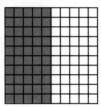

8.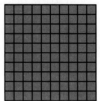

9.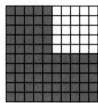

Look back at 6–9.

 10. What percent means one half?

11. Write three ratios that equal $\frac{1}{2}$.

12. What percent means the whole?

13. Write three ratios that equal a whole.

14. What does the percent in **6** describe? Write another ratio that compares the shaded area with the whole.

15. What does the percent in **9** describe? Write another ratio that compares the shaded area with the whole.

Summing Up

DATA This circle graph shows the different brands of sneakers that are sold.

16. Out of every 100 pairs of sneakers, how many pairs of Brand A were sold?

17. Which two brands account for about half of the sneakers sold?

18. What should be the sum of all the percents in the graph?

19. What percent of the sneakers sold are Other Brands?

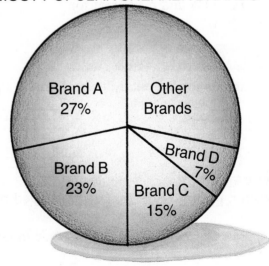

MOST POPULAR SNEAKER BRANDS

Brand A 27% · Other Brands · Brand B 23% · Brand C 15% · Brand D 7%

80% means 80 out of 100. Explain how a student can score 80% on a test that does not have 100 questions.

Percent

Mr. Ruiz is experimenting with a new kind of seed. He planted 100 seeds. During the week, 45% of the seeds had sprouted. Write the decimal and fraction for 45%.

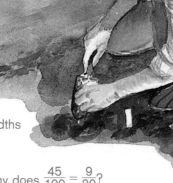

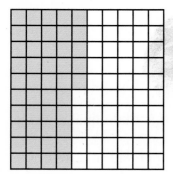

Think 45% is 45 hundredths

$$45\% = 0.45$$

$$45\% = \frac{45}{100} = \frac{9}{20}$$ Why does $\frac{45}{100} = \frac{9}{20}$?

More Examples

a. Write the fraction for 20%.

Think 20% is 20 hundredths

$$20\% = \frac{20}{100} = \frac{1}{5}$$

b. Write the decimal for 3%.

Think 3% is 3 hundredths

$$3\% = 0.03$$

Check Your Understanding

Write each as a percent, a decimal, and a fraction in lowest terms.

1.

2.

3.

4. eighteen percent

5. six per hundred

6. fifty-two hundredths

Share Your Ideas   Explain why $\frac{3}{10}$ is not 3%. What is the correct percent for $\frac{3}{10}$?

Practice

Write each as a percent, a decimal, and a fraction in lowest terms.

7. 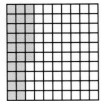   **8.** 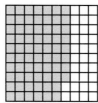   **9.**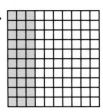

10. three per hundred   **11.** fourteen percent   **12.** 82 per hundred

13. nine hundredths   **14.** sixty percent   **15.** forty-one hundredths

16. one-half   **17.** three-fourths   **18.** four-fifths

Tell whether each is closer to 0, 50%, or 100%.

19. 3%   **20.** $\frac{87}{100}$ **21.** 0.45   **22.** $\frac{17}{100}$ **23.** 0.6   **24.** 12%

25. $\frac{9}{10}$ **26.** 0.05   **27.** 100%   **28.** 54%   **29.** $\frac{49}{50}$ **30.** 0.38

What part of each bar is shaded? Choose the best estimate.

31.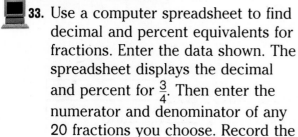

a. 48%   **b.** $\frac{1}{2}$ **c.** 0.59

32.

a. 0.42   **b.** 20%   **c.** $\frac{1}{3}$

Problem Solving

33. Use a computer spreadsheet to find decimal and percent equivalents for fractions. Enter the data shown. The spreadsheet displays the decimal and percent for $\frac{3}{4}$. Then enter the numerator and denominator of any 20 fractions you choose. Record the decimal and percent for each fraction.

Logical Thinking

Explain why each situation is impossible.

34. Shelly drank 110% of her milk.

35. In the sixth grade, 48% of the students are girls, 44% are boys.

	A	B	C	D
1	numerator	denominator	decimal	percent
2	3	4	A2/B2	C2*100

Name the percent that is found halfway between the fractions $\frac{6}{10}$ and $\frac{8}{10}$.

Midchapter Review

Write each ratio in two more ways. pages 416–417

1. $2:9$

2. 7 to 3

3. $\frac{4}{1}$

4. $10:20$

Write three equal ratios for each. pages 418–421

5. 3 items for $5

6. 400 meters in 50 seconds

Multiply or divide to find the value of *n*. pages 420–421

7. $\frac{2}{5} = \frac{n}{45}$

8. $\frac{1}{3} = \frac{12}{n}$

9. $\frac{24}{60} = \frac{n}{5}$

10. $\frac{250}{500} = \frac{1}{n}$

Use the scale drawing to find the actual length and width of each. pages 422–423

11. front hall

12. living room

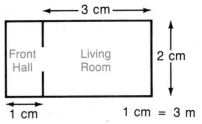

Write each as a percent and as a fraction in lowest terms. pages 426–429

13. 0.67

14. 3 per hundred

15. 5 hundredths

16. 0.5

Write each as a decimal and as a fraction in lowest terms. pages 426–429

17. 82%

18. 25%

19. 75%

20. 6%

Complete each sentence.

21. _____ means per hundred.

22. The _____ on a map compares two distances.

23. A _____ whose second term is 100 is called a percent.

Words to Know
ratio
percent
scale

Solve.

24. A photographer needs 4 hours to develop 1 roll of film. One week she developed film for 28 hours. How many rolls of film did she develop?

25. Carl won 75 out of 100 points in a computer game. Write a percent, a decimal, and a fraction in lowest terms to describe Carl's score.

Exploring Problem Solving

Will the Flowers Mature?

Farmers wonder whether it is worth their while to plant delicate flowers in a cool area of the country. About 1 day out of 4 days is too cold for the flowers. The flowers are killed by frost after 3 consecutive cold days. The flowers take 45 days to grow to maturity.

Thinking Critically

Would you plant these flowers? Tossing a penny and a dime and recording the results can help you find a solution. When your group has finished its work, you may want to combine your results with those of other groups.

Analyzing and Making Decisions

1. What are the chances that a day will be too cold for the flowers? How many consecutive cold days does it take to kill the flowers?

2. Toss both coins. The chance that they will both be tails is 1 in 4. How can you use the coin toss to simulate the weather for each day?

3. Simulate the weather for the flowers. How many days will you have to simulate the weather? How will you know if the flowers survive? If you can, try this 6 times.

4. If possible, combine your group's results with the results obtained by other groups. How many times did the flowers survive? How many times did the flowers die?

5. If you were a farmer, would you grow the flowers? Explain.

Look Back   **What if** it took 4 straight days of cold weather to kill the flowers? Would you grow them?

Problem Solving Strategies

Logic

Ann, Brad, Carol, and David each have a pet gerbil that is running through a maze. They are experimenting to see which gerbil can run the fastest. Ann's gerbil was ahead of Brad's, but it was not first. Carol's gerbil was behind Ann's, but it was not last. In what order did the gerbils finish?

Some problems require you to use logic. Often a diagram will help you solve the problem.

Solving the Problem

Think What is the question?

Explore What facts does the problem contain? Make a drawing to show the order in which the gerbils finished. Draw a line and put Ann's gerbil on it. Where does Brad's gerbil go? David's gerbil? Carol's gerbil?

Solve In what order did the gerbils finish?

Look Back David's gerbil is not mentioned in the clues. How did you know where to put it?

Share Your Ideas

1. Rewrite the clues so that the gerbil who came in first comes in last.

Practice

Solve. Use a calculator where appropriate.

2. Carol, Ann, Brad, and David own four gerbils named Winken, Blinken, Nod, and Feather. Carol watched Brad take Blinken home each night. The number of letters in one gerbil's name is the same as the number of letters in its owner's name. David's gerbil is not Feather. Who owns each gerbil?

3. A science class tested different types of plant food on some geraniums. By the end of the experiment, the red geranium had grown twice as high as the pink geranium. The white geranium had grown 1 inch less than the red geranium. The pink geranium had grown 4 inches. How many inches had the white geranium grown?

4. During the experiment, the plants were kept on a sunny window sill. The pink geranium was at the left. The red geranium was between the white one and the purple one. The white one was between the pink and the red geraniums. In what order were the plants placed on the window sill?

5. Miki and Dorene need exactly 4 quarts of water for an experiment. They have only two containers. One holds 8 quarts, and the other holds 3 quarts. How can Miki and Dorene use these containers to measure exactly 4 quarts?

Mixed Strategy Review

Use this information to solve 6–7.

Recipe for birdseed:
1 lb of pumpkin seeds
2 lb of sunflower seeds
3 lb of millet

6. Samantha wants to make 30 lb of birdseed. How much does she need of each type of seed if she follows the recipe?

7. Look at Samantha's recipe. **What if** she only wants to make 15 lb of birdseed?

Create **Your Own**

Write a problem about an experiment.

Exploring Experiments and Outcomes

Ramon is tossing a number cube. He wonders which number will be on top most often.

Recording the frequency of numbers tossed is an example of an **experiment.**

Each possible result in an experiment is an **outcome.**

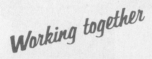
Working together

Materials: number cube with faces labeled 1–6

A. Toss the cube. What number is on top? Toss the cube again. What is the outcome?

B. Copy this frequency table.

Outcome	Tally	Frequency
1		
2		
3		
4		
5		
6		

C. Toss the cube. Mark a tally in the table to show the outcome. Toss the cube and record the outcome until 20 tallies have been marked.

D. Count the tallies for each number. Record the total for each in the frequency column.

Sharing Your Results

1. Combine the results of each group's experiment into a class table.

2. Which outcome occurred most often? least often?

3. Are the chances of tossing each number the same? Explain.

4. **What if** the cube were labeled 1, 2, 2, 3, 4, and 5? Would the chances of tossing each number be the same? Explain.

Practice

Ramon and Sara are playing *Toss and Compare* with two coins. If either coin lands tails up, Ramon scores one point. If both coins land heads up, Sara scores one point.

Ramon tosses the coins first and records the winner of the point in a chart. Then it is Sara's turn to toss the coins.

They toss the coins 30 times altogether. The winner is the person with the greater number of points.

Toss and Compare	
Ramon	I I I I
Sara	I

5. Do you think Ramon or Sara will win the game? Why?

6. Play *Toss and Compare* with a partner.

7. What are the possible outcomes in *Toss and Compare?*

8. In how many of the outcomes does at least one coin land tails up?

9. In how many of the outcomes do both coins land heads up?

10. Which do you have a better chance of tossing, at least one tail or both heads?

Summing Up

11. Do you think the rules give each player of *Toss and Compare* an equal chance to win? Explain why or why not.

12. Write a set of rules for *Toss and Compare* that gives each player an equal chance to win. Write another set that does not.

13. Play the game using your new rules. What did the results show?

Exploring Making Predictions

Mattie is tossing a coin. What are the possible outcomes?

What if Mattie tossed the coin 20 times? How many times do you think the coin would land heads up?

Working together

Materials: a coin

A. How many times do you think a coin will land heads up if it is tossed 20 times? Record your prediction.

B. Toss a coin 20 times. Record your results in a frequency table like the one at the right.

Outcome	Tally	Frequency
Heads		
Tails		

Sharing Your Results

1. Combine the results of each group's experiment and make a class table.

2. How many times did the coin land heads up? tails up?

3. Compare your experimental results with your prediction. How close was your prediction to the actual results?

Practice

These ratios can be used to show the results of your experiment.

$$\frac{\text{number of heads}}{\text{number of tosses}} \qquad \frac{\text{number of tails}}{\text{number of tosses}}$$

4. Use the results of your experiment to write both ratios.

5. Use the class results to write both ratios.

6. Write your prediction as a ratio.

7. **Look back** at **4–6**.
   Is the ratio of your results or the class results closer to your prediction?
   Did you expect this? Why or why not?

Summing Up

8. **What if** two coins are tossed? Predict the number of times both coins will be heads up if they are tossed 20 times.

9. These are the results of an experiment where two coins are tossed. List the results using a ratio.

Outcome	Frequency
heads, heads	30
heads, tails	27
tails, heads	32
tails, tails	31

10. About what fraction of the time does each outcome occur?

What did Tara mean when she said, "I'll take a chance! Maybe Mr. Jones won't collect our homework today."

Finding Probabilities

Five checkers are placed in a bag. Two checkers are red and three are black. Kevin thinks he will pick a red one. What are his chances?

There are 5 checkers so there are 5 **possible outcomes.** Each checker has the same chance of being picked. Two checkers are red so there are 2 **favorable outcomes.**

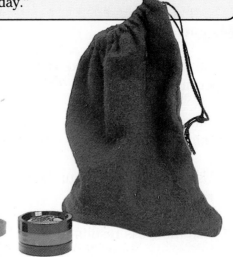

An **event** (E) is one or more outcomes of an experiment. Choosing a red checker is an event with two possible outcomes.

▶ The **probability** of an event is the ratio of the number of favorable outcomes to the number of possible outcomes.

$$\text{Probability } (E) = \frac{\text{number of favorable outcomes}}{\text{number of possible outcomes}}$$

The probability of choosing a red checker is $\frac{2}{5}$.

Another Example

What is the probability of choosing a black checker?

$$\frac{\text{favorable outcomes}}{\text{possible outcomes}} \longrightarrow \frac{3}{5}$$

The probability is $\frac{3}{5}$.

Check Your Understanding

What if these cards are in a box and you choose one of them?

1. What are the possible outcomes?

2. What is the probability of choosing the card with the number 9?

3. What is the probability of choosing a red card?

4. What is the probability of choosing a card with a number less than 6?

Share Your Ideas Explain the difference between a possible outcome and a favorable outcome.

What if you have cards with pictures of these coins in a bag? Find the probability of getting each, if you pick only one picture.

5. a penny

6. a nickel

7. a dime

8. less than 10¢

9. a silver-colored coin

10. a nickel if you have already spent one of the dimes

A cube has the faces numbered 1 through 6. Find the probability that each of the following will land on top if you toss the cube.

11. 4

12. a number less than 4

13. an even number

14. a prime number

Problem Solving

15. How many checkers would you put in a bag to make 10 possible outcomes?

Look back at 15.

16. **What if** the probability of choosing a red checker was $\frac{4}{10}$? How many red checkers would be in the bag? how many black checkers?

17. **What if** the probability of choosing a black checker was $\frac{7}{10}$? How many black checkers would be in the bag? how many red checkers?

What if there are 9 checkers in a bag? The probability of picking a black is $\frac{1}{3}$. How many black checkers are in the bag?

Mixed Review

1. $6{,}543 - 1{,}979$

2. $4.59 + 8.03$

3. $1.75 \div 5$

4. 3×4.5

5. $\frac{1}{6} + \frac{1}{2}$

6. $1\frac{1}{5} - \frac{3}{10}$

7. $\frac{3}{8} \times \frac{1}{2}$

8. $327 \div 3$

9. $59 + 125 + 17 + 9$

10. $2\frac{1}{3} + \frac{1}{4}$

11. $100 - 23.8$

12. 304×7

13. $\frac{1}{3} \div \frac{3}{5}$

14. $12 \times 1{,}000$

Give the number of sides in each polygon.

15. quadrilateral

16. hexagon

17. pentagon

18. triangle

19. parallelogram

SUMMING UP

Describe an event that is certain to happen.
Describe another that is impossible.

Certain and Impossible Events

What if you picked one marble without
looking? Is it likely that you will pick the
blue marble? Why?

Numbers can be used instead of words
to describe whether an outcome is
possible, impossible, or certain.

Outcome	Chance	Probability
blue marble	possible	$\frac{1}{10}$
red marble	possible	$\frac{9}{10}$
white marble	impossible	$\frac{0}{10} = 0$
any marble	certain	$\frac{10}{10} = 1$

▶ The probability of an event is always
  0, 1, or a number between 0 and 1.

▶ An **impossible event** has a probability
  of 0. A **certain event** has a probability
  of 1.

More Examples

a. What is the probability of March
having 32 days?
March never has 32 days.
The probability is 0.

b. What is the probability of April having
30 days?
April always has 30 days.
The probability is 1.

Check Your Understanding

**Tell whether each means that the probability is 0,
close to 0, close to 1, or 1.**

1. rarely   **2.** never   **3.** always   **4.** probably

Share Your Ideas   Explain why the probability of an
event can never be greater than one.

Tell whether the probability of each is *0, close to 0, close to 1,* or *1*.

5. The school bus will start in the morning.

6. The sun will set in the evening.

7. Summer vacation will last 4 months.

8. We will all have perfect attendance next year.

Choose the best probability for each.

9. impossible	10. sure	11. doubtful	12. expected
a. 0	a. 0	a. 0	a. 0
b. $\frac{1}{3}$	b. $\frac{1}{4}$	b. $\frac{1}{5}$	b. $\frac{1}{10}$
c. $\frac{2}{3}$	c. $\frac{3}{4}$	c. $\frac{4}{5}$	c. $\frac{9}{10}$
d. 1	d. 1	d. 1	d. 1

Use the dominoes to answer 13–16. Imagine that they are turned face down and mixed together. Tell whether the probability of picking each is *0, close to 0, close to 1,* or *1*.

13. a blank domino

14. a domino with 10 dots

15. a domino with more than 3 dots

16. a domino with more than 12 dots

Describe the numbers on a cube for which the probability of rolling a 3 is

17. 1.

18. close to 0.

19. $\frac{1}{2}$.

20. close to 1.

Logical Thinking

21. Carrie had a domino set like the one shown above. Now she has only 27 dominoes which have a total of 157 dots. What is Carrie missing from her set?

Use examples from everyday life to explain why possible and probable do not always mean the same thing.

SUMMING UP

Using Problem Solving

Arrangements

The coach is trying to decide in what order Jon, Paul, and Lena will run the relay race. How many different arrangements must he consider?

How many different arrangements do you think there are? more than 10? less than 10?

One way to find all the arrangements is to use a tree diagram.

First⟶   Jon   Paul   Lena

Second⟶ Paul   Lena   Jon   Lena   Jon   Paul

Third⟶ Lena   Paul   Lena   Jon   Paul   Jon

Sharing Your Ideas

1. Use the tree diagram to list all the possible arrangements.

2. How did your estimate compare to the actual number of arrangements?

3. How many choices are there for the first runner?

4. After the first runner is chosen, how many choices are there for the second runner?

5. After the first and second runners are chosen, how many choices are there for the third runner?

6. **Look back** at **3–5.** How does the number of possible arrangements of runners relate to the product of $3 \times 2 \times 1 = 6$?

Practice

Suppose a fourth runner, Matt, joins the relay team.

7. Estimate the number of arrangements that you think are possible for four runners.

8. How many choices are there for the starter?

9. After the starter is chosen, how many choices are there for the second runner?

10. After the first and second runners are chosen, how many choices are there for the third? for the fourth?

11. Write a multiplication sentence to show the choices. What is the meaning of the product?

12. Compare your estimate for the number of arrangements with the actual number.

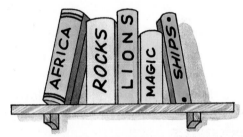

Use the books for questions 13–15.

13. Suppose you are arranging the books on a shelf. In how many different ways can the books be arranged?

14. What if it takes you 1 minute each time you rearrange the books? How many hours would it take you to make all the possible arrangements?

15. What if you arrange the books on a shelf without looking at the titles? What is the probability that they will be in alphabetical order?

Summing Up

Hal and Sally collect hats. Hal will choose a hat without looking and then Sally will choose a hat.

16. In how many different ways can the hats be chosen?

17. In how many of the ways does either Hal or Sally choose the magician's hat?

18. What is the probability that either Hal or Sally will choose the magician's hat?

443

Chapter Review

Write each ratio in two other ways. Then write an equal ratio for each. pages 416–421

1. $7 : 2$

2. 24 to 12

3. $\dfrac{9}{3}$

Find n. pages 420–421

4. $\dfrac{2}{3} = \dfrac{8}{n}$

5. $\dfrac{4}{5} = \dfrac{n}{35}$

6. $\dfrac{12}{20} = \dfrac{3}{n}$

7. $\dfrac{40}{100} = \dfrac{n}{10}$

Find each actual length. pages 422–425

8. The distance between two cities on a map is 4 cm. The scale is 1 cm = 30 km. What is the actual distance between the cities?

9. A room on a scale drawing is 5 cm long. The scale is 1 cm = 2 m. What is the room's actual length?

Write a ratio and a percent for each. pages 426–427

10. 15 out of 100

11. 20 per hundred

12. 33 out of 100

Write a decimal and a fraction in lowest terms for each percent. pages 428–429

13. 30%

14. 25%

15. 12%

16. 5%

Use the spinner for questions 17–19. pages 434–441

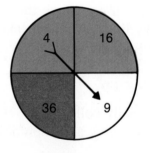

17. What if you spin the spinner 20 times? Predict the number of times *red* will be chosen.

18. What is the probability of an even number?

19. What is the probability of *blue*?

Choose the correct word to complete each sentence.

Words to Know
outcome
certain
impossible

20. A _____ event has a probability of 1.

21. An _____ event has a probability of 0.

22. Each possible result in an experiment is an _____.

Solve. pages 431–433, 442–443

23. There are 6 books on a shelf. In how many different ways can the books be arranged?

24. A certain whole number is less than 10. Twice the number is greater than 5. Three times the number is less than 10. What is the number?

Chapter Test

Write each ratio in two other ways. Then write an equal ratio for each.

1. 1:5

2. 4 to 16

3. $\frac{3}{2}$

Find _n_.

4. $\frac{1}{5} = \frac{9}{n}$

5. $\frac{3}{8} = \frac{n}{48}$

6. $\frac{18}{36} = \frac{1}{n}$

7. $\frac{75}{100} = \frac{n}{4}$

Find each actual length.

8. The distance between two cities on a map is 6 cm. The scale is 1 cm = 20 km. What is the actual distance between the cities?

9. A room on a scale drawing is 3 cm wide. The scale is 1 cm = 3 m. What is the room's actual width?

Write a ratio and a percent for each.

10. 16 out of 100

11. 39 per hundred

12. 50 out of 100

Write a decimal and a fraction in lowest terms for each percent.

13. 75%

14. 10%

15. 7%

Use the spinner for questions 16–18.

16. What if you spin the spinner 20 times? Predict the number of times _blue_ will be chosen.

17. What is the probability of an odd number?

18. What is the probability of _red_?

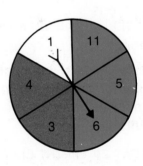

Solve.

19. There are 3 trophies on a shelf. In how many different ways can the trophies be arranged?

20. Pat, John, and Sue ran a race. John was not first. Sue finished between the other two. Who won the race?

THINK   Joan had $100 in her savings account. She withdrew 15%. How much money was left in the account?

Exploring Probability

A bag contains 1 blue, 1 green, and 2 red marbles. Suppose you pick one marble. Do you think that it will be blue? green? red?

The probability of picking a blue marble is

$\dfrac{1}{4}$ ← number of blue marbles
← total number of marbles

What is the probability of picking a marble that is green? red? white?

AT THE COMPUTER

Materials: Logo

A. The computer simulates picking a marble from a bag by randomly choosing one of the colors in a list. Define the procedure CHOOSE. Then enter PRINT CHOOSE several times. Describe your results.

```
TO CHOOSE
OP ITEM 1 + RANDOM 4 [BLUE GREEN RED RED]
END
```

B. Use the REPEAT command below to have the computer choose a color 20 times. Count the number of times each color prints. Record your results.

```
REPEAT 20 [PRINT CHOOSE]
```

C. Repeat the simulation in **B** four more times. Record the number of times the computer picked each color.

D. Which color was picked the greatest number of times? Tell why you think that happened.

Sharing Your Results

1. **Look back** at the probability of choosing each color. How many times would you expect to choose each color out of 100 times?

2. Compare your results to the expected number of times for each color. Are they the same? Why or why not?

Extending the Activity

3. Complete the following procedure by filling in the blanks. A color is chosen from a list that contains BLACK four times, YELLOW three times, BLUE two times and RED one time.

```
TO CHOOSE2
OP ITEM 1 + RANDOM _____[BLACK, _____, _____, _____,
                        YELLOW, _____, _____,
                        BLUE, _____, RED]
END
```

Type as one line.
Remember that
OP means output

4. Predict the number of times that the computer will pick each color if a color is chosen 100 times. Explain how you made each prediction.

5. Use the computer to simulate choosing a color one hundred times. Record your results in a chart.

BLACK	YELLOW	BLUE	RED

6. Compare your results with your predictions. What do you notice?

Summing Up

7. Create your own probability experiment. Make up a list of any colors you choose. Predict how many times each color will be picked. Then use the computer to simulate the experiment.

Simple Trees

Eight students signed up to compete in the Junior Tennis Open. How many matches need to be scheduled to determine the champion?

This tree diagram shows how the matches could be played.

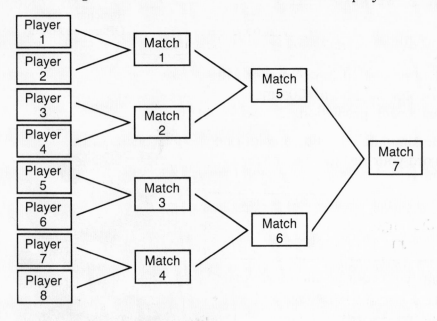

1. How many matches should be scheduled?

2. **What if** 11 players entered the Open? Sketch a tree diagram to show how many matches should be scheduled.

3. Choose any number of players and find the number of matches that need to be played.

4. Record your results for **1–3**. What do you notice about the number of players and the number of matches that need to be scheduled?

Family Math

In the last three chapters of this book, we studied how to multiply fractions; how to find ratios, percents, and probabilities, and how to find the perimeter, area, and volume of figures.

Does Your Floor Need A Carpet?

Mathematics is used in many ways in everyday life. Carpeting a floor is one example.

As a family activity, choose a room that you would like to carpet. Look for advertisements for carpeting in the newspaper or in a magazine. Choose 3 or 4 advertisements and write the information in a chart like this.

Carpet Type	Price per Square Yard	Total Cost
1.		
2.		
3.		
4.		

Now measure in feet the length and width of the room you want to carpet. If the room has a measurement that includes inches, round up to the next foot. It's better to have a small amount of carpet left over than not enough carpet!

Compute the area by multiplying the length of the room by the width. Since carpeting is measured in **square yards,** you will need to convert your measurement. There are 9 square feet in a square yard. Divide the number of square feet by 9 to get the number of square yards.

Now you are ready to find the total price for each of the 3 carpets you chose. Use a calculator if you wish.

Carpeting a floor is only one example of using mathematics in everyday life. Ask your family members to share other ways that they use mathematics to do things around the house.

Final Review

Choose the correct answers. Write A, B, C, or D.

1. Write the standard numeral for 216 million, 3 thousand, 84.

  A 216,384   **C** 216,030,840

  B 216,003,084   **D** not given

2. 56,821
   − 4,362

  A 52,459   **C** 52,541

  B 52,569   **D** not given

3. 620 × 232

  A 18,660   **C** 143,840

  B 6,042   **D** not given

4. 16,034 ÷ 62

  A 271 R32   **C** 259

  B 258 R38   **D** not given

Use the line graph for 5 and 6.

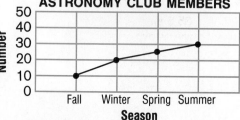

5. Which season had the fewest members?

  A fall   **C** spring

  B winter   **D** not given

6. How many members were in the Astronomy Club in the spring?

  A 10   **C** 25

  B 20   **D** not given

7. Identify angle *ARM*.

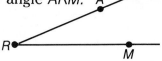

  A right angle   **C** obtuse angle

  B acute angle   **D** not given

8. 2 − 0.48

  A 0.46   **C** 1.52

  B 0.28   **D** not given

9. 2.5
   × 0.8

  A 2   **C** 20

  B 200   **D** not given

10. 45.25 ÷ 5

  A 9.5   **C** 9 R5

  B 9.05   **D** not given

11. What is the decimal for $\frac{7}{25}$?

  A 7.25   **C** 0.7

  B 0.28   **D** not given

12. Compare. $\frac{3}{4}$ ⬭ $\frac{9}{10}$

  A <   **C** =

  B >   **D** not given

13. $8\frac{1}{6} + 10\frac{1}{3}$

  A $18\frac{2}{9}$ **C** $18\frac{2}{3}$

  B $18\frac{1}{2}$ **D** not given

Choose the correct answers. Write A, B, C, or D.

14. $10\frac{1}{2} - 4\frac{2}{5}$

   A $6\frac{1}{3}$ **C** $6\frac{1}{10}$

   B $14\frac{3}{7}$ **D** not given

15. $\frac{3}{5} \times \frac{2}{7}$

   A $\frac{6}{35}$ **C** $\frac{5}{12}$

   B $\frac{1}{7}$ **D** not given

16. $2\frac{1}{2}$ ft = _____ in.

   A 24   **C** 36

   B 30   **D** not given

17. Find the area.

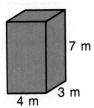

8 cm, 20 cm

   A 160 cm^2 **C** 28 cm^2

   B 80 cm^2 **D** not given

18. Find the volume.

7 m, 4 m, 3 m

   A 12 m^3 **C** 81 m^3

   B 28 m^3 **D** not given

19. A map scale is 1 in. = 16 miles. What is the actual distance for 6 inches on the map?

   A 96 miles   **C** 66 miles

   B 6 miles   **D** not given

Solve.

20. There are 5 bird feeders. They are numbered 1–5, starting at the top. A bird started at the top feeder and went down 2, down 1 more, and up 3 levels. What level was it on?

   A bottom   **C** 3rd level

   B top   **D** not given

Solve.

21. Mrs. Philips allowed $200.00 for travel expenses for her business trip. $\frac{1}{10}$ of this was spent on gas and tolls. $\frac{1}{2}$ of what was left was for food. How much was left for hotel expenses?

   A $100.00   **C** $90.00

   B $180.00   **D** not given

Use the figure to solve 22 and 23.

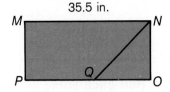

35.5 in.

22. The area of *MNOP* is 568 in^2. What is the length of *MP*?

   A 532.5 in.   **C** 29 in.

   B 16 in.   **D** not given

23. What is the area of figure *MNOP* if base *ON* of the triangle is 6.5 in.?

   A 230.75 in.^{2} **C** 460 in.^{2}

   B 108 in.^{2} **D** not given

Extra Practice

Write each number in standard form. pages 2–3, 6–7

1. sixty million, five hundred two
2. nine million, four thousand, thirty
3. eight hundred seventy-one billion
4. one billion, two thousand, fifty

Compare. Write <, >, or = for ● pages 8–9

5. 6,148 ● 6,184
6. 20,380 ● 2,038
7. 17,699 ● 17,698
8. 73,812 ● 73,812
9. 433,334 ● 344,443
10. 156,276 ● 165,267

Round each number to the place named. pages 10–11

tens

11. 473
12. 1,685
13. $703
14. 49,297

thousands

15. 6,513
16. 278,871
17. 60,444
18. $17,402

Find n. pages 18–19

1. $n + 19 = 48$
2. $28 + n = 81$
3. $n + 40 = 76$
4. $12 + n = 33$
5. $n - 37 = 21$
6. $n - 16 = 42$
7. $71 - n = 30$
8. $85 - n = 63$

Estimate each sum or difference. pages 20–21, 26–27

1.   59
   $+ 82$

2.   225
   $+ 279$

3.   483
   $- 171$

4.   6,744
   $+ 5,246$

5.   8,044
   $- 2,658$

Estimate. Then find each sum. pages 22–25

1.   46
   $+ 88$

2.   667
   $+ 49$

3.   255
   $+ 189$

4. $742
   $+ 885$

5.   1,400
   $+ 2,931$

6.   5,417
   $+ 894$

7.   4,387
   $+ 8,273$

8.   16,237
   $+ 45,765$

9.   51,501
   $+ 84,748$

10.   63,746
   $+ 78,489$

Subtract. Add to check. pages 28–31

11.   47
   $- 29$

12.   103
   $- 81$

13.   205
   $- 97$

14. $4,000
   $- 1,750$

15.   19,030
   $- 4,809$

16. $136,417 - 94,729$

17. $802,601 - 384,792$

452

Set A

Find each product mentally. Use patterns. pages 44–45

1. $\begin{array}{r} 50 \\ \times\ 9 \\ \hline \end{array}$
2. $\begin{array}{r} 60 \\ \times\ 70 \\ \hline \end{array}$
3. $\begin{array}{r} 400 \\ \times\ 20 \\ \hline \end{array}$
4. $5{,}000 \times 900$
5. $60 \times 5 \times 40$

Set B

Estimate first. Then multiply. pages 46–49

1. $\begin{array}{r} 29 \\ \times\ 7 \\ \hline \end{array}$
2. $\begin{array}{r} 438 \\ \times\ 3 \\ \hline \end{array}$
3. $\begin{array}{r} 207 \\ \times\ 6 \\ \hline \end{array}$
4. $\begin{array}{r} 3{,}124 \\ \times\ 2 \\ \hline \end{array}$
5. $\begin{array}{r} 4{,}709 \\ \times\ 5 \\ \hline \end{array}$

6. 278×5
7. 8×910
8. $9 \times 3{,}582$
9. $2{,}061 \times 3$

Find the LCM for each pair of numbers. pages 50–51

10. 3, 5
11. 8, 6
12. 20, 16
13. 10, 12
14. 18, 24

Set C

Multiply. Estimate to be sure each answer makes sense. pages 58–59

1. $\begin{array}{r} 37 \\ \times\ 34 \\ \hline \end{array}$
2. $\begin{array}{r} 89 \\ \times\ 26 \\ \hline \end{array}$
3. $\begin{array}{r} 76 \\ \times\ 19 \\ \hline \end{array}$
4. $\begin{array}{r} 265 \\ \times\ 64 \\ \hline \end{array}$
5. $\begin{array}{r} 2{,}714 \\ \times\ 32 \\ \hline \end{array}$

6. 58×80
7. 65×434
8. 93×207
9. $16 \times 3{,}050$

Estimate each product. Then multiply. pages 60–61

10. $\begin{array}{r} \$.63 \\ \times\ 7 \\ \hline \end{array}$
11. $\begin{array}{r} \$4.25 \\ \times\ 12 \\ \hline \end{array}$
12. $\begin{array}{r} \$7.89 \\ \times\ 8 \\ \hline \end{array}$
13. $\begin{array}{r} \$10.70 \\ \times\ 11 \\ \hline \end{array}$
14. $\begin{array}{r} \$31.47 \\ \times\ 26 \\ \hline \end{array}$

15. $8 \times \$.79$
16. $4 \times \$21.16$
17. $64 \times \$7.92$
18. $45 \times \$42.68$

Estimate first. Then use a calculator to multiply. pages 62–63

19. $\begin{array}{r} 971 \\ \times\ 316 \\ \hline \end{array}$
20. $\begin{array}{r} 4{,}312 \\ \times\ 277 \\ \hline \end{array}$
21. $\begin{array}{r} 809 \\ \times\ 502 \\ \hline \end{array}$
22. $\begin{array}{r} 7{,}297 \\ \times\ 333 \\ \hline \end{array}$
23. $\begin{array}{r} 68{,}002 \\ \times\ 894 \\ \hline \end{array}$

Set D

Write two related division examples for each. pages 74–74

1. 6×2
2. 3×9
3. 8×7
4. 6×4
5. 1×5

Estimate each quotient. pages 78–79

6. $4\overline{)97}$
7. $9\overline{)105}$
8. $6\overline{)348}$
9. $8\overline{)500}$
10. $7\overline{)399}$

Extra Practice

Set A

Divide. Check by multiplying. pages 82–85

1. 4)84   2. 3)73   3. 6)91   4. 7)73   5. 8)63

6. 5)435   7. 2)647   8. 9)846   9. 4)945   10. 3)750

11. 612 ÷ 8   12. 91 ÷ 7   13. 777 ÷ 5   14. 792 ÷ 6   15. 403 ÷ 9

Find each quotient. pages 86–87

16. 3)309   17. 8)483   18. 6)638   19. 7)735

20. 913 ÷ 9   21. 601 ÷ 2   22. 752 ÷ 5   23. 883 ÷ 4

Set B

Find each quotient. pages 92–93

1. 4)2,176   2. 9)9,981   3. 6)8,341   4. 2)5,555

5. 14,861 ÷ 5   6. 76,230 ÷ 8   7. 42,019 ÷ 7   8. 63,046 ÷ 3

Divide, using the short form. pages 94–95

9. 6)216   10. 5)807   11. 9)1,944   12. 2)37,148

13. 609 ÷ 3   14. 609 ÷ 4   15. 3,710 ÷ 7   16. 5,040 ÷ 8

Find each quotient. pages 96–97

17. 3)$.75   18. 2)$3.98   19. 7)$10.50   20. 9)$72.45

21. $49.60 ÷ 8   22. $79.80 ÷ 5   23. $36.72 ÷ 4   24. $8.40 ÷ 6

Find each average. pages 100–101

25. 71, 83, 10, 64   26. $1.39, $2.75   27. 1,102, 3,203, 2,604

Set C

Divide. Check by multiplying. pages 114–115

1. 20)800   2. 20)8,000   3. 90)270   4. 90)2,700   5. 80)5,600

6. 60)180   7. 40)3,600   8. 30)1,500   9. 70)490   10. 50)450

Estimate each quotient. pages 116–117

11. 28)730   12. 52)1,354   13. 33)617   14. 81)2,935

15. 3,711 ÷ 65   16. 8,437 ÷ 93   17. 4,294 ÷ 67   18. $950 ÷ 24

Set A

Divide. Check by multiplying. pages 118–121

1. 40)65   2. 60)298   3. 90)278   4. 80)482   5. 20)169

6. 31)83   7. 82)475   8. 64)453   9. 38)160   10. 57)456

Set B

Divide. Check by multiplying. pages 122–123

1. 51)3,468   2. 94)1,128   3. 60)4,568   4. 33)1,089

5. 49)2,503   6. 82)6,724   7. 16)812   8. 45)488

9. 71)1,562   10. 28)2,936   11. 26)16,120   12. 11)33,080

Set C

Divide. Check by multiplying. pages 128–133

1. $3,176 \div 51$ 2. $2,280 \div 48$ 3. $41,126 \div 73$

4. $53,017 \div 96$ 5. $7,236 \div 35$ 6. $7,510 \div 70$

**List the factors for each. Then tell
whether the number is prime or composite.** pages 136–139

7. 30   8. 37   9. 49   10. 53   11. 55   12. 56

Set D

Complete. pages 146–147

1. 5 wk = ____ d   2. 120 h = ____ d   3. 6 h = ____ min

4. 400 s = ____ min ____ s   5. 6 wk 2 d = ____ d   6. 581 min = ____ h ____ min

**Estimate the time to the nearest half hour.
Then find the exact time.** pages 148–151

7. from 1:05 P.M.   8. from 7:40 A.M.   9. from 9:55 A.M.
   to 4:30 P.M.   to 2:20 P.M.   to 12:00 noon

Add or subtract. pages 148–149

10.   4 h 25 min   11.   7 h 50 min   12.   3 h 20 min
    + 1 h 45 min   − 2 h 15 min   − 1 h 45 min

Extra Practice

Use the graph to answer each question. pages 152–153

1. Which grade has the most bus riders?

2. How many grade 4 students ride the bus?

3. How many more third graders than fifth graders ride the bus?

4. How many students are there in the sixth grade?

5. How many students in grades 3–6 ride the bus?

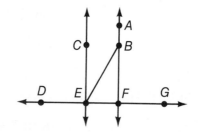

STUDENTS WHO RIDE BUS TO SCHOOL	
Grade 6	
Grade 5	
Grade 4	
Grade 3	

Each 🚌 is 10 students.

Set B

The table shows Randy's scores on the first five mathematics tests. pages 152–155, 158–159

1. Make a bar graph or a line graph to display the scores.

2. Use the graph to tell when his score improved the most.

3. If Randy gets a 60 on the next test, can you graph it on your graph?

4. Repeat **1** and **2** for your scores on your last 4 mathematics tests.

Test	Score
1	84
2	79
3	80
4	89
5	83

Set C

Use the figure to name each. pages 178–185

1. two segments with endpoint A

2. two rays with endpoint B

3. a right angle with vertex F

4. the measure of ∠ABE

5. two acute angles with vertex E

6. a line perpendicular to $\overleftrightarrow{CE}$

7. a line parallel to $\overleftrightarrow{AF}$

Draw a polygon with the number of sides. Write its name. pages 186–187

8. six

9. three

10. eight

11. five

Set A

Use dot paper and these figures. pages 192–199

a. 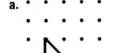   b.   c. 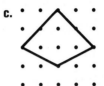   d.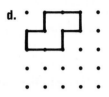

d. no symmetry line

1. Draw a similar polygon for each. Double the length of each side.

2. Trace each polygon. Draw any lines of symmetry.

3. Trace each polygon. Draw a congruent polygon that is a turn image.

Set B

List all names that apply to each polygon. pages 200–201, 204–205

1. 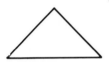   2.   3.   4. 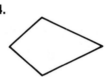   5.

Use the figure at the right to name each. pages 206–207

6. three radii

7. two chords

8. a semicircle

9. a diameter

Set C

Wite the decimal for each. pages 218–219

1. fifty-one hundredths

2. twelve thousandths

3. seven tenths

4. ninety-six thousandths

5. one and two tenths

6. four thousandths

Compare. Use >, <, or = for ⬤. pages 220–221

7. 0.8 ⬤ 0.6

8. 0.21 ⬤ 0.12

9. 0.77 ⬤ 0.7

10. 1.23 ⬤ 1.32

11. 3.08 ⬤ 4.08

12. 6.66 ⬤ 6.666

Extra Practice

Set A

Round each number to the place named. pages 222–223

ones   **1.** 4.59   **2.** 6.27   **3.** 11.48   **4.** 51.09

hundredths **5.** 0.174   **6.** 0.216   **7.** 1.345   **8.** 77.777

ten cents   **9.** $.83   **10.** $1.49   **11.** $2.31   **12.** $6.98

Estimate each sum or difference. pages 228–229

13. 8.4 − 3.8   **14.** $1.49 − $.25   **15.** 47.83 − 16.45

Set B

Add. Estimate to see if your answer makes sense. pages 232–233

1. 4.7   **2.** 7.6   **3.** 3.2   **4.** 1.79   **5.** 6.743
   + 2.9   + 5.2   + 0.64   + 0.09   + 0.8

6. 6.2 + 0.83 = n   **7.** 8.888 + 7.7 = n   **8.** 4.646 + 1.356 = n

Subtract. Estimate to see if your answer makes sense. pages 234–235

9. 1.8   **10.** 7.2   **11.** 5.3   **12.** 10.4   **13.** 3.078
   − 0.7   − 3.8   − 0.3   − 5.28   − 1.481

14. $9.49 − $7.75 = n   **15.** 6.2 − 3.38 = n   **16.** 4.444 − 0.55 = n

---

Set C

Estimate each product. pages 250–251

1. $.55   **2.** 6.2   **3.** 3.8   **4.** 50   **5.** 112
   ×   12   × 15   × 2.4   × 6.4   × 4.5

6. 72 × 3.2   **7.** 295 × 5.8   **8.** 176 × 2.2

Find each product. pages 254–255

9. 6.3   **10.** 8.9   **11.** 1.23   **12.** $.59   **13.** 6.04
   × 7   × 4   ×   7   ×   8   ×   5

14. 0.23 × 9   **15.** 0.501 × 8   **16.** 4.8 × 19

Multiply. Estimate to be sure each answer makes sense. pages 256–259

17. 4.8   **18.** 7.5   **19.** 6.27   **20.** 0.08   **21.** $.02
   × 0.3   × 0.9   ×   0.8   × 0.08   ×   75

Set A

Divide. Check by multiplying. pages 262–263

1. $4\overline{)3.84}$ 2. $7\overline{)8.47}$ 3. $6\overline{)15.6}$ 4. $5\overline{)\$.85}$ 5. $32\overline{)60.8}$

6. $9\overline{)7.65}$ 7. $3\overline{)0.108}$ 8. $16\overline{)1.12}$ 9. $8\overline{)0.72}$ 10. $20\overline{)1.04}$

11. $\$59.85 \div 45$ 12. $8.064 \div 8$ 13. $64.7 \div 10$

Set B

Choose km, m, cm, or mm for each measurement. pages 268–269

1. width of your classroom   2. width of this textbook

3. distance from Houston to Dallas   4. thickness of a pencil

Complete. pages 270–271

5. 2 km = _____ m   6. 1.3 m = _____ cm   7. 40 mm = _____ cm

8. 5.1 m = _____ mm   9. 600 m = _____ km   10. 7.25 cm = _____ mm

Choose kg, g, mg, L, or mL for each. pages 272–275

11. weight of a postage stamp   12. your weight

13. weight of a marble   14. capacity of a medicine dropper

15. capacity of a picnic jug   16. capacity of a paint can

Write cold, comfortable, or hot for each temperature. pages 276–277

17. 22°C   18. 6°C   19. 35°C   20. ⁻3°C   21. 18°C   22. 40°C

Set C

Write each fraction as a decimal and each decimal as a fraction. pages 286–287

1. $\frac{2}{5}$ 2. 0.73   3. $\frac{1}{10}$ 4. 0.3   5. $\frac{3}{4}$ 6. 0.09

7. 0.25   8. $\frac{49}{100}$ 9. 0.5   10. $\frac{7}{10}$ 11. 0.15   12. $\frac{3}{100}$

Find each missing number. pages 290–291

13. $\frac{3}{4} = \frac{\square}{12}$ 14. $\frac{1}{3} = \frac{\square}{24}$ 15. $\frac{\square}{6} = \frac{10}{12}$ 16. $\frac{1}{4} = \frac{\square}{16}$ 17. $\frac{1}{2} = \frac{\square}{60}$

18. $\frac{3}{5} = \frac{\square}{30}$ 19. $\frac{5}{8} = \frac{\square}{24}$ 20. $\frac{\square}{5} = \frac{40}{50}$ 21. $\frac{1}{6} = \frac{\square}{30}$ 22. $\frac{\square}{4} = \frac{5}{20}$

Extra Practice

Write each fraction in lowest terms. pages 292–293

1. $\frac{8}{16}$
2. $\frac{6}{10}$
3. $\frac{12}{30}$
4. $\frac{24}{32}$
5. $\frac{10}{12}$
6. $\frac{35}{50}$

7. $\frac{85}{100}$
8. $\frac{15}{40}$
9. $\frac{21}{24}$
10. $\frac{48}{60}$
11. $\frac{36}{120}$
12. $\frac{8}{48}$

Use the LCD to rewrite as like fractions. pages 294–295

13. $\frac{3}{4}, \frac{7}{12}$
14. $\frac{1}{2}, \frac{2}{3}$
15. $\frac{5}{8}, \frac{9}{16}$
16. $\frac{1}{4}, \frac{1}{3}$
17. $\frac{3}{5}, \frac{3}{4}$

Set B

Tell whether each number is closer to 0, $\frac{1}{2}$, or 1. pages 300–301

1. $\frac{4}{7}$
2. $\frac{6}{100}$
3. $\frac{1}{9}$
4. 0.79
5. 0.18
6. $\frac{5}{12}$

Compare. Write >, <, or = for ●. pages 302–303

7. $\frac{5}{8} ● \frac{7}{8}$
8. $\frac{2}{3} ● \frac{1}{4}$
9. $\frac{5}{8} ● \frac{5}{9}$
10. $\frac{3}{6} ● \frac{4}{8}$
11. $\frac{7}{10} ● \frac{7}{8}$
12. $\frac{3}{4} ● 0.5$

13. $\frac{5}{6} ● \frac{4}{5}$
14. $\frac{3}{16} ● \frac{3}{8}$
15. $\frac{4}{5} ● \frac{7}{10}$
16. $\frac{5}{6} ● \frac{7}{8}$
17. $\frac{7}{12} ● \frac{2}{3}$
18. $\frac{6}{8} ● \frac{9}{12}$

Write each mixed number as an improper fraction. Write each improper fraction as a mixed number or whole number. pages 306–307

19. $4\frac{1}{2}$
20. $\frac{9}{4}$
21. $2\frac{4}{5}$
22. $\frac{10}{3}$
23. $3\frac{3}{4}$
24. $\frac{18}{6}$

Set C

Estimate each sum or difference. pages 324–325, 330–331

1. $\frac{2}{3} - \frac{1}{4}$
2. $\frac{3}{5} + \frac{1}{3}$
3. $\frac{5}{6} - \frac{3}{8}$
4. $\frac{2}{5} + \frac{4}{9}$

5. $3\frac{1}{8} + 4\frac{4}{5}$
6. $12 - 3\frac{1}{4}$
7. $6\frac{7}{8} - 5\frac{1}{6}$
8. $4\frac{2}{3} - 1\frac{3}{5}$

Set D

Use mental math, fraction strips, or drawings to solve. pages 316–317, 320–321

1. $\frac{3}{5} - \frac{1}{5}$
2. $\frac{3}{8} + \frac{3}{8}$
3. $\frac{9}{10} - \frac{7}{10}$
4. $\frac{8}{9} - \frac{2}{9}$
5. $\frac{5}{8} + \frac{3}{8}$
6. $\frac{9}{16} + \frac{3}{16}$

7. $\frac{5}{12} + \frac{11}{12}$
8. $\frac{3}{4} - \frac{3}{4}$
9. $\frac{5}{8} + \frac{7}{8}$
10. $\frac{3}{10} + \frac{1}{10}$

Set A

Write each sum or difference in lowest terms. pages 318–319, 322–323

1. $\dfrac{3}{4}$
   $-\dfrac{1}{2}$

2. $\dfrac{2}{3}$
   $+\dfrac{1}{6}$

3. $\dfrac{3}{10}$
   $+\dfrac{2}{5}$

4. $\dfrac{1}{3}$
   $-\dfrac{1}{6}$

5. $\dfrac{7}{8}$
   $-\dfrac{1}{2}$

6. $\dfrac{3}{4}$
   $+\dfrac{5}{8}$

7. $\dfrac{3}{4}$
   $-\dfrac{5}{8}$

8. $\dfrac{1}{10}$
   $+\dfrac{4}{5}$

9. $\dfrac{2}{3}$
   $-\dfrac{1}{4}$

10. $\dfrac{7}{8}$
    $+\dfrac{1}{2}$

11. $\dfrac{1}{2}$
    $+\dfrac{3}{10}$

12. $\dfrac{5}{6}$
    $-\dfrac{1}{2}$

13. $\dfrac{2}{3} - \dfrac{1}{6}$

14. $\dfrac{7}{12} + \dfrac{1}{3}$

15. $\dfrac{1}{12} + \dfrac{1}{6}$

16. $\dfrac{3}{4} - \dfrac{1}{6}$

Set B

Add. Write each sum in lowest terms. pages 332–333

1. $2\dfrac{1}{4}$
   $+ 5\dfrac{1}{4}$

2. $6\dfrac{1}{8}$
   $+ 1\dfrac{3}{8}$

3. $5\dfrac{1}{4}$
   $+ 6\dfrac{1}{2}$

4. $8\dfrac{7}{8}$
   $+ 3\dfrac{7}{8}$

5. $1\dfrac{1}{2}$
   $+ 6\dfrac{1}{6}$

6. $4\dfrac{7}{10}$
   $+ 2\dfrac{9}{10}$

7. $3\dfrac{4}{5}$
   $+ 2\dfrac{3}{5}$

8. $1\dfrac{1}{4}$
   $+ 4\dfrac{1}{3}$

9. $3\dfrac{3}{4}$
   $+ 3\dfrac{3}{4}$

10. $6\dfrac{5}{6}$
    $+ 1\dfrac{2}{3}$

11. $\dfrac{5}{16}$
    $+ 3\dfrac{1}{2}$

12. $7\dfrac{3}{4}$
    $+ 9\dfrac{5}{6}$

13. $\dfrac{2}{5} + 4\dfrac{1}{2}$

14. $2\dfrac{5}{8} + 3\dfrac{7}{8}$

15. $12 + 3\dfrac{1}{2}$

16. $2\dfrac{7}{8} + 5\dfrac{3}{16}$

Set C

Subtract. Write each difference in lowest terms. pages 334–337

1. $5\dfrac{7}{8}$
   $- 2\dfrac{3}{8}$

2. $4\dfrac{3}{4}$
   $- 1\dfrac{1}{4}$

3. $6\dfrac{7}{10}$
   $- 2\dfrac{2}{5}$

4. $3\dfrac{1}{2}$
   $- \dfrac{1}{3}$

5. $7\dfrac{1}{4}$
   $- 3\dfrac{1}{8}$

6. $9\dfrac{5}{6}$
   $- 2\dfrac{1}{3}$

7. $4\dfrac{2}{5}$
   $- 1\dfrac{4}{5}$

8. $5\dfrac{1}{2}$
   $- 3\dfrac{7}{8}$

9. $6\dfrac{1}{3}$
   $- 2\dfrac{1}{9}$

10. $1\dfrac{1}{4}$
    $- \dfrac{3}{4}$

11. $8\dfrac{1}{10}$
    $- 4\dfrac{1}{5}$

12. $7\dfrac{1}{6}$
    $- 6\dfrac{1}{2}$

13. $8\dfrac{3}{5} - 5\dfrac{1}{10}$

14. $3\dfrac{1}{2} - 2\dfrac{3}{8}$

15. $12\dfrac{1}{2} - 7$

16. $6\dfrac{2}{3} - 5\dfrac{3}{4}$

17. $4 - 1\dfrac{1}{4}$

18. $5\dfrac{1}{4} - 2\dfrac{3}{8}$

19. $8\dfrac{1}{4} - 3\dfrac{1}{2}$

20. $7\dfrac{2}{5} - 2\dfrac{1}{2}$

Set D

Multiply. Write each product in lowest terms. pages 350–351, 354–355

1. $\dfrac{1}{4} \times \dfrac{1}{2}$

2. $\dfrac{1}{5} \times 30$

3. $\dfrac{1}{3} \times \dfrac{1}{6}$

4. $\dfrac{1}{2} \times \dfrac{2}{5}$

5. $\dfrac{1}{3} \times \dfrac{5}{8}$

6. $\dfrac{1}{4} \times \dfrac{2}{3}$

7. $\dfrac{3}{8} \times 12$

8. $\dfrac{3}{5} \times \dfrac{1}{6}$

9. $36 \times \dfrac{7}{8}$

10. $\dfrac{1}{4} \times \dfrac{3}{4}$

11. $\dfrac{2}{3} \times \dfrac{5}{6}$

12. $\dfrac{4}{9} \times 15$

Extra Practice

Set A

Choose inch, foot, yard, or mile to measure each. pages 360–361

1. length of a fish
2. height of a tree
3. distance across Lake Michigan
4. length of tape in a cassette
5. length of softball bat
6. altitude of top of a mountain
7. distance a duck can fly
8. width of a computer screen

Complete. pages 362–363

9. 2 yd = _____ in.
10. $\frac{3}{4}$ ft = _____ in.
11. 100 yd = _____ ft
12. _____ ft = 6 in.
13. _____ yd = $\frac{1}{2}$ mi
14. 2 yd 2 ft = _____ in.

Choose ounce, pound, or ton to measure the weight of each. pages 364–365

15. serving of cat food
16. an apple
17. a horse van
18. a lamb

Complete. pages 364–365

19. 64 oz = _____ lb
20. _____ lb = $\frac{3}{4}$ T
21. $\frac{1}{2}$ lb = _____ oz
22. 10,000 lb = _____ T
23. 5 lb = _____ oz
24. 1 T = _____ oz

Choose cup, pint, quart, or gallon to measure each. pages 366–367

25. cider in a jug
26. water in a fish tank
27. milk for a cake recipe
28. water for bathing a dog

Complete. pages 366–367

29. 32 fl oz = _____ c
30. _____ pt = 10 c
31. $\frac{1}{2}$ gal = _____ c
32. 5 gal = _____ qt
33. 12 pt = _____ qt
34. 6 c = _____ pt

Set B

Choose the most likely temperature. pages 368–369

1. a hot summer day	**a.** 60°F	**b.** 90°F	**c.** 120°F
2. ice skating on a pond	**a.** 20°F	**b.** 50°F	**c.** 80°F
3. room temperature	**a.** 48°F	**b.** 68°F	**c.** 88°F
4. water to make hot chocolate	**a.** 92°F	**b.** 152°F	**c.** 212°F

Extra Practice

Set A

Find the perimeter or circumference. pages 378–381

1. 10 cm, 4 cm

2. 1.3 m, 1.2 m, 0.5 m

3. 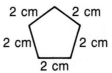 2 cm, 2 cm, 2 cm, 2 cm, 2 cm

4. 10 cm

Find the area. pages 382–383, 386–389

5. 1.5 m, 0.8 m

6. 45 cm, 45 cm

7. 18 cm, 20 cm

8. 4 m, 3 m

Set B

Name each space figure. pages 394–395

1.
2.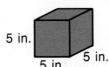
3.
4.
5.

Set C

Find the volume of each rectangular prism. pages 400–401

1. 12 in., 3 in., 6 in.

2. 5 in., 5 in., 5 in.

3. 30 ft, 10 ft, 10 ft

4. l = 2 ft, w = 2.5 ft, h = 3 ft

Set D

Use the points in the graph to complete the table. pages 402–405

	First Number	Second Number	Ordered Pair	Point
1.		5	(2, 5)	
2.			(6, 1)	
3.				F
4.	5	2		
5.				C
6.	9			I
7.			(4, 6)	K
8.		1		J
9.	3	8		
10.				L

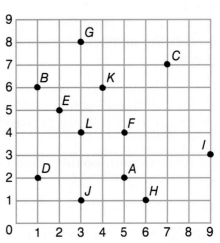

463

Extra Practice

Set A

Compare the number of odd digits with the number of even digits in each. Write each ratio three ways. pages 416–417

1. 21,741   **2.** 486,123   **3.** 77,222   **4.** 641.89   **5.** 987,654

Write three equal ratios for each. pages 418–421

6. 7:3   **7.** 40¢ for a dozen   **8.** $\frac{8}{16}$ **9.** 1 to 5

Use each scale to complete. pages 422–425

Scale: 3 cm = 1 m

	length in scale drawing	actual length
10.	6 cm	
11.		6 m
12.	15 cm	
13.		10 m

Scale: 1 in. = 20 mi.

	length on map	actual distance
14.	3 in.	
15.		80 mi
16.	15 in.	
17.		10 mi

Write a percent, a decimal, and a fraction in lowest terms for each. pages 428–429

18. six percent   **19.** 40 per hundred   **20.** two hundredths

21. 79 out of 100   **22.** eleven percent   **23.** 25 per 100

Set B

A column from a page of a telephone book contains names, addresses, and telephone numbers. Consider only the last digit of the telephone numbers. pages 434–437

1. What are the possible outcomes for the last digit?

2. If there are 90 telephone numbers in the column, predict the number of times each outcome will occur.

3. Use a column from a telephone book to count the number of times each possible outcome occurs.

4. What fraction of the time did each outcome occur?

Pick a card without looking. Find each probability. pages 438–441

5. triangle   **6.** hexagon   **7.** quadrilateral   **8.** polygon

—————————————{ Set A }—————————————

Solve. Use a calculator where appropriate. pages 13–15, 34–35

1. The signpost shows mileage from Kansas City to other cities. Which city is the farthest away?

2. Make a table with the mileages in order from least to greatest.

3. The Antonio family lives in St. Louis. They will drive to Kansas City and then on to Denver. How many miles will they travel?

4. In early July, the Bretts drove from Kansas City to Dallas and back. Later in July, they drove to Chicago and back. How many miles did they drive in the two trips?

5. How much farther is it from Kansas City to Denver and back than from Kansas City to St. Louis?

6. How much farther is it from Kansas City to New Orleans than from Kansas City to Chicago?

Atlanta 822
Chicago 542
Dallas 505
New Orleans 839
Denver 606
St. Louis 257

—————————————{ Set B }—————————————

Solve. Use a calculator where appropriate. If too little information is given, list the information needed. pages 53–55, 66–67

1. Ray Ralston worked 8 hours at Madison Greenhouses on Tuesday. How much did he earn?

2. In one week Ray worked 8 hours each day from Wednesday through Saturday. How many hours did he work during that week?

3. To prepare a hanging basket of impatiens, it costs $2.40 for the plant, soil, and planter. Each basket sells for $8.95. How much will you have to pay for two baskets?

4. Ray estimates that it costs $.55 a week to water and feed each impatiens basket. Find the cost of food and water for an impatiens basket that was prepared 4 weeks ago.

5. The Madison Greenhouse sells plant food for $2.89 for a 16-ounce package. Can you buy 4 packages for $10.00? Explain.

6. The greenhouse pays $17.54 for a case of 12 packages of plant food. Can they buy 50 cases this month?

Extra Practice

Solve. Use a calculator where appropriate. pages 89–91, 98–99

The town library charges fines for overdue books: $.01 for one day, $.02 for two days, $.04 for 3 days, and so on—doubling the fine for each additional day.

1. Make a table that shows the book fines for each day up to 12 days.

2. What will be Mr. Sawyer's fine for a book overdue 5 days?

3. How many days can a book be overdue and have a fine less than $1.00?

4. Pang has four overdue books. He will owe for 4, 6, 8, and 9 days. What will be his fine?

5. Peter has a book that is 10 days overdue. The book costs $7.50 to replace. Should he pay for the book or pay the fine? Explain.

6. The library is having an amnesty period—only a $.50 fine for each overdue book. How much will Laura save if she has three books, each 7 days overdue?

7. The library is sending 75 books to another library on an inter-library loan. A box holds 9 books. How many boxes are needed?

8. Yesterday, the library collected fines of $.04, $.16, $.08, and $.32. What was the average fine?

Solve. Use a calculator where appropriate. pages 125–127, 134–135

1. Alice had to toss a coin 5 times until she got heads a second time. Use a coin to do the same experiment. Did you get two heads in fewer tosses? How many fewer?

2. Look back at 1. What is the least number of tosses needed so that 2 heads in a row could occur?

3. Do the experiment in 1 five times. Find the average number of tosses until heads showed a second time.

4. A small school bus has seats for 21 people. Will the bus hold your class for a trip?

Use the information in the table to solve 5 and 6.

5. The Serinese family spent $37 on tickets to a show. Which tickets did they buy?

6. On Wednesday the tickets are half price for adults. How much would it cost the Serinese family to go to the theater on Wednesday?

TICKETS
$12 adults
$ 5 Children aged 12 and over
$ 3 children under 12

Set A

Solve. Use a calculator where appropriate. pages 161–163, 170–171

1. Bananas cost $.35 each and oranges $.20 each. Felipe paid $1.30 for 5 pieces of fruit. How many of each kind did he buy?

2. At the Pick-Em Orchard, Louise picked twice as many apples as her brother Sumner. Together they picked 51 apples. How many did Louise pick?

3. In the 5th grade election, Emma got 2 more votes than Taro. Together they had 48 votes. How many did each get?

4. Tickets to Wild Animal Park cost $5.00 for adults and $3.00 for children. Mrs. Sank paid $19.00 for her family. How many children were there?

5. The record store manager sold 25 compact discs, 7 cassette tapes, and 6 albums in three hours. How many of each recording did he sell in 6 hours?

6. A compact disc costs $10 and a cassette tape costs $8. Mandy bought 7 tapes. How much did she spend?

Set B

Solve. Use a calculator where appropriate. pages 189–191, 202–203

Draw the next two figures in each pattern.

1.
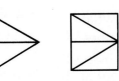

2.
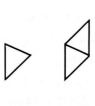
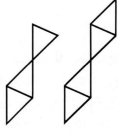

4.
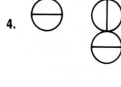
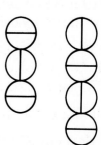

3.
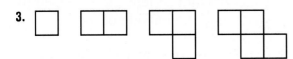

5. Marilyn had 78 baseball cards. She and her cousins divided them equally. Each person received 13 cards. How many cousins did she have?

6. Phil and Ron together rode their bikes 25 miles in one week. Ron rode his bike 5 more miles than Phil. How many miles did each of them ride?

Extra Practice

Set A

Solve. Use a calculator where appropriate. pages 225–227, 236–237

1. The Computer Store sells disks for $.75 each or $6.95 for a box of 12. How much is saved by buying a box?

2. Leona had a score of 79 on each of 3 tests. Her next test score was 87. What is her average score on the 4 tests?

3. Next-Day Delivery Service charges $9.80 for a package up to 2 pounds and $3.50 for each additional pound. What is the charge for a 6-pound package?

4. Toshio bought 3 cassettes for $1.49 each. How much change did he receive if he gave the clerk a $5 bill?

5. Nancy bought a scarf for $9.95, gloves for $12.50, and a hat for $8.75. How much change did she receive?

6. Lin and Stan together picked 42 apples. Lin picked 4 more apples than Stan. How many apples did each boy pick?

Set B

Solve. Use a calculator where appropriate. pages 265–267, 276–277

1. Jan lives 18 blocks directly south of Ana. Flo lives 8 blocks directly north of Ana. Yoko lives in a straight line halfway between Jan and Flo. How far does Yoko live from Ana?

2. Alani has photographs 12 cm wide and 9 cm high. She wants to mount them on paper 25 cm wide and 28 cm high. How many can she fit on a page?

3. From a statue Jacy walks 5 blocks west and 4 blocks south. Then he walks 9 blocks east, 7 blocks north, and 4 blocks west. He now sees the statue. How far away is it?

4. The reflecting pool at the office plaza is 25 meters wide and 40 meters long. Around it is a walkway 5 meters wide. How much fencing is needed to go around the outside of the walkway?

5. Larry spent $21.98 for calculators. The store charges $12 for the first 3 calculators and $4.99 for each additional calculator. How many calculators did Larry buy?

6. Look back at **5. What if** Larry bought 10 calculators? How much would they cost? What would be the average cost of each calculator?

Set A

Solve. Use a calculator where appropriate. pages 297–299, 308–309

1. Mr. Li wants to put a fence along the back edge of his property. The distance is 80 ft. He can buy fencing in sections 8 ft long, and each end will have to be attached to a post. How many sections and how many posts does he need?

2. For a team race, bean bags are placed 10, 20, and 30 yards from the starting point. Runner 1 gets the first bag and brings it to the starting point. Runner 2 gets the second bag, and brings it to the starting point, and so on. What is the total distance run by the 3 runners?

3. The fitness trail in the park has exercise stations every 100 yards, including a station at the start and finish. There are 14 stations in all. How many yards will Jason jog if he completes the trail?

4. One side of a playground is 30 ft long. The PTA planted 6 shrubs at equal intervals along the side. One shrub was planted at each end. How much space will there be between each shrub?

Four towns are on a straight road. Allentown is 10 km from Beattyville. Beattyville is 30 km from Denton. Denton is 40 km from Allentown. Carolltown is half-way between Denton and Beattyville.

5. How far is Carolltown from Beattyville?

6. How far is Allentown from Carrolltown?

Set B

Solve. Use a calculator where appropriate. pages 327–329, 338–339

1. Rick spent $4.00 on baseball cards at a card show. Some cost $.15 each, and the rest cost $.25 each. He bought more than 10 and less than twenty $.15-cards. How many of each kind of card could he have bought?

2. At a school fair, $\frac{2}{3}$ of the booths were games, and $\frac{1}{5}$ of the booths sold food. What fractional part of the booths were for other things?

Sam and Fred are playing a game on grid paper. They start from the same point. Sam moves 3 squares to the right, 4 squares to the left, 6 squares down, and 2 squares to the right. Fred moves 5 squares up, 3 squares to the left, 2 squares down, and 4 squares to the right.

3. How far apart are they?

4. How much closer to the starting point was Fred than Sam?

5. How many squares must each boy move to return to the starting point?

Extra Practice

Solve. Use a calculator where appropriate. pages 357–359, 370–371

1. One half of the money raised at the school fair was for playground equipment. The rest was split equally between the library fund and assembly committee. The library fund received $150. How much money was raised at the fair?

2. One-third of the people at the fair were students at the school. Three-fifths were parents. All others were children who did not attend the school. What fraction of the total was this group of children?

3. Mrs. Orbon saw a sweater priced at $18.00. The clerk took $\frac{1}{3}$ off that price. What was the final price?

4. Mr. Kwan sold $240 worth of crafts at a fair. One-eighth of his income paid for the booth, and $\frac{1}{3}$ was for materials. The rest was his profit. What was his profit?

5. David wants to buy 3 model cars. A sports car costs $5.50, a police car costs $4.75, a convertible costs $5.80, and a taxicab costs $4.60. He has $16. What models might he buy?

6. Maggie bought 12 model cars. One-third of the models were sports cars, $\frac{1}{4}$ were police cars, and the rest were antique cars. What fractional part of the models were antique cars?

Set B

Solve. Use a calculator where appropriate. pages 391–393, 406–407

1. Chris and Marty are siblings. One is a boy, and the other a girl. The boy is younger than the girl. Marty is older than Chris. Who is the boy?

2. In a store, a sweater was marked $\frac{1}{3}$ off the regular price. It cost $24. What was the regular price?

3. A certain whole number has only one digit. Twice the number is greater than 15. Three times the number is less than 25. What is the number?

4. The perimeter of a square is less than 40 inches. The area of the square is greater than 75 square inches. How long is a side of the square?

5. At the craft show Neil spent $\frac{1}{3}$ of what he had earned by delivering newspapers. This was $\frac{1}{2}$ of what he spent at the book store. He earned $24 delivering newspapers. How much money did he spend at the craft show?

6. Mr. and Mrs. Flynn and their son Dennis sat in seats 21, 22, and 23 at the circus. Mr. Flynn was not in seat 21. Dennis sat between his parents. Who sat in seat 23?

Set A

Solve. Use a calculator where appropriate. pages 431–433, 442–443

1. Mr. Romero's students sat in 3 rows of the auditorium. One-half of them sat in one row, and one-half of those who were left sat in a second row. The remaining 4 students sat in the third row. How many students were in the class?

2. Alice, Bobbi, Carrie, and Dena sat in the first four seats. Alice was not on either end. Bobbi was between Alice and Carrie. Dena was not in the first seat. In what order were the four girls seated?

3. Eva and Nina need exactly 1 cup of water for an experiment. They have only two containers. One holds 5 cups, and the other holds 2 cups. How can Eva and Nina use these containers to measure exactly 1 cup?

4. Three different postage stamps of different values are put in a row on a letter. If they are randomly placed, what is the probability that the stamps will be in order of value from least to greatest?

5. Ana, Betty, Cal, and Donna sit in the same row in the classroom. In how many different arrangements can they be seated in the four chairs in the row?

6. Alicia, Tom, Stan, and Betty live in Maine, Texas, Florida, and Hawaii. Alicia's state is not an island. Tom and Stan do not live in a state that borders Canada. Betty's state is famous for the Alamo. Tom's state has volcanoes. In which state does each live?

Skill Hints

HINT When adding and subtracting estimate first.
An estimate helps you check for reasonable answers.

Estimate by:

Adding the value of the front digits

$$351 \longrightarrow 300$$
$$+ 208 \longrightarrow 200$$
$$500$$

500 is a good estimate of this sum.

Rounding each number

$$1,573 \longrightarrow 2,000$$
$$- 1,142 \longrightarrow 1,000$$
$$1,000$$

1,000 is a good estimate of this difference.

Estimate. Then add or subtract.

1. $\begin{array}{r} 57 \\ + 73 \\ \hline \end{array}$

2. $\begin{array}{r} 93 \\ - 28 \\ \hline \end{array}$

3. $\begin{array}{r} 187 \\ + 93 \\ \hline \end{array}$

4. $\begin{array}{r} 206 \\ - 121 \\ \hline \end{array}$

5. $\begin{array}{r} 3,075 \\ + 5,486 \\ \hline \end{array}$

6. $\begin{array}{r} 2,742 \\ - 1,486 \\ \hline \end{array}$

7. $\begin{array}{r} 32,409 \\ - 18,367 \\ \hline \end{array}$

8. $\begin{array}{r} 29,473 \\ + 56,931 \\ \hline \end{array}$

9. $\begin{array}{r} 4,000 \\ - 2,873 \\ \hline \end{array}$

10. $\begin{array}{r} 62,835 \\ + 69,378 \\ \hline \end{array}$

11. $\begin{array}{r} \$26.50 \\ + 14.75 \\ \hline \end{array}$

12. $\begin{array}{r} \$38.25 \\ - 21.75 \\ \hline \end{array}$

13. $\begin{array}{r} \$172.00 \\ - 51.25 \\ \hline \end{array}$

14. $\begin{array}{r} \$387.42 \\ + 106.87 \\ \hline \end{array}$

15. $\begin{array}{r} \$7,493.38 \\ + 647.50 \\ \hline \end{array}$

16. $\begin{array}{r} 43 \\ 107 \\ + 29 \\ \hline \end{array}$

17. $\begin{array}{r} 187 \\ 432 \\ + 506 \\ \hline \end{array}$

18. $\begin{array}{r} 4,321 \\ 2,876 \\ + 3,407 \\ \hline \end{array}$

19. $\begin{array}{r} 28,709 \\ 42,321 \\ + 14,006 \\ \hline \end{array}$

20. $39 + 278 + 6$

21. $\$83.42 + 27.67$

22. $2,000 - 873$

One method of estimating products is to round each
factor to its greatest place value.

You can also round up and down to find the range of
the product.

	Round down		Round up

$$\begin{array}{r} 1,786 \longrightarrow \quad 2,000 \\ \times \quad 19 \longrightarrow \times \quad 20 \\ \hline 40,000 \end{array}$$

$$\begin{array}{r} 300 \longleftarrow \quad 326 \longrightarrow \quad 400 \\ \times \quad 10 \qquad \times \quad 18 \qquad \times \quad 20 \\ \hline 3,000 \qquad\qquad\qquad 8,000 \end{array}$$

40,000 is a good estimate.

The product is more then 3,000
but less than 8,000.

Estimate. Then find the product.

1. $\begin{array}{r} 19 \\ \times\ 7 \\ \hline \end{array}$ 2. $\begin{array}{r} 28 \\ \times\ 4 \\ \hline \end{array}$ 3. $\begin{array}{r} 721 \\ \times\ \ 6 \\ \hline \end{array}$ 4. $\begin{array}{r} 3,942 \\ \times\ \ \ \ 8 \\ \hline \end{array}$ 5. $\begin{array}{r} 8,702 \\ \times\ \ \ \ 5 \\ \hline \end{array}$

6. $\begin{array}{r} 26 \\ \times\ 14 \\ \hline \end{array}$ 7. $\begin{array}{r} 39 \\ \times\ 23 \\ \hline \end{array}$ 8. $\begin{array}{r} 297 \\ \times\ \ 44 \\ \hline \end{array}$ 9. $\begin{array}{r} 381 \\ \times\ \ 72 \\ \hline \end{array}$ 10. $\begin{array}{r} 9,406 \\ \times\ \ \ \ 83 \\ \hline \end{array}$

11. $\begin{array}{r} \$.72 \\ \times\ \ \ \ 8 \\ \hline \end{array}$ 12. $\begin{array}{r} \$3.75 \\ \times\ \ \ \ 12 \\ \hline \end{array}$ 13. $\begin{array}{r} \$8.39 \\ \times\ \ \ \ 9 \\ \hline \end{array}$ 14. $\begin{array}{r} \$11.35 \\ \times\ \ \ \ 21 \\ \hline \end{array}$ 15. $\begin{array}{r} \$20.30 \\ \times\ \ \ \ 34 \\ \hline \end{array}$

Find the least common multiple (LCM) for each pair of numbers.

16. 3, 7   17. 2, 3   18. 12, 15   19. 8, 6   20. 10, 8

21. 6, 9   22. 8, 12   23. 4, 10   24. 8, 4   25. 4, 9

Skill Hints

H I N T To estimate quotients use numbers close to the original numbers that can be divided mentally.

$87 \div 4$

Think $80 \div 4 = 20$

A good estimate of this quotient would be 20.

$287 \div 29$

Think $300 \div 30$

A good estimate of this quotient would be 10.

Estimate each quotient. Then divide.

1. $3\overline{)95}$

2. $9\overline{)77}$

3. $6\overline{)251}$

4. $8\overline{)348}$

5. $7\overline{)523}$

6. $8\overline{)2,456}$

7. $9\overline{)1,832}$

8. $5\overline{)548}$

9. $6\overline{)3,614}$

10. $7\overline{)3,534}$

11. $76,230 \div 7$

12. $\$129.68 \div 8$

13. $\$40.72 \div 4$

H I N T You can use short division when dividing by one-digit numbers.

$$7\overline{)1\,0\,.^3 0^2 6^5 6} = 1,438$$

Think $10 - 7 = 3$
Place remainder in dividend in front of next digit.
Think $7\overline{)30}$

Use short division to find quotient.

14. $4\overline{)868}$

15. $3\overline{)1,556}$

16. $2\overline{)10,232}$

17. $7\overline{)6,466}$

18. $9\overline{)\$113.04}$

H
I If the remainder is greater than the divisor, change
N your estimate of the quotient.
T

$$16\overline{)64}$$

Think $20\overline{)60}$

Try 3

$$\begin{array}{r} 3 \\ 16\overline{)64} \\ -48 \\ \hline 16 \end{array}$$ ← Remainder must
be less than divisor
change quotient to 4.

Divide.

1. $17\overline{)153}$ 2. $14\overline{)95}$ 3. $21\overline{)147}$ 4. $34\overline{)277}$ 5. $67\overline{)216}$

6. $24\overline{)440}$ 7. $47\overline{)954}$ 8. $83\overline{)3,908}$ 9. $32\overline{)\$386.56}$ 10. $31\overline{)3,317}$

11. $71\overline{)14,271}$ 12. $28\overline{)8,428}$ 13. $38\overline{)3,969}$ 14. $65\overline{)13,154}$ 15. $26\overline{)5,366}$

16. $5,290 \div 43$ 17. $2,172 \div 63$ 18. $\$5,729.36 \div 56$

19. $25,224 \div 28$ 20. $34,051 \div 57$ 21. $26,970 \div 87$

Find the greatest common factor (GCF) for each pair.

22. 6, 8   23. 10, 15   24. 8, 12   25. 9, 21   26. 12, 18

27. 14, 28   28. 10, 9   29. 12, 21   30. 20, 30   31. 8, 10

Skill Hints

To change time to a smaller unit, multiply.
To change to a larger unit, divide.

$2\,h = \_\_\_ min$
Minutes are smaller than hours.
$2 \times 60 = 120\,min$

$20\,d = \_\_\_ wk$
Weeks are larger than days.
$20 \div 7 = 2\,wk\,6\,d$

Complete.

1. $136\,min = \_\_\_ h \_\_\_ min$ **2.** $5\,h = \_\_\_ min$ **3.** $3\,wk = \_\_\_ d$

4. $2\,yr = \_\_\_ wk$ **5.** $18\,mo = \_\_\_ yr \_\_\_ mo$ **6.** $100\,s = \_\_\_ min \_\_\_ s$

7. $2\,wk\,3\,d = \_\_\_ d$ **8.** $1\,yr\,3\,mo = \_\_\_ mo$ **9.** $3\,yr = \_\_\_ mo$

When times are subtracted, regroup 1 h as 60 min.

```
  3 h   78 min
  4 h   18 min        Think    1h = 60 min
  1 h   20 min                 18 min + 60 min = 78 min
  2 h   58 min
```

Add or subtract.

10.   3 h 15 min
        + 2 h 45 min

11.   8 h 40 min
        − 2 h 25 min

12.   2 h 18 min
        + 5 h 20 min

13. $7\,h - 2\,h\,30\,min$ **14.** $3\,hr\,10\,min + 45\,min$ **15.** $1\,h\,35\,min + 1\,h\,40\,min$

Find the elapsed time.

16. from 2:05 P.M.
     to 4:30 P.M.

17. from 6:20 A.M.
     to 1:30 P.M.

18. from 10:15 A.M.
     to 12 noon

ᴴᴵᴺᵀ Use range, median, mode, and mean to describe a collection of data.

$$\underbrace{20, 18, 17, 17, 17, 14,}_{\text{5 data items}} \underbrace{13, 12, 10, 9, 7}_{\text{5 data items}}$$

The range of this data is $20 - 7$ or 13.

The median is the middle data item or 14.

The mode is the data that appears most, or 17.

The mean is the average of the data, or $154 \div 11 = 14$.

Find the range, median, mode, and mean for each of the following collections of data.

1. 22, 27, 22, 30, 28

2. 100, 76, 74, 73, 73, 70, 69

3. 38, 10, 14, 10, 19, 6, 8, 9

4. 52, 43, 48, 46, 48

Find the missing number.

5. The median of 3 numbers is 25. Two of the numbers are 30 and 15. What is the third number?

6. The range of a set of data is 23. If the least data item is 18, what is the greatest?

7. The mode of 5 numbers is 8. Four of the numbers are 10, 7, 8, and 3. What is the fifth number?

8. The mean of 3 numbers is 15. If two of the numbers are 16 and 14, what is the third number?

9. In the collection, 10, 8, 6 what number can be added so the mean is 8?

10. The mean, median and mode of 3 numbers is 10. One of the numbers is 10. What are the other two?

Skill Hints

Triangles are named according to their sides and angles.

No sides congruent **Scalene**	Two sides congruent **Isosceles**	Three sides congruent **Equilateral**	One right angle **Right**

Name each triangle. Some may have more than one name.

1.

2.

3.

4.

5.

6.

Quadrilaterals are named by their sides and angles.

trapezoid	parallelogram	rectangle	square	rhombus
one pair parallel sides	two pairs parallel sides	two pairs parallel sides 4 congruent angles	two pairs parallel sides 4 congruent angles and sides	two pairs parallel sides 4 congruent sides

List all the names which apply to each polygon.

1.

2.

3.

4.

478 FOCUS: Geometry

^H
^I The decimal point separates the whole number and the
^N decimal fraction. It is read as the word "and".
^T

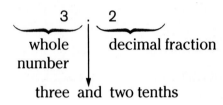

three and two tenths

Write a decimal for each.

1. six and one tenth

2. one hundred four thousandths

3. three hundredths

4. eighty-four thousandths

5. one hundred and five thousandths

6. forty-six hundredths

Compare. Use >, <, or = for ⬤.

7. 0.8 ⬤ 0.08

8. 3.2 ⬤ 3.20

9. 0.25 ⬤ 2.5

10. 0.112 ⬤ 0.14

11. 7.3 ⬤ 0.73

12. 1.01 ⬤ 10.1

Round each number to the place named.

ones	**13.** 3.24	**14.** 5.017	**15.** 18.39	**16.** 0.897
hundredths	**17.** 1.302	**18.** 3.617	**19.** 0.514	**20.** 0.386
ten cents	**21.** $4.52	**22.** $0.87	**23.** $10.03	**24.** $1.51

Skill Hints

To add or subtract decimals, line up the decimal points.
Then use zeros to hold places.

$$3.12 + .687 + 5 \qquad 5 - 2.3$$

$$
\begin{array}{r}
3.120 \\
0.687 \\
+\ 5.000 \\
\hline
8.807
\end{array}
\qquad
\begin{array}{r}
\overset{4\ 10}{5.0} \\
-\ 2.3 \\
\hline
2.7
\end{array}
$$

Estimate. Then add or subtract as shown.

1. $\begin{array}{r}0.3\\+\ 0.6\end{array}$		**2.** $\begin{array}{r}1.3\\+\ 0.8\end{array}$		**3.** $\begin{array}{r}0.9\\+\ 0.8\end{array}$		**4.** $\begin{array}{r}2.13\\+\ .87\end{array}$		**5.** $\begin{array}{r}2.06\\+\ 1.3\end{array}$	

6. $\begin{array}{r}5.38\\-\ 2.13\end{array}$		**7.** $\begin{array}{r}5.3\\-\ 2.13\end{array}$		**8.** $\begin{array}{r}5.\\-\ 2.13\end{array}$		**9.** $\begin{array}{r}\$21.42\\-\ \ \ 5.37\end{array}$		**10.** $\begin{array}{r}\$5.00\\-\ \ 4.29\end{array}$	

11. $4.3 + .98 + 2$ **12.** $\$18 - \$11.75$ **13.** $32.1 - 17.697$

Find the sum.

14. $\begin{array}{r}286.28\\+\ \ \ 43.076\end{array}$		**15.** $\begin{array}{r}98.031\\+\ 42.068\end{array}$		**16.** $\begin{array}{r}476.09\\+\ 283.947\end{array}$	

17. $24 + 14.3 + .876$ **18.** $\$21.76 + \$42 + \$.85$ **19.** $21.43 + 18.9 + 7.26$

Find the difference.

20. $42.3 - 18.76$ **21.** $100 - 42.18$ **22.** $18 - 0.65$

^H_I_N_T The number of decimal places in a product is the same as the total number of decimal places in both factors.

$$3.2 \longrightarrow 1 \text{ decimal place}$$
$$\underline{\times\ \ .5} \longrightarrow 1 \text{ decimal place}$$
$$1.60 \longrightarrow 1 + 1 = 2 \text{ decimal places in product}$$

Multiply.

1. 52.3×1.3
2. 7.08×1.2
3. 31.6×2.5
4. $\$32.65 \times 15$
5. $\$105.25 \times 4$

6. $3.7 \times .7$
7. $51.08 \times .6$
8. 0.5×0.3
9. $0.03 \times .2$
10. 0.016×0.5

^H_I_N_T When dividing by a whole number, place the decimal point in the quotient above the decimal point in the dividend.

$$18 \overline{)\ 18.90} \quad \begin{array}{l} 1.05 \end{array} \leftarrow \text{add zero to continue dividing}$$

$$\underline{18}$$
$$090$$
$$\underline{90}$$

Divide.

11. $3\overline{)3.93}$
12. $5\overline{)0.085}$
13. $9\overline{)18.27}$
14. $4\overline{)25.1}$
15. $3\overline{)\$8.64}$

16. $32\overline{)57.6}$
17. $42\overline{)91.56}$
18. $18\overline{)73.836}$
19. $12\overline{)0.18}$
20. $50\overline{)4.2}$

21. $\$10.25 \div 25$
22. $10 \div 4$
23. $38.6 \div 10$

Skill Hints

To find equivalent fractions, multiply or divide both the numerator and denominator by the same number.

$$\frac{3}{4} = \frac{\square}{100}$$

Think $4 \times ? = 100$

$$\frac{3}{4} \times \frac{25}{25} = \frac{75}{100}$$

$\frac{3}{4}$ and $\frac{75}{100}$ are equivalent

$$\frac{6}{10} = \frac{\square}{5}$$

Think $10 \div ? = 5$

$$\frac{6}{10} \div \frac{2}{2} = \frac{3}{5}$$

$\frac{6}{10}$ and $\frac{3}{5}$ are equivalent.

Find the missing number.

1. $\frac{1}{2} = \frac{\square}{10}$

2. $\frac{3}{4} = \frac{\square}{20}$

3. $\frac{1}{8} = \frac{\square}{128}$

4. $\frac{2}{3} = \frac{\square}{60}$

5. $\frac{2}{5} = \frac{\square}{10}$

6. $\frac{3}{8} = \frac{\square}{72}$

7. $\frac{1}{2} = \frac{\square}{364}$

8. $\frac{1}{3} = \frac{\square}{393}$

Write each fraction in lowest terms.

9. $\frac{6}{8}$

10. $\frac{5}{10}$

11. $\frac{9}{12}$

12. $\frac{4}{6}$

13. $\frac{10}{20}$

14. $\frac{6}{24}$

15. $\frac{75}{100}$

16. $\frac{5}{100}$

17. $\frac{8}{10}$

18. $\frac{20}{200}$

19. $\frac{3}{150}$

20. $\frac{12}{24}$

The least common denominator (LCD) of unlike fractions is the least common multiple of their denominators.

$$\frac{2}{3} \text{ and } \frac{1}{5}$$

multiples of 3: 0, 3, 6, 9, 12, $\boxed{15}$, 18,…

multiples of 5: 0, 5, 10, $\boxed{15}$,…

15 is the LCD of $\frac{2}{3}$ and $\frac{1}{5}$

Find the LCD. Then write like fractions.

21. $\frac{2}{3}$, $\frac{1}{4}$

22. $\frac{3}{5}$, $\frac{3}{10}$

23. $\frac{1}{2}$, $\frac{2}{3}$

24. $\frac{3}{8}$, $\frac{3}{4}$

HINT To compare unlike fractions, use LCD to write them as like fractions.

Then compare numerators.

$$\frac{2}{3} \text{ and } \frac{5}{8} \quad \text{LCD} = 24 \quad \frac{2}{3} = \frac{16}{24} \qquad 16 > 15 \text{ so } \frac{2}{3} > \frac{5}{8}$$
$$\frac{5}{8} = \frac{15}{24}$$

Compare. Write $>$, $<$, or $=$ for ⬤.

1. $\frac{3}{4}$ ⬤ $\frac{1}{4}$ 2. $\frac{1}{5}$ ⬤ $\frac{3}{5}$ 3. $\frac{5}{10}$ ⬤ $\frac{6}{10}$ 4. $\frac{3}{8}$ ⬤ $\frac{5}{8}$

5. $\frac{1}{3}$ ⬤ $\frac{1}{2}$ 6. $\frac{3}{4}$ ⬤ $\frac{3}{8}$ 7. $\frac{5}{10}$ ⬤ $\frac{1}{2}$ 8. $\frac{25}{100}$ ⬤ $\frac{1}{4}$

9. $\frac{5}{8}$ ⬤ $\frac{3}{4}$ 10. $\frac{2}{3}$ ⬤ $\frac{3}{5}$ 11. $\frac{3}{4}$ ⬤ $\frac{2}{3}$ 12. $\frac{1}{2}$ ⬤ $\frac{5}{8}$

Order the fractions from least to greatest.

13. $\frac{2}{3}$, $\frac{1}{2}$, $\frac{3}{4}$ 14. $\frac{3}{10}$, $\frac{2}{5}$, $\frac{1}{4}$ 15. $\frac{5}{8}$, $\frac{6}{10}$, $\frac{3}{4}$

HINT To change an improper fraction to a mixed number, divide the denominator into the numerator.

$$\frac{7}{3} = \square \qquad \text{Think } 3\overline{)7} \; {}^{2R1}$$

$\frac{7}{3}$ is the same as $2\frac{1}{3}$

Write each improper fraction as a mixed number or whole number.

16. $\frac{8}{5}$ 17. $\frac{10}{3}$ 18. $\frac{9}{4}$ 19. $\frac{7}{2}$ 20. $\frac{10}{5}$

Write each mixed number as an improper fraction.

21. $3\frac{2}{3}$ 22. $4\frac{1}{2}$ 23. $2\frac{3}{5}$ 24. $1\frac{1}{8}$ 25. $2\frac{3}{4}$

Skill Hints

HINT Estimate fraction and mixed number sums by rounding each fraction to $\frac{1}{2}$ or 1. Then add.

$\frac{2}{3} \longrightarrow \frac{2}{3}$ rounds to 1

$+ 1\frac{1}{4} \longrightarrow \frac{1}{4}$ rounds to 0

$\frac{2}{3} = \frac{8}{12}$

$+ 1\frac{1}{4} = 1\frac{3}{12}$

$1\frac{11}{12}$

The estimate of this sum is 2. $1\frac{11}{12}$ is a reasonable answer

Estimate. Then add. Remember to write sums in lowest terms.

1. $\frac{3}{4} + \frac{1}{3}$ 2. $\frac{3}{8} + \frac{1}{5}$ 3. $\frac{7}{10} + \frac{1}{4}$ 4. $\frac{3}{100} + \frac{3}{4}$

5. $\frac{5}{8} + \frac{1}{8} + \frac{7}{8}$ 6. $\frac{2}{5} + \frac{4}{5} + \frac{1}{5}$ 7. $\frac{2}{10} + \frac{9}{10} + \frac{5}{10}$

8. $\quad 1\frac{1}{4}$ 9. $\quad 3\frac{2}{3}$ 10. $\quad 8\frac{7}{8}$ 11. $\quad 5\frac{1}{2}$ 12. $\quad 4\frac{8}{10}$

$+ 2\frac{1}{2}$ $+ 2\frac{1}{4}$ $+ 2\frac{3}{8}$ $+ 2\frac{3}{4}$ $+ 9\frac{6}{10}$

13. $\frac{3}{5} + 2\frac{1}{2}$ 14. $18 + 6\frac{1}{2}$ 15. $3\frac{7}{8} + 8\frac{5}{16}$

HINT Rename the mixed number if you can not subtract the fractions.

$3\frac{1}{3}$ Rename. $3\frac{1}{3} = 2\frac{4}{3}$

$- \frac{2}{3}$ $- \frac{2}{3} = \frac{2}{3}$

Think   you can not subtract $\frac{2}{3}$ from $\frac{1}{3}$. $2\frac{2}{3}$

Subtract. Write each answer in lowest terms.

16. $\frac{3}{4} - \frac{1}{4}$ 17. $\frac{5}{8} - \frac{3}{8}$ 18. $\frac{5}{6} - \frac{2}{3}$ 19. $\frac{1}{2} - \frac{3}{8}$

20. $\quad 2\frac{1}{3}$ 21. $\quad 5\frac{1}{8}$ 22. $\quad 4\frac{2}{3}$ 23. $\quad 3\frac{2}{5}$

$- \frac{2}{3}$ $- 2\frac{3}{8}$ $- 1\frac{3}{4}$ $- 1\frac{7}{10}$

To multiply fractions and whole numbers, write the whole number as a fraction.

Then multiply numerators by numerators and denominators by denominators.

$$\frac{3}{4} \text{ of } 12 = \frac{3}{4} \times \frac{12}{1} = \frac{3 \times 12}{4 \times 1} = \frac{36}{4} = 9$$

Multiply. Write the products in lowest terms.

1. $\frac{1}{2} \times 12$

2. $\frac{1}{4} \times 16$

3. $\frac{1}{5} \times 20$

4. $\frac{1}{8} \times 32$

5. $\frac{3}{4} \times 20$

6. $18 \times \frac{2}{3}$

7. $\frac{3}{5} \times 10$

8. $40 \times \frac{5}{8}$

9. $\frac{2}{3} \times 19$

10. $\frac{3}{4} \times 27$

11. $15 \times \frac{3}{8}$

12. $36 \times \frac{2}{5}$

13. $\frac{1}{3} \times \frac{1}{3}$

14. $\frac{1}{4} \times \frac{1}{4}$

15. $\frac{1}{5} \times \frac{3}{5}$

16. $\frac{2}{3} \times \frac{1}{4}$

17. $\frac{3}{8} \times \frac{4}{5}$

18. $\frac{2}{3} \times \frac{7}{10}$

19. $\frac{5}{8} \times \frac{3}{4}$

20. $\frac{2}{5} \times \frac{2}{3}$

21. $\frac{1}{3} \times \frac{3}{8}$

22. $\frac{1}{2} \times \frac{2}{9}$

23. $\frac{3}{5} \times \frac{5}{7}$

24. $\frac{5}{6} \times \frac{6}{7}$

25. $\frac{1}{4} \times \frac{4}{5}$

26. $\frac{1}{7} \times \frac{7}{10}$

27. $\frac{3}{8} \times \frac{8}{9}$

28. $\frac{2}{3} \times \frac{1}{2}$

29. $\frac{1}{3} \times \frac{1}{3} \times \frac{1}{3}$

30. $\frac{1}{4} \times \frac{1}{3} \times \frac{1}{5}$

31. $\frac{2}{3} \times \frac{1}{8} \times \frac{3}{4}$

Skill Hints

HINT The height in a parallelogram or triangle always makes a right angle with one of the sides.

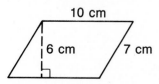

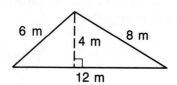

base = 10 cm   height = 6 cm
$A = b \times h = 10 \times 6 = 60 \text{ cm}^2$

base = 12 m   height = 4 m
$A = \frac{1}{2} \times b \times h = \frac{1}{2} \times 12 \times 4 = 24 \text{ m}^2$

Find the area of each figure.

1.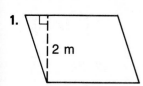

2.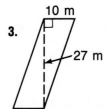

3.

4. triangle
   base = 12 m
   height = 8 m

5. parallelogram
   base = 13 m
   height = 22 m

6. triangle
   base = 104 m
   height = 37 m

HINT To find the volume of a rectangular prism, multiply the length, the width, and the height.

Volume = $l \times w \times h$
= 14 × 7 × 10
980 m³

h = 10 m
w = 7 m
ℓ = 14 m

Find the volume of the following rectangular prisms.

7. l = 20 cm
   w = 5 cm
   h = 9 cm

8. l = 13 cm
   w = 8 cm
   h = 12 cm

9. l = 100 m
   w = 42 m
   h = 2 m

10. l = 17 m
    w = 4 m
    h = 25 m

To find an equal ratio, multiply or divide both parts of
the ratio by the same number.

$$\frac{5}{12} \times \boxed{\frac{3}{3}} = \frac{15}{36}$$

$\frac{5}{12}$ and $\frac{15}{36}$ are equal ratios.

Find the equal ratios. Use = or ≠ for each ⬤.

1. $\frac{1}{2}$ ⬤ $\frac{10}{5}$

2. $\frac{2}{3}$ ⬤ $\frac{4}{6}$

3. $\frac{1}{4}$ ⬤ $\frac{2}{5}$

4. $\frac{3}{7}$ ⬤ $\frac{9}{21}$

5. $\frac{3}{4}$ ⬤ $\frac{75}{100}$

6. $\frac{2}{5}$ ⬤ $\frac{40}{100}$

7. $\frac{1}{3}$ ⬤ $\frac{3}{1}$

8. $\frac{3}{8}$ ⬤ $\frac{18}{23}$

Multiply or divide to find the value of *n*.

9. $\frac{1}{4} = \frac{6}{n}$

10. $\frac{26}{30} = \frac{n}{15}$

11. $\frac{5}{6} = \frac{10}{n}$

12. $\frac{3}{4} = \frac{30}{n}$

13. $\frac{2}{5} = \frac{n}{100}$

14. $\frac{16}{800} = \frac{n}{100}$

15. $\frac{3}{10} = \frac{30}{n}$

16. $\frac{39}{51} = \frac{n}{17}$

A percent is a ratio whose second term is 100.
% means "for each hundred".

$$30\% \text{ is the same as } \frac{30}{100} = \frac{3}{10}$$
is the same as .30

Write each as a percent, a demical, and a fraction in lowest terms.

17. eighteen per hundred

18. eight percent

19. seven hundredths

20. one-fourth

21. three-fifths

22. thirty eight percent

Glossary

acute angle An angle with a measure less than 90°. p. 182

addition An operation on two or more numbers to find the sum. p. 16

angle Two rays with a common endpoint called the vertex. p. 180
Example:

area The number of square units needed to cover a region. p. 382

associative (grouping) property of addition The way that addends are grouped does not change the sum. p. 16
Example: $(2 + 3) + 4 = 2 + (3 + 4)$

associative (grouping) property of multiplication The way that factors are grouped does not change the product. p. 42
Example: $(2 \times 3) \times 4 = 2 \times (3 \times 4)$

average The sum of the addends divided by the number of addends. pp. 100, 168

bar graph A graph with bars of different lengths to show information. p. 152

chord A line segment with both endpoints on the circle. p. 206

circle A closed plane figure. All the points on a circle are the same distance from a point called the center. p. 206

circle graph A graph that shows how a total amount has been divided into parts. p. 154

circumference The distance around a circle. p. 380

common factor A factor that is the same for each of two or more numbers. p. 136
Example: 1, 2, and 4 are common factors of 4 and 8.

common multiple A multiple that is the same for two or more numbers. p. 50
Example: 6, 12, and 18 are multiples of 2 and 3.

commutative (order) property of addition The order of the addends does not change the sum. p. 16
Example: $9 + 7 = 7 + 9$

commutative (order) property of multiplication The order of the factors does not change the product. p. 42
Example: $2 \times 3 = 3 \times 2$

compass An instrument used to construct a circle. An instrument used to show direction. pp. 206, 424

compatible numbers Numbers that are easy to compute mentally. p. 16
Example: $5 + 15 = 20$

composite number A whole number greater than 1 that has more than two factors. p. 139

cone A space figure with one circular flat surface (face) and one vertex. p. 394

congruent figures Figures that have the same size and shape. p. 194

cube A space figure with six congruent square faces. p. 394

customary system A measurement system that measures length in inches, feet, yards, and miles; capacity in cups, pints, quarts, and gallons; weight in ounces, pounds, and tons; and temperature in degrees Fahrenheit. *See* Table of Measures. pp. 346, 360

cylinder A space figure with two parallel bases that are in the shape of congruent circles. p. 394 *Example:*

decimal A number with one or more places to the right of a decimal point. p. 214
Examples: 0.7, 1.8, 2.06, 0.175

degree (°) A unit for measuring angles. p. 180

denominator The number below the fraction bar in a fraction. p. 286
Example: $\frac{2}{5}$ The denominator is 5.

diagonal A segment that joins two vertices of a polygon but is not a side. p. 204

diameter A line segment that passes through the center of a circle and has both endpoints on the circle. p. 206

difference The answer in subtraction. p. 26
Example: $9 - 4 = 5$ The difference is 5.

digit Any of the symbols used to write numbers: 0, 1, 2, 3, 4, 5, 6, 7, 8, and 9. p. 2

dividend The number to be divided. p. 76
Example: $6\overline{)36}$ or $36 \div 6$ The dividend is 36.

divisible A number is divisible by another number if the remainder is 0 after dividing. p.102

division An operation on two numbers that results in a quotient. p. 76

divisor The number used to divide another number. p. 76
Example: 7)28 or 28 ÷ 7 The divisor is 7.

edge The segment where two faces of a space figure meet. p. 394
Example:

endpoint A point at the end of a line segment or ray. p. 178

equal ratios Ratios that describe the same rate or make the same comparison. p. 418
Example: $\frac{3}{10}$ and $\frac{6}{20}$ are equal ratios.

equation A number sentence with an equal sign. p. 16

equilateral triangle A triangle with all sides congruent. p. 200

equivalent fractions Fractions that name the same number. p. 290
Example: $\frac{1}{2}$ and $\frac{2}{4}$

estimate To give an approximate rather than an exact answer. p. 20

event One or more outcomes of an experiment. p. 438

expanded form A number written as the sum of the values of its digits. p. 6
Example: 200 + 80 + 7 is the expanded form for 287.

experiment To carry out a plan in order to test a prediction. p. 434

exponent A number that tells how many times the base is used as a factor. p. 70
Example: $10^3 = 10 \times 10 \times 10$
The exponent is 3, and the base is 10.

face A flat surface of a space figure. p. 394

factor tree A diagram used to show the prime factors of a number. p. 139
Example:
```
        18
       /  \
      6  ×  3
     / \
    2 × 3 × 3
```

factors The numbers that are multiplied to give a product. p. 136
Example: $3 \times 5 = 15$ The factors are 3 and 5.

flip image An image made by reflecting a figure about a line. p. 198

fraction A number that names part of a whole. p. 286
Example $\frac{1}{2}, \frac{2}{3}, \frac{6}{6}$

frequency table A table used to record and summarize the number of times something occurs. p. 157

graph A drawing used to show information. p. 152

greatest common factor (GCF) The greatest number that is a factor of each of two or more numbers. p. 136
Example: The greatest common factor of 5 and 10 is 5.

hexagon A polygon with six sides p. 186

horizontal axis A horizontal line on a coordinate plane. p. 154

identity property of addition The sum of any number and zero is that number. p. 16

identity property of multiplication The product of any number and one is that number. p. 42

improper fraction A fraction in which the numerator is greater than or equal to the denominator. p. 305
Examples: $\frac{4}{3}, \frac{6}{6}$

intersecting lines Lines that cross at one point. p. 184

inverse operations Two operations that are opposite in effect. Addition and subtraction are inverse operations. Multiplication and division are inverse operations. pp. 18, 74

isosceles triangle A triangle with two congruent sides. p. 200

key The part of the map that explains the map symbols. p. 294

least common denominator (LCD) The least common multiple of the denominators of two or more fractions. p. 294

Glossary

least common multiple (LCM) the least number other than 0 that is a multiple of each of two or more numbers.   p. 50
Example: The least common multiple of 3 and 5 is 15.

like fractions Fractions that have the same denominator.   p. 294
Example: $\frac{3}{4}$ and $\frac{1}{4}$

line The collection of points along a straight path that goes on and on in opposite directions. A line has no endpoints.   p. 178

line graph A graph used to show changes over a period of time.   p. 154

line of symmetry A line that divides a figure into two congruent parts.   p. 196

line segment A part of a line having two endpoints.   p. 178

lowest terms A fraction is in lowest terms when the greatest common factor of the numerator and the denominator is 1.   p. 292
Examples: $\frac{1}{4}$ and $\frac{3}{5}$ are in lowest terms.

mean The average of the numbers in a set of data.   p. 168

median The middle number or average of the two middle numbers in a collection of data when the data are arranged in order.   p. 168

metric system A measurement system that measures length in millimeters, centimeters, meters, and kilometers; capacity in milliliters and liters; mass in grams and kilograms; and temperature in degrees Celsius. *See* Table of Measures.   p. 270

mixed number A number written as a whole number and a fraction.   p. 305
Example: $3\frac{4}{5}$

mode The number that occurs most often in a set of data.   p. 168

multiple The product of a whole number and any other whole number.   p. 50
Example: 0, 3, 6, 9 . . . are multiples of 3.

multiplication An operation on two or more numbers, called factors, to find a product.   p. 40

number sentence An equation written in horizontal form.   p. 18
Example: $3 \times 4 = 12$

numerator The number above the fraction bar in a fraction.   p. 286
Example: $\frac{2}{5}$ The numerator is 2.

obtuse angle An angle with a measure greater than 90° but less than 180°.   p. 182

octagon A polygon with eight sides.   p. 186

order of operations The order in which operations are done in calculations. Work inside parentheses is done first. Then multiplication and division from left to right, and finally addition and subtraction from left to right.   p. 108

ordered pair A pair of numbers used to locate a point in a plane.   p. 402

outcome A possible result in a probability experiment.   p. 434

parallel lines Lines in the same plane that never intersect.   p. 184

parallelogram A quadrilateral with each pair of opposite sides parallel and congruent.   p. 204

pentagon A polygon with five sides.   p. 186

percent A ratio whose second term is 100. Percent means parts per hundred.   p. 426
Example: 87% is read "eighty-seven percent." It means 87 parts per hundred.

perfect square A whole number whose two factors are identical.   p. 131
Example: 25 is a perfect square whose factors are 5 and 5.

perimeter The distance around a polygon.   p. 378

period A group of three digits of a number, separated from other digits by a comma.   p. 2

perpendicular lines Two lines that meet to form right angles.   p. 184

pi (π) The ratio of the circumference of a circle to its diameter. $\pi = 3.14$ or $\frac{22}{7}$.   p. 381

pictograph A graph that shows number information by using picture symbols.   p. 152

place value The value of a digit determined by its position in a number.   p. 2

plane A flat surface extending endlessly in all directions.   p. 178

point An exact location in space.   p. 178

polygon A closed plane figure made up of line segments.   p. 186

prime number A whole number greater than 1 with only two factors—itself and 1.   p. 139
Example: 5, 7, 11, and 13 are prime numbers.

prism A space figure with two parallel and congruent bases in the shape of polygons. p. 394

probability The ratio of favorable outcomes to possible outcomes of an experiment.   p. 438

product The answer in multiplication.   p. 42
Example: $4 \times 8 = 32$ The product is 32.

proper fraction A fraction in which the numerator is less than the denominator.
p. 305
Examples: $\frac{3}{4}, \frac{5}{8}$

protractor An instrument used to measure or draw angles.   p. 180

pyramid A space figure whose base is a polygon and whose faces are triangles with a common vertex.   p. 394

quadrilateral A polygon with four sides.
p. 186

quotient The answer in division.   p. 76
Example: $24 \div 3 = 8$ or $3\overline{)24}$ The quotient is 8.

radius A line segment with one endpoint on the circle and the other endpoint at the center.   p. 206
Example:

radius

range The difference between the greatest and least numbers in a set of data.   pp. 56, 168

ratio A comparison of two quantities.   p. 416
Example: 3 to 5, 3:5, $\frac{3}{5}$

ray A part of a line that has one endpoint and goes on and on in one direction.   p. 178

rectangle A parallelogram with four right angles.   p. 200

rectangular prism A space figure whose faces are all rectangular.   p. 394

regroup To use 1 ten to form 10 ones, 1 hundred to form 10 tens, 12 ones to form 1 ten and 2 ones, and so on.   p. 22

remainder The number that is left over after dividing.   p. 82
Example: $42 \div 8 = 5$ R2 The remainder is 2.

rhombus A parallelogram with all sides congruent.   p. 204

right angle An angle that measures 90°.
p. 182

right triangle A triangle with one right angle.
p. 200

Roman numerals A number system using the symbols: I, V, X, L, C, D, and M. It was used by the Romans.   p. 38

rounding Expressing a number to the nearest ten, hundred, thousand, and so on.   p. 10
Example: 43 rounded to the nearest ten is 40.

scale The ratio of the measurements in a drawing to the measurements of the actual objects.   p. 422

scale drawing A drawing made so that actual measurements can be determined from the drawing by using a scale.   p. 422

scalene triangle A triangle that has no congruent sides.   p. 200

semicircle A half circle.   p. 206

similar figures Figures that have the same shape but not necessarily the same size.
p. 192

slide image An image formed by moving a figure along a line.   p. 198

space figure A geometric figure whose points are in more than one plane.   p. 394

sphere A space figure with all points an equal distance from the center.   p. 394

square A rectangle with all sides congruent.
p. 204

standard form A number written with commas spearating groups of three digits.   p. 2

subtraction An operation on two numbers to find the difference.   p. 18

Glossary

sum The answer in addition.   p. 16
  Example: 8 + 7 = 15. The sum is 15

tally marks Marks used to record the frequency of the data.   p. 157

terms The numerator and denominator of a fraction.   p. 286

transformation The turning, sliding, or flipping of a plane figure.   p. 198

trapezoid A quadrilateral with only one pair of opposite sides parallel.   p. 204

triangle A polygon with three sides.   p. 186

triangular prism A prism whose bases are triangles.   p. 394

turn image An image formed by moving a figure about a point.   p. 198

unlike fractions Fractions that have different denominators.   p. 294

  Example: $\frac{1}{2}$ and $\frac{2}{3}$

vertex The point where two rays meet. The point of intersection of two sides of a polygon. The point of intersection of three edges of a space figure.   p. 180, p. 186, p. 394

vertical axis A vertical reference line on a coordinate system.   p. 154

volume The number of cubic units that fit inside a space figure.   p. 398

zero property of division 0 divided by any number except 0 is 0. You cannot divide a number by 0.   p. 74
  Example: $0 \div 12 = 0$

zero property of multiplication The product of any number and 0 is 0.   p. 42
  Example: $5 \times 0 = 0$ and $0 \times 5 = 0$

Computer Terms

BACK *n* (BK *n*) Moves the turtle backward *n* turtle steps.

BASIC A computer language.

cell A unit of a spreadsheet located by a column and a row.

CLEARSCREEN (CS) Clears the screen. In some versions, also homes the turtle.

FORWARD *n*(FD *n*) Moves the turtle forward *n* turtle steps.

HOME Positions the turtle in the middle of the screen, heading straight up.

IF condition [ ] [ ] If condition is true, executes command(s) in first [ ]. If false, executes command(s) in second [ ].

ITEM *n* [ ] Returns the *n*th item in a list.

LEFT *n* (LT *n*) Turns the turtle left *n* degrees from its current heading.

Logo A computer language.

MAKE "X *n* Assigns the value *n* to the variable named.

OUTPUT (OP) In a procedure, returns a value.

PENDOWN (PD) Allows turtle to draw again.

PENUP (PU) Allows turtle to move without drawing.

PRINT (PR) A Logo command that shows information on the screen.

procedure Creates a new Logo command that can execute a specified set of commands. A procedure is called by entering its name.

RANDOM *n* Returns a whole number from 0 to $n - 1$.

REMAINDER *n*1 *n*2 Returns the remainder of $n1 \div n2$.

REPEAT *n* [ ] A Logo command that repeats commands within brackets *n* times.

RIGHT *n* (RT *n*) Turns the turtle right *n* degrees from its current heading.

SETPOS [*n*1 *n*2] Positions the turtle at a specified point (*n*1, *n*2). (Some versions of Logo)

spreadsheet Data arranged in rows and columns. A computer spreadsheet records data and performs calculations.

TO procedure name . . . END Defines a procedure

Measures

Metric

Length

1 centimeter (cm) = 10 millimeters (mm)
1 decimeter (dm) = 10 centimeters
1 meter (m) = 10 decimeters
1 kilometer (km) = 1000 meters

Mass/Weight

1 kilogram (kg) = 1000 grams

Capacity

1 liter (L) = 1000 milliliters (mL)

Area

1 square centimeter (cm^2) = 100 square millimeters (mm^2)
1 square meter (m^2) = 10000 square centimeters

Customary

Length

1 foot (ft) = 12 inches (in.)
1 yard (yd) = 36 inches, or 3 feet
1 mile (mi) = 5,280 feet, or 1,760 yards

Weight

1 pound (lb) = 16 ounces (oz)
1 ton (T) = 2,000 pounds

Capacity

1 cup (c) = 8 fluid ounces (fl oz)
1 pint (pt) = 2 cups
1 quart (qt) = 2 pints
1 gallon (gal) = 4 quarts

Area

1 square foot (ft^2) = 144 square inches $(in.^2)$
1 square yard (yd^2) = 9 square feet

Time

1 minute (min) = 60 seconds (s)
1 hour (h) = 60 minutes
1 day (d) = 24 hours

1 week (wk) = 7 days
1 month (mo) = 28 to 31 days, or about 4 weeks
1 year (yr) = 12 months, or 52 weeks, or 365 days

Symbols

=	is equal to	2:5	ratio of 2 to 5	$\overleftrightarrow{AB}$	line AB
>	is greater than	%	percent	$\overline{AB}$	line segment AB
<	is less than	π	pi (approximately 3.14)	$\overrightarrow{AB}$	ray AB
≈	is approximately equal to	°	degree	<ABC	angle ABC
...	and so on, in the	°C	degree Celsius	$\overarc{AB}$	semicircle (arc) AB
	same manner	°F	degree Fahrenheit	‖	is parallel to
		10^2	ten to the second power	⊥	is perpendicular to
				(3,4)	ordered pair 3,4

Formulas

$P = a + b + c + d$ Perimeter of a quadrilateral
$A = l \times w$ Area of a rectangle
$A = \frac{1}{2} \times b \times h$ Area of a triangle
$C = \pi \times d$ Circumference of a circle
$V = l \times w \times h$ Volume of a rectangular prism

Index

Index

Index

Credits